Human Services and Social Work Responsibility

Second NASW Professional Symposium

Papers presented at the Second NASW Professional Symposium on Human Services and Professional Responsibility, held prior to the Annual Forum of the National Conference on Social Welfare, May 24–26, 1968, San Francisco, California.

Willard C. Richan, Editor

Associate Dean, School of Social Administration
Temple University, Philadelphia, Pennsylvania

NATIONAL ASSOCIATION OF SOCIAL WORKERS, INC.
1425 H Street N.W., Washington, D.C. 20005

Copyright © 1969 by the
National Association of Social Workers, Inc.
Standard Book Number 87101-053-4
Library of Congress Catalog No. 72–108195

Printed in the U.S.A.

3

Contents

Part II. Bringing Services Closer to the Consumer

Part III. New Manpower Resources

Part VI. Is Social Work Equal to the Challenge?

Contributors

Titles of the contributors are those at the time of the symposium
(May 1968)

Paul A. Abels, Assistant Professor of Social Work, School of Applied Social Sciences, Case Western Reserve University, Cleveland, Ohio

Dale A. Albers, Director, Social Work Services, Wyoming State Hospital, Evanston, Wyoming

Mrs. Amelia B. Barnard, Executive Director, Health Resources Center, Denver, Colorado

Bertram J. Black, Executive Director, Altro Health and Rehabilitation Services, New York, New York

Mrs. Irene Blickstein, Associate for Professional Personnel, Department of Family Services, Community Service Society, New York, New York

Neil F. Bracht, Assistant Dean, Extramural and Community Affairs, College of Human Medicine, Michigan State College, East Lansing, Michigan

Earl C. Brennen, Associate Director, Interprofessional Relations Project, University YMCA, Berkeley, California

Albert Comanor, Professor, Department of Social Work Education, San Francisco State College, San Francisco, California

William H. Denham, Director of Training and Research, Community Mental Health Center, Area B, Howard University–District of Columbia Department of Public Health, and Teaching Associate, Division of Psychiatry, Howard University College of Medicine, Washington, D.C.

Msgr. Robert E. Gallagher, Acting Director, Catholic Charities, Bronx Center, Bronx, New York (deceased)

Douglas Glasgow, Associate Professor, School of Social Welfare, University of California, Los Angeles, California

Charles H. Goodrich, MD, Director of Ambulatory Care and Associate Professor of Community Medicine, Mount Sinai Hospital, New York, New York

Alvin E. Green, Caseworker, The Menninger Foundation, Topeka, Kansas

Emanuel Hallowitz, Assistant Professor, Albert Einstein College of Medicine, Lincoln Hospital Mental Health Service, Bronx, New York

Abraham Kaplan, Professor of Philosophy, University of Michigan, Ann Arbor, Michigan

Ivor Kraft, Associate Professor of Social Work, School of Applied Social Sciences, Case Western Reserve University, Cleveland, Ohio

Arnold M. Levin, Consultant, Illinois Youth Commission Diagnostic Center, and Chairman, Technical Advisory Committee, Juvenile Protective Association, Homewood, Illinois

Mrs. Gertrude T. Leyendecker, Senior Associate, Department of Family Services, Community Service Society, New York, New York

Robert Mejia, Community Organization Worker, Sophie Wright Settlement, Detroit, Michigan

John S. Morgan, Dean, School of Social Work, University of Pennsylvania, Philadelphia, Pennsylvania

Robert Morris, Professor of Social Planning, Florence Heller Graduate School for Advanced Studies in Social Welfare, Brandeis University, Waltham, Massachusetts

Nelly A. Peissachowitz, Director, Neighborhood Service Center No. 1, Bronx, New York

Mrs. Ruth W. Ravich, Co-ordinator, Patient Service Representative Program, Mount Sinai Hospital, New York, New York

Helen Rehr, Associate Director, Social Service Department, Mount Sinai Hospital, New York, New York

Martin Rein, Associate Professor, Carola Woerishoffer Graduate Department of Social Work and Social Research, Bryn Mawr College, Bryn Mawr, Pennsylvania

Russell H. Richardson, Southeast Regional Director, Planned Parenthood–World Population, Atlanta, Georgia

Marvin L. Rosenberg, Director of Social Welfare Planning and Policy, Council of Churches of Christ of Greater Cleveland, Cleveland, Ohio

Anne R. Sarcka, Community Organization Specialist, Lincoln Hospital Mental Health Services, Bronx, New York

Marvin S. Schreiber, Executive Director, Senior Centers of Dade County, Miami, Florida

Mrs. Eunice O. Shatz, Associate Director, New Careers Training Program, Community Mental Health Center, Area B, Howard University–District of Columbia Department of Public Health, and Teaching Associate, Division of Psychiatry, Howard University College of Medicine, Washington, D.C.

Sheldon S. Steinberg, Director, New Careers Training Program, Community Mental Health Center, Area B, Howard University–District of Columbia Department of Public Health, and Assistant Clinical Professor, Division of Psychiatry, Howard University College of Medicine, Washington, D.C.

Caryl J. Stewart, Co-ordinator, Rehabilitation Division, Burlington Welfare Department, Burlington, Vermont

Cordell H. Thomas, Casework Supervisor, Family and Children's Services of the Episcopal Church, Philadelphia, Pennsylvania

Alan D. Wade, Dean, School of Social Work, Sacramento State College, Sacramento, California

Paul E. Weinberger, Associate Professor, Department of Social Work, San Francisco State College, San Francisco, California

Lyn Woods, Student, School of Social Work, University of Michigan, Ann Arbor, Michigan

Editor's Preface

A collection of papers can have a variety of uses—as a souvenir of a conference, a means of decorating a professional bookshelf or the list of publications in an author's *vita,* a convenience for the harried teacher, a money-maker, or a serious attempt to impart wisdom. The intent of this volume is to perform the last-mentioned function.

A deliberate effort has been made to avoid producing a souvenir of the 1968 Professional Symposium; souvenirs are meant to be preserved, but it is hoped that copies of this book will become well worn by use. The second use—that of decoration—is tempting, because the succulent turns of phrase in some of the papers make them decorative as well as instructive. The teacher will find that the papers are less of a crutch than a stimulant; of this, more is said below. It is a commonplace of the publishing industry that learned papers are notoriously poor money-makers.

This brings us to the final use: the imparting of wisdom. Such a goal involves risks, for it implies a demanding test of success. It is not with arrogance but with real humility that the producers of this volume have sought to provide a means by which practicing social workers, social work students, and others with a stake in social welfare can be apprised of current issues and developments in the field. No claim is made that this volume is comprehensive. At the same time, the range of issues and strategies covered by the symposium presentations was impressive.

This book has been composed with specific audiences in mind. One is social work professionals—those now manning the welfare and educational establishments across the country. It is believed that they will find the organization of the material lends itself to a focused examination of key issues and innovations in relation to significant aspects of social service delivery. The examination can be as general or intensive as is desired.   Toward this end, introductory material has been provided for each of the six major parts of the book rather than being lumped together in this introduction.

A second major audience is social work students.   The papers are related more to some parts of the curriculum than others.   In particular, the book should be useful in courses in social welfare policy and services and the professional seminar.   Teachers of administration should also find much relevant material here.   Specific articles are germane to the various method sequences.   This volume may be used as a supplement to a text or a major source in courses that do not use a primary textbook.

Finally, it is believed that these papers need to be known beyond the confines of the professional social work community.   Otherwise we are in danger of simply talking to one another.   If any single message comes through in these selections, it is that social work has neglected to "tell it like it is" in the arena beyond our own fraternity.

TIMELINESS

In approaching the papers in this volume, the reader should keep in mind the historical context in which they were written.   The U.S. Supreme Court is said to follow the election returns.   The same can be said of social work.   The year 1968 saw a possibly unprecedented sharpening of issues within the social work profession.   The spirit in which the 1968 Professional Symposium was forged was one of controversy and challenge.   The symposium followed by one month an NASW workshop on the urban crisis whose tone was as sharp as its name suggests.   These two events came in the midst of a period in which the association leadership sought to respond to urgent calls for reform.

These developments within NASW were clearly in response to major upheavals in the social and political fabric of society.   Nineteen sixty-eight was also a time when the nation's leadership was shaken fundamentally by forces of change.   At points the connection between events within and outside the social work profession was clear and direct, most notably the emergence of black self-awareness and self-assertion.   At points the internal issue was more one of becoming relevant and effective in the face of rapid social change.   Social work students asked, appropriately, whether they are being prepared for tomorrow's problems with yesterday's tools.

The reader is reminded of this historical context because from time to time he may come across a reference that seems anachronistic.   In this sense a set of papers that seeks to engage urgent issues risks the same fate as that most urgent of publications, yesterday's newspaper!

But it is believed that the issues with which these authors are grappling will still be alive for years to come. Their proposals and attempted solutions will still be timely. One could only wish, in fact, that social work and the social services would make such rapid strides in the coming decade as to render this book of little more than historical interest. Alas, it is likely that the papers will have as much immediacy and many of the proposed solutions be as untested years from now as at present. The reader can consider himself challenged to give the lie to this prediction.

Nor is time the editor's only enemy. Another is the fact that the papers appeared in one format, for one purpose; they have now been converted into something else. In developing the 1968 symposium, the association sought to challenge its members as much as to inform them. Five major papers (those by Comanor, Kaplan, Morris, Kraft, and Wade) were intentionally strong in tone and intended to call forth a response at the time they were given. Comanor and Kraft spoke to small groups via closed-circuit television, with group discussions following immediately, to strike while the iron was hot. The written word cannot convey the exact impact of the direct presentation.

This challenge was combined with more specific presentations that had as their major purpose the imparting of knowledge. In the spirit of encouraging maximum participation, social workers were invited to present their ideas and experiences. National units of NASW also planned special presentations, and concurrently four major workshops were offered. Not surprisingly, the symposium authors spoke in a mixture of tongues ranging from highly technical treatises on theory to descriptions of "where it's at" in the vivid idiom of the urban ghetto. Since it is believed that these various strands have equal importance to the job of making human services effective, they have been included in this volume.

CONTENTS AND ORGANIZATION

The papers are arranged in six parts. Part I deals with perhaps the most crucial question of all: How relevant are social services to human needs? Part II examines the problem of *delivery* of services in its narrowest sense: How can we deal with the fragmentation and inaccessibility of social welfare benefits?

One of the central issues in provision of services is the quantity and quality of social welfare manpower. Part III deals with the promise and problems encompassed in the utilization of indigenous nonprofessionals. In Part IV, the role of the consumer as change agent is explored.

Part V engages a set of problems that are perhaps the most vexing to those who would change social services: obduracy on the part of social agencies. It is obviously part and parcel of the more basic obduracy of a society that has always approached its social responsibilities haltingly. Part VI may be the most interesting to professional social workers. It is doubtful that its contents will fail to stir some kind of reaction in its readers. The authors have been unsparing as they dealt with the question "Is Social Work Equal to the Challenge?" But they also offer suggestions for making the answer to that question affirmative.

The reader may find this book discomfiting. It could not be otherwise with a frank appraisal of an institutional complex that we have all sensed was in deep trouble in recent years. Any human enterprise, stripped of its defense system, suffers embarrassment. But, as with the client who has woven a web of rationalization around his self-defeating behavior, the pain of acknowledgment is a necessary condition for progress.

The authors of the papers included in this volume are clearly not seeking to induce the kind of self-flagellation that tends to immobilize. In some papers the tone is abrasive and unsettling, but each is a constructive attempt to find better solutions. Each, therefore, is a sign of hope.

WILLARD C. RICHAN
Consultant, NASW Service Delivery Project

Philadelphia, Pennsylvania
October 1969

Acknowledgments

Any statement of appreciation to those who contributed to this volume and the symposium that led to it will necessarily fall short. It is inevitable that some will be slighted. Yet certain individual contributions deserve special mention.

Our debt to the authors of the papers that comprise this book is obvious. It is hoped that publication goes a small way toward discharging the obligation. But other contributions are less obvious.

The one person perhaps most responsible for the success of the undertaking was Chauncey A. Alexander, chairman of the NASW Task Force on Service Delivery. He was invited to engage in a taxing effort, not a ceremonial function. He met the challenge gladly and went far beyond mere duty.

Mr. Alexander received excellent support from the other task force members, whose names appear elsewhere in this volume. Not only did most members attend the working sessions of the task force religiously, they also gave generously of their time and talents in reviewing manuscripts, making editorial suggestions, and handling other vital details.

The symposium itself was aided by many, many other NASW members. Because of the number involved, blanket acknowledgment must be made. Especially important to the total endeavor was the support and encouragement received from Bernard Russell, chairman of the NASW Division of Practice and Knowledge, and NASW President Charles I. Schottland.

There is a tradition in social work for professional staff to stay out of sight and avoid the limelight. It is a foolish tradition that ought to pass from the scene, especially when the "laymen" are professional colleagues. Mrs. Mildred Kilinski, director of the NASW Department of Social Work Practice, was instrumental in the publication of this volume and also

15

helped turn the "grand design" of the symposium into a living, breathing reality.

It goes without saying that Mrs. Beatrice Saunders, director of the NASW Department of Publications, and Mrs. Patricia Ann Lynch, senior editor, had central roles in every step of the production of the book. Mrs. Saunders gave helpful consultation on its format and overall contents, and more than anyone else has helped to make the difference between a professional product and what might otherwise have been an amateur effort.

Supporting Mrs. Kilinski and Mrs. Saunders were other department directors and their staffs. It was gratifying to see the entire machinery of the NASW national staff, from Executive Director Joseph P. Anderson on down, give their time and assistance in helping to make the 1968 symposium a significant milestone in NASW history.   —W.C.R.

Foreword

The social work profession, its values, and its programs face a crisis of relevance to the social problems erupting in virtually every community in the United States. Health and welfare programs, agency structures, and professional methodology are all under attack. Social workers themselves tend to be demoralized, critical of themselves and their colleagues, and disorganized.

It was in this environment that the NASW Division of Practice and Knowledge, with its many councils and commissions, sought to respond to the professional challenges and advance social work practice. A study conducted by the Commission on Practice determined that delivery of social services and manpower were central concerns of all division units. The Task Force on Service Delivery was appointed to organize a symposium at which these issues would be examined.

The task force members were themselves critical of the weak leadership given by the social work profession and NASW in meeting these challenges. As they expressed their own criticisms and examined the crises in society and in health and welfare in particular, it became clear that the social service agencies and NASW were reacting defensively to the crises rather than giving leadership. NASW seemed to be seconding motions made by the federal agency administrations on Great Society programs. Important professional contributions such as the Regional Institute Program and many chapter activities were being overlooked in the wave of frustration and complaints. Within NASW an artificial division between social action and practice was creating sectarian groupings and power struggles.

As the task force members worked to develop a national symposium, they reached important insights into the current problems and arrived at certain convictions. The focus on service delivery provided a consumer-centered emphasis that encouraged objective evaluation of pro-

duction and avoided the myopic concentration on professional technology. It brought values, purpose, knowledge, and action together for
examination.

The task force adopted the idea of using the symposium to provide
a professional learning experience for participants rather than as a
sterile forum for papers by members of the professional Establishment.
The event was thought of as an opportunity to set in motion a process
of professional analysis, dialogue, and action related to service delivery.
Task force members planned to involve participants as much as possible
and hoped to stimulate their concern with examining and improving
their own practice, their agencies' service, and their NASW chapters'
relevance to the health and welfare scene. These insights and convictions
became the three symposium objectives:

1. To provide a significant professional and educational experience
for NASW members.

2. To examine the relevance of social services and the social work
profession to human needs.

3. To initiate a process of change by the social work profession in
the delivery of social services.

These objectives led to a three-part program organized around the
questions: What are the states of the service delivery system, the social
work profession's responsibility, and the profession's understanding of
how to approach the problems? What is the social work profession's
conception of the issues and strategies in social service delivery? What
possible future strategies exist for service delivery and for the social work
profession?

The second national NASW Symposium on Human Services and
Professional Responsibility, held prior to the Annual Forum of the National Conference on Social Welfare, May 24–26, 1968, in San Francisco, California, opened, not with the usual mass assembly, but with
small groups of up to twenty-five participants meeting with discussion
leaders in some forty individual rooms. The opening speech, by Albert
Comanor, was telecast by closed-circuit television to these rooms. It
was a critical assault on the entire social service delivery system, pre-
designed to shake any complacency about the severity and depth of the
problems.[1] With all participants' attention focused on the speaker and
subject, and without the usual environmental and time displacement
distractions, immediate discussions ensued. The second speaker, Ivor

---

[1] "Social Service Delivery in the United States," this volume, pp. 27–49.

Kraft, made a similar assault, more narrowly focused on the role of the profession and the professional organization, NASW.[2] The opportunity for the participants' immediate reaction was the same. Following these critiques, Abraham Kaplan finished the half-day session with a treatment of ways of thinking about the problems presented.[3]

The second phase of the symposium devoted an entire day to examination of the multiple views of the issues and strategies surrounding social service delivery. All programs provided opportunities for questions and discussion. Four workshops examined key delivery problems intensively: the challenge of poverty, the manpower crisis, evaluative techniques, and funding patterns.

On the same day, national NASW units considered service delivery from the standpoint of their primary specialties. Fourteen different programs presented in the half-day session offered an opportunity for examining and discussing the key professional issues in knowledge and practice, professional standards, and social policy. A second half-day session, concurrent with the workshops, was designed to provide maximum opportunity for any NASW member or chapter to present papers on issues and strategies of service delivery. Some sixty papers, selected from over three hundred abstracts submitted, were presented and discussed in twenty sessions open to all participants.

The final session, paralleling the first two critical papers, offered possible strategies for changing systems of service delivery and for making NASW a more effective action system. Robert Morris presented the former paper and Alan Wade the latter.[4]

There was no closing summary of the symposium. This omission was intentional. Seen as the beginning of a change process, the symposium was intended to shatter old conceptions, introduce new methods of thinking, present views of key problems, and then suggest some alternate strategies for approaching the problems. Participants were asked to continue the process when they returned home. To aid in the process, the five major speeches had been tape-recorded so that they would be available—in whole or part—to NASW chapters and other groups to enable

---

[2] "The State of the Social Work Profession," this volume, pp. 343–366.

[3] "New Perspectives on Problems of Service Delivery," this volume, pp. 97–104.

[4] Robert Morris, "Strategies for Innovation in Service Delivery," and Alan D. Wade, "In Pursuit of Community: A Platform for NASW," this volume, pp. 281–293 and 367–379 respectively.

them to reproduce the examination of social service delivery and aid in professional action toward change.

Reactions to the symposium have varied widely. A few persons considered it a radical attack on social work leadership, while some considered it the Establishment's way of cooling criticisms of NASW conservatism. But it seems safe to say that the intense involvement sought was achieved.

The reader of this volume will find here a reflection of the status, the faults, and the hopes of the social work profession. Only time will measure whether the second NASW Professional Symposium and this publication will contribute to the objectives of change to improve social service delivery.

CHAUNCEY A. ALEXANDER, *Chairman*
NASW Task Force on Service Delivery

Introduction

The history of social work has been closely intertwined with the history of social welfare services. It was, after all, the social service industry that gave birth to the social work profession. From time to time we are told that this relationship should be renounced in behalf of a private entrepreneurial model or a political action model, that the profession should disengage itself from so-called residual welfare programs and move entirely into frontline systems. But while each of these thrusts becomes ingested and works its influence, it is doubtful that the social work profession can ever end its close involvement in the institutional complex known as social welfare.

Most social workers are employed in established social services, but we are highly implicated in some fields employing relatively few members of the profession. Take, for example, the field of income maintenance. At most, a miniscule percentage of professional social workers have ever been employed in income maintenance programs in the United States. Yet it would be fair to say that these programs have been a major preoccupation of the social work profession, as an organized professional community, over the past three to four decades.

The official NASW *Goals of Public Social Policy* devotes the bulk of its fifty-nine pages to needs and programs that fall under the rubric of social services.[1] For better or worse, then, the profession is implicated in the delivery of social services. Therefore, it is incumbent on us to do our utmost to assure that those services are accessible, effective, and relevant to human needs. Any lesser commitment would be professionally irresponsible.

But this responsibility poses at once two major problems: One is the vastness of the social service enterprise and the corresponding vast-

---

[1] Rev. ed.; New York: National Association of Social Workers, 1967.

21

ness of the challenge to a profession with limited resources. At times an attempt has been made to resolve this dilemma by redefining more narrowly the scope of the charge to the profession. It would seem to the writer that this is no solution. Better to struggle with the disparity between aspirations and accomplishments, even if this produces a kind of professional anomie. Nor should we disavow the even broader commitment to mankind, which leads us well beyond the boundaries of social services.

The second major problem posed by our responsibility is the fact that the target of our concern, the social service industry, envelops the professional life of most social workers. It is at once the source of life and the source of anguish. And it is all too clear that when these considerations are in conflict, the anguish tends to become muted. Again, an attempt has been made to resolve the dilemma by redefining social work's concerns to conform with concerns of the industry. Again, the "solution" is no solution. Unless the profession qua profession can assert its independence and authority, it is doubtful that it will ever be able to meet its responsibility for the provision of effective human services.

The concern of the NASW Symposium on Human Services and Professional Responsibility was social work's role in the effective delivery of services to people in need. The phrase "delivery of services" signifies the importance to social workers of what actually happens to those in need of help. Put negatively, a service not delivered when and where needed is not a service at all—any sharp dichotomy between service and delivery is a false one. In some fields, one can talk about production and distribution processes as separate and distinct, but in social work these are two aspects of the same thing.

From a purely logical standpoint, then, it is artificial to refer to delivery as something apart from an integral process called service. But this emphasis on delivery becomes important because of a special failing of social work in the past: The profession has tended at times to focus on one aspect of the total process—the refinement of intervention techniques—with little regard for whether these were "delivering" anything of real significance to the people most in need of help. Largely because of this tendency, social work now faces a major crisis: the crisis of its relevance.

But relevance to what? It is by answering this question that meaning is given to the word. It seems clear that the pressing problems of human deprivation pose the most urgent issues for the social work profession. And so the central question for the social services is this: Are they truly relevant to the needs of the poor and the disenfranchised?

While one should not minimize society's obligation to deal with the needs of all its citizens, whether of high or low state, our prior concern should be those segments of the population that are systematically shut out of full opportunities for self-fulfillment.

The reader will find one thread running throughout most of these papers: professional concern with the poor. The book might have been titled *Human Services and Social Work Responsibility to the Poor*. There are two reasons why this was not done. First, society has already segregated the poor in its concerns sufficiently. The editor prefers not to imply, even by indirection, that this is a book only for those social workers who are concerned with the poor. But more important, the poor share that same burden that has hung over all victimized minorities throughout history: they are only the most intensive and disturbing expression of what plagues the whole. The destruction of freedom and fulfillment in the urban ghetto or the rural backwater is a threat to the freedom and fulfillment of all.

It is no accident that social work has always been directly implicated in the lives of such minorities. This places on the profession a unique burden and a unique opportunity. We are in a position to see the warnings and respond in relevant fashion: to work toward the reform of social welfare services and to "tell it like it is." Failure to do so is an abdication of our professional responsibility.

PART I

Relevance of Social Services to Social Needs

Comanor sounds the theme of this book, as he did the theme of the 1968 symposium. By using an adequate social service investment and design as the standard against which to compare the present reality, he demonstrates how far the field is from its goal. The assault is caustic and provocative, but it is not angry. Comanor has emphasized what is problematical, because the problematical should have priority on our agenda if we are to take seriously our responsibility to make social services better.

Morgan engages the problems of service delivery in a broad framework. His orderly analysis of trends he sees in the U.S.A. and other countries provides a useful structure for examining a subject that has defied conceptual order over the years.

Rein asks: Can a more rational system of financing lead to a more rational system of social services? His paper is especially timely in view of the flux in which both the structure and financing of social services now find themselves, and in particular because of the current interest in block grants as a possible solution.

Peissachowitz and Sarcka describe a mental health program that went through a major transformation in response to the manifest needs of the clientele. Clearly, no advance blueprint can assure that a social service will be relevant, especially in this period of rapid change. Likewise, Stewart tells of the changes a public welfare agency's program went through as a result of survey findings and clinical observations.

The final paper in Part I sets forth general ground rules by which social workers can test the relevance of social services. Kaplan is a philosopher, but his grasp of both social work language and issues is impressive.

Social Service Delivery in the United States

ALBERT COMANOR

No one can or ought to find satisfaction in the deficits and deficiencies of this country's social service system revealed by an unsparing inquiry. In fact, we more commonly find cause and temptations to point to the progress that has been made and the various achievements of the system —and admittedly, some of the services that will be cited here as poorly designed and some of the tragic circumstances described do show continuing improvement. But a defensive or bland posture is incongruous in a society in crisis. The issue for social welfare today is the disparity between where it is and where it might and must be. To know the dimensions of that disparity and the barriers to reducing it significantly requires merciless analysis and unillusioned practice.

The writer's intention is not to promote pessimism, but to underscore the necessity for critical analysis. This paper can only sample the kinds and locations of system inadequacy and it therefore makes not the slightest pretense to be a comprehensive analysis. It does, however, seem appropriate to take note of indicators of defects in quite different system dimensions.

Data that are commonly available reveal that (1) the lack of provision for adequate assessment of social services is itself a major defect of the system, (2) dysfunctional service design and malfunction in service execution are the general condition in social welfare, (3) there is a gross disparity between the quantity of social want and problems on the one

27

side of the scale and the quantity of service provision on the other, (4) from a macro-perspective, the social welfare system is seriously defective in its historical state of development, technology, structure, position in the social economy, and its ability to plan (restated, it is defective in its goals, means, performance, rationality, and capability).

FAILURES OF SERVICE DESIGN

A systematic formulation of design principles does not seem to exist, even though a framework of determinants would be desirable for service construction and inspection. A suggestive list could include such designations as the principles of size and scope (i.e., the fit or congruence of a service with what it is intended to do), response to want, precision, operability, internal logical construction, economy, functional utility, and feedback.

It can be hypothesized that failure to apply these principles will result in defects in the social services. Such defects might be described as service insufficiency or incompleteness, distortion, confusion, ineptness, malformation, inflexibility, and inutility. All of these defects—but in proportions and quantities that are not reported—confound the system of social service delivery in the United States.

Public assistance will serve to illustrate some of these failures of design. Moreover, it illuminates another important point, the interdependence of defects.

Assistance Budget and Grant

The first item to be considered will be the assistance budget and grant. Among design imperfections in this area are incompleteness, insufficiency, distortion, and inutility. The definition of *need* is left to the individual states, most of which have interpreted the maintenance of health and decency to mean minimum subsistence. Separate state determination invites differences, and the consequent variations in grant amounts are considerable. This in itself announces that entire assistance-receiving populations are being treated inequitably.

The summary analysis of White is pertinent. Thus, she reports, a family of four, consisting of a mother and three children of specified ages, could have a budget base as stated in the schedules of the various states ranging from a low of $124 monthly to a high of $295.[1] Her

---

[1] Gladys O. White, *Yardstick for Need* (Washington, D.C.: Bureau of Family Services, U.S. Department of Health, Education & Welfare, 1964),

illustrations of actual and specific assistance budgets carry their own implications. This family of four in a state with middle-range practices is allowed a budget of $215 monthly ($2,580 annually), which is higher than the national median of $191. That budget, however, does not include a number of items that are standard even for a minimum health and decency budget. Consequently, the family must spend money on unbudgeted items such as newspapers and church attendance and perhaps pay $50 for rent rather than the allowed $40. The amount left for food might come to $80, one-fifth less than the amount so identified in the schedule. Consequently, each child will have one cup of milk daily rather than the three or four recommended by the Consumer and Food Economics Research Division of the U.S. Department of Agriculture.[2] Fats and cereals will constitute their major fare.

In another state, where there is an arbitrary maximum payment, there is a gap between the state's own definition of minimum subsistence ($2,124 for a family of four) and the amount provided to families receiving assistance. In this case the food allowance for this family of four is $52.67.[3] To determine the degree of insufficiency for the achievement of health and decency, this budget is contrasted with other standards. It should be noted that the poverty level "is based on the restricted variety of foods suggested in the Department of Agriculture economy food plan," which is for emergency use.[4] Another—and higher—standard is appropriately called the "low-level standard" rather than "minimum adequate" to avoid confusion with still another standard, the Bureau of Labor Statistics' " 'modest but adequate' city worker's family budget, which is 50 per cent higher. . . ."[5] So this family with a yearly income of $1,680 was provided with 79 percent of the state's own oppressive standard of $2,124, 55 percent of the national poverty line of $3,040, 44 percent of the low-level standard of $3,790, and, referring to that "modest-but-adequate" standard, has one-third of the money needed to live in health and decency.

The issue of completeness of service design can be posed as a question:

---

p. 3. The public assistance data and illustrations that follow are drawn from this report. The budget figures are from 1961.

[2] *Food for Fitness: A Daily Food Guide,* Leaflet 424 (Washington, D.C.: U.S. Department of Agriculture, Agricultural Research Service, Consumer & Food Economics Research Division, March 1958).

[3] White, *op. cit.,* pp. 9–11.

[4] Mollie Orshansky, "Recounting the Poor—A Five Year Review," *Social Security Bulletin,* Vol. 29, No. 4 (April 1966), pp. 20–21.

[5] *Ibid.*

Once what the product should be is formulated, what happens if part of it is omitted? The inquiry has to be made item by item, service by service, to determine if there is a "breaking point," the point at which the product cannot possess the intended utility or is even dangerous or destructive.

The notion, then, that any product is better than none—that the giving of money is ipso facto positive and virtuous—is deceptive and diversionary. The producers of goods and services are accountable not solely for the act of production, as if any kind of product were worthy of commendation, but for the whole of what is produced and for its consequences. Nor is this accountability relieved by consumer ignorance or by the willingness of human beings, out of their desperate drive to survive, to take what they are given in the absence of what they require.

The product package in public assistance is below the breaking point: it is a construct that has destructive consequences. The 7.4 million persons receiving public assistance are relegated to a continuing state of poverty—at a level well below the upper boundaries of that condition.[6] The destructive concomitants of poverty can be countered, it is recognized, only by bringing people "off the periphery" to become "a functioning part of the community."[7] Public assistance functions as an important social mechanism for locating people within the community structure; it places the millions who receive it on the periphery.

Service Distortion

Another cluster of defects may be described as service distortion, which refers to the inclusion in a service of deceptions and anomalies, analogous to a rider on a bill. In the market these are known as "sharp practices." For example, Perkins has observed that "the amounts of money we give are so grossly inadequate that no one—not even the most expert manager—could manage them to meet the cost of even the barest living essentials."[8] It is assumed, however, that recipients will be "rational" in preferring dire necessities and in making economic purchases. When they do not they are presumed to need help in budget management, which becomes an auxiliary service associated with the grant. There is

---

[6] The figure given is for June 1965.

[7] Lola M. Irelan, ed., *Low-Income Life Styles* (Washington, D.C.: U.S. Department of Health, Education & Welfare, 1966), p. 9.

[8] Ellen J. Perkins, "Let's Try Money," p. 3. Paper presented at the Ohio Welfare Conference, Columbus, Ohio, November 1966. (Mimeographed.)

a real problem of consumer protection and counseling, and some successful efforts of an "unorthodox" nature are reported, such as dealing with the market (e.g., welfare group buying co-ops) and concentrating on groups especially vulnerable to victimization.[9] The association of such services with the granting of assistance places the onus on client capability rather than on the unworkability of the grant, client victimization in the market, and so on.

Another anomaly is the use of an apparently scientific design procedure to develop a defective product. A technology is developed to construct tables of consumer requirements; its use is then successively corrupted with the technical label being retained. Of course, it is understood that the real intent is to determine who is to be excluded from the system rather than to create something that enhances effective use. But this process contributes to an illusion that there has in fact been an individualization of services, that what has been evolved has some specific significance for the recipient's well-being. Since the grant amount has been so carefully calculated, it takes on an aura of legitimation that persuades practitioners in the field that they have done something important and suppresses the client's ability to say it is not enough.

Yet another form of distortion is the inclusion in a service of conditions, supplementary interventions, and secondary outcome expectations that the client, if he had freedom of choice, would refuse. Classically, this is seen in the idea that a service provides access to other interventions. It has taken the form of "worthiness" as a condition for material relief, such as, in the case of housing, the concept of "desirable tenants." Thus it is reported:

> Housing authorities see their role as that of protecting society, rather than rehabilitating families. The attempt to exclude "undesirable families" has often resulted in arbitrary [use of] power without adequate safeguards to protect families from its exercise. [So they] have attempted to exclude families for engaging in political activities, for having illegitimate children, or because a member of the family was imprisoned. . . .[10]

Services frequently become vehicles for attempts to enforce social norms and thrust specific notions about desirable life-styles on a "captive" population, of which the moralizing in the Aid to Families with

---

[9] Irelan, *op. cit.*, p. 84.

[10] Michael B. Rosen, "Tenants' Rights in Public Housing," in Norman Dorsen, ed., *Housing for the Poor: Rights and Remedies* (New York: New York University School of Law, 1967), p. 156.

Dependent Children program is a dramatic example. Such imposition and manipulation tend to appear in some form whenever the consumer is compelled to take what is offered; it is one of the hazards of monopoly.

Adding to the effects of monopoly is another element that invites supplier arbitrariness in service design and delivery. This is the social welfare field's preoccupation with need, which saturates the professional language. A primary problem with this is that it bypasses such things as wants and consumer demand. Service designers have to make judgments about how to transform needs into useful services; that is, they made decisions for people about what they want. This invites decisions about what people *ought* to want. If the guesses are wrong and the consumer is not persuaded to want what is proffered, he is likely to be seen as resistant or unappreciative. Control over service variability is a fundamental task in service design. This is dependent on feedback, which is seriously reduced in social welfare by a paucity of outcome analysis and expression of wants.

Assistance Categories

The design problems in assistance have hardly been touched on. The assistance categories, to add another, violate the principles of internal logical consistency and economy. Originally accepted as a strategy for squeezing as much as possible out of the nonrational biases, sentimentality, and political assessments of reluctant policy-makers, they continue as a permanent institutionalization of inequity, a hierarchy of differentiated deprivation. In December 1965, the average monthly payment per recipient for old age assistance was $79.87; for the blind, $92; for the disabled, $87.27; and in AFDC, $35.53.[11] Administration of the categories is costly. Their existence increases the complexity of the program. Moreover, the necessity to define the categories leads to obstructive and arbitrary requirements that further block the availability of assistance.

Administrative Malfunctions

The problems of administration require comment. The administrative malfunctions in assistance are legion—its excessive complexity, its procedural compulsiveness. Detailed procedural arrangements promote ri-

---

[11] Advisory Council on Public Welfare, *Having the Power, We Have the Duty* (Washington, D.C.: U.S. Department of Health, Education & Welfare, June 1966), pp. 28–29.

gidity, arbitrariness, and denial of service to clients. An example is the budget item for "special needs," in which a combination of worker subjectivity, uncertain resources, and the need in some jurisdictions for supervisory authorization produces tremendous variations. Having a decent bed often is a matter of chance and depends on the client's delivery team—worker, supervisor, and office. Habituated patterns of work distribution and task deployment, unreal expectations about staff interests and abilities, are deeply rooted and unexamined. The Midway findings report this: "Both workers and supervisors invested most of their time in work for which they were not specifically prepared." [12]

EFFECTS OF SERVICE DYNAMICS

It is time to summarize these service dynamics and consider some effects. For a person without money, the immediate issue is to get some. Having satisfied the entrance rites of public assistance, the client soon becomes aware that he still needs money. He has moved from the initial stress of poverty into a new state of stress of which the agency, originally conceived as a salvation, is a perpetrator. The worker is denied the satisfaction of truly helping his clients, and is induced to become an expert in diverting and cooling out client dissatisfaction. To transfer the primary issue upward in the agency hierarchy is futile; it can be taken as evidence of the worker's inability to divert the client's attention from money to other things, such as the greater accommodation to reality known as resignation.

It is evident that the program's administrators do not think highly of what it is or does or of those it serves. Its facilities commonly are disrespectful of the client. The agency is isolated from the community and its services are not advertised. There seems to be a reluctance to let potential service recipients become aware of what might be available to them. What is offered is contradictory and compromised, an excellent demonstration of T. S. Eliot's comment on history: ". . . and what she gives, gives with such supple confusions that the giving famishes the craving." [13] What can be said of a service that stigmatizes the people who use it simply because they use it? Perhaps the term is service contamination. The social recognition that people without money must

---

[12] Edward E. Schwartz and William C. Sample, *First Findings from Midway* (Chicago: University of Chicago, School of Social Service Administration, 1966), p. 5.

[13] "Gerontion," *The Collected Poems of T. S. Eliot* (New York: Harcourt, Brace & Co., 1930), p. 44.

have it has always been haunted by the notion that to be given it is worse than not to have it. Once this was termed pauperism; now it is called dependency.

So workers are caught in the contradictions and negative feedback of the service. They are handicapped by bureaucratic ritualism, confused by inappropriate assignments, suppressed by conservative and often authoritarian administrations, and tend to have a high turnover rate. The program is short on personnel; it has been suggested that from ten to fifteen thousand caseworkers and two to three thousand supervisors are needed.[14] But their value is dependent on improvement in the nature and circumstances of their work.

The potentials of public assistance have been aborted and converted to tragedy. It has been observed that the mortality of nonwhite infants is proportionately much higher than for white infants.[15] There was little change between 1950 and 1966. For neonatal and postnatal deaths combined, the rate has been about two to one; that is, in every thousand live births in 1966, 20.6 white babies and 38.8 nonwhite babies died. In other words, in any recent year approximately 12,000 infants died because they failed to receive the service package that was available to other infants. The ingredients of this death prescription are multiple, but it can be observed that a disproportionate number of minority group mothers live on what public assistance provides and we have just reviewed the fact that they accommodate to the insufficiency of the grant by nutritional deficiency and slow starvation. Public assistance might have been expected, even if decency were not intended, to do away with hunger in the United States. But the most recent report "finds that 10,764,000 Americans are suffering from hunger, and that 20 million more are not adequately fed." [16] If this is the test, public assistance has failed.

There is another indicator. In June 1965 it was estimated that there were then 35.1 million noninstitutionalized poor, of which 7.4 million received public assistance. Described as "categorically eligible" under the public assistance titles of the federal Social Security Act was a

---

[14] Advisory Council on Public Welfare, *op. cit.*, p. 79.

[15] U.S. Bureau of the Census, *Statistical Abstract of the United States: 1967* (Washington, D.C.: U.S. Government Printing Office, 1967), Table 64. *See also* Helen C. Chase, "White–Non-white Mortality Differentials in the United States," *HEW Indicators* (June 1965), pp. 30–31.

[16] "News Report," *New Republic*, Vol. 158, No. 19 (May 11, 1968), p. 4. Compare *Report of the Board of Inquiry into Hunger and Malnutrition in the United States* (Washington, D.C.: Citizens' Crusade Against Poverty, 1968).

larger number of people than those receiving assistance—8.7 million people, including 3.5 million children.[17]

SERVICE LINKAGES

With some divergence, we have been looking at one service, inward at its design and outward at its effects. Now the application of service design principles will be considered from the perspective of service linkage. Briefly touched on will be service sequence, splitting, and co-ordination, output mix, and the issue of size. Dysfunctional indications in the present situation will be noted.

A point previously made is that a useful service is constructed to fit its task. Key processes are (1) specification of the task, which includes its proportions, and (2) establishing task-service congruence. The part played by the service in the whole task is important, so a specified service might have total responsibility, be responsible for some part of the task, or work in conjunction with other services.

There are numerous examples of inattention to these considerations, the result being a ritualistic gesturing rather than a real service, or an aborting of the overall intent. The fragmentation and isolation of agencies is a major structural expression of this defect. Among commonly observed consequences are clients confused when confronted by the maze of agencies or the difficulty in bringing combinations of service into co-ordinated alignment for families with multiple problems. Studies report that agencies are often not only unable to provide services to applicants, but are unable to connect the applicants to other agencies. Agencies seem commonly to lack awareness not only of each other's services, but of each other's very existence.[18]

Service Sequence

One form of this disorder appears when services follow one another sequentially. Much so-called referral is futile, because it is not seriously designed to enable those referred to get to and use services strategically

---

[17] Ellen J. Perkins, "Estimated Numbers of the Noninstitutional Poor by Individual and Family Characteristics, by Category and by Public Assistance Status, June 1965" (Washington, D.C.: U.S. Department of Health, Education & Welfare, Bureau of Family Services, October 8, 1965).

[18] See *Community Organization of Child Welfare Services* (New York: Child Welfare League of America, 1955); and "Proposals for Better Delivery of Services" (New York: Citizens' Committee for Children of New York, 1965). (Mimeographed.)

responsive to their circumstances. It is too frequently a ritual, a pretense, of assumption of responsibility. Another illustration is the frequent discontinuity in institutional and community services that require a tight symbiosis if, in some cases, either is to come to anything.

Service-splitting

A variant of the linkage problem is the splitting of a unitary service construct into parts, each of which is thought to be a service. It took a long time for the concept of the mental institution as a therapeutic milieu to be generally accepted—the idea that the whole institution was therapeutic, not that one part of it provided therapy and other parts had no therapeutic effect on the patient population. In the provision of many services there is an odd quality of split identity, with casework being the part that "counts" and other aspects of the service, although necessary, not having the same significance. The author has said elsewhere that social work has been so hungry for essence that it has derogated its substance, failing to understand that its expertise with the social material it organizes and administers is the central dimension of its uniqueness and utility.[19]

Service Co-ordination

In its attempt to achieve scope, social welfare has largely utilized the mechanism of a loose linkage of independent services that require co-ordination. Examination suggests that the failures of co-ordination either to overcome tendencies to system disorganization or in achieving effective service linkages vastly outweigh its successes. Existing co-ordination reveals a number of defects.

For example, co-ordination fails to begin with the delineation of tasks and to contrast the purported scope of the co-operative system with the task. Recognition of these defects in problem definition and in scope has stirred up some talk but little service or program revision or development. On the community level, interagency co-ordination has been the main thrust. Restricted in orientation, understaffed, with incomplete participation, lacking reliable indicators of what operational relationships would lead to what results, these formal efforts have not resulted in any significant degree of co-ordination. Co-ordination frequently be-

---

[19] Albert Comanor, "The Situation as a Model for Practice: Discussion of a Paper by W. W. Boehm." Unpublished paper presented at the National Conference on Social Welfare, Dallas, Texas, May 1967.

comes a euphemism for sustaining a habituated pattern of unmet needs. There is also persistent concern about duplication of services, which provides a minor note of the ludicrous in a tragedy of nonexistent and insufficiently supported services.

The assumptions in co-ordination can be challenged. Innumerable community and agency studies have been made—and ignored—producing a survival crisis for agency co-ordinative planning. The current trend is toward a multiplication of planning centers.[20] The initial assumption in this process has been challenged, as witness this comment by Levine:

> It is safe to say that in most communities and within most states no single agency is charged with the responsibility of coordinating the activities of other health and welfare organizations. [While some may claim this role], it appears in reality that most agencies are not prepared to invest in a single person or agency the responsibility of establishing priorities for other agencies. . . . Thus, while a number of agencies often decry the lack of planning and coordination and express the need for greater interaction and cooperation with other agencies, they have been less prone to accept, in practice, the direction or even the active leadership of another agency that may infringe on their own jurisdictions.[21]

A *realpolitik* of welfare would acknowledge that co-operation is being sought in an atmosphere of interagency competition for scarce funds, of functional rigidity, and of more reciprocal distrust than is openly admitted. Nor is this matter advanced when complaints about agency autonomy issue forth from some federations and funds whose transparent interest is to consolidate central power over organizations and which know little and care less about the services than do the agencies they hope to dominate.

Output Mix

One of the functions of a system of services is to establish the proportions and quantities among them, which is called output mix. There is a

[20] *See* Robert Morris and Martin Rein, "Emerging Patterns in Community Planning," in *Social Work Practice, 1963* (New York: Columbia University Press, 1963), pp. 155–176.

[21] Sol Levine, "Organizational and Professional Barriers to Interagency Planning," in David G. French, ed., *Planning Responsibilities of State Departments of Public Welfare* (Chicago: American Public Welfare Association, 1967), pp. 54–55.

theory in social welfare, analogous to the "unseen hand" theory of classical economics, which supposes that needs will result in products by a rational process running from need-awareness to need-satisfaction. The decisions, however, are affected by factors extraneous to consumer wants. Services are specialized, and some are more prestigious than others—they seem to offer a better unit payoff for the fiscal and man-power investment and are more likely to obtain financial support. The system may not earn monetary profits, but it is supplied by psychological concomitants of profit: control of future earnings, comparative status, power over decisions affecting others. Decisions about what services to give preference to are frequently made with an eye to these profit concomitants rather than to need. Consequently, an analogue to economic submarginality develops in which some services, compared to others, are low in the mix and poorly supported in money and sentiment, quite without respect to the need for them.

Despite feeble attempts at "scientific" priority planning, which largely sum up competing interests, there is no reason to believe that product mix is functionally correlated to need. Indeed, there is considerable evidence to the contrary. So there are unmet needs, inexplicable variations in service proportions, geographic imbalances, obstinate survivals of obsolete organizations and practices, and so on.

Scope and Size

Large problems produce large tasks that call for intervention on an appropriate scale. Against the character of present issues, what is done is insufficient in design and intent. Some program labels admit to the need for magnitude—the War on Poverty, Comprehensive Mental Health, Model Cities. But what a disparity there is between what they portend and their substance! Perloff has observed that the federal government, which is so centrally important in enterprises of such scope,

> has become involved in urban affairs at the wrong level and in the wrong way. It is still largely mixed in the neighborhood project (the individual public-housing unit, the small urban-renewal project, the neighborhood poverty program, and the like), instead of being concerned with the metropolitan and megalopolitan region as a whole and with the rules of the game.[22]

---

[22] Harvey S. Perloff, "Modernizing Urban Development," *Daedalus*, Vol. 96, No. 3 (Summer 1967), p. 797.

Altogether missing from the analysis—almost absent from our knowledge—is that understanding of the human scene that is suggested by the concept of human ecology. The construction of an environment in which each individual and group has a niche conducive to fulfillment is a task not yet seriously begun.

The Service and the System

A major fault in the system is that it is not oriented, at the point of service delivery, to the use of its potentials; rather, it is preoccupied with the often fortuitous use of specific services. The present hegemony of specialized treatment-oriented agencies contributes to the unserved problems that fall between them, to the frustration of the client lost in the agency maze, to the provision of services that are not the strategies of choice, to the narrow self-absorption of agencies in their walled-off specializations.

Initial contact points in social welfare do not operate as entrance portals to the system as a whole. Primary tasks do not generally include strategy determination and the exploration, creation, and organization of opportunity. Such an orientation is seen in the proposals for establishment of Neighborhood Information Centers, but these are only now appearing.[23]

INDICATORS OF DYSFUNCTION

Indicators of dysfunction in other areas of the welfare system will now be sampled, with special notice given to the quantitative disparity between problem and provision. An extremely rough indicator, although it makes the point, is the fact that the general state of service provision runs from zero to about half of what is required for minimum adequacy. National expenditures in child welfare were $396 million in 1966; "an adequate program would cost another $400 million." [24]

By 1962, 8 million mothers with children under 18 years of age were working. Of these mothers, 3 million had children under 6 years of age. The capacity of all reported licensed day care facili-

---

[23] *See* Alfred J. Kahn, *Neighborhood Information Centers* (New York: Columbia University School of Social Work, 1966).

[24] Alexander L. Crosby, "The Price of Utopia," *Monthly Review,* Vol. 19, No. 12 (May 1968), p. 24.

ties in the United States (day care centers and family day care homes) was estimated at 185,000 children.[25]

The U.S. population not within the coverage area of voluntary family service agencies in 1966 was 43 percent, and 47 percent of the agencies had waiting lists.[26]

Draft rejections for medical reasons and international comparisons of life expectancy and infant mortality underscore the inadequacies of the nation's health services. A doubling of the present national annual expenditures for health services of $48 billion could, it is proposed, achieve across-the-board adequacy if accompanied by reconstruction of the delivery system.[27] The cost of all government assistance programs now comes to about $4.6 billion. To raise all grants to the poverty line would require about $11 or $12 billion a year. Similarly, to bring social insurance payments to the aged to the poverty line would cost about twice as much as is presently spent.[28]

A comprehensive program of legal aid "would cost at least $100 million more than the estimated $50 million being spent." [29] As for all legal services for the poor, it is estimated "that at least 14 million [legal] problems arise each year for clients who are poor." Adding up and estimating all services provided by all arrangements and programs, the outside figure of legal cases handled annually is 900,000.[30]

The Joint Commission on Mental Illness and Health found that "80 percent of the nation's 277 state mental hospitals had not kept in step with modern advances in treatment and still provide custodial care rather than treatment for their patients." [31] The number of children under 14 estimated to be in need of psychiatric care is between 2.5 million and 4.5 million.

---

[25] Leon Richman, "Day Care," in Harry L. Lurie, ed., *Encyclopedia of Social Work* (New York: National Association of Social Workers, 1965), p. 245.

[26] *Family Service Statistics,* Part III, Summary of 1965, Table 11, and Summary of 1966, Yearly Report, Questionnaires, Chart II (New York: Family Service Association of America, 1965 and 1966).

[27] Crosby, *op. cit.*

[28] *Ibid.,* p. 26.

[29] *Ibid.,* p. 25.

[30] Stanley Zimmerman, "Introduction," *Housing for the Poor: Rights and Remedies,* Project on Social Welfare Law, Supplement No. 1 (New York: New York University School of Law, 1967).

[31] Quoted in *Health Care Issues of the 1960s* (New York: Group Health Insurance, 1963), p. 10.

The situation in 1963 points up the tragic paucity of services [with] less than one in ten, 295,000 children and young people below the age of 18, . . . being seen in outpatient psychiatric clinics . . . [and] only 2500 . . . receiving full-time treatment in [the] forty recognized treatment centers.[32]

A summary of these fiscal comparisons is provided in the A. Philip Randolph Institute's *A Freedom Budget for All Americans.*[33] Contrasting fiscal year 1968 with the annual expenditure if adequacy were to be achieved, the figures are $19.6 billion and $43.8 billion. Another, more inclusive, projection estimates an additional net annual cost of $55 billion.[34]

Such quantitative disparities are intermixed with qualitative and outcome issues. From the perspective of the single operation, poor conceptualization, lack of ingenuity, inept merchandising, and design defects may be factors in the inability of the service to catch public interest. Such faults can initiate a domino effect, closing out component elements in the construct, obstructing a clientele, discouraging support. The case of payments to foster parents seems to be of this order. The program design is distorted by an attitude that has interpreted the acceptance by foster parents of monetary recompense as contraindicative of appropriate motivation. There is, then, wide variation in payment ("from $32 to $88 a month for each child in average cases"), denial of foster home opportunities for certain kinds of children, and a shortage of foster parents.[35] In family service, design restriction is suggested by the fact that group treatment is reported by only 43 percent of member agencies of the Family Service Association of America.[36] Only one-third of such agencies seem to have services directed specifically to the needs of older people, such as foster placement of adults or homemaker services.[37]

A thread running through the history of the social services is the blocking of the extended use of improved designs, a clumsiness and

---

[32] *Planning Psychiatric Services for Children* (Washington, D.C.: American Psychiatric Association, 1964), pp. 3–4.

[33] New York: 1966.

[34] Crosby, *op. cit.,* p. 30.

[35] Haitch, *op. cit.*

[36] Booz, Allen & Hamilton, Inc., *Summary of Study of Philosophy and Objectives, Program, Organization, Planning and Financing for the Family Service Association of America* (New York: Family Service Association of America, November 1967), Exhibit III.

[37] *Family Service Statistics,* 1966.

weakness of the system that has caused a huge, if uncalculated, waste. There does not seem to be an adequate means of diffusing new developments throughout the field, or their acceptance in professional thinking has commonly not been accompanied by sufficient support in public sentiment, policy, and funding to produce full service coverage. Many demonstration projects considered productive died because they failed to obtain permanent funding. A recent dramatic example was Project ENABLE, a major extension of the practice orientation of the family field and an interesting effort in interorganizational service provision. It had rapid impact, but was abruptly ground out of existence by congressional cuts in the programs of the Office of Economic Opportunity.

Albee charges services for the retarded with an output mix problem. The service focus has been on the development of clinics oriented to biomedical treatment. In contrast to the 40,000 children served annually in medically directed clinics, he points to the almost 6 million mildly retarded adults and children who desperately need teachers, sheltered workshops, social workers, volunteers. He asserts:

> Where medical care is truly needed to prevent retardation, and where it has not been available, [is] in the prenatal and perinatal care of "medically indigent" expectant mothers in our large cities. Our efforts are out of balance and out of joint.[38]

It is when groups or classes of people are subjected to the effects of the ideologies of degradation that the services are most irrelevant, deformed, and destructive. Clear examples of nonexistent services are seen in the cases of the Negro migration from rural to urban areas and the situation of the migratory worker. The lack is especially evident in the former case, since tested models of planned resettlement programs do exist.

How seriously ideology can corrupt services is most brutally to be seen in the treatment of criminals and of nonwhite minorities. The treatment of crime is probably the most dramatic case of the failure of a technological society to come up with a technology. Daniel Bell speaks of crime as an "American Way of Life." [39] This country does not have an environment of personal safety, a society of equal justice, or effective and enlightened means of confronting offenders. Imprisonment, whatever its alleged necessity, is a barbaric horror in spite of cur-

---

[38] George W. Albee, "Needed—A Revolution in Caring for the Retarded," *Trans-action*, Vol. 5, No. 2 (January-February 1968), pp. 40–41.

[39] Quoted in Harvey Wheeler, "A Moral Equivalent for Riots," *Saturday Review*, May 11, 1968, p. 20.

rent reforms. It depends for its continuance on the social dynamic that Everett C. Hughes crystallized in the the title of a paper, "Good People and Dirty Work." [40] The dynamic is the process by which society mandates practices it deprecates. Aside from this, what is provided with the intent to be modern is in poor shape. Correctional schools are overcrowded; case loads are too high; parole, a prison without walls, is loaded with role confusion and contradiction.[41]

As for the minorities, the condition of the American Indian bespeaks the state of service provision. The American Indian Fund summed it up in a fund-raising letter:

> In return for the wealth of his forests, and plains, and fields, the Indian has received the least portion of America's bounty. Here is where he stands today: Schooling, 5 years; life span, 43 years; family income, $1500; unemployment, 45%.

As for the black American, the National Advisory Commission on Civil Disorders says of present policies and provisions that they advance from imperfection to crisis.[42] But as Wheeler points out, the real quality of this crisis of societal failure has not yet been grasped:

> Violence must be looked at in terms of the violation of the dignity of human beings. In these terms, violence is merely the sporadic counterresponse when one's humanity and one's dignity has been violated. . . . This country . . . has been a personality-violating culture since its birth.[43]

A group of black educators, addressing a conference at Harvard, referred to the ethnocentric ideology of society as "bent on the genocide of all black people." [44] The term is accurate: the destruction of dignity and identity is also a death. Against this horror of psychosocial degradation some elements of social welfare struggled, some evaded the issue, and some have shared in it.

---

[40] *Social Problems*, Vol. 10, No. 1 (Summer 1962), pp. 3–10.

[41] See Elliot Studt, *The Re-entry of the Offender into the Community*, Pamphlet 9009 (Washington, D.C.: U.S. Department of Health, Education & Welfare, 1967).

[42] *Report of the National Advisory Commission on Civil Disorders* (New York: Bantam Books, 1968).

[43] *Op. cit.*, pp. 19–20.

[44] Five State Organizing Committee for Community Control, "Position Paper," *Phi Delta Kappan*, Vol. 49, No. 4 (April 1968), p. 450.

THE ABSENT ASSESSMENT

One of the remaining two categories of system imperfection listed at the beginning of this paper is the lack of comprehensive assessment. Refer-ence is made to an "intelligence gap" that

> is rooted *in one-sided, missing, distorted, misinterpreted, or unused information.* The initial impact of the intelligence gap is that national policy makers are misled. . . . In various degrees this is the *status quo* of our domestic intelligence in the critical fields of civil liberties, discrimination, human values, the mass media, crime and delinquency [and all other social fields].   [Italics added.] [45]

As a solution to this, it has been proposed that an annual presidential social report, account, or audit be made.[46] However, presentation of a report does not guarantee positive action; there are many examples of long-delayed response to good data. To turn to the issues social workers face at their desks, within their agencies, and in their communities, granted that the missing comprehensive assessment contributes to uncertainty, a vast amount of defect could have been reduced or eliminated without national, regional, or even community inventories.

The welfare system contains structures and orientations that obstruct development and use of system assessment. Thus the knowledge required for a continuing analysis of social service delivery must include examination of the functioning of an explicit set of service models. Since the classical models are defective and unable to provide outcome data, a concentrated attempt to redevelop a set of designs that can be studied and debated seems an elementary requirement. The considerable outflow of papers that suggest more and more models is indicative of the problem but does not constitute the kind of deliberate engineering that is needed. At various levels, data should provide an inventory of services and the functioning of organizations, as well as information that can get at service linkages.

The necessary involvement of many levels of the system exposes assessment to the resistance and malperformance that are readily dis-

---

[45] Bertram M. Gross and Michael Springer, "New Goals for Social Information," *Annals of the American Academy of Political and Social Science,* Vol. 373 (September 1967), pp. 209–218.

[46] *See* Bertram M. Gross and Michael Springer, "A New Orientation in American Government," *Annals of the American Academy of Political and Social Science,* Vol. 371 (May 1967), pp. 10–12.

cernible at the delivery and agency levels. Gross anticipates, for example, that

> people of humanistic bent . . . [will read inaccurate interpretations into systems analysis] and will prefer the Cassandra-like role of bewailing the loss in human values as against enlisting in a positive effort to restore human values to a central position in man's thought and action.[47]

Concern for a meaning beyond the problem, the task, or the role can be understood, but Wooton's charge that the expression of that concern as an action goal is arrogant cannot readily be set aside.[48] Given present knowledge and means, an attempt to transcend the empirical carries losses not to be deprecated.

A further difficulty is the general administrative backwardness and ineptness of the system's agencies and organizations. They are generally lacking in administrative technology, are fuzzy about their goals, and are forced to use client counts and work units expended as indicators of the outcome of service provision. The influence of the classical model of service directed toward improved personal capacity, when the outcome is predictive, forces outcome analysis back on induction from behavioral theory and "tacit knowing," and so exposes the service to a variety of errors.[49] Pertinent is the *Manas* editorial remark that "philosophy that is shaped and made viable in the grain of design and practical construction has a clear pragmatic sanction: it may have limits, but within those limits it is filled with demonstrable truth." [50]

"The major disease," it has been said, "that can afflict any data processing operation is a hardening of the categories." [51] This disorder is already pandemic in welfare: knowledge categories, venerated despite

---

[47] Bertram M. Gross, "Social Systems Accounting," in Raymond A. Bauer, ed., *Social Indicators* (Cambridge, Mass.: MIT Press, 1966), p. 260.

[48] Barbara Wooton, *Social Science and Social Pathology* (London, England: George Allen & Unwin, 1959), chap. IX.

[49] Fred G. Ikle, "Can Social Predictions be Evaluated?" *Daedalus,* Vol. 96, No. 3 (Summer 1967), pp. 741–742. "Tacit knowing" is defined as a cluster of mental abilities that includes "selecting and integrating regularities from inarticulate experiences without being conscious of the process of selection and integration."

[50] The editor, "The Designing Intelligence," *Manas,* Vol. 20, No. 7 (July 5, 1967), p. 8.

[51] Gross, *op. cit.,* p. 260.

their incomplete development and often dubious validity; service categories, unmovable despite their obvious limitations; method categories, often criticized but not readily displaceable.

Another obstacle is a ubiquitous "euphoria" in the welfare system. This has two forms: optimistic reports of achievement and celebration of bit-by-bit advances in welfare policy or financing that are unaccompanied by a cold review of whether they are even keeping up with negative change processes. This optimism seems intended to placate opposition and to encourage continued confidence in further effort. A serious consequence of social welfare's focus on the small, as well as its excesses of optimism, is that this feeds into the suppressive tactic of concealment of social problems. It is understandable and operationally appropriate that the change agent will undertake what is seen as possible and may construct strategies of accretive development. But what may seem operationally appropriate within a given condition of policy and practice may not yet be relevant and has historically usually been insufficient. To neglect to comprehend and communicate what is inappropriate or insufficient is a failure of accountability. What has developed in social welfare is a crisis of criticism and credibility.

THE HISTORICAL LOCATION OF SOCIAL WELFARE

To judge the general state of the welfare system requires a framework for judgment. One approach is to consider social welfare in its relationship to the economy. This might be restated as a question: Given the state of this country's knowledge and technology, its per capita income, its expectations—what then would be congruent for welfare? The United States is emerging from the transitional stage between preindustrial and industrial society, a period characterized by economic adventurism, scarcity, capital accumulation, and of attempted maximization of privilege. But deprivation and inequality—social rigidities having been previously loosened—invite disorder and social problems. A society possesses an array of techniques for dealing with such issues: (1) redistribution of privilege, (2) dealing with problem formation by prevention or with developed problems by restoration, rehabilitation, sedation, seduction, or sequestration, (3) dealing with overt disorder by sedation, suppression, and dehumanization. Included among these techniques is a variety of social services, which are presumed to affect the capability for and expression of social disturbances, which manifest themselves in part as "welfare contingencies." The operating principles are brinkmanship and trial and error. Social disturbance and social problems need to be controlled, but the preference for means other than improvement in the power and possessions of the economically depressed constitutes a manifest instigation of these same problems and disturbances.

Collective effort, such as the trade union movement, resulted in power shifts, but since changes achieved in this way reflect successes by groups with varying interests, the resulting pattern of services is spotty and uneven.

The industrial society is characterized by economic rationalism. It contends with economic instability by planning and with potential disorder by introducing the concept of a comprehensive minimum level of satisfaction—for example, the currently proposed guaranteed minimum income—that is assumed as a political right, not as a charity.[52] This arrangement is the core of the welfare state. It is accompanied by governmental administration and planning, by research to identify needs and effectiveness, and the transfer of system guidance from the locality to the federal government. Welfare control by local elites, often claimed as a means of assuring more empathic service to recipients, has in fact more commonly in practice reflected inequity, client invisibility, reduced provision, and prejudice.

The transition to economic rationalism is facilitated by improved knowledge of the contagious effect of social problems and the limited effectiveness of control processes. Primarily, emergence into an economy of abundance makes possible redistribution of goods and, to some extent, status, without significantly affecting prestige differentials. This is indicated by trend data on the proportional distribution of income. From 1947 to 1962, the portion of the total money income of the nation received by the bottom 20 percent of the population fluctuated between 3.2 and 3.6 percent, while that of the top 5 percent ranged between 16.8 and 18.9 percent.[53]

Convincing analyses show that the welfare state can be achieved.[54] The Freedom Budget proposes two key policy developments: an effective program of full employment and a guaranteed annual income. On these

---

[52] Harold L. Wilensky, "Introduction," in Wilensky and Charles N. Lebeaux, *Industrial Society and Social Welfare* (New York: Free Press, 1965), p. xii.

[53] S. M. Miller *et al.*, "Poverty, Inequality, and Conflict," *Annals of the American Academy of Political and Social Science*, Vol. 373 (September 1967), p. 22.

[54] *See* Leon H. Keyserling, "Employment and the 'New Economics,'" *Annals of the American Academy of Political and Social Science*, Vol. 373 (September 1967), pp. 116–119.

foundations a "moderately good" advance in the Gross National Product is anticipated. The accretive gains in abundance, described as the "economic growth dividend," would in a ten-year period be thirteen times as great as the cost of a general reform of the serious problem conditions of society as presently perceived—which would include poverty, housing, urban decay, conservation, air and water pollution, health, and education. The expenditure of $185 billion more in comparative ten-year periods would not require a tax revision.

Beyond the welfare state is economic and social maturation.[55] One term for postindustrialism is the "Service Society." In social welfare terms, the services to be made comprehensively available would not be associated with being underprivileged. This is anticipated in the concept of social utility.

CONCLUSION

The present reality, as the data presented here reveal, is a jagged line of advance that is still struggling to develop a condition in welfare to match the state of the economy. The definition of "level of satisfaction" is still under contention. The situation is not so much one of rational welfare planning as it is a continuing struggle of interests in a manner that combines "brutal, pragmatic realism and humanistic ideology." [56] Achievement of a planned condition of minimal satisfaction—obvious, necessary, and reachable—a goal, moreover, that does not yet confront some of mankind's most profound problems, is being contested. Wilensky writes: "We move toward the welfare state but we do it with ill grace, carping and complaining all the way." [57] There has been recent evidence of a continuing preference for brinkmanship, as indicated by the congressional enthusiasm for police control of riots rather than for the preventive programs recommended by the riot commission report and by the passage of what Ginsberg castigates as "the most punitive piece of welfare legislation passed in the history of the United States Congress." Perhaps more indicative is his cautionary speculation that "an overwhelming proportion of the American people," if given the opportunity,

---

[55] *See* the entire Summer 1967 issue of *Daedalus;* Walter A. Weisskopf *et al., Looking Forward: The Abundant Society* (New York: Fund for the Republic, 1966); Daniel Bell, "Notes on the Post-Industrial Society," *The Public Interest,* Nos. 6 and 7 (Winter & Spring 1967), pp. 24–35 and 102–118.

[56] Gross, *op. cit.,* p. 251.

[57] Wilensky, *op. cit.,* pp. xvi–xvii.

"would vote for even stiffer legislation against the people who are in our welfare programs and against the people who are poor and need help." [58]

In the historical context, the social services in the United States are considerably preindustrial and in a transitional stage toward an industrial society, have some incomplete and underdeveloped welfare state characteristics, and contain traces of postindustrial elements. The modalities of intervention run the entire spectrum from dehumanization to preventive social reorganization. In brief, the state of social welfare in the United States cannot yet be described as civilized.

There is an old saw that a community's welfare situation is what it deserves. But it is not just for the population of this country to remain unfulfilled by the obstructions to welfare maturity. The entire world depends on the contributions that might be made by the first nation to achieve a postindustrial economy. The issues seem linked, with man's continued progress imperiled by the inequalities among nations and the development of effective measures to reduce those inequalities being dependent on the internal social maturation of the economically advanced nations.

In the meantime, there are the social services. General societal reform does not depend on their improvement, but their imperfections do constitute an ingredient in the state of public confidence about them. The question of whether something can be done about them can be a factor in policy-making. In their present condition they are like the worst offender in the *Mikado,* who was condemned to play billiards "on a cloth untrue, with a twisted cue, and an elliptical billiard ball."

---

[58] Mitchell I. Ginsberg, *Changing Values in Social Work* (New York: Council on Social Work Education, 1968), p. 5.

The Changing Demand for Social Service

JOHN S. MORGAN

The inadequacy of this country's welfare programs has become more and more apparent in recent years. For example, the *Report of the National Advisory Commission on Civil Disorders* has this to say:

> The Commission believes that our present system of public assistance contributes materially to the tensions and social disorganization that have led to civil disorders. The failures of the system alienate the taxpayers who support it, the social workers who administer it, and the poor who depend on it. As Mitchell Ginsberg, head of New York City's Welfare Department, stated before the Commission, "The welfare system is designed to save money instead of people and tragically ends up doing neither." [1]

There have been many other trenchant analyses of the welfare system and detailed proposals for amendments and additions to it.[2] It remains true, as the commission's report makes clear:

> Although many of the present inadequacies in the system can be

---

[1] New York: Bantam Books, 1968, p. 457.

[2] Advisory Council on Public Welfare, *Having the Power, We Have the Duty* (Washington, D.C.: U.S. Department of Health, Education & Welfare, June 1966).

identified, and specific changes recommended, long-term measures for altering the system are still untested.

A first strategy is to learn more about how welfare affects people and what its possibilities for creative use are. . . .[3]

With this turbulent atmosphere of change in mind and these unanswered questions of strategy so clearly posed, the writer will examine this topic more in relation to the trends of change than to the changes that have already taken place. In the present situation the social work profession must be aware of the dynamics of today's society. All around us are unsettlement, instability, and uncertainty. The profession must examine its own contribution to the well-being of society as a dynamic element in change and not tether itself to preconceived ideas of what is important or useful to the people it seeks to serve.

Change now takes place at a rapid pace. The early industrial revolution took place over six or seven generations: a man went from a rural environment to practicing a craft, his son moved into a small factory, his grandson into an industrial complex, and his great-grandson into the world of technocracy and professionalism. The present turmoil of civil disorders, educational reorganization, and technological redeployment have made change a normal way of life for most people under 30 years of age—and that means for more than half the American people. It is now expected that people in underdeveloped countries—and indeed, many people in this country—will make enormous social, industrial, educational, and community changes, not in seven generations, not even within one lifetime, but within a short period of perhaps one-third of a lifetime. The strains and stresses required by this enormous and rapid adaptation of human life to the conditions of a modern industrial society are among the major sources of contemporary social dysfunctions and disorders. The things about which we are all so worried—the breakdown of families, the increase in mental illness, the alienation of the cities, the growing dissatisfaction and disengagement of young people —are not themselves diseases, but are symptoms arising from rapid and only partially assimilated changes in the human condition required of all of us in this tremendous and uncertain age.

MAJOR TRENDS

The seven major trends in the changing demands for social services that the writer detects in this country and throughout the world are as follows:

---

[3] *Op. cit.*, p. 461.

1. From curative to preventive services.

2. From individualized to universalized services and, in this connection, from small-scale to large-scale operations.

3. From private to public responsibility for the social services.

4. From services providing income only to services that provide income plus additional benefits.

5. From the criterion of poverty to the criterion of need in determining eligibility for social services.

6. From services with a treatment orientation to the social administration of large-scale services.

7. From a limited view of welfare as a palliative, based on current assumptions about the distribution of wealth or about personal responsibility for well-being, to a broader view of welfare as encompassing the human condition.

Each of these trends will be discussed as they appear in the current scene.

From Cure to Prevention

The change in program emphasis from the curative to the preventive is being discussed with regard to all of the various social services, at least by those who feel they should be expanded. A model for such an expansion exists in the public health services that developed in the late nineteenth and early twentieth centuries as an extension of the curative medical services. Unfortunately, there is as yet no science of social etiology. A great deal remains to be learned about the underlying conditions to which preventive social services should be directed. Without such knowledge, how can we know what service will prevent which unsatisfactory human condition?

Preventive social services will therefore have to be thought of in the same way that the public health services are viewed, namely, as services that are relevant for whole populations, not isolated groups. Social need is a normal and universal human phenomenon. All people experience a variety of problems at various points in the life cycle for which help of one kind or another is needed. And today people must look to the society to which they belong to provide them with the kinds of services that will enable them to function adequately and satisfactorily. To pursue this analogy, everyone has a need for healthy conditions of air and water; measures to control air and water pollution are therefore services for all people. It is not possible for there to be clean air and water for just some population groups.

In this connection, the generally preventive nature of an effective income maintenance system is obvious. In a money-based society an adequate income prevents many forms of social deprivation. As Lord (then Sir) William Beveridge indicated in his famous report, adequate income for a family must be thought of as a major preventive of generally unsatisfactory living conditions, malnutrition, and ignorance.[4] Do we in this country see income maintenance as having this function or are we hampered by the puritan ethic that espouses the moral value of work? In other words, do we think it is more important for people to work for an inadequate wage than to receive a sufficient income as part of the appropriate distribution of the enormous wealth produced by modern industrial society? The evidence is that this is the case, and it is this attitude that has been a major deterrent to institution of a system of guaranteed income in the United States.

In 1964 out of the total U.S. population of 189.9 million, 34 million persons could clearly be defined as living in poverty; of these only 7.4 million were receiving public assistance.[5] Poverty is therefore not a welfare problem but a social problem. It can be tackled preventively only by tackling its causes, by re-examining the nation's arrangements for distribution of the abundant wealth it is now capable of producing. Social security and public assistance can serve to mitigate the consequences of existing poverty, but they can never be either cures for it or preventive of it.

Viewing social services as preventive rather than curative requires us to think about them in at least three new dimensions: (1) a reconsideration of the services themselves and their application to society, (2) the causes of social illness, and (3) a more generalized concept of the services in terms of the needs of whole populations. The notion of prevention raises for the social work profession questions of values, practice, and education to which it will not be easy to find answers. It is clear that the time has come to make the effort and to brave the storms of anxiety that will be provoked thereby.[6]

---

[4] Lord William Beveridge, *Social Insurance and Allied Services* (New York: Macmillan Co., 1942).

[5] *The Dimensions of Poverty* (Washington, D.C.: U.S. Government Printing Office, 1965).

[6] These ideas are clearly expressed by Florence Haselkorn, "An Ounce of Prevention . . . . ," *Journal of Education for Social Work*, Vol. 3, No. 2 (Fall 1967), pp. 61–70.

From Individualization to Universality

It has become commonplace to draw attention to the fact that modern social services largely grew out of the individualized services and programs for specific population groups offered by private agencies and have drawn on contributions from the social sciences for insights into individual needs. But it is becoming increasingly clear that present-day social problems affect large populations. This immediately raises the question of the extent to which and the ways in which existing social services can be adapted to the needs of these greatly expanded client groups.

One global solution to a major social problem—poverty—that is gaining increasing acceptance is the idea of income maintenance. The emergence of the notion of a guaranteed minimum income is a manifestation of the beginning recognition of the importance of an income provision system that is valid for the whole population. Another example of a universalized benefit—and one that has been adopted in every industrial country in the Western world except the United States —is a program of family allowances or universal children's allowances.[7] The growing pattern of basic old age benefits for all residents with a wage-related supplementary benefit, notably in Sweden and more recently in Canada, is a further indication of the extension of the universalized income maintenance schemes.

This tendency is emphasized in the riot commission report:

> Our longer-range strategy, one for which we can offer only the most tentative guides, is the development of a national system of income supplementation to provide a basic floor of economic and social security for all Americans.[8]

There has not as yet been a serious examination of what it will mean for the profession to serve a clientele that is not economically dependent. The inception of Medicare and Medicaid has created administrative and economic chaos in the health care field and raised some startling ethical problems for the medical profession. For example, raising fees for medical care to "what the traffic will bear" is clearly unethical when tax funds are the main source of payment. The medical certifi-

---

[7] For a comprehensive coverage of family and children's allowances, *see* Eveline M. Burns, ed., *Family Allowances and the Economic Welfare of Children* (New York: Citizens' Committee for Children of New York, 1968).

[8] *Op. cit.*, p. 462.

cation of disability in order to obtain services or financial benefits for a patient must now often contain an ethical conflict among the practitioner's medical interest, the patient's financial and social interest, and the public interest in economy in the use of scarce resources. The social service professions and social work educators have an obligation to make a systematic analysis of and preparation for the time when the technical problems of providing a guaranteed minimum income have been resolved. Otherwise the profession may not survive. Titmuss has expressed the problem neatly:

> The challenge that faces us is not the choice between universalist and selective social services. The real challenge resides in the question: what particular infrastructure of universalist services is needed in order to provide a framework of values and opportunity bases within and around which can be developed acceptable selective services aiming to discriminate positively, with the minimum risk of stigma, in favour of those whose needs are greatest.[9]

But in relation to this trend, it is also important to note the widespread reactionary forces in society that place financial rectitude before human values. This can be seen in the unwillingness of Congress to press ahead with antipoverty legislation and in the restrictions it placed on the program of Aid to Families with Dependent Children in the 1967 amendments to the Social Security Act. This reflects the growing reluctance of people to whom the present industrial society provides a relatively good living to sacrifice any part of their own affluence for the benefit of those who have not so far gained any profit from the technological changes and increased affluence of our society.

In light of this wave of negative reaction, the social work profession will have to accept responsibility for interpreting the facts of social need and move more vigorously into advocacy as a mode of practice.[10] This has its problems, but it seems to be an inescapable imperative of today's social conditions.

Examination of the implications of this trend from individualized to universalized services emphasizes the need for development of the art and practice of social administration. This is in fact one of the outstanding findings of the recent United Nations reappraisal of its tech-

---

[9] Richard M. Titmuss, *Welfare State and Welfare Society* (London, Eng.: National Council of Social Service, 1967), p. 27.

[10] *See* George A. Brager, "Advocacy and Political Behavior," *Social Work*, Vol. 13, No. 2 (April 1968), pp. 5–15.

nical assistance programs. Social science knowledge can help to improve administration of the social services. Needed is fundamental knowledge of organization, systems, communication, and small group theory and of modern developments in personality theory.

The question of incentives and rewards will also have to be examined. It is clearly no longer sufficient to think only of monetary rewards. The kinds of expectations people have for rewards in the form of improved status, increased power, and a sense of achievement must also be considered.

But this will not be sufficient to provide an adequate base for social administration. Forms of administration must be found that are infused and shot through with human values and with the value system that is fundamental to social work practice. The objectives social work seeks to achieve are social objectives and they will be achieved only if the administrators themselves hold such values and work with people in ways that are not antagonistic to these objectives. Here lies the challenge to social work for the expansion and development of its notions of practice to include administration as a social work method.

From Private to Public

The third trend cited earlier is the steady shift of responsibility for the expansion and development of social services from the private to the public sector. It is not surprising to learn that there is a serious shortage of resources, manpower, teachers, money, buildings, and other essential requirements for good social services. The sheer scale of both needs and services as they affect whole nations and communities dictates the establishment of priorities. Ability to pay for service is no longer morally acceptable as a priority. Decisions must be made on the basis of public policy. For example, if a nation lacks the dentists needed to provide adequate dental care for its population, some decision must be made about who is to get the available dental services. Some nations, for example, Canada and Great Britain, decided to direct the services to children, on the sound principle that it is better to devote available dental resources to the preservation of the teeth of the next generation than to expand the provision of massive dental care for those whose teeth have already begun to show serious deterioration.

It is this need to establish priorities in the public interest as much as the need to mobilize massive resources that leads us to turn to the government as the basic resource for the new types of social service that are emerging. This in turn raises new problems with regard to the allocation of scarce resources. Foreign policy, industrial production, and agricultural policy are all now to be taken into account in the allocation of the nation's total resources. The social services have to be seen in the context of the total national economy, and decisions have to be made about the proportion of the national income and skilled manpower that can be devoted at any given time to the prevention of social disorder and to repairing and easing already existing social conditions that in the judgment of the community must be alleviated or cured.

Another consideration arises in relation to the provision of public services: the whole area of accountability. When a professional person such as a doctor, psychiatrist, or dentist is in private practice, the only persons to whom he is accountable are his clients and, with regard to his professional behavior, his profession. But when dental or mental health service is made a public provision, the provider of service must be accountable to the community as a whole for the way in which he uses *its* resources.[11]

This question is raised as a preliminary to the consideration of the private agency's place in the modern social service complex. The discussion so far poses the problem of relevance. Human needs are as varied as humanity. The private agency is a selective instrument that must now move out into new areas uncovered by the establishment of universal or even partially universal public services. For example, as gross poverty becomes essentially a public responsibility, specific types of poverty will be uncovered that are not capable of being dealt with on the basis of averages or by any general public service. This is an unexplored area in which the private agencies have a responsibility to examine their place as the explorers and forerunners of new services— and as the responsible agents of society—in taking care of the special areas now being uncovered.

The development of new social services on a selective basis to meet newly uncovered needs will require a high degree of individualization and selectivity, two characteristics of the private agency field that open the way to new and exciting adventures in the development of social services. It does, however, pose a number of serious problems for the social work profession. It will involve re-examination of much of present practice and of many current assumptions about the nature and character of service. It also imposes on the practitioner the responsi-

---

[11] This is only one aspect of the whole problem of social accountability to which Bertram M. Gross has given prominence in his recent writings, especially *The State of The Nation,* in which he examines some of the many difficult problems of social systems accounting (London, Eng.: Social Science Paperbacks, 1966).

bility for identifying and exploring, on a research basis, the frontiers of the existing and expanding services, in order to see where these new needs really are and what services are needed to meet them.

From Money to Services

It is evident from the legislation now proceeding through the legislatures of various countries that it has been recognized that the provision of money, while essential in itself, does not in fact enable many people to obtain basic services of which they have need. Illustrative of this point are the 1962 amendments to the Social Security Act, with their emphasis on services, or Titles XVIII and XIX, which provided Medicare and Medicaid. Most of these services require public action because they call for the mobilization of services to a degree that simply cannot be achieved by the individual. Nor indeed can the private agencies, out of their own resources, mobilize anything like the volume, variety, or quality of services that many of their clients need.

In a pluralistic society such as the one to which we belong, it is both reasonable and desirable that there should be more than one provider of service. Indeed, there is so much to be done that the writer is much more concerned with service gaps and inadequate co-ordination than with any question of service duplication. The private agencies are the guarantors of this essential pluralism. There is, however, a real need for private agencies to concentrate on the provision of new services as the public sector increasingly comes to absorb the mass programs.

From Poverty to Need

There has been a movement—at least on paper and in discussions— from the criterion of poverty as a test of eligibility for service to the criterion of need. It is no longer morally acceptable to the social work profession to provide social services only to those who are poor.

However, if poverty is removed as a criterion of eligibility for service, it must be replaced by some other test. So far, a satisfactory criterion has not been found. The recent developments under Title XIX of the Social Security Act do in fact make the test of eligibility for medical care an economic test. The fact that the various states in administering the Medicare program have set equally various maximum income levels as a criterion of eligibility for the service indicates the undesirability and unreliability of an economic test in relation to the need for medical care. But if the test is not to be a financial one, what is it to be and how is it to be administered? Here again is a problem of creating social administration—not financial or political administration, but administration that achieves social objectives by social means.

It is clear that if poverty is to be discarded in favor of some other criterion for the provision of social services, there is yet a long way to go in developing adequate, socially justifiable, and administratively feasible tests to establish eligibility for a service. The current trend in the public welfare field—the separation of income maintenance from service benefits—is an indication that awareness of the problem exists, but there is little evidence that the subsequent problem of achieving socially just and administratively feasible ways of testing the eligibility of clients for service has been tackled.

From Treatment to Administration

The sixth trend noted earlier is the movement from a treatment orientation to an emphasis on administration in the development of new social services. This does not and should not mean that treatment services will be diminished. Rather, it means that new large-scale, universalized services will be added in order to make available to people services that they can use if they need them, without any consideration of a specific treatment orientation. There needs to be a careful examination of the proposition that treatment implies assumption of responsibility by the professional for diagnosis and care of the problem, whereas with the newer universalized programs, the client has responsibility for seeking and using the service. The need for the development of information services as part of the social welfare service system is clearly indicated if the client's responsibility is to be fulfilled.

If these services are to be successful, the client must be involved in the administrative process in which he is an essential partner. This will require social work practice of a high order but with a new orientation. In order to achieve it, painstaking research and bold experimentation must be undertaken, based on the assumption that the use to be made of the service is primarily a matter for the client to decide.

From a Limited to a Broad View

The social services are coming to be concerned with the whole arena of human well-being. This raises a new array of problems:

1. First among these are the corporate responsibility of the community as a whole and the individual responsibility of the citizen as a citizen. The essential problem is to design social service operations that retain the essential responsibility of the client and make available

to a person services of a kind, of a quality, and in a quantity that are relevant to his need. Perhaps the best example of this new range of problems is to be found in the field of urban redevelopment and public housing. Here again, one of the major issues is that of the nature and quality of the administration of the services. The social and biological sciences must provide additional knowledge, but social work must supply know-how, and this know-how must now include the deployment of resources—including staff—in large-scale operations. The aim should be not a welfare state with passive recipients of bounty whether from public or private agencies, but a socially responsible state in which the citizen is able to take an active part in creating and operating as well as in using services.

2. Social work practitioners have a unique and significant contribution to make in the identification of problems. Unless this sort of identification is made, the probability is that plans will go ahead without the kinds of values, social objectives, or patterns of administration and management that ought to be provided by social workers, with their knowledge of human behavior, respect for human dignity, and capacity to recognize the fundamental elements of human need.

3. A real problem for social work will be identification of the social aspects of economic and political programs. All of these, on the first superficial examination, seem to be questions mainly for the economist. It is only when the impact of any one of these programs on the lives and habits of individuals and families at all levels of the social spectrum is examined that one realizes the immense power for good or evil of schemes for the management of the national economy and the introduction of massive public programs with implications for redistribution of the national income.

4. The concept of "professional practice" must be expanded to include (a) social administration and (b) other new forms of practice such as those to which attention is drawn in the papers on the antipoverty program and the implications of these programs for personnel recently published by the Council on Social Work Education.[12] These papers cover many areas of practice; for example, Slavin draws attention to the need for "skill in social policy analysis, formulation, development, and evaluation." He points out that, while at present social policy and services are thought of as an essential background for social work

---

[12] *Personnel in Anti-Poverty Programs: Implications for Social Work Education* (New York: Council on Social Work Education, 1967).

practice, they have now become "for many social workers, operational—a form of social work practice, a 'doing' as well as 'knowing.' " [13]

5. The fifth major problem is the redefinition and realignment of the main directions of social work education. This does not mean discarding what now exists. On the contrary, it means enriching and enlarging what we now have in order to incorporate what has been gained in terms of knowledge and practice understanding from the new types of professional activity aimed at the new needs that have been uncovered.

Efforts to contribute a responsible professional reaction to any major trends in changing demand for services and many of the problems for the profession cited will depend for usefulness and development on a considerable expansion of research. It is probably also true that one of the kinds of research to which a great deal more attention should be devoted is comparative study of situations in different types of communities and in different nations. A better understanding of the essentials of practice will be gained if they can be seen at work within the different cultural and social milieus of other communities and other countries.

6. Examination must be begun of the implications for the profession of social work as the skilled art and practice of encouraging and developing community change. This in a way may well be a return to the earlier traditions of Jane Addams and other social work pioneers who devoted their professional lives to changing not only the societies in which they lived, but also the institutions of social organization and community service provision. The difference will be that the present task, in some ways more exciting and in some ways more difficult, will require involvement of clients not only in the change process, but in problem diagnosis and determination of the directions in which problem solutions will be sought.

CHALLENGES TO THE PROFESSION

All of the trends and problems cited raise a number of challenges to the whole pattern of professional thought. First, it is often said, but far too often not accepted or fully understood, that poverty, ill health, unemployment, old age, disability, and many other forms of human disablement are not, in fact, either the responsibility of or capable of being dealt with by individual action of the persons most concerned. The difficulty here is not only to persuade the social work profession and the community to accept these as community responsibilities but also to find

---

[13] Simon Slavin, in *ibid.*, p. 22.

out how services to meet these needs can be provided while at the same time retaining for the individual client a real and genuine responsibility in his approach to and use of the services. There is a danger that in our anxiety to make services available, we shall so organize and administer them that they will be, so to speak, provided by the "anonymous state," and this may quite easily lead the ordinary citizen to regard the state as fair game for anything he can get out of it. The probability is that the value of the services to him will be markedly diminished, if not totally destroyed. This is one of the many problems the profession ought to examine.

The second group of challenges is of a more fundamental kind. It will probably be impossible to make any serious inroads on the appalling housing situation in the large cities if it is necessary to be as respectful of the rights of private property as has been the case in the past. The hitherto respected "right" of the landowner to extract the maximum market value (often a hypothecated capital increase) will have to give way to the public interest if land for low-cost housing is to be made available at prices that make housing within their means possible for low-income groups. The rights of landlords to extract market value under threat of legal action from the rent of properties will have to be subjected to criteria related not to the market but to the notion of a "just" rent for the type and quality of accommodation offered.

In the same way, in the development of services, especially services such as medical care that are in short supply, substantial progress is unlikely to be made so long as the overriding values of private enterprise must be respected.

Similarly, the view that work is itself a good and that money obtained from employment has in itself an inherent social value has been accepted too easily. This is a relatively recent idea in the history of human affairs. The rapid change in the productive capacity of machines raises questions about the whole assumption of the moral value of work and wages.

It is therefore disturbing that the riot commission assumes that "the capacity to obtain and hold a 'good job' is the traditional test of participation in American society." [14] All the evidence now available suggests that present-day society will not be able to provide "good jobs" on a steady lifetime basis for all the employable people in it. The unemployment rates for the age group 16–19, whether white or black, continue to be two, three, and even four times the unemployment rates for the labor force as a whole, indicating the inability of the current

---

[14] *Op. cit.,* p. 453.

labor market to absorb them, a situation exacerbated by the lack of preparation they are given in the educational system for effective membership in a modern labor force. The current efforts to create jobs may be essential for today, but they represent last desperate efforts to restore work to a place in our social and industrial organism that cannot be sustained. Twentieth-century technocracy makes this an obsolete solution to a complex problem. Here is likely to be found the most serious resistance to change, not only among conservatives in the political arena, but especially among the captains of industry and leaders of organized labor, whose traditions have been based on the supremacy of work as a value and the virtue of wages as an incentive.

Last is the age-old question of class structure and status. One of the underlying discontents of most urban societies today is the apprehensiveness of citizens arising from their lack of social, economic, and political power in situations that profoundly affect their whole way of life.

Until the social work profession is prepared to examine objectively and without predetermined conclusions some of these sacred assumptions, we are unlikely to make any serious or effective approaches to problems such as housing, medical care, and poverty or indeed begin to comprehend the social needs of the alienated residents of the inner cities. These are not problems to be solved by statistical analysis, although it may well tell us where and when our judgments will be relevent and our decisions effective. In the last analysis, they are questions of good and evil in the whole context of human values in society. It is this interrelation of social, political, and economic policies within a moral framework that seems to set the stage for the kind of re-examination that the social work profession must undertake.

Service Delivery Problems
and Block Grants

MARTIN REIN

It is perhaps somewhat misleading to refer to the distribution of social services in the United States as a "system." Is this an appropriate framework within which to describe and understand the social services with their multiple, contradictory, and conflicting goals and the indefinite boundaries that distinguish public from social services (e.g., postal versus medical services)? What imagery should be used in describing these various services and their relationship to each other? The system analogy suggests that the parts are interrelated, functionally intertwined, and mutually reinforcing, with each unit contributing to some broader purpose than its own survival. To adopt this perspective is to confuse prescription with description and to blur the boundaries between myth and reality, practice and ideals. Moreover, unless the purposes of the "system" are specified, the discussion has not been extended very far, for no standards have been developed against which to evaluate its output.

Perhaps a geographic metaphor would be preferable. We would then be prepared to draw a map of the dispersal pattern of services by areas. This would be equally misleading, but for other reasons. In drawing a map, the boundaries of separate service regions can be distinguished, but this is precisely what is most problematic in the social services. Consider the case of the police department: It is clearly not a social service since its primary mission is social control and social protection of person and property. However, as James Q. Wilson has pointed out, the police can pursue many policies to achieve these aims, and some of these policies might justifiably be classified as social services. The Institute of Public Administration's budget analysis of youth services in New York City reports that the police department spent $1.7 million for individual, family, and community services, or 7 percent of the total amount spent by the city government for such services. Of even more interest is the fact that police department expenditures for these services amounted to half the total amount spent by the New York City Youth Board and more than the amount spent by hospitals.[1] This anomaly arises because the goals of social service are varied; they serve many purposes, including social control. They are not simply "humanitarianism in search of a method," as one influential writer in the field has suggested.[2]

A good case could be made for viewing social services as a mosaic in which the boundaries are vague, overlapping, and uncertain; reality and myth merge; and a participant's mood in observing developments of social policy shifts from euphoria to despair (as many who have been following the developments of the 1967 amendments to the Social Security Act must surely feel). But the analysis of problems in the organization of social services presumes a clear understanding of the purposes of social services and a reasonable definition of them. The classic illustration of the problem of definition is, of course, Titmuss's penetrating analysis, in which he argues that services performing similar functions should be grouped together.[3] Thus fiscal, social, and occupational welfare must be seen as part of the same system. The activities that are included or excluded from this more embracing definition affect not only total expenditure, but the characteristics of beneficiaries and the ultimate assessment of who pays and who benefits from the services. By this redefini-

---

[1] *The Administration of Services to Children and Youth in New York City* (New York: Institute of Public Administration, 1963), Table A-1, p. 56.

[2] Nathan Cohen, *Social Work in the American Tradition* (New York: Dryden Press, 1958).

[3] "Considered as a whole, all collective interventions to meet certain needs of the individual and/or to serve the wider interests of society may now be broadly grouped into three major categories of welfare: social welfare, fiscal welfare, and occupational welfare. When we examine them in turn, it emerges that this division is not based on any fundamental difference in the functions of the three systems (if they may be so described) or their declared aims. It arises from an organizational division of method, which, in the main, is related to the division of labour in complex, in individuated societies." Richard Titmuss, "The Social Division of Welfare," in *Essays on the Welfare Service* (New Haven: Yale University Press, 1959), p. 42.

tion Titmuss attempts to demonstrate that the major beneficiaries of the high-cost sector of the social services are the middle classes. As a result of the failure to redistribute benefits, a restructuring of the boundaries between these benefit systems must be sought.

The issues of purpose and boundary are closely interrelated. These questions are neither academic nor rhetorical, for they dramatically affect the way in which services are patterned and organized. But the boundaries of social services are not easy to define since institutions serve multiple purposes and it is difficult to isolate their primary and secondary functions. Ultimately, the definition of the problems of organizing a system should grow out of the assessment of the performance of institutions in relation to achieving their missions. It is the failure to achieve and the inability to state the outcomes sought that generate the administrative problems in the structure of social services.

For the reasons stated, agreement on purposes is indeed the most elusive and intractable issue in the social services. This is why the writer decided not to start with a classification of goals, but with the commonsense, traditional statement of the problems in the organization of services. It is a pragmatic approach, but one that, hopefully, will bring us closer to a clarification of the issues from which the principles for organizing social services can be developed.

The strategies of change must solve the problems of the present system. No one change will solve all the problems; hence it is necessary to clarify about which problems we are concerned and in what specific ways the restructuring and refinancing of services will contribute to reducing the problem at issue.

PERSISTENT PROBLEMS

It is possible to identify four persistent problems in the organization and distribution of social services. By and large, the delivery systems that will be created will be in response to one or more of these problems. Not all of the problems lend themselves to ready resolution.

Discontinuity

Many services are clearly interrelated, insofar as they contribute to the completion of a given task. Thus, recruiting, training, and placing individuals on the job are related activities in the sense that the same individuals may be involved in all of these activities over time. The problem of discontinuity arises when the flow of individuals among related programs is interrupted. This interruption may be related to structural and administrative difficulties that inhibit decision-making, as in the manpower system, or to philosophical, moral, and professional issues, as in the child welfare system, in which provision for temporary substitute parental care drifts into long-term permanent care. Protection of parental rights and a stubborn faith in their potentialities for rehabilitation inhibit long-term decisions. It is the nondecision system that poses the most challenging conceptual problems in creating a system to solve or reduce the problem of discontinuity.

As stated earlier, discontinuity arises when the flow of clients through the system of interrelated activities is interrupted. The flow can be impeded for many reasons. When scarcity produces a lack of resources, each service is bound to limit the number of individuals it can accept. This produces a backup in the sense that individuals are halted at the first stage of entry into the system. An entry backup can take the form of special institutions in which individuals await disposition for extended periods of time (overcrowded shelters and detention centers) or, in the case of community care, simply long waiting lists. Discontinuity may arise as well when each agency defines its boundaries through its intake policies in such a fashion as to reject graduates of other programs, for example, when a child guidance clinic will not accept children who have been in mental hospitals or an employment agency will not accept training program graduates with police records. In these examples, the flow from institutional to community care or from one service to another is halted because of conflicting agency policies. Finally, flow may be interrupted when referrals are based on faulty information or clients find it inconvenient to use the physical facilities of the next related program.

Reduction of Choice

In many, but not all, respects, social services can be regarded as social commodities that are distributed outside the market system. Simply providing cash to individuals may not, however, allow them to satisfy a social and personal demand with a marketable product, because the market does not respond instantly to consumer preferences. Factors such as professional monopoly inhibit the ability of the market to expand supply in the face of greater demands. The result, as in the case of medical care, is that a shift in demand only forces prices higher. Consequently, it is necessary to *plan* for the diversity and distribution of services to satisfy the preferences of individuals. Social services have traditionally been justified as social protection for those who fall out of the march of industrial progress and as an aid to those who lack the capacity to choose in adjusting to and making use of other institutions; it can be

extended to the concept of social provision to meet consumer preferences. But, characteristically, those who seek to influence the principles
on which social services are distributed have been fettered by the doctrine of efficiency or by paternalism masked as therapeutic intervention,
and have consequently neglected to take account of the role of consumer
choice in public provision. Many services have developed in such a
fashion as to narrow the range of choices and options available to individuals with low income and minority group status. For example, a
dual delivery system based on race has been created in child welfare,
and in medical care one based on income. Even within a given system,
choices are narrowed by preference being given to some services rather
than others, as the community care movement illustrates. The attempt
to match a specific service to a recognized need is dependent on the
development of firm knowledge demonstrating that a specific need will
be met best by a specific service. But this level of knowledge has not
yet been developed in relation to most services. There is thus little
justification for a policy of constraining choice in order to develop programs that are optimal to the solution of a given problem.

Support tends to be given to those services that are regarded as less
expensive. For example, the populations of mental and medical institutions are scattered into the community—often without adequate provision—guided by the belief that community care is to be preferred over
institutional care. The result can be not only less choice but increased
indirect costs, which are not taken into account because the social
arithmetic by which costs are added is too narrowly conceived. For
example:

> Considered only in financial terms, any savings from fewer mental
> hospital inpatients might well be offset several times by more
> expenditures on the police forces, on prisons and probation officers;
> more unemployment benefits masquerading as sickness benefits;
> more expenditures on drugs; more research to find out why crime
> is increasing.[4]

Without benefit of empirical evidence of program effectiveness and
without benefit of an accurate scheme of social accounting, it is necessary to create a delivery system that is explicitly based not on the principle of economy or the dominant professional fad but on the principle
of widening choices of consumers. Greater choice for consumers also
means more choice for professionals when they must act in the "best

---

[4] Richard Titmuss, *Commitment to Welfare* (London, Eng.: Allen &
Unwin, 1968), p. 106.

interests" of some clients. In other words, overlapping of services, which makes possible more choices, may be needed.

Functional Dispersion (Duplication)

This problem concerns the dispersal of a similar function among many different community agencies. Dispersal involves duplication. By and large, when this problem arises what is being discussed is the dispersal of personal social services, which are somewhat broader than are the social work functions. The problem of duplication is really the question of what these social services are and on what principles they should be organized, because we are, by and large, not seriously concerned about the availability of duplicatory or competitive programs in education, medical care, housing, or case transfers. Here pluralism is often regarded as the virtue of choice and not the vice of inefficiency.

Dispersal may be an effective strategy to obtain resources for a new or unpopular function, as in the case of manpower training at the federal level. At some stage in the process of development of such programs, there is interest in collecting, co-ordinating, or integrating these tasks and dispersal comes to be seen as a problem to be solved. The rationale often lies not in a concern about inefficiency but in a commitment to growth; by collecting hidden resources, visibility and power are increased, thus increasing the capacity to win more resources.

Incoherence

Specialized and differentiated services become fragmented when they cannot be combined in a coherent fashion so that they are relevant to the solution of a given problem. This difficulty arises when a single problem requires multiple interventions. For example, housing, medical care, education, and nutrition are all necessary in any coherent program to achieve a single target of reduced morbidity and mortality. Since the time phasing required to bring these activities together is often not self-evident (and different processes can be shown to yield different results), the problems of incoherence and discontinuity can be separated. That is to say, a distinction can be drawn among problems that require simultaneous interventions, those that require serial interventions, and those that require both. So defined, the problem of incoherence refers to simultaneous interventions that require planning for a mix of policies that take account of each other and reach the consumer at the same time so as to reinforce and build a new gestalt greater than the impact of each specialized service. But the intractable problem of incoherence arises when it becomes clear that multiple interventions also imply multiple goals. While it might be possible to develop a comprehensive plan (policy mix) in relation to a given goal, we have not yet defined a comprehensive goal to which all comprehensive programs can be subordinated. There are two problems of incoherence that need to be distinguished from each other: how to allocate and combine resources among differentiated programs to achieve a stated goal and how to distribute scarce resources among different programs that embrace different goals.

The Office of Economic Opportunity catalog of federal assistance programs for June 1967 lists a total of 459 programs to help people improve their social and economic positions. These are administered by fifteen different federal agencies and departments. The federal structure is paralleled by, in most but not all cases, state and local structures. Politically and conceptually it is more difficult to deal with the problem of incoherence, which requires concerting the efforts of different programs with different goals, priorities, and administrative arrangements so that they can concert their efforts on behalf of the same goal, the same population, or the same geographic or target area.

Achieving coherence is made even more difficult because of the daunting task of specifying program goals. A brief review of the experiences of the President's Committee on Delinquency and Crime, the Gray Areas programs, the War on Poverty, and more recently the Model Cities program makes possible identification of at least four competing and conflicting goals:

1. Improved competence of individuals and local communities. According to this conception, it is important that services be organized to enhance individual and group capability. Citizen participation is seen as crucial to implement this goal.

2. Improved competence of municipal government. Here the main purpose is to enhance the problem-solving capability of local government. The competence of managers rather than consumers is at issue here.

3. Maximum economic self-sufficiency. Here is a specific social problem—a single goal with multiple causes. No single program is capable of achieving maximum economic self-sufficiency. Education, manpower training, housing, medical care, and so on all seem relevant. No combination of programs may prove effective without an accompanying economic policy to assure full employment and adequate wage levels. Within these constraints, how can social services be organized to achieve this goal?

4. The redistribution of resources to the poor. Here the primary

concern is what proportion of the marginal rate of increase in economic growth should go to the poor. The goal is to alter the level of living of individuals with low income. The criterion of social progress is the reduction of economic inequality.

Thus, the question can now be restated: To what goals or social problems is the recombination of fragmented and specialized services oriented? The task is to allocate resources so that a coherent integration of social services is made possible. Yet efforts to solve the problem of incoherence have only created chaos in planning as an impressive number of comprehensive planning programs have been spawned in mental health, community action, Model Cities, delinquency prevention, and so on, thus exacerbating the problem that was to have been relieved. But there is no comprehensive plan that integrates all these comprehensive plans. Nor is development of one likely, since we cannot specify the social objective to which all these activities are to be subordinated. Hence it is doubtful if, in fact, principles for organizing these fragmented and incoherent services can be developed.

FINANCING AS A STRATEGY OF CHANGE

Can a new pattern, source, or level of financing solve these delivery problems? A preliminary clarification of some terms may be useful. By *pattern* is meant the form of funding: grants-in-aid, specialized matching funding, and block grants. By *source* is meant general revenues, earmarked taxes (e.g., social security), philanthropy, fees for services, and tax concessions. By *level* is meant the amount of funds, facilities, manpower, and other resources that are available. Even more important than the absolute level of financing may be the marginal rate of increase of the resources and especially whether they can grow more rapidly than prices and population increase (that is, the marginal rate of increase in per capita expenditures at constant prices).

Now to the heart of the problem posed. Can restructuring the financing of services rescue the delivery system from its endemic problems? Some people feel that there must be a move away from categorical financing (earmarked funding by specific programs) because it clogs the planning machinery and leads to an administrative game preoccupied with capturing the largest amount of federal resources, at the lowest level of financial commitment to the state or city. They urge that movement be toward a block grant rather than the categorical system at either the state, city, or neighborhood level. Many advantages are believed to accrue from such a scheme, one of which is the argument that block grants can become a way of concerting resources for social deficit areas. This approach alters the structure of financing rather than its overall level. Block grants could therefore be supported as a way of concentrating present resources in areas of geographic need. It is a strategy to promote territorial justice, especially if the grants are distributed on the principle of positive discrimination —i.e., areas with social deficits get more than other areas. More resources can be combined with more authority to make allocative decisions among the social services. The experience under the Economic Opportunity Act in experimenting with block grants that decentralize the locus of decision is informative.

The Office of Economic Opportunity set out to make block grants available to local communities. It was assumed that local control over resources could contribute to the reallocation of program priorities by the redistribution of these new funds. But this principle, while it was extolled in theory, was soon repudiated in practice. In time, more and more of the "free" uncommitted funds became tied to programs of national interest—Head Start, legal services, and the like —and in a short period of time a block grant system was converted into a categorical grant-in-aid system. The federal government had confronted a difficult dilemma. A block grant system might in principle enable the federal government to achieve more accountability through performance standards rather than through meeting established technical criteria that grant-in-aid programs follow. This could lead to a shift from input to output criteria. But the outputs have not been defined and the federal government does not appear to have the power to demand performance criteria even if it could define them. To achieve accountability, the federal government seems to have moved toward program specification, which, in effect, is the very grant-in-aid system from which it tried to depart.

But even if this dilemma could be resolved, yet another issue must be faced. New programs will have a difficult time getting launched, since a block grant system will respond to established institutions that have more clout than new institutions that have not yet been formed. Thus, to protect the development of new services, a special grant-in-aid would be needed. Clearly this form of financing promotes fragmentation, yet it has a stubborn vitality. It is likely to persist despite assaults on its negative consequences because it serves as a substitute for accountability and as protection for established and new services.

So much, then, for the administrative history of block grants under OEO. Can block grants solve the problems set out at the beginning of this paper? Block grants may contribute most to the solution of the problems of discontinuity and incoherence. But this is admittedly based on an untested, if plausible, assumption. It is known that the consistency of policies and the flow of clients through a system are inhibited when different levels (federal, state, and local) administer a program, each receiving funds from different sources. But if the present administrative structure were kept (in corrections, for example, state prisons, regional courts, and local aftercare facilities) and only the source of financing altered, discontinuity and incoherence could in principle be reduced by creating a common mechanism of fiscal accountability. But this reasonable argument remains inconclusive, for those who administer the block grant may lack the power to monitor, and if they have the power to monitor, they may lack the power to enforce decisions, and if they are given both powers, they may lack the resources to convert potential power into exercised power. The history of planning for the social services confirms this harsh but realistic assessment of the power to review and to act by planning bodies that control the allocation of funds.

The strongest case for an income-conditioned block grant system is that it might alter the dispersal of funds and hence the level of funds for special areas. This can be achieved without necessarily increasing the total amount of resources. This would not lead to a bigger pie, but one that is distributed differently. But can the level of resources have an impact on the delivery problems enumerated? Discontinuity and limited choice can be improved partially by higher levels of financing. This type of co-ordination among the social services can only be achieved by expanding the resources each service needs in order to collaborate with other services. When scarcity prevails, co-ordination fails. There is no sense in referring people for services that do not exist, and choice is constrained without sufficient funds to finance alternative programs. An adequate level of financing could, by contrast, facilitate the routing of individuals among related and alternative programs. It is doubtful, however, if it will contribute substantially to reducing the problem of incoherence.

It is widely assumed that financing can control the structure of social services. The principles of central financing—which in turn makes possible centrally organized and centrally co-ordinated services—are the basic ideas that inform the strategy of the United Funds. Yet UF has followed this model only to discover how difficult it is to create such concentrated power, given the American commitment to pluralism. At best, UF controlled only about one-fifth of all voluntary health and welfare funds.[5]   The Community Action Programs hardly did as well. Dispersed federal funds could not be made to flow through a central funnel into a central source and then be dispersed in a co-ordinated fashion.   Centralizing the diverse sources of the federal funds into a single local planning structure did not lead to co-ordination of different programs (coherence), simply because it could never be central enough. One billion dollars of CAP funds could not control the estimated $40 billion spent by federal, state, local, and private sources for services for the poor.[6]

SUMMARY

A modest restructuring of the source or expansion of the level of financing cannot solve the problems of dispersion and incoherence. Indeed, it may only exacerbate these problems by stimulating the development of new programs and by creating new centers to plan for these innovations. To alter the inefficiencies associated with the dispersion of similar functions and to promote the co-ordination of independent and unrelated functions (incoherence) would require a major concentration of funds, which would violate those established professional domains called specialization.   American society seems unwilling to accept this price to achieve coherence.   A new pattern of financing can, however, by concerting funds into limited geographic areas, affect *the level of resources,* and the level of financing services can in turn contribute to the reduction of at least the problems of discontinuity and limited choice. Redistribution of federal resources to areas of priority and need thus offers the greatest promise for improving the performance of local service delivery systems.   It is not the *pattern* for distributing resources that seems so urgently in need of reform, but the *level* of resources in areas of need.

---

[5] Alvin L. Schorr, "The Future Structure of Community Services," *Social Welfare Forum, 1965* (New York: Columbia University Press, 1965).

[6] This estimate is based on data prepared by Michael March, "Public Programs for the Poor," *Federal Programs for Human Resources,* Joint Economic Committee Report, Ninetieth Cong., 2d Sess., 1968.

Social Action Groups in a Mental Health Program

NELLY A. PEISSACHOWITZ AND ANNE R. SARCKA

A community mental health program meets its most severe challenges in a transient, low-income inner-city area. In such a neighborhood, the relationship between individual pathology, the rigidity and inadequacy of social institutions, and the illness that pervades society as a whole become inextricably interwoven. The mental health professional, who traditionally has been concerned with individual pathology, must reach the conclusion that if any positive impact on the mental health of the area's residents is to be made, intervention at all levels is a matter of the greatest urgency.

The crisis of relevance that is the theme of this symposium is a crisis that pertains not only to social workers but to everyone in the mental health field. While social work has been allied with social action throughout its history and many social workers have been on the front lines of social change, the field is still too heavily invested in methods that are no longer sufficiently relevant. This paper describes one aspect of an effort by Lincoln Hospital Mental Health Services to forge a community mental health program that would be relevant to the specific needs, hopes, and choices of a specific community, New York's south Bronx.

Within that community there has been a dramatic shift during the past few years from a neighborhood with a rather stable, low-to-middle-income working population, predominantly white, to one made up largely

75

of transients, mostly Negro and Puerto Rican, who have been pushed out of other neighborhoods. It is an area with little tradition of organization and few stable ties.

The social and health indexes of the area are appalling.[1] Institutions and agencies were not able, did not know how, or did not care to prepare for the change that has taken place; they are not equipped to cope with the present situation.

In view of these problems, it was obvious that new forms of service delivery would have to be devised in order to offer any meaningful help to the neighborhood's inhabitants. Lincoln Hospital Mental Health Services staff began to search for innovative means to provide services that would cover a broad spectrum from primary prevention to clinical treatment, be based where people lived, be staffed insofar as possible by local residents, and be directed toward strengthening and expanding the community's abilities to cope and implement its own choices.[2]

These aims necessitated exploration of alternative concepts and modes of service and required staff to deal with their own resistance to change. In the process, many mistakes were made. What stands out, however, is the commitment to forging a creative and viable program that would be responsive to community needs. Some of its dimensions included developing new points of intervention, developing new personnel categories, and changing the relative use of available tools to incorporate more of the technologies of such fields as political science, creative arts, anthropology, the civil rights movement, and community development.

---

[1] Compared with the Bronx as a whole, most of the Lincoln area falls into the lowest quartile of median family income ($3,700–$5,400) and educational attainment (7.6–8.8 years). The unemployment rate is about twice that of the Bronx average. The amount of overcrowded housing and school facilities is about twice that of the Bronx as a whole. Furthermore, (1) there is a 110 percent higher rate of public assistance cases, (2) the rate of venereal disease among youths under 21 is up to 300 percent higher, (3) there is a 45 percent higher admission rate to state hospitals, (4) the juvenile delinquency rate is 25 percent higher, (5) the rate of out-of-wedlock births is over 50 percent higher, (6) the rate of premature births is close to 20 percent higher, (7) the infant mortality rate is 20 percent higher, and (8) the number of newly diagnosed cases of tuberculosis is 100 percent higher than the Bronx average.

[2] See Harris B. Peck, MD, Seymour R. Kaplan, MD, and Melvin Roman, "Prevention, Treatment and Social Action: A Strategy of Intervention in a Disadvantaged Urban Area," American Journal of Orthopsychiatry, Vol. 36, No. 1 (January 1966), pp. 57 ff.

NEIGHBORHOOD SERVICE CENTER

One of the new services developed was the Neighborhood Service Center program. Staffed by nonprofessional community mental health workers (mostly residents of the area) under professional supervision, the centers were seen as one means of bridging the gap between the community and the resources available to it, including the hospital.[3] In these storefronts, help with almost any kind of problem was given on a walk-in basis. Through their many contacts with community residents, center staff came to see the need to mobilize people not only in relation to their individual difficulties, but also to those of the environment in which lay the roots of many of these problems. Staff believed that attacking the sources of environmental pressures could have a significant impact on people, both by alleviating some of those pressures and by developing a sense of self-worth and power through involvement in bringing these changes about. Thus social action became an important part of the program's armamentarium in terms both of individual and institutional change.

The first step was to provide the kind of immediate help that would make it possible for the individual to cope more effectively with recurring crises. At the same time it was necessary to move beyond this level; there had to be a shift of power. The goal was to get people to speak for themselves rather than to rely on the professional or social agency to be their spokesman, to release these people's ability and develop their power to affect the outside forces on which the poor are dependent, and ultimately to achieve participation of the residents in decision-making.

In an attempt to attack the causative factors behind the residents' feelings of defeat, despair, and powerlessness, social workers at the Neighborhood Service Centers, community mental health workers, and clients initiated activities on many issues related to these forces. They organized a tenants' council and conducted voter registration campaigns; lobbied in New York City, Albany, and Washington for stronger anti-poverty, housing, and welfare legislation; testified at hearings and met with officials and legislators. They fought the introduction of a food stamp plan and cutbacks in Medicaid, became active in Model Cities

---

[3] *See* Emanuel Hallowitz, "The Role of the Neighborhood Service Center in a Community Mental Health Program," *American Journal of Orthopsychiatry,* Vol. 38, No. 4 (July 1968), pp. 705–714; and Frank Riessman and Hallowitz, "The Neighborhood Service Center—An Innovation in Preventive Psychiatry," *American Journal of Psychiatry,* Vol. 123, No. 11 (May 1967), pp. 1408–1413.

planning. While all of these activities include experiences relevant to the topic of this paper, only two will be presented in detail: the process of organizing a welfare group and intervention in a community crisis.

To involve people—any people—in action is an enormous task, even when dealing with those groups whose energies are not being consumed by their daily struggle with problems of survival. To build a viable core group of the poor can present overwhelming difficulties. The challenge thus became to find the issue, a modest goal that could be reached, and a proper target for a takeoff point.

ORGANIZING A WELFARE GROUP

At the Neighborhood Service Center the many different needs of the individual could be approached in such a way that there was no fragmentation of service. This fact proved to be essential to the achievement of goals. It was concrete, immediate needs that brought people to the center. Underlying problems were not those for which people could mobilize in seeking help. Most initial requests had to do with difficulties with the Department of Welfare, often reflecting the department's own built-in inadequacies of policy and procedure. Helping the individual welfare recipient became a never ending, hopeless task. It was necessary to look for other methods, and so staff began to develop group approaches and social action techniques.

As a beginning, every effort was made to maximize the client's own ability to deal with his problems. Information was provided while at the same time an attempt was made to develop in him a feeling that he was *entitled* to certain things as a right. Emphasis was put on accepting each person as a human being with dignity, which was especially important to people whose self-image had been damaged by their life experiences.

As a relationship developed between worker and client and a feeling of trust resulted (a new feeling for many), the client was able to accept the worker's suggestion that he join with others having similar problems in finding ways to deal more effectively with the Department of Welfare. While playing an essential part in the group meetings, the worker continued to work with individuals as they became freer to bare their deeper many-sided problems.

It became evident through working with the group that other needs had to be filled and gratifications provided before "organizing" could be thought of. The need to get out of the oppressive, crowded apartment, to be free of responsibility for the ever present children (the center arranged for group baby-sitting and a program for children while mothers attended meetings), to socialize, to ventilate feelings, and to share experiences was common to all. Recurring themes were the need for clothing and other essentials; the frustrations, humiliations, and feelings of powerlessness in relation to the Department of Welfare; their inability to get into work training programs because of poorly advertised patronage systems, and the desire to "get off welfare."

Development of Group Feeling

Initially there was little carryover of the social experience, the sharing of common concerns, from the meetings to the members' private lives. The group members did not visit each other between meetings. They related to each other only through the worker. However, exposure to warmth, acceptance, and respect gradually generated positive feelings in them. Some of their fears and negative self-image began to diminish. Members began to break down the protective wall of the "rejected"—suspicion and hostility—and to respond to each other and to staff in new ways. The direct involvement of the center director—an authority figure, professional, and a representative of the Establishment—contributed significantly to new feelings of self-worth. As time went on, those participating brought neighbors to the meetings. Interest was expressed about other issues and other people. A feeling of isolation gradually gave way to one of belonging.

Although current welfare topics were discussed and systematic information was given about welfare policies and entitlements, there was deliberately no set agenda. Formal organization was not emphasized, but after awhile individuals began asserting themselves in a leadership capacity. Structure emerged and could be formalized. Participants began to insist on their entitlements and were able to move on their own with more confidence. At the same time, issues were sharpened, the target defined, and possible strategies weighed. Those more able to absorb information became sought after by others and quickly achieved status within the group and in the neighborhood.

The group's first action was disappointing. They sent a letter to the commissioner of the Department of Welfare requesting special grants for Christmas, "So we, too, as other parents, can give to our children without the degrading necessity to make the rounds of charitable organizations. . . ." This letter did not yield any concrete results. The goal was too ambitious, since it required a basic policy change.

A demonstration to obtain clothing, however, produced important results. On-the-spot grants were authorized. When the checks were distributed, those who received theirs first did not leave the welfare center but waited for others to get theirs, aware of their impact as a group. Not only did the number of people involved provide the group with needed strength and confidence, but their common goal added an important dimension: "All of us—we are the same—cut off and poor." Identification with this feeling served to unite the group and made the bridging of ethnic barriers feasible.[4] The necessity to move together was recognized as a *must*.

The group began to have a feeling of identity. Being part of a successful action increased their feeling of confidence and provided much-needed gratification. This, combined with relief from their frustrated feelings, began to break down their deep resistance to and fear of affiliation with any organized group.

Faith in collective action aimed toward a common goal gradually took root. Contact could then be established with local welfare recipients' groups, the city-wide movement, and eventually with the National Welfare Rights Organization. Knowing these organizations were there to back them up added power to the local group. At the same time, involvement with others counteracted some of their feelings of isolation and generated a feeling of strength in individual members.

Shifting Power

In view of staff's commitment to a shift of power, it was felt essential to break the prevailing pattern of communication. People without money and power have rarely been able to obtain access to influential persons. To bring about direct communication between welfare recipients and those in decision-making positions, the worker had to withdraw as expediter and spokesman. For people to trust in their own strength, it was essential that they be given proof that they could indeed negotiate with the relevant center of power. The professional social worker and the community mental health worker had to act as models, using various techniques to demonstrate ways in which communication could be accomplished.

It was found, however, that for welfare recipients attempts at direct confrontation with authority figures often produced inordinate fear.

---

[4] With the inevitable competition for limited antipoverty funds, the distance between Negro and Puerto Rican members of the community had deepened. Because of the power certain jobs carried with them, fierce contests arose, such as for positions with the Concentrated Employment Program and Model Cities.

Their life experiences had contributed significantly to feelings of helplessness and worthlessness. This fear had to be viewed in the context of the total life situation of the individual; it could not be characterized as individual psychopathology.[5] Pent-up anger also had to be viewed as an appropriate response to reality. To provide a constructive outlet for this anger is essential. An accumulation of intense hostility was the result of the unconscionable "give as little as possible" policy of the Department of Welfare. The majority of welfare recipients were without the most essential basic items. While procuring these items was seen as essential, at the same time it was viewed as a constructive way to rechannel repressed or displaced anger onto appropriate targets and thus bring them into the service of healthy self-assertion.

The lack of essentials was a need around which people could be rallied. To force the welfare department to grant a maximum of entitlements and to change its policy, the "minimum standards" campaign was launched. This effort was precipitated in New York by Mobilization For Youth, Inc., and was continued by the Citywide Coordinating Committee of Welfare Groups, and at the national level by the Poverty/ Rights Action Center in Washington, D.C.

The basic tool of this campaign was a form listing the minimum household and clothing items to which welfare recipients were entitled by the established welfare standards. Recipients were to check off those items they needed. For example, the form indicated that each member of a family was entitled to a kitchen chair, so that the family could eat together rather than in shifts. Similarly, each person was entitled to three sheets per bed, specific eating utensils, and so on. If a person had fewer than the items to which he was entitled, he could request whatever was lacking.

The completed forms were sent collectively to the supervisor or worker in the welfare department. If the request was not met within a specified time (usually two weeks), a group of clients would go together to the welfare center to insist that their requests be honored. If that—and sometimes more drastic tactics—failed to result in the needed grant, a fair hearing was requested from the state Department of Social Welfare. Often this request alone produced substantial grants for needed items.

The importance of this campaign can hardly be overestimated. Across

---

[5] Warren C. Haggstrom, "The Power of the Poor." Revised version of paper presented at the 71st Annual Meeting of the American Psychological Association, Philadelphia, Pa., August–September 1963.

the nation, welfare recipients, social workers, welfare department staff, students of law and medicine, and many others became aware for the first time of the glaring discrepancy between what had been determined as being necessary for a minimal standard of living and the actual practice of the welfare department. The effects of this effort will be felt for a long time to come.

While the campaign brought about a much-needed modification of the environment, increased feelings of self-confidence also resulted. There was a swell of hope among recipients, of determination to stand up for their rights to get *all* the entitlements provided by law. The actions culminated in the testing and use of legal but previously unknown and unused grievance channels. With the aid of the Citywide Coordinating Committee and civil rights lawyers, fair hearings became a power tool for welfare clients. Thousands of dollars in grants were issued as a result. Actions of welfare recipients across the nation stirred up considerable controversy and to a significant degree contributed to consideration of alternatives to the present welfare system.

With the minimum standard and fair hearing campaigns, a further step forward had been made. The group now sought participation in the decision-making processes of the surrounding community. Members became active participants in a local Model Cities planning group; some were nominated to its executive board. They moved on to other vital issues, issues that neither related to welfare nor directly affected their own individual situations. From an assembly of individuals seeking some way to improve their own conditions, a united force with a sense of identity, independence, pride, direction, and collective goals had developed.

For the individual, involvement in the group had stimulated growth, self-assertion, self-respect, and a feeling of belonging and community. Reporting on the National Convention for Welfare Rights, a community mental health worker stated:

> I also found that Mrs. B. [the group's president] by going to the convention found strength—she has found unity with City-Wide and with other Spanish groups . . . she proved this to me when she called a meeting to discuss the Convention and I was not even asked to attend. The group now has plans to join the national movement. Mrs. A. is also calling a meeting of all the Spanish groups in Manhattan, Bronx and Brooklyn so that they could get together and have a meeting with City-Wide which, at this point they feel is weak and maybe together they could make it stronger. They feel that the time is near when all groups joined together could

make a happier, decent world to live in even if you are poor and on Welfare.[6]

For many participants, new patterns of functioning resulted. While some have gained in social experience, others have become helpers and leaders themselves. They have become able to find and use opportunities and push for their right to become independent of welfare. One of the members is now a mental health worker in the program; another has become a social service aide. Some are in job training programs. Still others have essential roles as representatives on the local welfare center's advisory committee and on the commissioner's committee.

Know-how in regard to finding and using power has become evident; there is no longer any hesitation about establishing direct communication on higher levels. Making their weight felt as voters, group members made frequent demands of their elected officials. Even fruitless efforts did not have such shattering effects as before. There was a sharpened awareness of issues affecting the community and readiness to participate actively. They developed a sense of having some power over their own fate.

While some see changes as beginnings and take encouragement from microscopic progress, for others the inevitable frustrations of setbacks and the fact that the welfare system has not undergone *real* change have hardened cynicism and reinforced the feeling that they are without voice, power, or influence. The termination of the three-year demonstration grant of the Neighborhood Service Center program, which necessitated the closing of the center, provoked anger and disillusionment. However, energies were quickly turned into intense activity to pressure federal, state, and city officials to keep the center open. Simultaneously the group prepared to set up its own program; it incorporated, drew up creative and ambitious proposals for funding, and submitted these to numerous sources.

The group first received funding for the summer and later for a year-round program. A former community mental health worker is now its full-time director. The program has its own storefront head-quarters and a staff of thirteen. The group deals with many facets of the problems of the area's residents. Welfare is still one of the major issues, but the group has broadened its scope and also deals effectively

---

[6] Sonia Rivera, "Report on First National Welfare Rights Convention, Washington, D.C., August 1967," p. 3. Informal report to the director of the Neighborhood Service Center.

with some of the complex problems arising out of the Model Cities planning in the area.

A unique aspect is a reaching-out effort to the affluent communities of Long Island and Connecticut to try to counteract the negative stereotype of the AFDC mother. Mrs. B, a mother of six and a welfare recipient herself, has written up her own life history, which she effectively presents at such meetings as a case in point. The group feels that their presentations have a salutary effect and offer hope for some changes in perception of and attitudes toward the welfare recipient. The group knows how to cultivate and make most productive use of its allies, such as clergymen, to the best advantage of the neighborhood.

Another group activity is in the area of housing. Rather than concentrating on code enforcement only, the group attempts to involve the small property owner by providing landlords with information that will facilitate their obtaining loans and funds from heretofore unknown and untapped resources in order to upgrade and improve their buildings. This group is an incentive to others in the community to begin to assert themselves more forcefully.

The role of the worker was crucial. Sound organization and tactics were essential to the development of progressively greater decision-making power in the group. At the beginning stage the worker had to be the leader, be active and yet sensitive to the pace; had to adapt his stance as leadership developed, nurture leaders, work with individuals between meetings, and move into the background as the group became stronger. The worker then became a resource person, the one to set the stage, ready to move in when needed. This required flexibility and constant reassessment of the group as well as the goals. In the choice of issues it became crucial to present alternatives that would provide the needed modest success with both short-term and more demanding long-term goals, since failure carried the risk of adding to destructive feelings of powerlessness, despair, and cynicism.

For the Mental Health Services staff the intimate involvement with the welfare group highlighted the close interaction between social and individual pathology. Prevalence of incestuous relationships, promiscuity, violence, rage, and apathy are often the direct results of deprivation in a concrete sense: shared beds, overcrowding, lack of privacy, and other intolerable environmental conditions. Provision of separate beds for brothers and sisters, adequate clothing for teen-agers attending school, bedrooms for parents with doors that can be closed, sufficient chairs to permit a family to sit together at mealtime are crucial.

The social worker in this setting was faced with the challenge of transmitting his professional skills to the community mental health worker rather than being the doer himself. The social worker had to become a generalist: advocate, educator, negotiator, expediter, counselor, organizer, and the person who transmits and sustains a conviction about the strength of people to lift themselves out of the trap of their situation.

Facing the issues, one has to choose sides, to show partisanship; one cannot remain neutral. Our basic premise is not to help people adjust to a reality to which no one should have to adjust. Adjustment only means sinking into passivity and the destructive feelings of powerlessness. While the staff's commitment is to persevere in bringing about change in some of the societal institutions that permit these conditions to exist, it was learned that creating radical changes in institutional functioning is at best a slow process and often impossible to achieve. We may be successful only in sharpening sensitivity to the way services are delivered and in making sure they *are* delivered. We may not change attitudes, but we can change behavior.

ORGANIZING IN A CRISIS

The activity described next differs from the preceding one in that it had relevance for the entire community, rather than only to welfare recipients. Service was not a component. There was a clear task orientation.

The threatened closing of a much-needed local hospital created a great amount of anxiety and anger. Residents came to the center asking what the staff would do. In contrast to the experience with the welfare group, people wanted to be part of the action and therefore could be mobilized instantly, even those heretofore uninvolved in any activity that was not directly connected with their own personal concerns. It is important that the issue be easily defined and the target—the "external enemy"—be identified by the people themselves. It was possible to broaden the base of the groups involved and thus achieve the threat of greater numbers. Although the hospital was a voluntary one, the position taken was that it was the city's responsibility to provide health services when needed.

The movement gained in momentum, with the support of legislators and other political representatives being enlisted. Action culminated in a confrontation of politicians and city officials at a mass meeting and in the joining of forces with hospital employees and militant physicians who spearheaded direct action. With the closing of the hospital looming before them, many who had been passive or reluctant to participate during planning sessions felt the increasing urgency and joined in demonstrations at City Hall. Participants risked arrest at a "chain-in" at the commissioner's office and testified at a public Board of Estimate hearing, to present in their own words—many in Spanish—and from their own experiences the urgent need for continued hospital services. Those testifying keenly felt the impact on the board members. For most it was their first encounter with city power and city apparatus: an abstraction had become a reality.

While much political maneuvering and many power struggles were behind the issue, the city capitulated to the waves of protest and agreed to take over the hospital. City officials and the press stated publicly that community pressure had been responsible for "saving" the hospital.

The impact of this success was great. Expressions such as, "Imagine if we had not gone down, they would have just gone ahead and let them close it," "When I got there with the mayor sitting there and looking at me, all of a sudden I was no longer afraid. After all, I'm somebody too." "You *can* fight City Hall if you want to," are results of carefully chosen and persevering efforts to get people to trust themselves, to stand up for themselves and make demands, to see themselves in a new light.

The fact that the group had been instrumental in forcing a change of events had effects that carried over to other areas. Small groups formed spontaneously around other community concerns. Yet the story of this hospital is not entirely a success story; many of the services promised were never provided. Staff, too, failed to keep these task-oriented groups together and to build from there. The issue was not kept alive. There was insufficient grass-roots leadership, and other organizations did not pick up where we left off. Other priorities, lack of staff, and perhaps lack of know-how were responsible.

However, increased readiness for participation and a feeling of power on the part of neighborhood residents were pervasive. Equally important, public officials remained sensitive to community demands. For example, they yielded quickly in a situation in which already-allocated money earmarked for an urgently needed crash renovation program at the local municipal hospital was tied up and the community set a deadline for action.

When the hospital issue came to life again, the community found that it could rally its forces quickly and effectively. Based on previous experiences, the city quickly withdrew its attempts to impose its own health service plans and deferred to community wishes. An acceptable compromise was then worked out mutually.

SOME IMPLICATIONS

What has really happened as a result of the experiences described here?
Has anything really changed? Some changes can be seen; these are due
to many factors: to the civil rights movement, the War on Poverty, the
testing of traditional boundaries of authority currently taking place on
many fronts. While these have all had an impact, involvement in action
with the centers has for many been an initial experience. Encouragement is found in the following:

1. Established institutions and agencies are beginning to develop new
relationships with the users of services. "Poor power" is beginning to
make itself felt. Decision-makers are now being challenged when they
make unilateral plans for the community. There is growing recognition
that communities should be involved in decisions that affect them.

2. The climate in the community is beginning to change, and some
of the people have changed as well. Anger and frustration are more apt
to be directed at appropriate targets. There is less awe of authority,
more inclination to claim their rightful dues. Feelings of isolation have
been lessened. Many people now identify with the community and its
struggles and are ready to participate in efforts to bring about improvement. They are aware of their potency and have begun to demand a
role in planning and decision-making. They realize that their voices *do*
count and that they *can* be heard (a basic requirement for the mental
health of people). Some have gone into education programs or employment training, have become active in other organizations, and have
begun to help their neighbors toward greater independence. Others
have recognized their power as voters and now make use of their elected
officials.

For some of the neighborhood children, their mothers' activities have
become a source of pride and have given them a new model to follow.
Some have helped in preparations for and participated in demonstrations.
Inevitably, there have been negative results as well. This community
is largely comprised of women and children, many women being heads
of households. Some have become so absorbed in community activities
that their children and husbands have been neglected. This may com-
pound problems in families in which the man's position as head of the
household may already be in jeopardy. So newfound involvement and
strength may also have negative mental health implications. On balance,
we believe that there is much more to be gained than lost, but these are
considerations that should be kept in mind.

In social action, new, broadening experiences resulted for participants.

Environmental pressures were used as a catalytic agent, while available healthy ego strengths were uncovered and made use of.[7]   However, it has become our conviction that social action is of sufficient importance in itself to be an integral part of any program.   Indeed, it must become part of the social worker's function in any setting.

For staff, involvement in community activities raised formidable questions when issues having political relevance were concerned.   Since staff were seen as representatives of a powerful medical school and university, there was always fear, especially on the part of local groups struggling for power themselves, that staff's true intentions were not being revealed, and that we might buy them off or swallow them up if they were not on constant guard.   While the burden of suspicion fell primarily on the professional staff, nonprofessionals were also subject to some doubts.   Mental health workers who were also community residents had to cope with the problem of being, on the one hand, representatives of the hospital's Mental Health Service and, on the other, representatives of the community, with the accompanying conflict of interests and biases.

A further issue for staff was the recognition that because of their positions as employees of a city hospital, a medical college, and a university, there might be certain actions of the Neighborhood Service Center groups in which they would not be able to participate fully.   This caused considerable concern as a theoretical issue, but, as it happened, never became a practical one.   Many of the actions taken represented bold steps for the Mental Health Service, which would not have been possible without the firm and even courageous support of the administration when action became hot and political pressure mounted.

While certain limitations were present, staff were able to use the cover provided by the city-wide welfare rights movement.   Another tactic was the use of a neutral organizational auspice under which to carry out those aspects of a campaign that were apt to be most provocative. Since it was our policy to strengthen existing organizations by staffing some of their committees, it was appropriate for staff to work closely with those having similar concerns.   This provided other groups with needed manpower and gave us a base for action on a variety of fronts. The structure and interests of a powerful institution can become cumbersome and moves can be made more quickly under the neutral umbrella

---

[7] See Rudolph M. Wittenberg, "Personality Adjustment Through Social Action," *American Journal of Orthopsychiatry,* Vol. 18, No. 2 (April 1948), p. 220.

of a local organization. The advantage of using affiliations with other groups should not be overlooked.

The relationship to those institutions that were on the receiving end of protest activities became complex, to say the least. Repercussions were inevitable. Some welfare center administrators retaliated against both clients and staff. Others, impressed with the growing power of the recipients' groups, began to handle complaints more efficiently. A few, recognizing the need for revisions of policy, welcomed this pressure, since it strengthened their position and helped to produce change in the face of the opposition of an entrenched bureaucracy.

Involvement in so many crucial community issues provided exposure that led to deeper understanding of and closer relationships to the community's residents, agencies, and many of the concerns that were held to be most significant. During these efforts, clients and staff had a rare opportunity to work together. Each had something to teach and something to learn. Staff members thrown into new experiences had to sharpen their skills. The agency had to examine its commitments. Community residents' chronic mistrust of the hospital was lessened; some even began to see it as an ally.

Clearly, a commitment to social change should include an examination of the structure, policies, and practices of one's own agency as well. The fact that agency staff have stimulated others in this direction but have not made sufficient efforts to follow these principles at home is a complex topic that warrants separate discussion.

In one sense, any involvement in basic issues becomes a problem, since taking sides inevitably creates suspicion and hostility. No matter how seemingly benign, any issue may have political implications and repercussions. But failure to become involved leads to even greater problems. Our position is that it is better to be damned for doing than for not doing. Through being involved, we build on and broaden the narrow traditions of the past. Then our role becomes not only that of enabler, but also one of worker engaged with others in the building of new communities and of the sense of community now so painfully absent and so urgently needed throughout the nation.

Making Clinical Services Relevant to the Poor

CARYL J. STEWART

Two perspectives on the identification of social problems of the poor and the development of relevant intervention techniques will be described in this paper: one gained from a research study and one derived from the clinical findings of a small rehabilitation division of a local public welfare department. The city described is Burlington, Vermont, the largest city in the state. It has a population of 35,000, with an additional 50,000 persons in its immediate environs. Its present growth rate is among the highest in the country. A study of the ecological correlates of low income in the greater Burlington area reveals a pattern of inner city and suburbia similar to the pattern so commonly described among the large population centers of the country.

RESEARCH PERSPECTIVE

During the period June 1965–August 1967 a study was conducted of the population of the city of Burlington that sought to identify the poor and their problems in ways meaningful for intervention.[1] For that reason, the basic unit of study was the family or household. Data were

---

[1] Results of this study were published in Caryl J. Stewart, *The Burlington Social Survey* (Burlington, Vt.: George Little Press, August 1967).

90

collected by means of household interviews administered to a probability sample of the city's population. Identification of poverty was established by applying the formula developed by the Social Security Administration and in wide use throughout the country.[2] By this formula, the sample indicated that 22 percent of Burlington households, containing 25 percent of the population, existed below the poverty level.

Types of Poverty Households

Analysis of the findings showed two types of households that are significantly related to poverty status. The first is the single-member household, which on examination was found to comprise primarily the elderly. Analysis of this group led to the following characterization:

> Typically the individual is an elderly widow eking out an existence, perhaps in a single, poorly-equipped room, on the income of her social security or on old age assistance. She may be physically unable to work. She probably would not successfully gain employment were she to try. She really is not expected to be an income-producer, though she might still like to be. She is probably depressed. Thirty-three percent of the poverty households [in Burlington] are of this type.[3]

Besides the primary economic problem that must be faced on the level of public social policy, services for the aged, especially those aimed at alleviating the problems of isolation and alienation, are desperately needed. Despite some notable work being selectively done that has been reported in the literature, the social work profession has by no means begun to face up to the social service needs of this group.

The second significant poverty group identified was the large intact family of six or more members (the average size being eight). The father was working, was poorly educated, and had an average annual income of $3,200. Looking at this type of family from the point of view of service delivery, it was found that they are served, if at all, by

---

[2] *See* Mollie Orshansky, "Counting the Poor: Another Look at the Poverty Profile," *Social Security Bulletin*, Vol. 28, No. 1 (January 1965), pp. 3–29; and Orshansky, "Who's Who Among the Poor: A Demographic View of Poverty," *Social Security Bulletin*, Vol. 28, No. 7 (July 1965), pp. 3–32.

[3] Stewart, *op. cit.*, p. 66.

the least-equipped and most traditional of public welfare categories—general assistance. In Burlington it has meant for some that their large hospital bills were paid by the local welfare department, that government surplus food commodities were obtainable, and that, among the least stable or poorest, occasional general assistance was provided within the traditional philosophy of negative sanctions and in the form of vouchers, usually for food.

Recently, federally aided work experience programs in the welfare system began groping attempts to help this type of family. There is little evidence, however, that at the service delivery level there is an adequate conception of and capability for carrying out this task. Recent congressional action transferred this program to the Department of Labor, which—again at the delivery level—has shown an even less adequate grasp of what is involved in serving this group.

The vocational rehabilitation system, while more experienced, has up to now appeared to be concerned mainly with defining disabilities and with the seeming need to make taxpayers out of all of their clients. Other structural problems interfere with their responsiveness to this group, although the changes now being fashioned on the federal level in the Department of Health, Education, and Welfare and in Congress make one more optimistic that someone up there is also concerned with this.

The voluntary agency system deals periodically with members of this type of family as the members individually develop problems that fit the service patterns of the separate agencies. These agencies—which employ a large percentage of professional social workers—are usually focused on types of sociobehavioral problems. Their established methods of intervention have not proved successful in reaching the poor. Thus these families emerge and recede and are seen in fragmented ways by many institutions at points when they or society find it necessary.

Identifying this large intact family is of course another way of arriving at the important fact that so much of the poverty population consists of children. In the study sample it was found that 40 percent of school-age children (that is, between 6 and 15 years of age) were in poverty households. Of this large group no less than 72 percent were from large intact families.

These, then, were the two most important poverty groups in the study. In the total population sample the two types of households accounted for 35 percent of all individuals. Among the poverty segment they made up 64 percent of the population. The relevance of existing social service systems to these two kinds of households is questionable.

Identifying Family Problems

What, then, are their problems? The second important aspect of this study was to try to identify family problems as they are perceived by families themselves. The researchers were under no illusion that they were compiling a complete dossier of family problems. The assumption was that problems families are willing to describe are relevant to them and are therefore significant for the social service system.

The problems cited here were developed from spontaneous replies by adult members of sample families to an open-ended question asking them to describe any important problems or changes that had occurred in the immediately preceding twelve-month period. These responses were analyzed by a professional social worker and sorted into specific categories that were then re-sorted into three general categories.

These categories were as follows: (1) dependency, that is, any problem having to do on some level with economic well-being, (2) health, which is self-explanatory, and (3) adjustment. This last category comprised two subgroups that had different implications. One subgroup was designated behavioral adjustment problems and encompassed categories such as marital, alcoholism, and family relationship problems. The second was designated stress problems and referred to problems a family undergoes that are reactive to stressful life experiences such as the death of a family member.

Seventy percent of the respondents were willing to describe problems to the interviewer. Analysis showed that broad differences do indeed exist in the perception of problems by the poor and the nonpoor. Poor families perceived the majority of problems reported—68 percent—in the categories of dependency and health. Nonpoor families perceived 77 percent of their reported problems in the area of adjustment. Related data compiled on a sample of health and welfare clients revealed a similar relationship when all known problems were assessed, although they further revealed that the poor had more problems in all categories than the nonpoor.

This must be assessed against the knowledge that the profession's most highly refined intervention techniques are related to problems of adjustment. Whatever historical reasons account for this development, the fact is that we have been seduced into devoting our energies toward modifying behavior. We have operated on an implicit assumption that there are sufficient supports in the environment to reinforce and reward improved behavior, to say nothing of even allowing it to take place.

It is now understood that this is not so. Poverty families do not even think to mention stressful life experiences as problems. Their problems are lack of money, illness, poor housing. And that is what they tell us when we take the trouble to ask.

CLINICAL PERSPECTIVE

Next the clinical findings of the small rehabilitation unit that carried out this study will be described briefly. The twin goals of this unit in the beginning were to study the needs of the poor and to provide a comprehensive social work service to a selected group of welfare families. The approach contained a few givens: (1) a bias toward family therapy techniques and concepts, (2) an interest in the chronic welfare family, (3) an approach by which an attempt would be made to diagnose and make explicit the entire range of problems troubling a family and assume the responsibility of bringing to bear the corrective resources for them all, if possible, and (4) the unit would provide the primary therapeutic relationship with the family through which it was hoped their dysfunctional behavior patterns might undergo some modification. Even given this framework, the unit was committed above all else to pragmatism and to monitoring the appropriateness of the attempts at comprehensive intervention.

The lesson learned has been what the study showed—namely, that the most important (i.e., disabling) problems of poor families are their problems of economic dependency and health. Adjustment problems are there of course, but amenable to modification only in relation to the other two.

A summary of the clinical findings would include the following:

1. The unit was highly successful in establishing a therapeutic relationship with the family. This is noteworthy because it was a completely voluntary relationship and because the unit was part of an agency whose negative sanction techniques were known intimately to its clients.

2. The role of advocate became important early as the extent of negative treatment from environmental sources became obvious. Unit members were constantly interpreting, educating, and seeking to modify behavior toward the client families—behavior that kept them dysfunctional.

3. An often incredibly intricate relationship was found between adjustment and health problems wherein somatic symptoms played an important role in the emotional vicissitudes of individuals in ways that defied intervention even when medical and psychotherapeutic techniques were closely collaborated. At the same time there were indications that lessening of economic dependency problems was related to lessening of certain somatic symptoms.

4. Improvement in economic dependency problems was seen to be followed by improvements in both health and adjustment areas. Often dramatic evidence was noted that family relationships were especially responsive to improvement of economic status.

5. A phenomenon was noted that was named "the therapeutic employer syndrome." This describes the achievement of stabilized employment by men with erratic work histories following certain job placements in which they worked under men with especially warm and sensitive personalities. One of the unachieved goals was the attempt to discover more of these therapeutic employers throughout the community, since it was felt that this might well bring important results with men whose developmental deficits have resulted in personalities too frail for the usual give and take of competitive employment.

In summary, it was found that work with deprived families must differentiate problems and interventions on the following levels: (1) the environment in which the family functions, (2) the interaction between the family and that environment, and (3) the internal functioning of the family and its individual members. Over time, the unit found its focus moved more and more toward the first two—namely, attempted modification of the social institutions and conditions that impinge in an important way on the families and improving the relationship between the families and these important institutions. With regard to the second, it is important to understand that protective mechanisms built up over the years among poor families can make it difficult for them to relate constructively to social institutions, often even when the institution is attempting to forge a more constructive relationship with them. It was found that it is in this area that modified family casework techniques can make timely contributions in helping families change their adaptive patterns.

CONCLUSIONS

The implications of these findings for social work lead to the following conclusions:

The social work profession must turn to the refinement and strengthening of community organization methods. In the present case, professional staff efforts shifted steadily over the two and a half years of the project from a family therapy orientation to what must be called a community organization orientation, although the techniques used would not fall too comfortably within that method.

In the unit's approach it was the problems of the client families in their relationships with social institutions that provided the points of entry from which staff attempted to modify negative environmental forces. This usually had to do with trying—and often failing—to get institutions to change the way they behave toward a family. It usually involved playing the role of advocate. It sometimes meant joining forces with other groups in attempting to solve a social problem such as poor housing. It usually meant becoming involved in some degree of conflict, which attempts at change seem to create. And it often meant the recourse of simply making sure that decision-makers were told about problems uncovered and given recommendations for their alleviation. The minimal goal was always at least to identify the problems; denial is more difficult when facts and their meanings have been stated.

Social workers have much to contribute in bridging the gap of understanding the causal relationships between social institutions and dysfunctional behavior. Because of this we must also become expert and involved in planning for the broad spectrum of social services, including both health and welfare. It is at this level that many pattern changes in service delivery will take place.

If social work is to be relevant to the problems of the poor, then we must not turn away from the task of refining techniques. For delivery of service *is* the application of some kind of intervention technique. The fact that our most refined techniques are irrelevant to the poor is no argument against the refinement of techniques. It is simply a warning that we must develop—and refine—techniques that *will* bring important services to the poor.

New Perspectives on Problems of Service Delivery

ABRAHAM KAPLAN

The task of philosophy has always been one of meeting what has been aptly called "the crisis of relevance." This is a crisis that afflicts not only the social work profession, but perhaps most of the traditional activities in society. I will therefore try to put into perspective what seem to be the thought processes involved in the profession's actions. I will first consider ways of thinking about the problems of social work, then the data for them, formulation of the hypotheses that enter into treatment of these problems, testing these hypotheses, and, finally, application of the findings. These are what some would call dull abstractions, but dull or not, they seem to be the abstractions in which social work must necessarily be conceptualized. They can be made less dull by being made more concrete.

FORMULATING PROBLEMS

The way in which the social work profession formulates its problems exhibits a human tendency that can be identified in the physical sciences as well. It is the habit of looking at problems, not in terms of what the problems themselves call for, but in terms of what problem-solving tools are available to bring to the situation. We tackle not the most serious difficulties, but the easiest ones, so that we can experience the gratification of achievement and the encouragement of success. We direct our search, not to the areas where it is most likely that we will find what we are seeking, but where it is easiest for us to continue the search. Comanor pointed out that each of the states has its own way of defining the need for assistance; I would go further and say that each agency and perhaps even each individual social worker has his own way of conceptualizing need.[1]

Another tendency is to define problems in terms of the repertoire that is already available for dealing with them. An excellent illustration of this is the notion that the 1935 Social Security Act provides the basis for the solution of all the problems the profession faces: all that is necessary is to amend it, to adapt it to changing conditions.

It is not to be wondered at that the profession views the social scene as posing just those problems that can most effectively be dealt with by the means already in its possession. Problems are seen in terms of existing skills, existing resources, existing facilities—but with one qualification: the need for more of the same thing. This is not to say that the social services are getting enough money but use it inappropriately. A vastly greater share of the total resources of society must indeed be directed to the problems with which social work is concerned. But we might do well to ask ourselves whether the problems have already been defined in the most effective way. If more money were provided for the social services, would the same things continue to be done, only more of them? I hope that the profession will allow itself rather more imagination than is to be found in the "more-of-the-same" way of thinking.

For example, there is in this country a great myth concerning the values that are embodied in what is called "the Home." When people talk about what is wrong with the family as an institution they immediately give statistics having to do with the stability of the family—increasing divorce rates and so on—as though the only thing wrong with the family is its instability, and the only dimension for the formulation of the problem is the quantitative one. Instead, it may be that in some cases not only the children but the adult members of the family as well would be better off if the family were dissolved. More than stability has to be taken into account. The problem may not always consist in keeping the family together; it may be to find ways of separating the partners, or at any rate of breaking their mutually destructive patterns and replacing these by quite other patterns. Here is a concrete instance in which our thinking is too much bound up with presuppositions.

---

[1] Albert Comanor, "Social Service Delivery in the United States," this volume, p. 28.

Before going on to discuss the data in terms of which problems can meaningfully be formulated, there is one aspect of the way in which problems are conceptualized that ought to be mentioned. This is the question of whether problems are to be thought of in the spirit of what Kraft has called the "accommodationists" (or the "gradualists").[2] It is by no means my intention to argue for gradualism, but instead to put renewed emphasis on the value of reason and on the power of human intelligence to cope with human problems. I repudiate the notion that whenever somebody wants to be reasonable and to behave with the full resources of his humanity, he has then and there identified himself with the Establishment, with preservation of the status quo.

SOCIAL WORK DATA

It is extremely difficult to get the data that bear on the problems social work is attempting to solve. It is easy to fall into the trap of supposing that the data obtained in habitual and routine ways are what is called for. In fact, the situation is the other way around. Habitual and routine data pre-empt the whole area, so that soon one begins to think that data of this kind are all that can meaningfully be sought.

The history of science, as well as of human relations, gives many instances of what can easily be identified (in retrospect) as "invisible data"—things that now seem so clear it is incomprehensible why they were not seen before. Comanor spoke about the danger of "hardening of the categories"; this is a risk in every categorical framework.[3] No categorical system can be expected to remain useful for long. Most social workers function within certain bureaucratic frameworks, perhaps even within legal structures. They work with all sorts of categories, subject to definitions that probably remain rigid far beyond the point of usefulness. This rigidity may be inescapable, but one should at least allow to one's own thinking the freedom that is denied to the organization or that, at any rate, is not implemented by the organization.

Two specific recommendations can be made about the gathering of data:

1. Few if any systematic observations are made in order to obtain data that are thought to bear significantly on the further development of the profession. Data-gathering task forces are organized at times of crisis to obtain information on specific problems, such as the study made

---

[2] Ivor Kraft, "The State of the Social Work Profession," this volume.

[3] *Op. cit.*, p. 45.

of the Watts riot, but there is a great need for the same sort of under-taking in noncrisis situations.[4] Some portion of the profession's re-sources should be allocated to the task of making systematic observations, at least to provide base lines for the estimates that constantly must be made even in day-to-day operations.

2. There is no science in which instruments of observation are used without being calibrated. No biologist would use a microscope, no astronomer would use a telescope, no physicist would use a Geiger counter without learning something about the capacity and limitations of the instrument that feeds him the data on which his work is based. The instrument with which the social worker makes observations is himself. The social worker himself is not only significant as the instrument of observation; he is the most significant of all the resources at the profession's disposal. A greater effort should be made to calibrate the instrument. This means that a social worker must learn something about himself and about what happens to him when he enters into a situation in which he is involved professionally. What is he likely to see or over-look? What is he likely to distort? In short, what are the operating characteristics of the instrument? Finding answers to such questions will become an increasingly important part of whatever training is called for to improve professional competence.

FORMULATING HYPOTHESES

Every social worker would recognize at once that he does indeed make observations, he does gather data. At the very least, he asks people about themselves. What they answer is recorded, processed in various ways, and tabulated. Presumably, that makes the data scientific. But in order to think fruitfully about any subject matter, not only data are needed, but also hypotheses; only in this way can data become meaning-ful. It is a real question, however, whether hypotheses enter into social work thinking at all.

This is not said in a depreciatory way. It is risky to make hypotheses. When we work with something of great value—and what could be of greater value than the human lives with which social workers deal?—if a mistake is made much can be lost. However, hypotheses do not necessarily have to be hypothetical in the colloquial sense. To think in terms of hypotheses is only to be willing to think in terms as great as one's intellectual reach. It means not to be afraid of ideas, general-

---

[4] Nathan E. Cohen, "The Los Angeles Riot Study," *Social Work*, Vol. 12, No. 4 (October 1967), pp. 14–21.

izations, or abstractions, but to welcome them as giving a more vivid appreciation of the specific, the particular, and the concrete.

It is distressing to hear of the opposition between the clinician and the field worker, between casework and community organization, between working with an individual case and working on broad general policies. You cannot work effectively with a concrete, individual case unless you understand what you are working with, and to understand means always to think in terms of general and abstract categories. On the other hand, nothing effective can be done with general and abstract forms unless they are constantly checked against and corrected by the particular and the concrete. What is needed is not to resolve the opposition in favor of one or the other or to make some compromise between them, but to intensify both sorts of work in such a way that each not only tolerates but welcomes what is being done by the other and recognizes how much each has to give to the other.

When we formulate hypotheses we are as much tied down by, as much influenced by, our specific backgrounds and interests as is true in data-gathering. Comanor talked about the way in which ideology corrupts services.[5] It does something else; it also contaminates our thinking about the services we are providing. It is not only our ideology that does that, but also our professional involvements and commitments.

Kraft spoke eloquently of the rich who will not get off the backs of the poor because they have a stake in their position and are not about to let go.[6] There is no one who does not also have his stake in his profession, in his specific professional situation, in everything he has given himself to so far, in the mistakes he might make and the successes he might achieve. For example, there are agencies the avowed purpose of which is to help people find jobs, but which in fact operate in such a way as to *prevent* people from effectively being absorbed into the labor force. This is not to say that unemployment is the result of agencies' mistakes. Nevertheless, it can become so easy to find fulfillment in the continued concern with placing a man in the "right" job that both worker and client arrive at job-seeking as a way of life. Something similar happens with the alcoholic, who goes through a cycle of drunkenness and repentance. He and his family have arrived, without full awareness on the part of any of the people involved, at a satisfying behavioral pattern for all concerned. Kraft was right when he said that every Establishment has a way of making a virtue out of necessity.[7] But it

---

[5] *Op. cit.*, p. 45.

[6] *Op. cit.*

[7] *Ibid.*, p. 352.

is not easy to get out of this bind simply because it is intrinsic to organization.

There is a more general paradox of organization, which can be formulated in this way: An organization always sets up certain ends, but often it turns out that because of the organization's own interests and needs those ends become deflected and the organization pursues other goals, sometimes even directly contrary to what its original goals were. We have to live with this dilemma of being enmeshed in organizations that have their own stakes, their own commitments. All we can do is recognize the dilemma, take it into account, and try to deal with it.

The oppositions cited are artificial, intensified by the various institutional and personal commitments each person has. We begin to say, "As a taxpayer, I feel such and such; as a father, I feel so and so; as a member of this organization. . . ." So it goes, although the unity is there, regardless of how we fragment it in our thinking.

TESTING HYPOTHESES

Suppose you have a few hypotheses that make some sense in the light of the existing data. You know a little bit about what is going on and have a few ideas about how to deal with it. At this point little effort is directed toward testing your hypotheses, verifying your ideas about what is called for, checking whether a certain problem has indeed been solved. There is little outcome analysis; the tendency is to accept the level of analysis that is sufficient to meet the organizational or personal needs of the specific situation.

The question should be asked: "When is a file really closed?" Is there an assessment of whether what has been done succeeded in really meeting the requirements of the specific case? For instance, there is at work here a kind of mystique of quantity: Numbers loom large in our sense of outcome and achievement, and quite understandably. We have a certain budget with which to work—a certain allocation of funds— and must make certain reports. How satisfying it is to be able to make these reports in quantitative terms! What enters into such statistics has great weight in establishing the success or failure of a specific program.

Some people suffer from the complementary error, a kind of mystique of quality. They have the notion that quantity does not count at all, and that as soon as we have established measurable categories we have lost sight of the human dimension. I have as little sympathy with the one point of view as with the other. What is being urged is a heightened awareness of the hidden agenda that everyone brings to these human encounters, of the secret tasks we are trying to perform, and of our tendency to suppose that we have succeeded in our work when all that we have done is to take care of the items on our hidden agenda.

Dehumanization has become so widespread and so deeply rooted in our culture that we must cherish every manifestation of a real concern for other human beings. Social workers are not exempt from the forces at work throughout the rest of society that create this dehumanization. Martin Buber has pointed out the difference between being to someone in an "I-Thou" relationship and being only in an "I-It" relationship with that person, in which the other is not a person at all but an object, having significance only in terms of fitting into the needs you have brought into the situation. He becomes a *client;* you also are correspondingly dehumanized—you become a *social worker.* The institution is dehumanized as well—it is an *agency,* without human feeling and understanding. If we were prepared to test our ideas about human beings without quite so much influence from presuppositions and commitments of which we are not aware, we might be more willing to deal with these problems in straightforward human terms. That would imply dealing with ourselves in such terms as well.

PROTECTING VALUES

In what is said by legislatures, in newspaper editorials, and sometimes even from pulpits, much hostility is expressed toward the programs in which social work is involved. Social work's efforts seem to be barely tolerated by society. What is at work in the minds and hearts of the people who hold these views? What are their own guilts and anxieties that are being masked by their opposition to social work?

People say that more severe and punitive legislation is needed. Many of them attack welfare programs, apparently in the belief that the more severely the poor are punished for their poverty the more ennobled their behavior will be. Yet this is so obviously false, from what little is known about human behavior, that there must surely be something else involved in the demand for punishment. Are these people perhaps inviting punishment directed against themselves, so that they can hold onto their values? If I am able to see such anxiety and guilt in them, I might be able to undertake the more difficult task of seeing similar mechanisms at work in myself. How tempting it is to feel that I am the only human in a world of barbarians!

Some of the greatest dangers today to the values to which we are all committed come from our fears of knowledge, of science. It is true that knowledge is power, but power is not intrinsically evil. I am disturbed to hear students talk about "the power structure" as something that must be destroyed; I doubt if they would be happy with a powerless structure. To be sure, power can be used to manipulate others and destroy them, but it can also be used to make man free. Those who are determined to protect our values from what they see as the onslaught of the scientists and the intellectuals must face up to the consequence that in taking this stance they have made it impossible to provide scientific support for these values. This means, in turn, that values are left to the not very tender mercies of tradition, prejudice, and violence.

Value questions underlie social work activity, as they underlie all human activities worthy of the adjective. These questions are contained in the very word "social," one of the meanings of which is "the opposite of antisocial." With this recognition, the value component becomes explicit, and something has to be done with it. Social workers can face up to such values and do so in ways that do not contrast with a scientific temper of mind but invite it and its contribution.

We are suffering, not only in the social work field but with regard to all of today's basic problems, from an enormous intelligence gap; a great deal more knowledge is needed. But there is an even greater need than this: the determination to put into practice the knowledge we already have. From that determination, both practice and knowledge can benefit greatly.

PART II

Bringing Services Closer to the Consumer

In the past few years the delivery of social services has become a major social welfare concern. Several factors contribute to this concern, among them the increased awareness that social work has been notably unsuccessful in reaching certain population groups. New federally aided programs have at the same time greatly enhanced the resources for the delivery of services and greatly complicated the process.

The papers that follow in Part II, which focuses on the problem of accessibility of services to the consumer, follow a logical progression. The co-ordination of traditional social services based in existing institutions may be considered a first level of innovation. Gallagher describes a central intake and referral unit for a number of Catholic service agencies in the Bronx, and Barnard deals with the development of an integrated social service program for a number of Denver hospitals.

A second level of innovation is the development of a new form of service to meet emerging needs. Schreiber describes the evolution of a multiservice center for older persons. Although based on familiar conceptions of service within an agency structure, this program involved a number of significant new steps.

A further departure from traditional social services is seen in the dispersal of social services in community-based centers. It is clear that the new neighborhood health and mental health centers do not represent simply the idea of geographic accessibility. Among other aspects is a change in the relationship between purveyor and consumer. Black and Bracht point out some major implications of these programs for social work practice and professional education. But, lest social workers jump on this new bandwagon with too little forethought, Albers and Pasewark bring up a number of issues regarding the "new" comprehensive mental health centers. Their raising of these questions has greater importance for the reader than their statement of a specific viewpoint would have had.

In the final paper in Part II, Richardson asserts that social workers' timidity about the birth control issue has resulted in the profession's failure to play a meaningful role in making family planning services accessible to potential consumers. He points out a number of ways in which he believes the profession can begin to alter this situation. The topic is family planning; it could have been any number of service delivery problems that social workers have in the past avoided engaging.

Packaging Social Services

ROBERT E. GALLAGHER

"Though large amounts are being spent on social service programs for families, children and young people, few of these programs have been effective." [1] This blunt, direct indictment was made by the National Advisory Commission on Civil Disorders. The traditional defense by the social work Establishment has been a cry for more money and more manpower. Meanwhile, however, the growth of professional specialization superimposes additional functional boundaries both within and among agencies. Priorities are misdirected toward the maintenance of the professional rather than direct service to the client. The consequent professional stratospheres absorb the already inadequate manpower pool, and the plea is repeated.

Meanwhile, the poor increasingly refuse to accept the services offered in the traditional forms. In frequent instances, they are subtly excluded by such convenient devices as referral to a "more appropriate resource" —usually nonexistent—by being placed on a long, inactive waiting list, or by the agency's decision to close the case because the client was not "motivated." Too often traditional agencies have insulated or isolated themselves from the poor.

---

[1] *Report of the National Advisory Commission on Civil Disorders* (New York: Bantam Books, 1968).

Within this context this paper will describe the organization and functioning of a unified social service center by the Catholic Charities of the Archdiocese of New York in a borough of New York City. New York Catholic Charities, established almost fifty years ago, is comprised of 203 affiliated agencies ranging from a foundling hospital to homes for the aged. Annually it renders service to half a million individuals and families. Under its aegis are a variety of direct service agencies, each operating under separate administrative control, with contractual relationships with various governmental agencies and in some instances housed in separate locations. The result frequently has been an overlapping or duplication of services and referrals back and forth between agencies—in sum, poor delivery of social services.

ESTABLISHMENT OF THE CENTER

Catholic Charities has during the past several years been engaged in a critical self-study and reorganization with professional management assistance. One of the basic questions posed was how to provide prompt, appropriate, and unduplicated social services. An effort toward a solution was the establishment in July 1967 of a Catholic Charities Center in the Bronx.

The Bronx is one of the three boroughs of New York City within the Archdiocese of New York, which also includes ten counties outside the city. The Bronx, with a population of over a million and a half, is equivalent in population to Detroit, the fifth largest city in the nation. It includes one- and two-family private homes, high-rise co-operatives, rundown tenements, and a large variety of public housing. Its population includes the rich, the poor, and the middle class. Within its boundaries is a Model Cities area, one of the largest private housing developments in the nation, a police precinct with the highest crime rate in the city, a magnificent botanical garden, five designated poverty areas, eight universities and colleges, and the world-famous Bronx Zoo.

The Catholic Charities agencies and services relocated at the Bronx Center were formerly at separate locations. An immediate gain—imperative in the face of rising costs—has been the pooling of supportive services, i.e., switchboard, receptionist, secretarial and clerical staff, bookkeeping, supplies, and maintenance. Central administrative controls have been established, including budgeting and expenditures within a single corporate entity. Central registration and a single set of files are being designed to avoid duplication. A common application form adaptable to a variety of services has been developed. Also planned is an information retrieval service for research and planning purposes.

Within the center the following services are now available: family counseling; homemakers for families, the aging, and the chronically ill; psychiatric and ancillary clinical services for children; psychiatric evaluation of adults; emergency financial assistance; services to unmarried mothers; child placement; services to the aging and chronically ill in their own homes and placement in nursing homes or the Home for the Aging; volunteer Big Brothers; and services for children and families being brought before the family court. Also located at the center are the Catholic Youth Organization, St. Vincent de Paul Society, the "city office" of a child care institution, and an office for a group residence program another institution operates in the Bronx.

The center staff includes graduate social workers, psychiatrists, psychologists, case aides, homemakers, and office staff. Fieldwork placements are provided for graduate social work students and planning is under way with Fordham University for a two-year training program. A corps of volunteers is also available.

CENTRAL INTAKE

The first pivotal program feature of the center is central intake. Formerly requests for service—whether made directly or by community agencies—were made to the specific service agency, with resultant inevitable shuffling of requests from one service to another, acceptance of inappropriate referrals or duplication of effort, and the lack of interagency communication. Client "shopping" for service and frustration were frequent.

A single call to one number at the Bronx center is now all that is necessary for those requesting information or direct service. The value of a central information service is indicated by the assortment of information requests received: Individuals call for domestic help, baby-sitters, companions for the aged, names of private boarding schools or camps, procedures for adopting or boarding children; to donate clothing, furniture, and surplus stock; or to volunteer their services. Agencies, schools, physicians, and other professionals call for information on available services. Troubled and confused persons call to talk about their problems, many never requesting tangible services, but seeming only to be in need of a sympathetic ear.

All inquiries and requests for service including walk-ins are received and handled by assigned desk workers. To the fullest extent possible, an attempt is made on the telephone to determine the problem and whether the center can provide assistance, on the premise that it makes no sense for people to come to an agency only for referral elsewhere. On the other hand, proper initial handling of requests saves both the agency's and the client's time. Additional calls to the appropriate agency ensure follow-up. An invitation to the client to return if the referral does not work out is not merely a nicety but indicates the advocacy posture of the worker and the agency. Although the process can be demanding of staff time, it is an important aspect of good service delivery.

When the requested service appears to be available within the center, a definite appointment is offered to the client directly or through the referral source. An appointment clerk has at hand the scheduling of each staff member, and intake, continued service appointments, and conferences are scheduled centrally. This device ensures maximum utilization of staff time and spares the professional one time-consuming chore.

The intake worker is responsible for following through and arranging the continued service based on the intake study. If necessary, he may consult with the appropriate service unit supervisor, e.g., homemakers, volunteers, clinic, and district. The availability of the indicated service is always, of course, a primary consideration. If, for example, psychiatric time is booked far ahead or a social worker is not available to undertake a difficult marital counseling situation, alternate planning is required to avoid as far as possible the building up of a treatment or other waiting list. In turn, an overall commitment to short-term intervention is crucial to ensure prompt delivery of service.

One worker continues responsibility during this process. The same worker is ready to communicate with the referral source and other agencies. Most important, the same worker is available to the family and holds an interpretive interview to explain the ongoing treatment program to be rendered within the center or helps the client to tie in with the needed community resource. In effect, one worker packages and delivers service.

PACKAGING OF SERVICES

The second major program gain achieved through the center has been the meaningful packaging of continued services as needed and as part of total treatment. The following cases are illustrative:

A couple with six children, aged 1½–13, were referred by their pastor. The husband was unemployable owing to a chronic illness and the wife was unable to manage on his low disability allowance. The husband refused to apply for supplemental public assistance and was becoming more and more withdrawn. With the help of the worker, they agreed to accept financial assistance and the husband received medical attention. After a two-month hospitalization, he died and the family immediately began to disintegrate. The mother lost control of the situation, the children reacted in a negative manner, and three of the older ones refused to attend school. Psychiatric consultation was available to the social worker as he dealt with the mother's feelings and the children's problems. Homemaker service was initiated to help the mother in a supportive and educational way. The two older boys were assigned Big Brothers, and summer camp placement was planned for the younger children. Throughout the history of this case there was one worker.

In another case, the mother of eight children separated from her alcoholic and abusive husband. The center worker assisted her to receive support and protection through the family court and public assistance. Homemaker services were provided during an illness she had, and one child is receiving psychiatric attention. The older boys are receiving the guidance of Big Brothers, and camp care is planned. Again, throughout this case a single worker has provided the mother with management and budgeting advice and supportive casework and has mobilized a variety of services on behalf of this troubled family.

CONCLUSIONS

The center operation has made possible unified, unduplicated services to families with a minimum of the traditional fuss of referral, repetitive intake, summaries, separate records, conferences, and the other impediments that so frequently fragment, delay, or sabotage service delivery. The most important factor in achieving smooth delivery of services has been the professional and personal communication among the center staff. Professional boundaries and prior agency allegiances do not crumble easily. There have been disputes and frank professional jealousies to overcome. However, the success to date of the Bronx Catholic Charities Center is exclusively due to the willingness of staff to respond to the total requirements of those seeking services and their readiness to take a fresh look at their professional roles.

Finally, the unified service concept has been extended into a local neighborhood. A staff person has been assigned full time and the center staff has been organized into multidisciplinary task forces to explore current services and unmet needs. The purpose is to determine the role of the agency and those services that would be relevant to the needs and aspirations of a ghetto community. Already evident is the need for radical changes in the types of service and methods of delivery.

In summary, the Bronx Catholic Charities Center is an effort by a large voluntary federation to overcome duplication and fragmentation. It is a result of critical study and reorganization. Administrative changes have improved efficiency, reduced costs, and alleviated to some extent the chronic manpower shortage. To a significant degree the center has produced prompt, unduplicated, and efficient delivery of social services.

Co-ordinated Clinical Social Service: Home, Hospital, and Nursing Home

AMELIA B. BARNARD

The present era, characterized by pressures for "instant change" on the one hand and the vested interests and relatively fixed nature of traditional social and health institutions on the other, places stress on all members of the so-called helping professions. "So-called" because the professions are told more and more often about their failure to help and are challenged to defend many principles and practices that have evolved as experientially sound.

The burgeoning of new legislation, new programs, new ideas, and new funds with which to try to find new ways to deliver needed services is exciting; the danger is proverbial—must we throw out the baby with the bath water? Conversely, are we tempted to translate the known and the proved into new terms, new labels, and new titles and in the process to disguise the fact that what passes as innovative or new has a solid knowledge base gained through experience?

This brief paper will deal with a program that borrows heavily from the traditional model of delivery of clinical social work services, but which has made some major structural alterations in that model. The structural change has as its objective those three important but often elusive goals of (1) better utilization of social work manpower, (2) continuity of patient care, and (3) co-ordination as contrasted with fragmentation of social work services. Central to the sustenance of the program is the dedication of staff, board, contributors, and contracting

113

agencies to these goals; time alone will tell whether traditionally disparate and autonomous bodies will continue to see practical gains in a program based on the theoretical value of the co-ordinated approach.

ORIGIN OF THE PROGRAM

In capsule, the program of the Health Resources Center of Denver originated with a specialized referral service in the health field and has expanded to include the provision of social work services to interested private hospitals, certified home health agencies, and nursing homes on a contractual basis.   At present five hospitals, six nursing homes, and two home health agencies are participating in the program; a system of centralized record-keeping has been developed.   The staff consists of eleven graduate social workers, four social work assistants, and two clerical employees; the agency has also served as a placement facility for students from the University of Denver School of Social Work. The major source of funds is contracts with participating agencies; in addition, seven voluntary health agencies have upheld an annual contribution for support of the program and it has a three-year grant from the U.S. Public Health Service.   Most recently the center has instituted a nursing home clearinghouse giving a daily figure for available beds in the Denver metropolitan area, which is paid for by approximately half of the hospitals (both public and private) in the area.

The center's program grew out of community concern with health and medical care and was funded initially in March 1962 by the Colorado State Department of Public Health using U.S. Public Health Service moneys.   In brief, the objectives of the center are (1) to serve as a clearinghouse for information about available community resources and as an appropriate referral source, (2) to document evidence of unmet needs within the community, not for use by the agency itself, but for any group interested in examining the need for additional programs, and (3) to serve a co-ordinating function in the health field.

In the process of trying to reach those persons not otherwise known to health and social agencies, the physician in private practice was identified as the person coming into daily contact with this segment of the community.   In order to involve physicians in the center's work, they were asked to serve on what was then an executive committee and is now an incorporated board of directors.   Representatives are included from each of the four county medical societies, and it is largely—if not entirely—because of them that in June 1964 the center was invited to move to rent-free housing within the Denver Medical Society, which meant far more than simply space from which to operate: It signified the open support and endorsement of the program by the medical community.

Meanwhile pressures were building rapidly toward the passage of Medicare and Medicaid legislation. The physicians in the area were reluctantly coming to grips with the broad implications of health care concepts as contrasted with the narrower and more traditional view of medical care, and it became possible to talk about the value of ancillary services to the private sector of medicine. The Health Resources Center, with its board of directors comprised of key professionals from both the public and private sectors of the health field, was a natural focal point for discussion of these concerns.

It is noteworthy that at that time not one private general hospital in the Denver metropolitan area had incorporated social work as part of its program. As interest in extension of social work services to additional segments of the medical community began to be voiced by hospital administrators and physicians, a committee worked during the late summer and early fall of 1965 to examine ways and means of so doing. Impetus in the direction of staffing private hospitals gained added momentum as the probable impact of passage of Titles XVIII and XIX of the Social Security Act on private hospital programs was considered. Freedom of choice of physician and hospital by the medically indigent, it was felt, would tend to some extent to disperse the concentration of medical care for this group from university and city hospitals to community facilities. This does not imply that social work services were expected to be limited in any way to the medically indigent, but rather that private hospitals would be serving an increasing number of such patients. In point of fact, present hospital case loads show equal numbers of private and service patients.

As the idea of a co-ordinated structure emerged, the center was forced to consider the related problems of recruitment and the manpower shortage; thus, initially the program was limited to hospitals. However, in short order the potential for inclusion of a similar contractual relationship with certified home health agencies and interested extended care facilities was seen.

OPERATION OF THE CENTER

Essentially, what the center is now doing is centralizing much of the supervisory and nearly all of the administrative responsibility in the central office. Staff is recruited from there and employed by the agency for assignment to a specific facility. Contracts or letters of agreement are signed between the agency and the outside facility on an annual basis and include what might be termed a job description for a social work department. The cost to the facility includes the salaries of the workers assigned to it plus a percentage to cover administrative costs of the central office.

Staffing patterns in contracting agencies range from one half-time person in a 200-bed nonteaching hospital with no service cases to a staff of seven in a private children's hospital. An attempt is being made to make maximum use of social work assistants under close supervision by a professional staff member. The model followed is, of course, the traditional structure of the large social service department in a university hospital, in which social workers are assigned to specific services in the hospital and are responsible administratively to the chief of service and to the director of the social service department for their professional performance. The senior staff member, when there is a social service department, carries the title of director of social service and participates in programming at the department head level; a worker in a one-man facility carries the title of clinical social worker and also meets with other department heads. The executive director of the Health Resources Center relates to the institution's administration much as the social service director in a university medical center relates to chiefs of services and has supervisory relationships of the traditional kind with staff. All staff wear the usual white coat but have a small pocket insignia identifying them as HRC Social Service. Since many physicians are on the attending staff of more than one affiliated facility, this serves to identify the central agency.

Some problems with dual identification on the part of staff were anticipated. None has arisen—a fact that unquestionably reflects the caliber of staff who have been attracted to the program. Perhaps another analogy to the traditional model is in order, namely, the similarity to the role of university-employed field instructors. Of proved value is the usefulness of weekly staff meetings for a variety of purposes including in-service training for social work assistants, case presentation by students and staff for professional stimulation and growth, and, most important, exchange of information and experiences.

The system of centralized records was developed in the interest of continuity of patient care. Within the private sector of health care—perhaps within any sector—there is considerable mobility from home to hospital to nursing home. Records are kept in the worker's office while the patient remains in the institution and returned to the central office when the case is closed, for distribution to another facility should the patient move there. A master file card is kept on every case, which in addition to identifying data indicates where the record is at any point in time. Dictation is done by means of telephone and electronic equipment housed in the central office, where records are transcribed for return to the worker; this is not much different in principle from the secretarial pool.

The system allows any institution, once the social work program is established, to elect to continue the department separate from the Health Resources Center. This option has been taken by one hospital that had been affiliated with the center for two years. The social work staff was absorbed by the hospital. The hospital administration expressed great appreciation for the center's help in establishing a sound program, but felt that a contractual arrangement for any part of the hospital program violated basic concepts of sound management. The consensus of the center's board, staff, and other participating administrators was that this attitude toward management responsibilities was unique to this specific hospital. Certainly, however, the structure has built-in potential for such a development. At the start of the program it was stated that the important thing was development of sound social work programs in this segment of the health community. However, the center has become sufficiently impressed with the value of the co-ordinated approach that deep regret was felt at this hospital's decision. Out of this, however, has come an interest in examining means of defining differing levels of affiliation.

PRINCIPLES

Some of the principles on which this program has evolved are as follows:

1. The advantage to the physician in private practice, as well as to others in the health field, of having one agency to which to turn for appropriate use of clinical social service.

2. The potential to become a centralized source of information about specialized health resources to meet specialized health needs.

3. Continuity of patient care; the ability of one agency to follow patient and family through a series of health facilities.

4. Co-ordination of knowledge regarding continually changing agency programs and community resources for use by staff providing casework services.

5. Maximum use of available manpower by centralizing administrative and supervisory functions.

6. For the smaller hospital department of one to four members, the centralized structure permits resident social work staff to maintain positive working relationships when policy matters are at issue and to utilize the strength of the Health Resources Center's board and administrative staff to negotiate a resolution with hospital administration.

Service Delivery in the Multipurpose Senior Center

MARVIN S. SCHREIBER

Viewed in perspective, the growth and development of the multi-purpose senior center—a uniquely American innovation—reflects a community awareness and social consciousness significant in the 1960s and holding much promise for the seventies. The center is a setting that lends itself to a community and neighborhood approach to meeting the social and health needs of the elderly in both rural and urban America. It can be described as a space-age vehicle capable of delivering a wide range of services to older people and seeking to preserve the values of dignity, self-worth, and concern for the individual associated with an older age.

A quarter of a century ago New York City social workers began to wage a war on poverty—the poverty of loneliness, isolation, and alienation; the poverty of opportunity for the elderly to have meaningful and creative leisure, to be of use to themselves and others, to discover, develop, and use new skills to achieve dignity in old age. Their perseverance led to the creation of the first senior day center in the former Bronx Borough Hall.[1] The success of the William Hodson Community Center gave impetus to the acceptance of the center as a community approach to meeting some of the needs of older people. It also demon-

---

[1] Susan K. Kubie and Gertrude Landau, *Group Work with the Aged* (New York: International Universities Press, 1953).

118

strated the social worker's ability to effect social change—the proportions of which are just beginning to make a significant contribution to the American social welfare scene.[2]

The upsurge of new senior centers has been phenomenal. In 1966 a directory published jointly by the Federal Administration on Aging and the National Council on Aging listed almost one thousand center programs. A new directory, now being compiled, is expected to list three thousand centers. The Older Americans Act, Economic Opportunity Act, and efforts at the local community level by public and voluntary agencies have spawned a new generation of centers. Today, 20 million Americans are over 65 years of age. In 1975 this age group could easily number 25 million.

Senior Centers of Dade County, Inc., is a voluntary social agency responsible for the development and operation of multipurpose centers, the first of which opened in 1961. Today, six centers having a multidisciplinary staff of social workers, public health nurses, educators, special instructors, food services personnel, and volunteers are open. The Miami Housing Authority, in connection with its extensive housing program for the elderly, provided for the construction of senior center facilities for the use of its tenants and other aged persons in the community. Enrollment in centers is open to all residents of Dade County over 60 years of age, without charge. Financial support is shared by the United Fund and the county—UF underwrites the planning and administrative costs, the county government, the operating budget, which is essentially for professional and specialist staff.

The goals of the multipurpose senior center relate directly to the provision of supportive social services. Social workers seek to promote the well-being of older persons through an environment conducive to the creative use of leisure time and abilities, forming satisfying interpersonal relationships, and the learning of new roles having meaning and value to the older person and the community. They further seek to promote good health habits and nutrition; encourage participation in volunteer service in the center and community; foster continued interest in self-education, retraining, and employment; and encourage participation in a variety of group activities. Included in the definition of supportive social services is the delivery of group and individual services, health maintenance programming, food services, and so on—all the interrelated areas of center program geared to support meaningful and independent living.

---

[2] Jean M. Maxwell, ed., *Centers for Older People: Guides for Programs and Facilities* (New York: National Council on the Aging, 1962).

PROGRAM SERVICES

Group services represent the broadest and most basic service in the center and include both large and small group activities developed from the expressed needs and interests of the elderly themselves. Group services seek to involve the older person in the planning and decision-making processes. Membership self-government, elected officers, and working committees of adults in their 60s, 70s, and 80s challenge the group worker to apply social work skills and knowledge of the aging in our society and to use community resources.

Casework counseling is a vital senior center service. The caseworker gives support to individuals and small groups at times of crisis and as part of an ongoing effort to help individuals use the center's services to enrich their lives. Counseling and referral bring to the older person the community's interest and concern for his well-being and assistance in making maximum use of the maze of public and voluntary agency programs. The older person's strengths are supported, and feelings of dignity and self-worth are enhanced. The group worker and caseworker, complemented by graduate students, form the direct service social work component of an interdisciplinary staff team. Among the mental health disciplines, it is the social worker who is uniquely equipped to serve the elderly in the center setting.

By definition, a multipurpose senior center must give leadership to the community in developing a wide range of supportive health and social services for older Americans. It is therefore not surprising that centers offer—directly and indirectly—recruitment, training, and employment opportunities; health education; counseling; and multiphasic screening programs among the services they deliver. The social work role in the development, structure, and effective delivery of these services requires a sensitive application of community organization, administrative, casework, and group work skills, as well as a readiness to experiment.

For example, there is a keen awareness among those having responsibility for center administration of the need for an appropriate health services program. In 1961, in enrolling its first members, Senior Centers learned that a high percentage were not receiving medical care; some had not seen a doctor for as long as twenty years. Yet many of these persons sought information from the social workers about the availability of medical help. This suggested the existence of a gap in available medical resources or in the older person's use of community resources.

A sizable group of the elderly resisted using available health services, believing that age is inevitably accompanied by chronic illness. They appeared to reason that their refusal to accept aging would indefinitely forestall illness and disability. Psychological denial was found to be prevalent. Center staff believed that it was unwise to tamper with this defense mechanism. They sought to help the older person understand his health needs and face the reality of his health status. Through a process of aiding the individual to achieve and maintain mental and physical well-being, the importance of prevention and the need for knowledge in the use of community resources are emphasized. Staff continue to be concerned for those individuals who pride themselves in not seeking medical care, who believe that apparent freedom from disease indicates youth, productivity, and self-worth. When illness destroys this pride, it is a shattering psychological experience. Staff have therefore sought to develop the concept of health maintenance as a way of life and to encourage its acceptance as an integral part of an individual's total center experience. Less is now seen of false pride, and for many individuals it no longer appears to be a focal point of ego structure.

The rationale for the center's intervention in the health area was that its warmly accepting environment helped the individual discuss his health needs and concerns easily, the peer group provided effective support, and the social worker and nurse in partnership delivered vital health maintenance services. In the process of developing health maintenance services, the administration needed to recognize and understand its role, contribution, and limitations and how it must relate to other agencies and professional disciplines, become involved with them, and work with them in the implementation of a health service in a social agency setting. This process is similar to the development of a social work program in a health services agency. The broad social work role is one of collaboration and teamwork among the health maintenance nurse, caseworker, and group worker. The importance of real teamwork becomes more obvious each year, as individuals give evidence of problems having both social and physical causes.

A LOW-COST MEALS PROGRAM

In enrollment interviews and casework counseling in five senior centers operated by Senior Centers between 1961 and 1965, it was evident that a high percentage of the more than fifteen hundred individuals seen denied themselves a noonday meal sufficient to meet minimal standards of good nutrition. Eating habits, especially among those living alone, reflected little attention to planning balanced meals, which was compounded by the fact that the limited incomes of the elderly prevented them from purchasing wide varieties of food. Limited knowledge of diet and nutrition was the norm, together with apathy and poor motivation. Shopping for food, especially "good buys," was often difficult, so that the elderly paid more for less.

Staff were well aware that an inadequate diet, coupled with loneliness and isolation, has an adverse effect on the health and well-being of older people. Since food is a basic human need, it was recognized that a balanced meal is essential to physical well-being and companionship in eating is essential to social well-being. Senior Centers chose to combine food with friendship.

In June 1966, following months of consultation with community agencies, board and staff members, and discussions by the elderly themselves, an application for a Low Cost Meals Demonstration Project was submitted under Title IV of the Older Americans Act. The mechanism proposed was a central commissary kitchen to prepare nutritious meals for all centers, and satellite or receiving kitchens to handle meals received in food warmers from the central facility, the program to be operated mainly by elderly workers.

The Administration on Aging of the U.S. Department of Health, Education, and Welfare awarded a $77,000 demonstration grant to help equip the commissary and satellite kitchens, purchase portable food warmers and a truck, and train and employ older workers. All income from the sale of meals was earmarked for the purchase of food and supplies. The price of a full meal was set at 40¢. The principal objectives included the following:

1. To serve low-cost, nutritious, carefully planned luncheons and take-out meals that provide a substantial portion of the minimum daily requirements of essential nutrients, as set forth by the National Research Council's recommended dietary allowances.

2. To distribute surplus federal food commodities to the elderly in the poverty or marginal income groups, instruct them in the storage and best use of these food commodities, and develop recipes in order to help stretch limited incomes.

3. To provide employment opportunities to the elderly living on social security and Old Age Assistance to help raise them above their low income level and provide a meaningful work experience to help keep them productive in their later years; to make available appropriate volunteer roles for those desiring to give such service.

4. To motivate the individual to practice good eating habits and learn to buy more economically, through demonstrations, cooking schools, lectures, and discussions, as well as through making full use of the low-cost meals program.

5. To provide opportunities for socialization through participation in the low-cost meals program, while being exposed to the opportunities available through the multipurpose senior center, including such vital services as health counseling, education, casework, and group work. Opportunities for community and volunteer service and the meaningful roles these provide were significant added goals.

CONCLUSION

The 1970's hold great promise for higher incomes, better housing, preventive health services, and employment opportunities for older Americans, and imaginative and creative social workers will be needed. The multipurpose senior center has demonstrated that it can be an effective vehicle for the delivery of community services. When related to a comprehensive and co-ordinated community program of services to the elderly, the social work role in centers will assume new dimensions in planning, collaboration, service delivery, and evaluation.

Social Work in the Planning and Delivery of Health and Mental Health Services

BERTRAM J. BLACK

During the past two decades, some significant changes have taken place in the thinking being done about the delivery of health and mental health services. Earlier, concern with the costly proliferation of hospitals had led to regional and district hospital planning. Report after report spoke of the need for neighborhood hospital outposts with more specialized and more fully equipped medical centers to be spotted at greater intervals. Thus began, in a sense, the geographic approach to structuring health care.

Ideally, a certain number of hospital beds would be available to a specific population, with so many X-ray machines and laboratories and special illness facilities for so many people. When all was built, then everyone would have access to a regular hospital bed if his doctor so recommended and to a place on a specialized service if his illness demanded it. No one could really complain about the concept. These plans seemed to be headed toward provision of better health services and greater efficiency in spending public funds.

The story of why better hospital planning did not always lead to better hospitals and rarely led to increased delivery of better health services is an old one. Among many other factors, it is now recognized that the needs for medical services and numbers of hospital beds are only partially correlated. Hospital planning, which was stepped up with the advent of the Hill-Burton program (the Medical Facilities Survey and Construction Act, PL 482), has greatly conditioned more recent thinking in planning other medical services.

GEOGRAPHIC APPROACH

The geographic approach to developing health and mental health resources started first with the concentration of scientific and technological resources in order to make them more useful and usable. The hospital evolved into the medical center. The medical centers became what Somers calls "institutionalized"—concentrations of equipment and manpower expected to provide better patient care.[1] However, as one hospital planning expert put it:

> As patient care has become better and better because of its increased specialization and mechanization, its component parts have also become more and more fragmented and, in effect, less and less available to the individual. The people in need of care have greater and greater difficulty in making effective contact with the complex system so as to find their way to the right place at the right time.[2]

The newer regional medical programs for integrated patient care and the heart, cancer, and stroke centers represent an advanced stage of such geographic institutionalization.

Some decentralization and attempts to bring service delivery closer to the population for whom the services are intended has come with the application of public health approaches. It has long been recognized that one aspect of epidemiology is the ecology of the patient and his disease. Control of infectious disease must be related to a specific geographic area or high-risk population. A poison control or a suicide prevention center, both modern preventive public health devices, must be related to well-defined geographic areas to be effective. It is partly in recognition of the fact that living conditions and societal structure are inextricably interwoven with illness and health patterns that mental

---

[1] Anne R. Somers, "Some Basic Determinants of Medical Care and Health Policy: An Overview of Trends and Issues," in "Dimensions and Determinants of Health Policy," *Milbank Memorial Fund Quarterly*, Vol. 46, No. 1 (January 1968), Part 2, p. 21.

[2] Robert M. Sigmond, "Health Planning," in "Dimensions and Determinants of Health Policy," *Milbank Memorial Fund Quarterly*, Vol. 46, No. 1 (January 1968), Part 2, p. 101.

health planners have turned to the concept of catchment areas for the new mental health centers.

This is, of course, not the main reason. It is actually easier to plan services, buildings, systems of monitoring programs, or data banks if a well-defined geographic area with a well-defined population is kept in mind. The writer agrees with Blasingame when he speaks of the recent concentration of medical services, that "it is obvious that we must apply our best thoughts and energies toward devising appropriate therapy," but the geographic approach to delivering health and mental health services is a fact of life.[3]

WHOLE-PERSON APPROACH

Before considering some of the concepts that derive from this approach and affect professional relationships and use of manpower, however, it is important to note that another set of systems for delivering health services has also evolved in this generation, sometimes independent of the geographic approach, sometimes intertwined with it. These will be referred to as embodying the "whole-person" approach to patterns of service.

Perhaps the oldest and most familiar of these is group medical practice. Sometimes group practice is related simply to economics—sharing of facilities—but more often of late it represents a merging of resources on behalf of the patients. This has become especially true of prepaid group plans (Health Insurance Plan, Permanente, Group Health Insurance). Such a program, in stupendous contrast to the outpatient department clinic pattern, recognizes that the delivery of health care must be to patients and not to illnesses or organ systems.

A few gems of whole-person medical care can be found in some hospitals and medical centers. These appear in the form of home medical care units in which the hospital's services to the severely chronically ill are transported to the patients' homes. A few good convalescent care programs have the same sparkle. Some forward-thinking hospitals, too, have tentatively suggested that mining the progressive patient care concept might yield pay dirt—sometimes with patients' benefits in mind, but more frequently couched in terms of hospital economies. Of course, that is not bad for the patients either!

The most recently enunciated whole-person health programs are

---

[3] F. L. J. Blasingame, MD, remarks before the House of Delegates, American Medical Association, Philadelphia, November 28, 1965.

those dubbed "comprehensive." The comprehensive programs most in evidence today, mainly in planning terms, but increasingly in functioning structure and program, are the comprehensive community mental health centers. Just over the hill are comprehensive health centers, and off on the horizon are comprehensive neighborhood service centers.

These comprehensive centers link the two approaches to delivering health care—the geographic and the whole-person approaches. The elements making up such comprehensive programs may be discussed in terms of the characteristics prescribed by the American Hospital Association for optimum health services.[4] These require the following:

1. A team approach to individual medical care (under the leadership of a physician).

2. A spectrum of services that must include diagnosis, treatment, rehabilitation, education, and prevention.

3. A co-ordinated community and regional system.

4. Continuity between the hospital and nonhospital aspects of patient care.

5. Continuity between 'in- and outpatient care.

6. Continuing evaluation and research on quality and adequacy in meeting the needs of patient and community.

Here, then, is the whole-person approach to designing delivery systems of health and mental health services, which, when linked to the geographic effect, has been coloring planning and program-building efforts during the past decade, if not really over the past generation. These approaches have faced the professional community as well as the consuming and supporting public with some concepts and issues that are at times bewildering. At least they precipitate thought about their effect on the utilization of professional manpower. Only a few will be examined here. Consideration will be given to whether modifications, if any, in role, methods, and techniques may be called for if social workers are to perform effectively in health delivery service systems.

A ROLE IN PLANNING

Sigmond has said: "Most simply stated, planning is advance thinking as a basis for doing."[5] Stripped of all the mystique of biometrics and

---

[4] *Statement on Optimum Health Services,* Publication S17 (Chicago: American Hospital Association, 1965).

[5] *Op. cit.,* p. 91.

demography, shorn of the process and committees of community organization, bereft of charts and computers, that is what planning is
all about—advance thinking, ever more in demand in the health fields,
too often bypassed on the excuse of limited time or manpower. Sigmond, a hospital planner himself, has pointed out that during the
past generation

> . . . the health care field has been expanding so rapidly and so
> continuously in almost all directions that institutions developed
> out of the most ineffective planning processes hardly ever seemed
> to "fail." This has led to a feeling that one can hardly go wrong
> and so need not plan in a tedious fashion. The need has appeared
> to be so great relative to the demand that anything done was better
> than nothing.[6]

The result of this state of affairs is that almost anyone who took
action to initiate a new or apparently innovative program has been
blessed as a planner. No wonder Lourie complained wistfully:

> Comprehensiveness is the "in" concept of the period. Soon com-
> prehensive neighborhood centers will need coordination to avoid
> incomprehensible comprehensive approaches. How many centers
> of planning can we tolerate? [7]

We must agree with Michael S. March of the federal Bureau of the
Budget that the shortcomings of present organizational patterns for
health as well as social services are significant and clearly evident.[8] The
target has to be the development of more effective and better articulated
service delivery systems designed to direct services beyond the individual to the family and the neighborhood.

To accomplish this calls for planning—for advance thinking as
the basis for doing. Planning of delivery systems of health and mental
health services is a complicated business. It is not only that health service is "amorphous in definition," as Brown put it, and that "the system
of medical care is more entrepreneurial than professional in orientation
. . . ," but that the design system must weave together existing pieces

---

  [6] *Ibid.,* p. 104.

  [7] Norman V. Lourie, "Orthopsychiatry and Education," *American
Journal of Orthopsychiatry,* Vol. 37, No. 5 (October 1967), p. 839.

  [8] Michael S. March, "The Neighborhood Center Concept," *Public Welfare,* Vol. 26, No. 2 (April 1968), p. 110.

of service with newer conceptual models. And to make planning more difficult in the field of health care, especially in matching services to needs, ". . . the product of the system is also the consumer of the system." [9]

Social workers have not been greatly called on in the planning of health care programs. Can this be because social work as a profession has little or nothing to offer this process?

Says Whitney M. Young, Jr.:

> As social workers, we are concerned, first and foremost, with the character and quality of life in an increasingly urban society. How can we make the urban environment human and humane? How can we avoid the dangers inherent in the hostility and alienation that come from anxiety and powerlessness? We must guarantee that the same skills, genius, and creative drive that have gone into brick-and-mortar progress, into the building of bridges and tunnels, into the smashing of the atom and flights into space, now go into planning with people for their own social needs.[10]

But Arkava asks of social work educators:

> Indeed, does social work have a real contribution to make to the solution of the problems concerned with racial integration, mental retardation, mental health, and income maintenance? . . . It is all very well to take a position on a subject, that position being determined by a set of values held by the profession or group; it is another thing to imply that one has taken a position because of some special knowledge about a particular problem or issue. It seems necessary to specify what it is that one knows about the problem or issue. Social work should, in honesty, specify what social work does, what it can do, and how that doing is unique.[11]

Can it be that social work has removed itself from "knowledge" and is only left with "concerns" about the social problems of those it tries

---

[9] Ray E. Brown, "Problems of the Planning Process," *Bulletin of the New York Academy of Medicine,* Vol. 44, No. 2 (February 1968), p. 107.

[10] Quoted in Marion O. Robinson, *Humanizing the City,* Public Affairs Pamphlet No. 417 (New York: Public Affairs Committee, April 1968), p. 2.

[11] Morton L. Arkava, "Social Work Practice and Knowledge: An Examination of Their Relationship," *Journal of Education for Social Work,* Vol. 3, No. 2 (Fall 1967), p. 11.

to serve?   If this is so to any extent, the profession had better start retooling fast to participate in planning.   It is failing miserably to prepare mental health and health service workers, including social workers, to participate in planning service systems.   Lip service to social planning as part of a curriculum in community organization is of limited consequence.   Planning has to be a responsibility of those who will be directing and delivering the services, not of some separate council or co-ordinating body.   Sigmond puts it well:

> Planning can be transmuted into action only by those with operational responsibility for the action.   Mischief will result if an attempt is made to give a planner authority to impose action if he is not, at the same time, to be held responsible for the results of the action.[12]

CONTINUITY OF CARE

If there is one concept in health services for which social workers have stood solidly, it is continuity of care.   We are all too familiar with the inadequate and discrete programs offered sick people in the name of health care.   The most infamous of these were—and still are—the outpatient clinics of general hospitals.   In the new mental health centers, it is planned to introduce continuity of care.   This raises the question of whether what is meant is continuity of care for the identified illness or for the person who has the illness.   Who better than the social worker should appreciate the consequences of lack of continuity?   However, there does not seem to be much evidence that the profession has imparted much of its experience to the more recent planning for continuity of health care.   In the early 1940's there were some well-organized clinical services, such as that directed by Eleanor Cockerill at Long Island University Hospital.   It is sad that this experience did not carry over to outpatient departments and is not even obliquely referred to today by those designing the juxtaposition of health service elements to provide the comprehensive package necessary for continuity of care.   Is this because social work experience in operating such programs—including the experience of veterans' service centers after World War II—is so far in the past that it can hardly be remembered?   Or did professional interests ossify or shift

---

[12] *Op. cit.,* p. 95.

away from concern with continuity of care? Is this why Blum and his associates can declare, in making the case for neighborhood multiservice centers:

> The family is now pitted not only against its own problems but must fight at least as hard to avoid being torn asunder by conflicting, even if independently valid, priorities posed by workers whose purposes are restricted in scope by the goals set by their agencies and whose outlook and efforts are circumscribed by the culture of their profession.[13]

COMMUNICATION WITH THE TARGET POPULATION

Social workers pride themselves on their professional ability to establish rapport with troubled people and to understand with realism the environment in which they find themselves. Much has been written and more is being said about the problems of gaining community understanding and support for the social and health programs the underserved populations need and deserve. With respect to three matters, professional social workers should have more to say:

1. As Dixon pointed out recently:

> . . . health producers may be trapped in a fantasy about the high priority of health services in people's minds. The available evidence would seem to indicate that health ranks below such other community concerns as jobs, votes, and perhaps even education.[14]

Social workers have had long experience in helping people with what they say they want and in helping them to clarify what they need. Therefore, the contrast between expressed needs and underlying or total needs should not faze us.

2. It is about time that the profession stopped beating its collective

---

[13] Henrick L. Blum, MD, Fred Wahl, Genelle M. Lemon, Robert Jornlin, and Glen W. Kent, MD, "The Multipurpose Worker and the Neighborhood Multiservice Center: Initial Experiences and Implications of the Rodeo Community Service Center," *American Journal of Public Health*, Vol. 58, No. 3 (March 1968), p. 459.

[14] James M. Dixon, "The Health Agenda for the Future," in "Dimensions and Determinants of Health Policy," *Milbank Memorial Fund Quarterly*, Vol. 46, No. 1 (January 1968), Part 2, p. 264.

breast about how middle class social work is and how it has forgotten or never learned how to deal with the lower classes. Some of those in the health and rehabilitation fields have never ceased serving the poorest and most handicapped of the population and have some knowledge and know-how to transmit.

3. The use of indigenous workers is not new, either in the history of social work or in public health. If social work can overcome the rigidity and self-protectiveness that come with professional maturity and keep its eyes on the health needs of people, it should be able to make good use of the help the people themselves can give. In other cultures, in other countries, this has been demonstrated well; in the newly recognized culture of poverty in a familiar geography, the profession should be able to do as well.

EPIDEMIOLOGY

To deliver health or mental health services without taking steps to seek out the sources of the illnesses or even to describe adequately the characteristics of the problems being dealt with would be poor policy. Of course, there are a variety of complications. The definitions of sickness and mental illness are by no means precise. The present-day tendency to identify many symptoms of social pathology and disorganization as evidences of mental illness makes it extremely difficult to measure incidence or prevalence.

Those community mental health and health service centers that are inclined to classify as illness a broad spectrum of personal and community disorders are perturbed that when they do offer good medical and public health resources, there is rarely an overwhelming consumer demand. As Thomas said:

> The appalling figures for perinatal and maternal mortality, venereal disease, illegitimacy, prematurity, malnutrition, family disintegration, narcotism, mental disease, and all the rest—which exist in all our slums and in all of our cities—are not due to the absence of physicians and public health clinics in our slums. They are due to the presence of the slums. More clinics and physicians will add to the comfort and feelings of security of the slumbound, but no one should think that the direct threat to human life that the slum itself poses will be changed. We must not underestimate what needs doing. To change the slums to places fit for

human beings and free the people who now must live there from their confinement is far, far more than a public health problem.[15]

The problem of service delivery in this instance is also an epidemiological problem—that of case-finding. But this kind of case-finding requires treading a narrow path between identifying the individual who needs the treatment, which has the effect of publicly labeling him, and preserving the personal, private integrity of the individual. Social work practitioners should have learned enough from their experience with the reaching-out process to be able to help health planners and administrators in this task.

CONSULTATION AND EDUCATION

It is extremely interesting and significant that the element of service required for comprehensive community mental health centers is "consultation and education" (as used in the Comprehensive Mental Health Center regulations, PL 88–164), not just mental health education. Many things are subsumed under this term, from the more traditional advice and counseling given to a physician by a psychiatrist, psychologist, or a social worker, to the formal courses in elements of psychiatric treatment given general medical practitioners in medical schools.

In many respects there is in the newer mental health centers a greater tendency to use social workers for consultative functions than for any other purpose. Actually, the relationship of school systems, police departments, courts, and churches with social service agencies has existed much longer than that between these "caretaker" elements of society and psychiatric agencies. The contacts between these elements and psychiatric clinics—when they did exist—have more often than not been carried on by the social worker on the clinic team. Whether the social worker could or should be the consultant or educator in the consultation-education program of a comprehensive community mental health center will depend in part on the purposes of the service. Is it to be direct treatment of ill persons? Is it to be case-finding? Is it to be educational in terms of imparting knowledge or teaching others to perform mental health functions? Or is the service directed toward communication with the target population the product as well as the consumer of the system?

---

[15] Lewis Thomas, MD, "Discussion of Thomas McKeown's Paper 'The Complex of the Medical Task,'" *Bulletin of the New York Academy of Medicine,* Vol. 44, No. 2 (February 1968), p. 104.

REHABILITATION

The whole-person and geographic approaches to delivering health services to people point up the glaring fact that the largest medical treatment problems in society today are not those of curing acute illnesses but of alleviating chronic conditions. While our future must deal with prevention, our present has to be concerned with how to maximize the functioning potential of the immensely large number of human beings who suffer from physically and mentally handicapping conditions.

When planning and negotiating were taking place over the development of the comprehensive community mental health centers, it was disappointing that rehabilitation was placed in the second group of essentials and was apparently not a necessary service for a facility to qualify as a mental health center. But now there is hardly a plan that does not at least stipulate that rehabilitative services will be provided along with the five essentials: inpatient, outpatient, and emergency treatment, partial hospitalization, and consultation and education. Even the neighborhood service center planners say:

> The effort to develop a better neighborhood service center represents an extension of the principle of rehabilitation to the provision of service to the socially and economically disadvantaged.[16]

Unfortunately, professional social work is a minority in the field of rehabilitation. Medical rehabilitation has long been the preserve of the physician, although to an increasing extent places on the treatment team have been yielded to the vocational psychologist and rehabilitation counselor. Mental health rehabilitation is for the most part a shared enterprise of the psychiatrist, psychologist, and vocational rehabilitation counselor, with the occupational therapist in a secondary position. There are few active rehabilitation programs for either the physically disadvantaged or the mentally ill in which the professional social worker is seen in any other guise than as ancillary to the rehabilitation team.

Fifteen years ago an effort was made by Ryrie Koch, Jane Hoey, and the writer to get major schools of social work to take on the training of rehabilitation counselors, which they would not do. They exhibited all of what Brown calls "the rigidity of our professional and institutional practices and the rigidity of the outlook of these

---

[16] *Op. cit.*, p. 99.

institutions." [17]   What came to pass is that another group of professionals—the vocational rehabilitation counselors—are being trained at the master's level, and their theoretical orientation is being accepted as more relevant in rehabilitative services than that of social work.   It may now be too late to reintroduce social workers to rehabilitative mental health services.   Time is still all too short to prepare them for the health service centers and the multiservice programs.

POOR PEOPLE, SICK PEOPLE

In the inner city, the ghetto, the poverty areas, community interest is focused more on jobs, education, housing, and other social and economic needs than on the need for more adequate health care. Those who work with the poor and have used the rehabilitation approach have demonstrated how inextricably bound together are social, psychological, economic, and medical problems.   Jobs are vitally important, but much of the job training efforts go to waste when the trainees have physical or emotional conditions that, if uncared for, stand in the way of their ever learning or functioning adequately on the job.   When Altro Health and Rehabilitation Services in 1967 examined the population of the youth branch of the State Employment Service in the Bronx, it was discovered—and not suprisingly—that seventy of one hundred youngsters had serious mental, emotional, or medical problems that had to be dealt with before job training could be effective and that the remaining thirty had unattended medical conditions that were serious barriers to their successful functioning as adult workers.[18]   However, something can be done, and this is attested to by the fact that, after they received rehabilitative services and vocational training, 80 percent of this group was able to find work or attend school.   The co-ordinating and highly skilled casework counseling efforts of the agency's social workers, functioning as community organizers on behalf of the client, made this high success rate possible.

The American Public Health Association is making a case for poverty's being a pathogen for ill health.   It is just as true that illness, especially chronic illness, can be seen as part of the syndrome of poverty.   The writer agrees with Lourie that social work "is clearly identified with relieving suffering and deprivation," but not with his

---

[17] *Op. cit.,* p. 108.

[18] Celia W. Benney, Herbert Hochhauser, and Jay Sloma, "Mental Health Services in a Youth Opportunity Center" (New York: Altro Health and Rehabilitation Services, 1968).   (Mimeographed.)

addition that "like the other mental health professions, however, we are still rooted in the middle class values which hamper full measure utilization of resources and manpower which are not now assigned to the most needy." [19]   That reassignment of priorities is necessary is no doubt true, for social work services have had the tendency of moving on with their old clientele into the more affluent society, leaving the new poor behind.   What is objectionable is the implied denigration of middle-class values.   In terms of our desires with regard to quality and quantity of health care—and this goes for mental health care as well—the profession would do well to hang onto its middle-class values.   The poor seem to want that kind of health care too.

CONCLUSION

Of course, it is clear that the concepts and issues listed are highly correlated with each other.   The common thread among them is made up of the responsibilities for planning and administration.   By linking a geographic system with what has here been called a whole-person system and addressing it to the needs of groups of people in local communities, factors are being emphasized that in the past it has been possible to avoid.   There is a need for direction and administration of social institutions that are new to society.   While their structure may not seem so different from things that have been tried before, today there is new knowledge and new impetus to deliver better health and mental health services.   Regardless of where the planners and administrators come from, whatever their professional discipline, the end result will be a new breed of community health managers.   They will not be carrying the same responsibilities as the director of a mental health clinic or the administrator of a hospital.   As Ginsburg put it, speaking of the mental health workers of the future:

> Obviously, no one discipline can ever hope to encompass all the needed knowledge and skills.   The weaknesses in the usual interdisciplinary approaches are well known; often they result in a confusion of highly specialized language and conceptualization, with no real integration.   Ideally, a mental hygienist should be trained in psychology and psycho-analysis, sensitive to the problems of community relationships, and skilled in group techniques and in the techniques of mass communication.   Such training may well grow out of some modification of the education for psychiatric

---

[19] Norman V. Lourie, "Social Change—Social Work—Mental Health," *Pennsylvania Psychiatric Quarterly,* Vol. 5, No. 1 (Spring 1965), p. 6.

social work, which at first glance, at least, seems the most suitable jumping-off place.[20]

Albee said:

I do not think the alternative to the sickness model [which he deplores] is likely to be a psychological model. Indeed I believe the new approach will be social-educational and is more likely to develop out of the field of education or social work than out of psychology.[21]

What are we waiting for?

---

[20] Sol W. Ginsburg, MD, *A Psychiatrist's Views on Social Issues* (New York: Columbia University Press, 1963), pp. 27–28.

[21] George W. Albee, "Psychological Point of View," p. 20. Paper presented at the Annual Meeting of the American Psychiatric Association, May 13, 1968, Boston, Mass. (Mimeographed.)

Medical School Sponsorship of Neighborhood Health Centers: Implications for Social Work

NEIL F. BRACHT

The development of neighborhood health centers funded by the Office of Economic Opportunity to deliver comprehensive multipurpose services to the poor has been rapid. These consumer-oriented and locally planned health centers are located, for the most part, in major urban ghetto areas close to the population to be served. They function on a twenty-four-hour emergency care basis, and a multidisciplinary health team provides family-centered, personalized care. Educational and training programs for the poor are built into these programs, and utilization of indigenous personnel is a paramount factor.[1] Among the sponsors of these centers are hospitals, public health agencies, medical societies, and nonprofit community groups. Ten of the centers are administered and directed by medical schools and, in the ensuing discussion, a special look will be taken at these centers, their goals and problems, and the implications for practitioners in both medicine and social work.

---

[1] James A. Kent and C. Harvey Smith, "Involving the Urban Poor in Health Services Through Accommodation—The Employment of Neighborhood Representatives," *American Journal of Public Health,* Vol. 57, No. 6 (June 1967), pp. 997–1003.

A total of fifty-two centers throughout the nation have now been approved for funding. What is a typical neighborhood health center like? What is new about its service delivery system?

> The neighborhood health center serves everyone in the target area who is living at the poverty level. Centers are located in either urban or rural areas, serving a population ranging from 10,000 to 30,000. The person who presents himself for service gets it immediately, without having to struggle through complicated and inflexible eligibility requirements. Through its family care professional group, the neighborhood health center provides comprehensive, high quality, personalized, and continuous health care. Services for the entire family are offered at a conveniently located facility, and all ambulatory services are offered under one roof. Patients can get help from practitioners of general medicine or highly technical specialists. If the patient needs hospital care, it is arranged by the center.[2]

The center belongs to the poor and they have a feeling of participation in it. For example, in the Watts Health Center in Los Angeles, residents have enhanced the decor of their health facility with an exhibition by local artists.

For social workers, these innovative service centers call for different kinds of interdisciplinary relationships and new skills in outreach and prevention. They even suggest a fundamental shift in the relationship between professionals and the poor. For the social work profession, the neighborhood health center not only poses complicated social policy questions (such as whether a separate system of health care for the poor should be continued), but even suggests certain alterations within the training programs of the schools of social work to make them "more relevant to the human condition."[3] These issues and their implications for social work will be covered later.

ROLE OF MEDICINE

Discussion of these new service centers will begin with an examination of the role of medicine, and in particular the role of the medical school

---

[2] *The Neighborhood Health Center* (Washington, D.C.: Office of Economic Opportunity, 1967), p. 4.

[3] Theme statement for the NASW Second National Professional Symposium, San Francisco, Calif., May 24–26, 1968.

vis-à-vis health and social services for the poor. Of crucial importance is an understanding by social workers of the fundamental and significant changes taking place in medical schools and programs of medical education. In fact, the surprising willingness of medical practitioners to leave the ivory tower of the university and move into the arena of the nation's most pressing domestic concern—the urban crisis—is the direct result of changes that have taken place in the last decade within many medical schools.

Changes in the Medical School

What are some of these changes? First, the medical school curriculum is changing. It is tailored more to individual student learning needs and includes more elective time for students to follow special interests. The social and behavioral sciences are considered by many educators as basic to medical education, and more course exposure to medical sociology is apparent. Medical students themselves are changing, as is evidenced by the formation of the national Student Health Organization, a social action group concerned with urban and rural poverty problems. Students have worked in ghettos with the poor on special health projects during their summer vacation.

Second, the concept of the medical school as an institution only for teaching and research has changed to include demonstration and service. Having long been separate and isolated from the community and its health problems, some medical schools are now becoming much more active in community health development. In the new medical school at Michigan State University, both faculty and students are committed to the use of the community and its agencies as a major laboratory for education and research.[4] It is no longer considered desirable for all training to occur within the university medical center setting.

This institutional change is reflected in two important ways. On the one hand, departments of community medicine are developing at a rapid pace within medical schools, and their orientation toward the community and its health problems is much in evidence. Neighborhood health centers at Columbia Points in Boston, Watts, Atlanta, and Nashville are similar in that the departments of community and preventive medicine within the respective sponsoring medical schools spearhead

---

[4] Andrew D. Hunt, Jr., MD, and Neil F. Bracht, "Medical Education and the Community," *Michigan Medicine,* Vol. 65, No. 12 (December 1966), pp. 1061–1066.

the major attack and organize the health program for the poor. As two medical spokesmen said recently, there has been "a failure of the medical school to keep abreast of its role in the dynamic and rapidly changing society which must anticipate the future and prepare the physician for practice in a changing social milieu." [5] It is interesting to note that in these and other departments of community medicine around the country significant new opportunities exist for social workers in innovative teaching and service programs.

In still another direction, which reflects this institutional change, a changing role is seen for social workers within the medical school itself. This is evidenced in the appointment of social workers to administrative posts in medical schools in order to develop and implement programs of community medicine and serve as a liaison between the medical school and community groups. After all, the ultimate objective of medicine is the maintenance and improvement of the public's health, and the medical school is more and more concerned with the delivery of health care and its impact on population groups. Social work is contributing to the field of health care research and will have to step up its participation in new federal planning programs such as the Comprehensive Health Planning Act and the Regional Medical Program (Heart Disease, Cancer, and Stroke).[6]

Strengths and Problems

Some of the fundamental changes taking place in medical schools have been outlined as a backdrop to a more specific analysis of the medical school as a sponsor of the neighborhood health center. What are the strengths that a medical school brings to a health center demonstration in an urban ghetto or rural poverty pocket as opposed to other sponsoring agencies? One cannot overlook the considerable prestige and talent a medical school can muster and bring to a service demonstration project. Medical school involvement provides some assurance of high-quality health care. Another important aspect is that the medical school has tremendous capability for becoming an effective change agent

[5] Kurt W. Deuschle, MD, and Hugh Fulmer, MD, "Community Medicine: A New Department at the University of Kentucky College of Medicine," *Journal of Medical Education,* Vol. 37, No. 5 (May 1962), p. 432.

[6] Elizabeth Watkins, "Low Income Negro Mothers—Their Decision to Seek Prenatal Care," *American Journal of Public Health,* Vol. 58, No. 4 (April 1968), pp. 655–667.

in community health.   In addition, some schools are well equipped through health service research centers to evaluate the impact of programs on populations served.   The attractiveness of medical school involvement is also an asset in recruitment of physicians and other health personnel to these projects.

On the other side of the ledger one can consider the special problems confronting the medical school as it takes on a major service commitment.   Foremost is the fact that with few exceptions the medical school has not had a strong orientation or past history of service to the community, especially in ghetto areas.   The medical school has not perceived its role as a change agent, and its major funding resources have been directed into teaching and research.   Only recently has it begun to develop mechanisms and arrangements for involvement in direct service projects that can also be used for educational programs.   Many leaders in medical education have been advocating involvement in demonstration programs for student learning.[7]   Another factor that presents problems for the medical schools is that they have been isolated from other resources of the larger universities in which they are located.   For example, urban affairs institutes and social science departments can provide significant help in co-operative endeavors to alleviate the problems of the poor, but all too often the medical schools remain autonomous and separate within the university.

Another interesting problem that faces the medical school in OEO programs is the fact that it has had little experience in direct confrontation with local citizen groups who have a direct policy-making role in determining certain activities and practices in the health center.   Heroic efforts have been made to transcend the cultural gap between medical center officials and the poor, but tension continues.   A recent illustration occurred in Newark, involving the New Jersey College of Medicine and Dentistry. While an OEO health center was not at issue, the poor were concerned about the fact that a $96 million medical college was to be built on a 150-acre site, uprooting some 20,000 Negroes from the area. Some believe the disenchantment within the Negro community over this "Negro removal project" was a precipitating factor in the Newark riots of 1967.   As a result of intensive negotiations and pressure, the college will now be built on the terms of the residents, using only 57 acres; the college has also guaranteed that it will take over operation of the Newark

---

[7] Lowell Coggeshall, MD, "Planning for Medical Progress Through Education," p. 38.   Report submitted to the Association of American Medical Colleges, Chicago, 1965.

City Hospital, invest $2.5 million in repairs to the hospital, and establish community health centers in the area.

In the neighborhood centers there is evident tension between community associations of the poor and the center personnel. While there are healthy elements to this tension, it does reflect realistic social and cultural barriers between the white physician, who is usually impatient with long delays and is oriented to quick decisions, once convinced of a course of action, and the slower process of community consensus and action. This lack of familiarity with the very process of community action and planning remains perhaps one of the most troublesome areas for the medical school staff. As a member of the Columbia Points project states:

> For many health professionals, the notion that members of the community served by a health care program should somehow be involved in its operation is an utterly absurd proposal. If coerced, they [the professionals] reluctantly agree to an advisory board, but it soon becomes clear to the community and to the institution that health professionals are simply not accustomed to taking advice from the laity.[8]

In summary, the medical school brings to the neighborhood health center a sense of new direction and enthusiasm, with extremely fine and talented resources that can provide high-quality health care to the poor. It lacks a tradition of and experience in working in urban areas, especially with the poor, and it has often been isolated from the more important resources within a university that could assist in community projects. The medical school has a strong tradition of powerful and autonomous departments, and a continuing education program within the faculty is required to keep morale high and commitment to community projects balanced with the other needs of teaching and research within the program.[9] In those medical schools in which there is a clear-cut commitment from the dean's office joined by departmental involvement, these problems are decreased.

---

[8] Count D. Gibson, Jr., MD, "Current Issues in Reorganization to Deliver Better Health Services, The Neighborhood Health Center, the Primary Unit of Health Care," p. 4. Paper presented at the American Public Health Association Convention, Miami, October 23, 1967.

[9] Jack Geiger, MD, "The Neighborhood Health Center—Education of the Faculty in Preventive Medicine," *Archives of Environmental Health*, Vol. 14, No. 6 (June 1967), pp. 9–12.

IMPLICATIONS FOR SOCIAL WORK PRACTICE

In the medical school's direct confrontations with local community residents over program development and policy decisions, the social worker can make a new kind of contribution. Social workers willing to move into new outreach situations and be involved in community organization are enlarging the role of medical social work. Even the traditional department of social service within the university hospital is adapting to the neighborhood concept, and it is interesting that in the Denver health center project, branch offices of the university's social services department have been established in two outreach OEO health centers.

This latter is but one example of the numerous implications these health centers have for social work practice and new delivery innovations. Foremost among the activities of social workers in all of the projects surveyed is the emphasis on education, training, and consultation with indigenous personnel. New positions are being created in most of the programs, such as "family health worker" (Bronx), "neighborhood co-ordinator" (Kaiser), and "health agents" (Watts). While social workers within the neighborhood health centers have moved enthusiastically to participate in educational training programs for the indigenous subprofessional groups, they have not totally come to grips with the new kinds of roles and relationships that will exist between the professional and the subprofessional. Nor have social workers considered the employment barriers with which these subprofessionals will be confronted by the institutional rigidity traditional in health and welfare agency hiring practices.

In the Mile Square project in Chicago, the major activity of the social worker is prevention. Knowledge and ability to apply public health and preventive concepts to social work practice are extremely important. The problem is that not many schools of social work are turning out graduates with formal course content in public health concepts and the application of preventive measures.

The family-centered approach in these health centers is certainly not new, but it does demand increased flexibility and independence of action on the part of social workers, especially within the new concept of the neighborhood health centers. Medical and psychiatric social workers are working more directly with neighborhood action groups and, therefore, a considerable part of their professional time is involved in more classical community organization work. Again, the opportunity for unusual integration of community organization and casework practice exists within the neighborhood health center, but schools have only recently begun to train people in multipurpose methods. Community organization as a sequence still attracts relatively few students. In some projects, social workers are being called on for their administrative ability in organizing and planning program development.[10] Again, this has implications for specialized advanced training of social workers in medical care organization, administration, and health care delivery systems.

BROADER POLICY QUESTIONS

Let us now consider some of the broader social and health policy questions that face the profession as it looks to the long-range development of neighborhood health centers. First, will the nation continue to have a separate arrangement for delivery of health care to the poor, or are these centers to be intermediary arrangements with the long-range goal of integrating the poor into the mainstream of health care delivery? Rein and Riessman favor a model in which the role of the Community Action Program "expediter is oriented toward expanding the system in order to achieve more equitable distribution of services for all clients in need." [11] A troubling question is, What will happen to these centers when OEO funds run out?

Another policy issue

> concerns the means test applied to residents of each area served by a free care health center. Families whose incomes fall below the arbitrary line are eligible for valuable medical care worth many dollars in purchasing power, but once a breadwinner breaks out of that income range, he and his family are automatically cut off from further care at the center.[12]

In terms of new institutional arrangements for the delivery of health and social services, we are witnessing the operation of a real model for the integration of health and social services within the neighborhood health

---

[10] Harold Light and Howard Brown, "The Social Worker as Lay Administrator of a Medical Facility," *Social Casework,* Vol. 45, No. 6 (June 1964), pp. 333–336.

[11] Martin Rein and Frank Riessman, "A Strategy for Antipoverty Community Action Programs," *Social Work,* Vol. 11, No. 2 (April 1966), p. 11.

[12] *A New Kind of Care—Better Health for the Poor* (Washington, D.C.: Office of Economic Opportunity, 1967), p. 4.

center. Can this innovative "merger" be applied within the traditional structures of health delivery?

Still another question involving the OEO neighborhood health center relates to the fact that most of these have been funded in urban areas, and only recently have funds gone to rural neighborhood health centers. It would be a mistake to focus concern on the urban poor and forget the real and chronic problems of rural America. In the Michigan project, the rural Community Action Program has contracted with the Michigan Department of Public Health as the delegate agency, with the new medical school at Michigan State University collaborating in the development of the project and providing consultation. From the outset, the intention to establish a nonprofit group that would eventually administer and receive gifts and grants for other programs in this area was paramount in planning.

CONCLUSION

In conclusion, the country's health care delivery system, as pointed out by the President's Commission on Health Manpower, is in a state of crisis.[13] Especially acute has been the system's inefficiency and its inadequacy in providing care for low-income groups. At the present time, rapid changes are occurring in medical schools and medical centers, in which medical educators in conjunction with their health and welfare colleagues in the community are taking a new look at their role and involvement in reducing the gap between health needs and provision of services to low-income populations.

This paper has focused on the neighborhood health center as a new delivery model. It has surveyed changing responsibilities for social workers in these centers and raised social policy implications for the profession. Issues related to the medical school sponsorship of these centers have also been discussed. In a recent article Randal states:

> Of all the innovations put forward by the Office of Economic Opportunity in its fight against poverty, the one that will perhaps eventually accomplish the most is its relatively recent neighborhood health center program. If Project Head Start was the first to

---

[13] *Report of the National Advisory Commission on Health Manpower,* Vol. 1 (Washington, D.C.: U.S. Government Printing Office, November 1967).

catch the public's fancy, the health center idea is likely to be of more direct benefit to the poor.[14]

Many social workers can personally give witness to the bright promise of these centers, but at the same time we live with the knowledge of the serious problems that are inherent within these programs. One of the most serious is the staggering backlog of unmet medical and social needs that the poor population brings to the neighborhood center. Obtaining adequate professional staff for these centers, in view of the national health manpower shortage, is a crucial factor in the continued development of the neighborhood health center concept. Despite these problems, the profession should support these innovative health delivery centers, which are "truly relevant to the human condition."

[14] Judith Randal, "The Bright Promise of Neighborhood Health Centers," *The Reporter,* March 21, 1968, pp. 15–18.

How New Are the "New" Comprehensive Mental Health Centers?

DALE A. ALBERS AND RICHARD A. PASEWARK

The present era in mental health has been viewed by some as a period of marked progress and advance. Hobbs, for example, speaks of mental health's "Third Revolution," and in a similar vein, Trast refers to "the current revolutionary development(s) in mental health. . . ."[1] Partially contributing to such feelings of progress and advance is the "bold new approach" inherent in the emerging concept of the comprehensive community mental health center—a program that has been described as the beginning of "a new era"[2] and one that is ostensibly designed to "provide facilities and services to prevent

---

[1] Nicholas Hobbs, "Mental Health's Third Revolution," George Peabody College for Teachers, March 10, 1964, p. 1 (mimeographed); Merton Trast, "Problems in Establishing Community Mental Health Centers in Major Urban Areas," in *Implementing the Community Center Concept*, proceedings of the 19th Annual Conference, Chief Social Workers in State and Territorial Mental Health Programs, Dallas, Texas, May 1967, p. 1.

[2] *The Comprehensive Community Mental Health Center*, Public Health Service Publication No. 1137 (Washington, D.C.: U.S. Department of Health, Education & Welfare, April 1964), p. 5.

148

and ameliorate the waste and tragedy of mental illness and mental retardation," [3] and "to correct the problems of the state hospital." [4]

Barton says the comprehensive community mental health center is "the most exciting and important concept in the field of psychiatry in many years." [5] In a more critical manner, Dunham refers to the notion of community psychiatry, of which the comprehensive community mental health center is an integral part, as "the newest therapeutic bandwagon," [6] and its application and relevance to the rural area has been treated as a "white elephant." [7]

An examination of the community model suggests that it represents only an incremental advance. It embodies nothing new that permits the identification of either a philosophical or technological breakthrough of a major dimension. All that has been encompassed has been intensification, repackaging, and redelivery of traditional services and resources that have long been known to the field, "resources that should have been available all along." [8]

There remains little doubt that more adequate service delivery will be provided through the basic services of hospitalization, partial hospitalization, outpatient treatment, emergency care, consultation, and education. These will be encompassed under the aegis of a single organiza-

---

[3] "A Bold New Program," *Community Mental Health Advances,* Public Health Service Publication No. 1141 (Washington, D.C.: U.S. Department of Health, Education & Welfare, 1964), p. 1.

[4] H. M. Forstenzer, "Planning and Evaluation of Community Mental Health Program," in S. Goldstone, ed., *Concepts of Community Psychiatry* (Washington, D.C.: U.S. Department of Health, Education & Welfare, U.S. Public Health Service, 1965).

[5] Walter E. Barton, MD, Introduction, in Raymond Glasscote, Davis Saunders, H. M. Forstenzer, and H. R. Foley, *The Community Mental Health Center, An Analysis of Existing Models* (Washington, D.C.: Joint Information Service of the American Psychiatric Association and the National Association for Mental Health, September 1964), p. xiii.

[6] H. Warren Dunham, "Community Psychiatry: The Newest Therapeutic Bandwagon," *Archives of General Psychiatry,* No. 12 (March 1965), p. 303.

[7] David N. Daniels, "Community Mental Health Centers and the Rural State: Is the Model a White Elephant?" (Palo Alto, Calif.: Department of Psychiatry, Stanford University, 1967), p. 1.

[8] Bertram J. Black, "Comprehensive Community Mental Health Services: Setting Social Policy," *Social Work,* Vol. 12, No. 1 (January 1967), p. 54.

tional structure—the comprehensive community mental health center. The distance between supplier and consumer will, to some extent, be reduced. Concomitantly, there is no question but that this more intensive and rapid delivery of traditional services will represent an improvement over present levels of practice.

What is the next step in the delivery of mental health services? What will replace the community model ten, fifteen, or twenty years hence? Is it possible to eliminate or bypass the community model in favor of other delivery models that will evolve subsequent to it? If so, how can this be done? It is quite possible that such an exploration and an examination of these kinds of questions has occurred, and without result. If so, apologies are in order. However, the fact that a no more far-reaching and imaginative concept than an extension of the settlement house model has emerged from these deliberations suggests an even greater reason to view, in more modest terms, the bold new approach that is to be undertaken.

TACIT ASSUMPTIONS

In committing ourselves to the community concept, it seems that greater cognizance should be paid to a number of tacit assumptions that underlie the model. While these assumptions may be correct, for the most part they remain untested. Among these are the following:

1. *The organization of mental health services under a single administrative structure will increase the quality, delivery, and efficiency of these services.* The implication here seems to be that by drawing together the five basic medical elements of service, traditional though they may be, the spirit and intent of the law are met. However, it also carries the presumption that there is sufficient competence for the task on hand and that matters pertaining to interpersonal and social systems that militate against individual well-being and prevention are secondary.

2. *The prescribed range and array of services are appropriate to all geographic locations.* Here the structure, organization, and delivery of services take on a definitely urban character. The view implicit here is that the range of services contained in the basic package has the same application to the state of Wyoming as it does to the state of New York. Wyoming has a population of approximately 315,000. It is ranked forty-ninth in population among the states and is ninth largest in area, covering over 97,000 square miles. Stated another way, its population is comparable to the city of Lansing, Michigan, and it covers an area slightly less than the combined states of New York, Connecticut, Maine, Massachusetts, and New Hampshire.

In terms of distance, a family living in Sundance, Wyoming, that finds it necessary to hospitalize a family member in the state hospital in Evanston would have much in common with a family living in New York City that finds it necessary to hospitalize a family member in Columbus, Ohio. There are five practicing psychiatrists in the entire state of Wyoming, two of whom are in private practice. The professional social work community is limited to thirty-six full-time employed individuals, and there are five psychologists in public service agencies. From these few facts it can be seen that the needs and resources of rural areas are quite different from those of urban communities, and unless a pattern of service with some freedom of movement to experiment with alternate delivery systems can be developed appropriate to the rural areas, the tired and worn cliché, "the rich get richer and the poor get poorer," may well be confirmed.

3. *The comprehensive community mental health center can at this time be truly comprehensive in nature or the model can "provide comprehensive services as needed for all persons, of all ages and for all types of psychiatric and emotional disorders, in the person's home community regardless of diagnosis. . . ."* [9] Concerning this third assumption, there is some preliminary evidence to suggest that the centers are presently unable to deal adequately with diverse problem populations. At least one of the centers, originally described as one of the eleven "existing models" of what constitutes a good mental health center, has encountered rather serious problems relating to the chronically ill. Initially only 2 percent of the center's patients were readmitted for a period of one year or longer. Four and a half years later this figure rose to 40 percent, and the center staff anticipates the readmission figure will soon exceed 50 percent.[10]

Problems associated with the treatment of the alcoholic, the drug addict, the chronic schizophrenic, the organically impaired, the legal offender, and the elderly have served to "pre-empt a growing share of the center's resources and are reducing the number of less sick patients who can successfully be treated." [11] The accumulation of chronic pa-

---

[9] Richard N. Elwell, "Philosophy and Purposes of Comprehensive Community Mental Health Centers." Paper presented at Florida Mental Health Council on Training and Research, University of Florida, June 14, 1967. (Mimeographed.)

[10] Allen M. Kraft, Paul R. Binner, and Brenda A. Dickey, "The Community Mental Health Program and the Longer Stay Patient," *Mental Hygiene,* Vol. 51, No. 4 (October 1967), p. 65.

[11] *Ibid.,* p. 69.

tients has prompted the center to ponder resolving its dilemma by restricting its admission practices to the "less sick," thus risking the accusation of being discriminatory and providing services somewhat short of comprehensive, or it may pursue another tack that has been suggested, that of developing "rear-echelon" services that take on the form of "back-up facilities," becoming a "custodial center which would remain essentially outside the mainstream of the nation's research effort and be only peripherally related to training centers." [12]   The author of this statement is indeed correct when he asks: "Doesn't this sound vaguely familiar?" [13]

4. *The development of future mental health services will be integrated with the community mental health center.*   A related danger exists that in our haste to implement the community model, two of its basic premises will be undermined—those of a continuity of organized care and lessening of the distance between the consumer and supplier of mental health services.

In regard to the former, it would appear that in establishing a community-based center under the auspices of a single agency, a rather restricted view of comprehensive services may follow, with the result being the establishment of a mental health enclave. What is lost sight of, and ultimately perhaps more difficult to achieve, is a broader view of comprehensive services that embraces the physical, social, and economic aspects of man and includes all health, economic, social, and rehabilitative services. Comprehensive services, without truly comprehensive planning that "expresses a concern for relevance, a breadth of scope and detail within," may result in the establishment of a dual service system or the creation of a superstructure that lacks corrective action.[14]

Concerning the reduction of distance between consumer and supplier of services, it would appear that inherent in the community model are certain elements that could possibly preclude the realization of this very goal. For example, if those mental health services that are now the responsibility of the center—services that implicitly define what is and

---

[12] *Ibid.,* pp. 69 and 70.

[13] *Ibid.,* p. 70.

[14] Donald E. Lathrope, "Comprehensive Planning for Social Work Services," p. 12. Paper presented at the Advanced Seminar on the American Family in the Army Community, Fitzsimmons Army Hospital, Denver, Colo., October 1967.

what is not mental health—remain focused in the community center, the possibility then exists that agencies other than the center will be instrumental in minimizing the social and physical distance between supplier and consumer. Further, it is not unreasonable to suppose that such a trend will be manifested by other service-oriented groups and disciplines, and that the provision of more immediate and available services may well be anticipated in the fields of welfare, general medicine, nursing, vocational rehabilitation, religion, and law enforcement.

It seems both unrealistic and unreasonable to assume that agencies and individuals responsible for providing these services will wish or will permit a co-ordination and a direction of their services simply by creation of the community mental health center. It can only be hoped that the center middleman will not feel challenged or resentful and that he will not erect stumbling blocks to impede the flow of such services or, as the member of a vested interest group, will not take action to incorporate these services and thus increase the distance between the provider and user of mental health services.

CONSEQUENCES

Some of the consequences associated with a major commitment to the community model should be realistically recognized. The advantages and benefits to be derived from the comprehensive community mental health center have been elaborated on by many. Unfortunately, goodness and light do not always accompany a social venture of such proportions. Thus, no matter how noble and humanitarian its declared purpose or intent, unintended consequences are frequently observed.

Primary is the danger of institutionalization—of rigidity and "hardening of the categories." In the community model, services have been formalized under a single institutional structure, replete with contractual arrangements, written agreements, and the sanctions of legal authority. Already there is some early evidence to suggest that the community center is well on its way toward a type of institutionalization previously experienced by its predecessor, the state hospital. Among such indications are these:

1. The immediate concern with the construction of elaborate edifices to house the concept.

2. A near canonization of the five basic services. All five are necessary—two, three, or four are not acceptable. At least, they do not qualify for matching funds even if supplemented by any number of different elements not prescribed by the basic list.

3. The relegation of evaluation and research to the list of supplementary or secondary services. This suggests, perhaps, that a degree of certainty exists and that the answer has been found. The course being steered is proper and the best of all possible courses. It further implies a certain reluctance to examine the ongoing or to explore alternative modes of operation, processes that frequently accompany the act of formal institutionalization.

Further, it is to be suspected that as manpower and funds are increasingly committed to the community model, the processes of institutionalization will intensify and solidify. Vested interests, both public and professional, will be created. Personal and professional energies will be devoted to perpetuating the system, and herein lies the danger that the model will become an end in and of itself. Such a possibility becomes enhanced when more professional manpower becomes committed to the model and there is less manpower available to explore and examine alternative models and solutions.

Perhaps, in fact, the reduction of distance and the more immediate provision of service are the essence of the contemporary approach. If so, it is unfortunate that the concept could not have been extended a step or two beyond, rather than becoming infused with, administrative orderliness and bricks and mortar.

Essentially, what is being suggested is that in its anxiety to appear industrious, ardent, progressive, knowledgeable, and assertive, the social work profession is overly prone to adopt the innovation syndrome. To reinforce an image of progress, it is especially vulnerable to a hasty commitment of resources that quickly institutionalize training and service approaches in a manner that makes it difficult to evaluate adequately the alternative prospectives and avenues that might otherwise have been available. Such, it is believed, is the case in the fervent adoption of the community center model, wherein enormous resources are being committed to a model whose ideological base is little more than administration and promotion of existing services.

It can, of course, be argued by opponents of this position that social progress is slow and gradual. Society does not ordinarily permit one to leap tall buildings with a single bound. Culture is unwilling to or cannot accommodate truly bold new approaches. Gradual evolution rather than revolution is the order of the day. Although this maxim might have a more general application to society as a whole, its application to more limited aspects of society—and especially to the health field—is seriously questioned.

For example, during the last generation the American public has permitted and supported radical innovations and procedures in the health field with little protest and much support; its children have served as the subjects and controls in testing the efficacy of the Salk vaccine and other immunization agents. Kidney and heart transplants are not only allowed, but their results are awaited with excitement and anticipation by a public that is very much aware of their exploratory nature. General optimism prevails, and optimism rather than repulsion is reinforced by the hope that primate donors might eventually provide for their human counterparts. In such a climate, it is doubtful that the new élan with a more thrustful approach to the problem of mental health would not be accepted and encouraged by the public provided such avenues do, in fact, hold the technological base for achieving the results desired.

Social Work's Neglected Responsibility: Delivery of Family Planning Services

RUSSELL H. RICHARDSON

Up to now the social work profession has been minimally involved in the development and delivery of family planning services. Social workers in both public and private agencies have largely ignored family planning as a possible referral service to be discussed with families. From available records it would appear that less than 5 percent of the approximately 700,000 medically indigent women who are currently receiving free or subsidized family planning services from public health clinics, hospitals, or Planned Parenthood clinics learned about the service from or were referred by social workers.[1]

Until quite recently many state welfare departments had policies that specifically forbade social workers to discuss family planning with their clients. From that unreasonable position some states began timidly permitting social workers to make referrals, but only if the client brought up the subject. Obviously, few social workers were sufficiently knowledgeable or had enough conviction on the matter to lead them to help clients initiate a discussion of this nature. Most of the restrictions have now been removed and the profession is beginning to be confronted with administrative policies and programs designed to encourage or require social workers to inform their clients about this important medical

---

[1] Annual Reports (New York: Planned Parenthood–World Population, 1965–66).

service. Several state plans are already beginning to implement a referral system using special forms and procedures. Can social work deliver?

DEVELOPMENT OF PROFESSIONAL POLICY

Prior to 1960 the social work literature contained practically nothing about family planning and relatively little has appeared since then. The family planning resolution passed by the NASW Delegate Assembly in 1962 was the first expression of concern by the profession. Unfortunately, it brought little, if any, action. The more recently approved policy statement passed by the 1967 Delegate Assembly reflects some progress in the profession's thinking and a maturing concern about the problem. However, the NASW policy statement continues to point up some of the profession's hang-ups. Its preoccupation with wanting to give casework service to everybody in the face of urgently needed social action is appalling. The profession is not directing itself to the primary need—i.e., to help remove the institutional roadblocks and rigidities that seem to withhold or impede the delivery of high-quality voluntary family planning services to the 5.3 million women who are dependent on either free or partially subsidized medical services. Only 14 percent, or about 750,000, of these women live in families whose major source of support is public assistance.[2] However, there is ample evidence that unless many of the remaining low-income families are helped with child spacing or family size limitation they will quickly join the growing ranks of welfare recipients. As a profession, social work has done far too little to help families remain independent of present forms of public assistance.

According to Sheppard:

> Family planning, or birth control, can be effective in creating the conditions for increased income—for taking people out of poverty. The incidence of poverty among families with one or two children under 18 is relatively low (11%), but steadily rises as the number of children increases—to 43% among families with six or more children.[3]

---

[2] "Five Million Women (Who's Who Among Americans in Need of Subsidized Family Planning Service)" (New York: Planned Parenthood Federation of America, 1967), p. 10.

[3] Harold L. Sheppard, "Effects of Family Planning on Poverty in the United States," p. 3. Unpublished paper, W. E. Upjohn Institute for Employment Research, Kalamazoo, Mich., October 1967.

LACK OF AWARENESS

Most social workers are unaware of the danger to mothers (and their babies) when pregnancies occur as frequently as is possible when no contraceptive measures are utilized. They do not know that maternal mortality is generally five times as high for the poor as for the nonpoor and that infant mortality is twice as high. They apparently do not know that more adequate child spacing and family size limitation can play a critical role in lowering these tragic figures.

With reference to prematurity and all of its accompanying problems and risks, social workers should know that recent studies clearly indicate that the percentage of premature births by mothers who space their pregnancies by twenty-four or more months is only 6 percent, whereas when pregnancies occur at intervals of less than twelve months the rate of prematurity is 17 percent.[4] This knowledge can save lives and prevent many serious and crippling problems. A prematurity rate three times as high with unspaced pregnancies compared to those more adequately spaced cries out for an aggressive educational program and marked expansion of services. Lest there be any doubt about potential interest and acceptance on the part of medically indigent mothers, an example can be cited of a situation that has been duplicated in hospital after hospital across the nation. Prior to 1960, few public or private hospitals offered family planning services in conjunction with the long-established pattern of a six-week postpartum examination. Although this examination is medically important in itself, prior to the addition of family planning services to the postpartum check-up, it was common for only 15–30 percent of the total number of women who delivered to return to the hospital for this service. With the simple addition of family planning, it is not unusual now for hospitals to report from 65 to 90 percent of new mothers returning for the check-up and family planning.

Many of these patients will need follow-up services and the special interest and skill that a social worker can provide if they are going to continue to practice contraception. They may become dissatisfied with the method prescribed and need encouragement and support in seeking a change, or they might need help with transportation in order to ensure a continuing supply of pills or contraceptive materials.

A recent study in New York City by Lawrence Podell further substantiates the interest welfare mothers have in family planning. Podell's

---

[4] Newton Long, MD, medical consultant, Southeast Region, Planned Parenthood–World Population, Atlanta, Ga.; personal communication to the author, March 1968.

study revealed that four out of five welfare mothers under the age of 45 do not want any more children. Some of his other findings indicate that of his sample of 2,179 welfare households, one-fourth of the mothers first became pregnant when 16 years old or younger. Further, the less educated the mother and the earlier the first pregnancy, the greater the number of children she had. This and other information should speak clearly of social work's past neglect of responsibility in the delivery of family planning services.

It may already be too late, because the strong tide of hostile, negative reaction to rising welfare rolls and costs is reflecting itself at national, state, and local levels. Certain amendments to the Social Security Act, although they did not pass Congress, addressed themselves to this strong shift in thinking and would have called for coercively directed family planning. Recently in a state generally known for progressive action and attitudes, the welfare board announced its intention to seek out ineligible persons receiving welfare payments by using private investigators; this was expected to be followed by regulations calling for cutoffs when the alcoholic content of the blood of recipients reached certain levels and requiring recipients to participate in birth control programs instead of seeking such help voluntarily. (The board's policy requiring an affidavit certifying that each "eligible" client had received birth control counseling was subsequently rescinded under orders from the U.S. Department of Health, Education and Welfare.) Surely social work bears some responsibility for the hostile misunderstanding that these attitudes reflect.

PRIORITIES

The first problem in order of priority, and the least understood, is the fact that in too many instances the needed family planning services simply do not exist. If they do exist, they are often not convenient for families either because of the hours they are open or their location.

Until recently only seven of the southeastern states provided family planning through public health clinics.[5] The federal government did not acknowledge that it was providing financial support for family planning and the limited funds available were carefully camouflaged. There are grounds for encouragement now, since it appears that substantial sums

---

[5] Alabama, Florida, Georgia, Mississippi, South Carolina, North Carolina, and Virginia. Almost all of the counties in Tennessee and three in West Virginia also offer family planning services. See Don Harting, "Family Planning Policies and Activities of State Health and Welfare Departments," *Public Health Reports*, Vol. 84, No. 2 (February 1969).

of money are to be made available for family planning through the 1967 amendments to the Social Security Act (PL 90-248). Starting July 1, 1968 (fiscal year 1969), not less than 6 percent of the total maternal and child health expenditures were to be reserved or earmarked for family planning services. The overall authorization for maternal and child health programs is to increase in steps from $250 million in fiscal year 1969 to $350 million in fiscal year 1973. Therefore, allocations for family planning would start at no less than $15 million in 1969 and go up to no less than $21 million in 1973.

States must provide at least "demonstration" programs in family planning under the state maternal and child health program. Under the public assistance program, the states must develop programs aimed at "preventing or reducing the incidence of out-of-wedlock births, and otherwise strengthening family life," and must assure that "in all appropriate cases family planning services are offered to [relatives, children, and individuals]." The amendments further provide that "the acceptance by such child, relative or individual of family planning services provided under the plan shall be *voluntary* and shall not be a prerequisite to eligibility for or receipt of any other service or aid under the plan." [6]

A second and significant priority is for the social worker to develop skill through experience in helping clients to obtain this important medical service. They need not concern themselves with the problem of motivating clients—this is not the client's problem! The social worker must, on the other hand, develop a sensitivity as to why the client has not already sought out the clinic and must not necessarily accept the first explanation given. The client may give a variety of reasons that have little or no bearing on the real problem. All too often they simply do not know that the clinic exists, or how and when to go there.

RECOMMENDATIONS

1. As a profession dedicated to the rights of all people, social work must be alert to the need to resist with all vigor and determination any tendency to introduce coercive elements into family planning services. The poor, including those who receive public assistance, must retain the right to determine whether and when they will be pregnant.

2. In order to establish and maintain this right all women must have access to high-quality comprehensive health services including family planning. Social workers have a responsibility in helping to establish

---

[6] Public Law 90-248, Ninetieth Cong., HR 12080, January 2, 1968, p. 58.

such community-level health services and an equal responsibility to inform persons about their availability.

3. Since social workers have historically had only limited involvement in the delivery of family planning services, the profession should address itself to giving this critically needed and important service sufficient priority to ensure that family planning will not continue to be neglected.

4. Graduate schools of social work should address themselves to including comprehensive information on family planning that will cut across the areas of specialization. Both public and private agencies should see to it that supervisory staff and training personnel are helped to achieve a position of real leadership in assisting those for whom they are responsible to develop competence in dealing with referrals for family planning. For caseworkers this will include considerable knowledge about contraceptive methods, available community resources, how to discuss family planning with clients, and how to be of help in the referral process. For community organization workers, it is important to understand the critical absence of comprehensive health services and especially the large gaps that exist in the area of family planning services. Their attention should be drawn to the need for expansion and co-ordination of services when these exist, but quite often this will mean the establishment of new services to meet the needs of the poor.

Dr. Allan Guttmacher, president of Planned Parenthood–World Population, in his testimony before the Senate Subcommittee on Employment, Manpower, and Poverty on June 8, 1967, stated:

> It is apparent that today in the United States, family planning is accepted as an important and necessary component of community health services. The question that faces us today is not whether family planning services are needed; it is not a question of beneficial results; it is not even a question of individual or societal acceptance—rather it is a question of the degree of priority we are willing to place on family planning services for the medically impoverished and how far we are willing to go to implement that priority.[7]

The writer can say no less for the social work profession.

---

[7] Quoted in Sheppard, *op. cit.*, p. 27.

PART III

New Manpower Resources

Utilization of indigenous nonprofessional workers in social service programs has tended to be discussed in ideological terms. Perhaps this should not be surprising in view of the context in which this development has emerged. The historical period has been one of crises and contention both within and outside of social welfare. And many programs that have made the greatest use of indigenous workers have also tended to be centers of controversy and sources of criticism of the Establishment.

But the papers in Part III of this volume are not ideological in tone. They suggest that we are now reaching the point at which there is no longer any issue as to whether indigenous nonprofessionals have a place in the delivery of social services. They quite obviously do. Now we face essentially the same problem as the administrators who take over in the wake of the revolutionaries: How do we make the new system work? These papers move us a long way toward obtaining useful answers to this question.

Hallowitz's honest account of the involvement of indigenous nonprofessionals in Lincoln Hospital's community mental health program points up a number of dilemmas for professionals in such a situation. The indigenous workers clearly did not see themselves simply as a manpower resource, but demanded active participation in decision-making.

Two papers by Shatz and her associates describe a New Careers training program in Washington, D.C. Denham and Shatz focus on the issue of the professional worker's response to the indigenous worker, and Shatz and Steinberg explore the problems involved in institutionalizing the role of the nonprofessional. It is one thing to bring such workers onto a staff on an experimental or demonstration basis. It is another to make them part of the ongoing machinery.

Brennen offers an alternative model, that of "planned replacement," in which there is a deliberate avoidance of socializing indigenous workers too fully to the agency culture. He points up the problem of developing a person who is sufficiently integrated in the service structure to allow him to function effectively, yet sufficiently outside it to retain his value as a member of a target community.

In many instances, one purpose of moving clients into new staff or quasi-staff statuses, whether stated or unstated, is therapy. Thomas describes a program in which an attempt was made to rid alcoholics of the "patient" role in order to speed their reintegration into a society dominated by work and member roles.

Use of Nonprofessional Staff: Issues and Strategies

EMANUEL HALLOWITZ

A spate of books and papers have extolled the virtues of the indigenous nonprofessional, not only as a new source of manpower, but also as an agent of change both within the community and the institution. Typically, new methods or techniques attract many rabid adherents and as many—usually less vocal—detractors. Also typically, the adherents tend to exaggerate the virtues of the new approach and ignore or minimize its disadvantages.

Lincoln Hospital has now had four and one-half years of experience with nonprofessional staff, who number seventy almost exclusively Puerto Rican and Negro community mental health workers, of whom 60 percent are women and 40 percent men. About 75 percent of them have completed high school, a few of whom have also had evening college courses; the other 25 percent did not complete high school. The age range is 20–72 years, but most are in the 30–40 bracket.

Elsewhere the writer has described in some detail the many tasks and roles these workers have assumed as members of Lincoln Hospital's psychiatric clinic, day hospital, and neighborhood service center staffs.[1]

---

[1] Frank Riessman and Emanuel Hallowitz, "The Neighborhood Service Center—An Innovation in Preventive Psychiatry," *American Journal of Psychiatry*, Vol. 123, No. 11 (May 1967), pp. 1408–1413; Hallowitz and Riessman, "The Role of the Indigenous Non-Professional in a Community

But those reports did not deal much with the special problems and stresses posed by the introduction into a community mental health center of a new source of manpower. The introduction of seventy nonprofessionals into an agency presents problems quite different from a case in which only two or three such workers are introduced. This paper will therefore focus primarily on these problems, the mistakes made, and the strategies that developed out of this experience.

PROBLEMS NONPROFESSIONALS PRESENT

The community mental health workers, coming as they do from an extremely disadvantaged population, bring to the job the same strong feelings toward the power structure that are evident in the target population: suspicion, distrust, and fear that they will be exploited, fired out of hand, and discriminated against because of color, ethnic background, or religion, together with the almost unconscious conviction that supervisors and administrative personnel are omniscient and omnipotent and that somehow, through simple association with them, they too may become all powerful. However, the countervailing conviction often exists as well that only they really care about the poor, only they really know what is going on, only they are down to earth and reality oriented. Another contradictory set of attitudes often observed is a wish to learn from the professionals combined with an anti-intellectual attitude in which reading, education, and knowledge are deprecated.

Insecure as individuals, the nonprofessionals gain their feelings of security and strength from the group. But when one person is singled out for special praise, the group may develop feelings of rivalry. Realizing, however, that such rivalry can threaten their group strength, they often counter this threat by interpreting being singled out as an attempt by the power structure to play favorites—to divide and conquer. This sort of dynamic is probably inevitable until the nonprofessionals become more secure as individuals.

At first delighted at being accepted into the system and happy with

Mental Health Neighborhood Service Center Program," *American Journal of Orthopsychiatry*, Vol. 37, No. 4 (July 1967), pp. 766–778; Hallowitz, "The Use of Indigenous Nonprofessionals in a Mental Health Service," paper presented at the National Conference on Social Welfare, Chicago, Ill., June 1966; Hallowitz, "The Role of the Neighborhood Service Center in a Community Mental Health Program," *American Journal of Orthopsychiatry*, Vol. 38, No. 4 (July 1968), pp. 705–714.

their new status as mental health workers, they soon discover that they are still low men on the totem pole. They then begin to struggle to define their role more clearly and to find a way to achieve a higher status than that originally assigned to them.

The professional working with nonprofessionals is equally subject to conflicting emotions and attitudes. He may enjoy the superior status and omnipotence with which the nonprofessional invests him, but he feels anxious and resentful when he cannot live up to these expectations. Similarly, although he is eager to see the nonprofessional develop skills and assume more complex tasks, he is reluctant to assign him responsibility or allow him much independence of action or judgment. The fear that the nonprofessional's functioning with clients will not be of high quality impels the professional to find ways of controlling and directing his activity.

The professional has been taught to gather facts, reflect, plan a course of action, and be deliberate in his interventions; the nonprofessional tends to be more active and immediate in response to client needs. He functions informally and spontaneously, often disregarding traditional channels of communication and authority. These differences in style create conflict, perhaps the sharpest of which arises from the professional's traditional ways of structuring programs and offering supervision and his difficulty in adapting these traditional techniques to the needs and style of the nonprofessional.

Furthermore, the professional, bringing with him an ingrained frame of reference generally learned in professional settings, tends to view the nonprofessional's behavior, attitudes, and work performance by traditional standards, in spite of his intellectual awareness that the old frame of reference no longer applies.

These difficulties cannot be attributed to either the professional or the nonprofessional alone, but are rather the result of a new type of interaction that calls for major and difficult readjustments in each group. The professional, because of his knowledge, self-awareness, and professional discipline, and in no small measure because he is in a position of power, will not only have to change himself but will also have to play a key role in helping the nonprofessional to change.

THE LINCOLN HOSPITAL EXPERIENCE

The balance of this paper will describe some of Lincoln Hospital's struggles in order to point out the common pitfalls in this situation, clarify further some of the dynamics of the interactions, and pinpoint the internalized blocks to the professional's own development.

First, some myths currently prevalent should be laid to rest. Specifically, the poor do not necessarily have special knowledge, insight, or intuition not available to the more affluent; neither is the poor person ipso facto more sympathetic to others in the same plight, nor does his poverty give him special knowledge about effective administration, program planning, interviewing skills, community action, and the like for the urban poor. He does not necessarily understand his community or culture better than an outside professional. On the whole, the poor and disadvantaged were found to be no more free of prejudice and snobbery than any other group in society. The one clear advantage of the indigenous nonprofessional is that he understands the language, style, and customs of his neighbors.

As a matter of fact, a good sociologist or anthropologist capable of gaining community acceptance can understand the community, in the various senses in which mental health professionals must understand it in order to operate in it effectively, much better than does or can a nonprofessional. This should not be a startling discovery. As in most urban slum areas, individuals tend to stay in their locale and associate with their own selected groups. Few have had enough experience with the community as a whole to generalize about it or even its parts in ways genuinely useful to the professional. Urban slum communities are much more heterogeneous than is customarily assumed.

There *are* individuals in the target population who have developed effective survival techniques and who are capable of warmth, sympathy, and empathy. Among them are some who are vitally interested in their neighbors' welfare. As a rule, these are individuals who, but for their life circumstances, would have been college graduates or professionals. When such persons can be identified and provided with some training and supervision, they can make important contributions to service goals.

Terminating Employment

Agencies that choose to hire nonprofessionals must decide before such a program is put into operation whether their goal is rehabilitation of the nonprofessional or service delivery, for, just as the nonprofessional has an inordinate fear of being fired out of hand, the professional has problems about firing personnel. If the agency's goal is to provide service, it must set realistic performance standards for the new personnel and then adhere to them. Granted that the nonprofessional will need time and help to achieve a minimum standard of performance, the question remains: How much time? And what should be done when someone slips through the selection process and it is discovered that he represents a case of serious psychological deviance? How much deviance can be tolerated? If therapeutic and social work interests override administrative judgment, action may be delayed (especially if this action is dismissal) not only at the expense of the program, but also possibly at the expense of the individual. The block here is emotionality. Supposedly, a mental health professional's original motivation in career choice was the wish to help, not hurt. Further, agencies are often afraid of hostility and delay termination of an employee for fear of the reaction of other staff members. Even when the issue is one of gross incompetence, agencies often hesitate to take such a step because to deprive someone of a job could mean, at best, difficulty in his finding another and, at worst, returning him to the welfare rolls. Speaking bluntly, such situations stimulate our guilt and we are emotionally unable to do what we know intellectually is necessary.

The uncomfortable fact is that if an agency is hiring nonprofessionals for service, it must accept its real responsibility, and that is the mandate to provide needed manpower and create job opportunities for those able to take full advantage of them. Every incompetent person retained on staff means that a competent person will be deprived of opportunity, as well as that one more critical service task may go unperformed. Diagnostic judgment must be used to identify the problem, decide what might improve the situation—that is, exactly what changes in a person's performance are necessary—and how much time this change process should require. If the changes do not occur, termination procedures must be set into operation. No small element in this is the fact that, when an incompetent person is retained for a protracted period of time, the other workers may interpret this as a sign that the administration is weak and basically indifferent to its real function. On the other hand, even taking timely action may reactivate the other workers' fears of being discriminated against or fired and produce a good deal of hostility. Nevertheless, one can usually depend on the workers ultimately to recognize the wisdom of the decision.

An even more difficult situation is one in which a person has been hired who has unusually high leadership ability, such that he becomes a charismatic figure for his group. If this leadership seems to be used destructively, for example, in a blind hostility toward authority, such questions as these must be asked: Is this person's need to battle authority amenable to change? Will he use it only to mobilize the other workers' latent hostility? If this is true, is it worthwhile to retain him because of the possibility that this kind of leadership will have long-range usefulness in stimulating more rapid emergence of leadership among the other workers, sometimes in opposition to him? If the decision is made to fire such a leader, the agency risks active and hostile confrontation from the rest of the group and must be prepared to cope with it.

If it is believed that such an employee's influence is basically destructive, then temporizing over his dismissal tends to lead the administration simply to learn to live with the situation and cope with each crisis he creates as it arises. That is why clinical judgment becomes so important for evaluating the worker's long-range potentialities and deciding how much risk the agency is willing to take. It must be remembered that people are hired for their survival characteristics: aggressiveness, assertiveness, and manipulativeness. We are delighted when these abilities are used effectively in working with other institutions, but we tend to react with anger when these same qualities are directed against us; in guarding against our counterreactions, we must be especially objective in evaluating those workers who arouse them.

Other Problems

Another issue of major importance in working with nonprofessionals is the necessity to guard against giving contradictory messages, for example, encouraging them to speak out at staff meetings, but then becoming angry and authoritative if they accept the invitation and speak out in an angry manner. It is easy to reject what they are saying on the grounds that they are being overemotional and neurotic, rather than listening to them. Other kinds of double messages are also given: at one time emphasizing all the things the workers still have to learn, and at another telling them how much they can teach the professional, thus unwittingly feeding a growing sense of grandiosity.

Supervision presents another problem. Out of their life experiences— probably largely out of their school experiences—nonprofessionals tend to see supervision not as a learning process, but as a threat. Their suspiciousness makes it difficult for them to believe that criticism is meant to be constructive, and it is not unusual for them to react defensively and argumentatively. Sometimes this leads to their withholding information and avoiding supervisory conferences. As this was examined by the Lincoln Hospital staff, we realized that we were more comfortable with a dependent—even overdependent—relationship that fed our narcissism and self-esteem, whereas the hostile reactions of the nonprofessionals threatened our potency and self-image and frustrated our wish to be of service. In an attempt to avoid this hostility, we too often placated the worker, a maneuver that he tended to see as a cop-out, or reacted with counterhostility, which simply tended to escalate the conflict and create a power struggle.

Paternalism is also an ever present danger. A review of the experience at Lincoln Hospital showed many areas in which this had operated as an unconscious factor. The professional who chooses to work in a disadvantaged area has a stake, both personal and professional, in the success of a nonprofessional employee program. Feeling that they are his charges, he may do battle for them or become their spokesman, rather than encouraging them to do their own battling and speak for themselves. Or, in the attempt to make the nonprofessional's task easier, the professional may introduce changes in procedures without consulting them or allowing them to participate in decision-making. If the nonprofessionals then reject or attack the changes, the professional tends to react with hurt, disappointment, or counterhostility.

The Issue of Participation

Actually, in the area of participation, not only paternalism but the issue of power created special problems. Often staff made it clear that the program belonged to the professionals. When we did say "ours," meaning it was a joint program, the nonprofessionals felt that we were trying to con them (and there may have been some truth in this). For although on an intellectual level there may be a desire to have the nonprofessionals participate in decision-making and policy and program direction, there is still an unconscious conviction on the professionals' part that they know better. Furthermore, they want to retain exclusive power, and the reality is that every increase in power for the nonprofessionals means a concomitant decrease for the professionals.

The struggle to find an appropriate level of participation for the nonprofessionals involved dealing not only with our own irrationalities but with theirs as well. From the outset, we defined the areas in which the workers had decision-making power but specified that in other areas the power of decision lay with the administration, although the nonprofessionals could participate in discussions directed toward making decisions. The workers felt that some of the areas we reserved for our own prerogative should properly have been theirs or that, at the very least, they should have had an equal share in the decision-making. A second, and even more delicate, problem arose when the nonprofessionals, having made suggestions that were solicited by the professionals, found their suggestions rejected. It was difficult, if not sometimes impossible, to make them understand that participation does not necessarily imply control. They want a democratic organization, with everyone having an equal voice and vote. It is hard for them to accept the reality that social agencies and institutions are at best benevolent dictatorships or constitutional monarchies, that social agencies are systems of delegated responsibility and authority, but that implicit in this system is accountability to a higher authority. Similarly, they find it even more difficult to accept the political reality that the agency itself may be accountable to any of a number of governmental structures.

The conflict around participation has not been resolved, but the confrontations have taught us much and moved us further along toward genuine participation of all levels of staff than had ever been contemplated. A few examples might illustrate:

In the fall of 1965 Lincoln Hospital was invited to send two delegates to each of three poverty conventions being held in the area, to be composed of delegates from all agencies and resident groups in the area. Each convention was to elect an antipoverty board. Lincoln Hospital Mental Health Services decided to send a professional-nonprofessional team to each convention, although it was really felt that two professionals would do a more effective job. The community mental health workers demanded to know why professionals were being sent at all, and why the administration felt it had the right to select the nonprofessional delegates. It was explained that the agency had been invited to send delegates and that it was an administrative prerogative to decide which persons could best represent the agency. The workers pointed out that the conventions were essentially community affairs, that they were members of the community working in it on the kinds of problems with which the conventions were concerned, and that they were entitled to a voice in who would represent the agency. After much discussion they agreed that under the rules of the convention, the administration had to be conceded the right to select three professionals, although they disapproved of the convention rules. But they insisted on the right to elect their own delegates. When one of the professionals voiced the fear that such an election would simply be a popularity contest, the workers demanded to know why it was thought that they did not have enough at stake in the conventions to elect the best representatives they could.

After much discussion and with some misgivings, the administration agreed to let the workers hold their own election. They accepted one of the original appointees, but substituted two others. All three were extremely effective participants—more effective, in fact, than the professionals, because they knew more people and were able to do more effective political maneuvering. One of them was elected to the board of one convention, and in another convention's election, the nonprofessional's politicking outside the convention was probably decisive in having the professional elected to the board, a position it is doubtful he could have won on his own.

Several months later, the hospital received a grant for professional staff to participate in a series of workshops and visits in Puerto Rico. At the last moment six places became available for nonprofessional staff. This time it was decided to permit the nonprofessional staff to select the six people who were to go. The administration was concerned that there would be conflict between the Negro and Puerto Rican staff members and that people would be elected on the basis of popularity rather than competence. For research purposes, the key administrators put down the names of the six nonprofessionals they thought could do the best job. The workers selected a chairman, developed criteria for selection, placed names in nomination, had the nominees give two-minute speeches, and then voted. They elected five of the six persons the administration would have selected. In retrospect, the administration was forced to recognize that again it had been guilty of unreasonable paternalism.

A third situation aroused much more anxiety among the professionals. The community mental health workers requested permission to meet as a group once a month on agency time without the presence of a professional. This meant, in effect, the development of an independent workers' group. A number of discussions were held with the group, exploring their reasons for wanting such sessions. There was concern that their sessions might be used to reinforce hostilities toward supervisors. Another possibility was that the meeting would be held to organize a union—an activity that was not opposed, but something they ought to do on their own time. The workers assured the administration that these assumptions were incorrect, that they simply wanted the freedom to talk together about such things as program development without the inhibiting presence of a professional. They felt further that they needed some sense of identity, which such a group could foster. They also saw it as a way to be of help to each other in sharing information about resources, programs, and so on. Reluctantly, the meetings were agreed to on condition that a joint evaluation be made after six months. It was also suggested that the meetings be held twice a month, since it was felt that one meeting a month would not permit enough continuity of process. The workers agreed and the meetings began.

At first the meetings did indeed focus on and aggravate the dichotomy between professional and nonprofessional staff, but this allowed acknowledgment of the split to become overt and open to much more candid discussion, thus making it easier to deal with. The meetings produced much more anguish for the workers themselves. Just as the split between nonprofessional and professional became more open and focused, so did the suspicion and distrust between the Negro and Puerto Rican staff members come to the fore. The situation was further complicated by internal struggles for power and control within the group.

After the first several meetings, some of the workers asked for permission not to attend the group. The professional staff took the position that attendance was required and helped these workers to think about ways in which they could influence the group's development. On a number of occasions consultation was offered to the group as a whole, but this was adamantly refused. The situation worsened, and the administration was often tempted to call the whole thing off, but recognized that if this were done, it would be seen as an arbitrary use of power and as implying lack of confidence in the workers' ability to handle their own differences.

About the fifth month more cohesion began to be seen in the group. Some of their organizational problems were resolved; others, although they were still apparent, were less intrusive. At the end of the sixth month, the joint evaluation was made. It was then clear that all the workers wanted the meetings to continue; they asked that even more time be set aside for them. The workers indicated that the meetings had enabled some of them to speak out more easily in staff meetings, that they had gained valuable information from colleagues and had a better appreciation of the limitations and assets of some of their colleagues. They also noted areas in which the organization of the independent group needed to be strengthened. It was clear that they were guarded in making negative comments about their own organization, but some of these did come through.

The professionals' response was more ambivalent. They too could point to specific gains in individuals, but they were more concerned about the fact that the independent organization gave a forum to those with the most hostile attitudes toward authority. They did recognize, however, that a more positive leadership was emerging. Nevertheless, they felt that the destructive elements were still in control, although not as much so as in the earlier phase of the group's development.

The independent workers' group continued and has now been in operation over three years. There is still no unanimity among the professionals, but by and large the positive elements outweigh the negative ones. The professional staff is in agreement that despite our fears, the confrontations forced on us that made us rethink some of our traditional methods of organization, procedure, and administration did enhance the program.

STRATEGIES

Lincoln Hospital's experience to date convinces us that the utilization of nonprofessionals from the target population has advantages that far outweigh the difficulties. In reviewing the experience, trying to look honestly at our mistakes and failures as well as our successes, we have formulated some recommendations that might be useful to other agencies:

1. Before undertaking a program using nonprofessionals, the professional staff needs to participate in the planning and determination of its goals. They must be alerted to possible areas of conflict and participate in developing expectations and standards of performance. They can participate in planning a training program and can help in clarifying the nonprofessional's role. In particular, they will need help in anticipating some of their own emotional reactions when the inevitable conflicts emerge, conflicts that are an essential and natural development.

2. It is equally essential that there be a period of preservice training for the nonprofessionals. Such training should concentrate on specific tasks, knowledge, and skills rather than on theory. There should be heavy use of role-playing and audiovisual materials. Stress should be placed on what they already know and how it can be utilized in the new program, so that group discussions on issues rather than formal lectures should predominate. It is important during this training period that individual conferences be held between the trainer and trainee that can be the forerunner of the supervisory process. Later, in-service training in small groups can be organized on a regular basis to introduce more formal teaching of theory and application. Even here the trainer or

supervisor has to be careful constantly to show the application of theory to practice.

3. For a long period of time the focus of the supervisory conference should be on what the worker finds exciting rather than on cases with which he is having difficulty. The supervisor will be well advised to note the common errors and misconceptions of his staff and to utilize these in group teaching and discussion rather than in individual sessions. Further, it must be kept in mind constantly that the supervisor is supervising the worker and not the case. While this has always been considered an important principle of supervision, professionals tend to lose sight of this when supervising nonprofessionals. Whenever possible the worker should be left free to accept or reject advice, that is, permitted to learn by his own mistakes.

4. Just as a nonprofessional will need supervision in carrying out his assignments, so will the supervisor of the nonprofessional need help. No matter how experienced the supervisor is, he is now undertaking a different assignment that will require some readjustment. During this period, the supervisor often needs help. To structure this from the beginning will be fruitful. We found a group meeting of supervisors to be extremely helpful. This can often replace individual supervision, except in the case of unique problems.

5. It is extremely important to provide nonprofessionals with opportunities to make decisions. It is important to bear in mind, however, that when staff members are given authority to make decisions, the administration has to be willing to live with those with which it may not agree.

Nonprofessionals also need opportunities to participate in an advisory capacity, with the administrator making the final decision but benefiting from their thinking. This should be made clear from the start so that the workers are not under the misapprehension that they will decide. As part of their development it is important to give them opportunities to gather information and make reports. Further, it is important to create opportunities for them to react to decisions and plans made by higher echelon staff, making it clear that their reactions and suggestions will be considered although not necessarily accepted. If their ideas are not accepted, they must be helped to work through their feelings about being asked to carry out decisions and plans not of their own making.

6. A structure must be created that permits the nonprofessionals to participate in the determination of personnel practices and grievance machinery.

7. It must be anticipated and accepted that in their growing sense of power they will make unreasonable, if not irrational, demands and that

they will abuse their power. In coping with these phenomena, it will help the professionals to see them in perspective and not react to the crisis with panic, counteranger, or unreasonableness of their own. Extreme patience and flexibility are needed. Unfortunately, too often we simply label our own rigidity as consistency.

8. Above all, merely confronting the nonprofessionals with their suspiciousness, distrust, hostility, or overdependence does not make the problem disappear. What is being dealt with are attitudes and behaviors that have been a lifetime in the making, and logical and rational confrontations cannot undo them in a day. This is a developmental and working-through process that will have its ups and down as it inches ahead. The administrators and supervisors of such programs must be careful about their own swings between elation and despair and keep before them the awareness that they are engaged in a process that involves two steps forward and one and a half steps backward.

Impact of the Indigenous Nonprofessional on the Professional's Role

WILLIAM H. DENHAM AND EUNICE O. SHATZ

This paper reports selective highlights of a demonstration project involving the use of indigenous workers in the human service agencies of Washington, D.C. Specifically, it will discuss the reaction of professionals operating at the delivery level to the introduction of indigenous nonprofessionals and issues and related questions emerging from this experience in terms of their implications for the delivery of human services in general and social services in particular.

The New Careers project was an experimental effort primarily based on opportunity theory.[1] It involved the development and implementation of a system of occupational opportunity for some 150 underprivileged youths and young adults, virtually all of whom were Negro. The system consisted of a two-pronged effort: (1) the development of a series of nonprofessional or aide jobs in the health, education, and welfare complex in Washington and (2) the selection, training, and placement of enrollees in the jobs. The emphasis in this paper is on the former. In the process, approximately ten nonprofessional job specialties were developed for that number of human service agencies.[2]

---

[1] Richard A. Cloward and Lloyd E. Ohlin, *Delinquency and Opportunity* (Glencoe, Ill.: Free Press, 1960).

[2] Positions developed included neighborhood workers and aides in day

178

The project lacked the resources that might have enabled systematic monitoring and analysis of role behavior. This problem, coupled with the fact that these programs were in the earliest stage of development, suggests that the ensuing material should be viewed as a tentative and impressionistic indicator of what promises to be a movement of major significance in the human service field.

EXPECTATIONS FOR PROFESSIONAL ROLE CHANGE

A major argument for the presumed benefits from use of indigenous non-professionals is that it will lead to more effective use of professional personnel. By effective use is meant that the skills, knowledge, and attitudes that are inculcated into the professional through university education and training should be more directly and consistently utilized in improving service to people. The nonprofessional is seen as furthering professional effectiveness in two ways: (1) freeing the professional to perform more consistently those tasks prescribed in his role that require a high degree of skill or (2) enabling him to experiment with and develop new tasks that could enhance the quality of his output. These purposes can be achieved by defining the nonprofessional role so that it serves either of two functions—maintaining or strengthening existing service delivery systems or changing them.

Maintaining or strengthening existing systems. This is achieved primarily through the mechanism of task relief, which means relieving the professional of tasks for which undergraduate or graduate social work training and education are not required and incorporating such tasks into the nonprofessional role. In this context the core functions of the professional are kept intact regardless of whether they involve direct service or supervisory activities. Supposedly the basic output of the professional will be enhanced by maximal and skillful performance of central functions as a result of his being relieved of peripheral or ancillary tasks.

Changing the system. The main change envisioned here is the improvement of service accessibility, defined as the means whereby the service products of an agency are offered in ways that will maximize

---

care, residential counseling, schools, nursing, geriatrics, recreation, and social service or case assistance. Participating agencies included the local school system; welfare, recreation, and health departments; and the Community Action Program and its delegate agencies (public and voluntary).

acceptance of them or use by potential clients. The principal vehicle for making service more available is the nonprofessional worker and the qualities allegedly resulting from his being indigenous—"psychosocial antennae" that enable him to reach out to an alienated population with a variety of tangible provisions. These might include giving information about agency service, rendering simple direct service aimed either at meeting clients' immediate needs for concrete help or motivating them toward more extensive relationships with the agency for assistance with complex problems, and referring clients to appropriate services when host agencies are unable to meet the expressed need.

In this model, the nonprofessional operates as a practitioner. The primacy of the professional as the person in charge of the service delivery unit is secured but his role is expanded to include a number of additional functions, depending on the nature of the service and how the role is defined. For example, the professional may function as an expert practitioner handling the most complex or demanding situations; he may become the team diagnostician, evaluator, or consultant; he may be expected to assume major responsibility for staff development and training; or any combination of these.

In addition to the expected alterations in professional role, two additional outcomes were anticipated by virtue of the professional's confrontation with the poor as co-workers rather than as service recipients. First, it was expected that the professionals would experience considerable role crisis as they were forced to determine what their attitudes and behavior toward the aides ought to be. Second, it was hoped that professionals would become resensitized to the needs and values of the indigent community as manifested through the indigenous worker and, conversely, that the nonprofessionals would develop more objective perceptions of human service professionals to counteract prevailing negative opinions about them and their agencies. This reciprocal sensitization was seen as reducing the social distance or alienation between these two categories of worker.

Before describing the outcome of these expectations it must be pointed out that virtually all of the programs using indigenous nonprofessionals suffered from minimal operational clarity, which was typical of demonstrations at the early stage in the antipoverty effort. Goals were still being articulated in funding proposals. In addition, programs frequently were impelled by political forces to begin operations without adequate staffing, structure, or administration. Consequently, role expectations of all staff, who were caught up in what was often a maelstrom of innovation and confusion, were inevitably fluid and changing.

OUTCOMES

In comparing the expected changes in the professional's role with what actually occurred, it was found that outcomes varied, depending on the predominance of three circumstances governing the use of indigenous nonprofessionals by the agencies: (1) situations in which indigenous workers were used to fill existing vacancies at the nonprofessional level, (2) when new positions for such workers were created to maximize the output of the professionals, or (3) when nonprofessionals were being used as part of a new approach to service delivery.

Impact and Reactions

In those instances in which trainees were used primarily to fill existing vacancies, the formal content of the professional role remained constant. The only change in occupational policy involved the adjustment of entry criteria to enable the hiring of aides. While there was no formal transfer of tasks from the professional to the nonprofessional, it was initially speculated that to a significant degree the professional would be relieved of performance of various lower-level tasks, thus increasing the time spent in direct practice, since he would no longer have to substitute for the nonprofessional. This, however, did not occur for a totally unexpected reason: In these agencies the shortage of nonprofessional staff had been so chronic as to have virtually become an integral aspect of the institutional culture. The professionals having to fill in for the nonprofessionals had little opportunity to use, let alone develop, the more highly technical skills usually required of such workers. Rather, they had become accustomed to performing routine functions.

For example, in the welfare counselor aide training program, the senior supervisory counselors in cottages to which the aides were assigned were for the first time in their employment required to function as training supervisors—a task that, although formally a part of their job description, had never been performed substantially or consistently. In most instances this responsibility was apparently beyond the competence of the supervisors. They reacted to this crisis with considerable anxiety, much of which was displaced on the aides, who were accused of being troublemakers and interfering with the old order. In other instances, when junior cottage staff complained about the aides, they were advised by the supervisor that the aides were only "temporary," the insinuation being that they would be replaced. The tension experienced by the professional over his deficiencies in supervisory skills was exacerbated by the inability of the agency to provide him with any support through staff training or development geared to the supervisory functions.

Agencies that tended to regard their manpower interests as being served by creating new roles for indigenous nonprofessionals were inclined to the view that more effective use of professional staff could be effected through the task-relief strategy, and the nonprofessionals' jobs were defined on this basis. However, in all such instances no formal restatement of professionals' duties or reallocation of their time responsibilities occurred. Furthermore, it was also expected informally that the professional would have major responsibility for supervising the nonprofessional. But here again, no administrative backup in the form of interpretation or training was ever provided. Consequently, the professional practitioner, given this new responsibility, in most instances had to perform it on a trial-and-error basis.

This was especially striking in the program that involved the training of school aides in the District of Columbia school system. Throughout the program, teachers grappled with but did not resolve such dilemmas as these: Were they to act as foremen, teachers, or supervisors vis-à-vis the aides? What repertoire of skills did they need to develop for what seemed to be a multidimensional role? How could the time demands inherent in aide supervision be reconciled with the learning needs of the class (an especially cogent issue since the addition of the auxiliary staff was supposed to provide more teaching time)? Should they give greater emphasis to such activities as curriculum development and evaluation, differential teaching methods, and so on? If so, were their skills adequate for these new challenges and if they were not, could this be acknowledged without jeopardizing professional reputations?

The expectation that additional time would accrue to the professional for performance of previously undone tasks requiring a high degree of skill or the assumption of new tasks was not realized in any patterned or sustained fashion. Here again, the major operative factor was the urgency of the new demand on the professional to supervise the indigenous worker. This, combined with the anxiety and uncertainty generated by the needs of such workers, seemed to absorb the energies of the professionals and cancel out the additional time that in theory might have been saved.

In situations in which nonprofessional positions were established as part of a new approach to service delivery, functional alterations in the professional role were primarily oriented to developing the nonprofessional role. The supervisory needs of the nonprofessionals were ubiquitous and virtually enveloped most of the professional time and energy that might have been utilized in giving service.

An added factor that further reduced the operating scope of the professional was the absence of any defined guidelines for his own role. Most official descriptions of the professional job in these programs were couched in unusually vague or ambiguous terms. In most instances the job descriptions gave professionals responsibility for supervision and/or in-service training of indigenous staff and held them accountable for ensuring that service was dispensed as expeditiously and fully as possible. Beyond this it was "every professional for himself" as far as determining what the nature of his other responsibilities in the area of service might be.

What is being argued here is not that professional role descriptions should be rigid. Quite the contrary—such descriptions should be developed in such a way as to allow professionals considerable discretion in selecting options for action. However, sound personnel policy requires that job descriptions provide reasonable direction to employees in the performance of tasks and responsibilities. This was not the case for most professional roles in the project. They were labeled rather than defined. Thus, whether intentionally or not, the nonprofessional in most of these programs functioned as the exclusive giver of service. In effect, he became *the* practitioner, carrying major responsibility for both rendering whatever service could be rendered and making it available to clients.

The professional reacted to these unanticipated developments with considerable tension and anxiety, which was often dysfunctional as far as the viability of the nonprofessional role was concerned. There was considerable acting out by professionals against the aides in such ways as threatening them with overly subjective and negative evaluations, limiting the aide's role to the more menial tasks, or "caseworking" the aide in an attempt to reverse his role from worker to client.

These factors of preoccupation with the supervisory component, ambiguity in the definition of role, and the resultant conflict engendered led to the speculation that no appreciable increase in the professional's involvement with service activities occurred. As far as accessibility of service was concerned, this was increased in many instances. However, it represented service that was made available and rendered primarily through the efforts of the nonprofessional. Quite apart from how effective such service was in meeting client need, its significance lay in the fact that it represented a new product without the traditional professional label.

Social Distance

The question of whether the interaction between professionals and non-professionals led to a reduction of social distance between them can be examined from the standpoint of the mutual expectations of each group. In the project it was noted that expectations of the professional by the nonprofessional tended to be expressed in terms of concrete needs. The latter was in an occupationally dependent position vis-à-vis the professional. As a subordinate in the relationship, he tended to look for five kinds of helping inputs from the professional: (1) help in surviving in a highly tenuous role, (2) help in developing practical skills and acquiring knowledge to meet the task requirements, (3) help in learning to negotiate his way in the agency, (4) help in realizing his aspirations for advancement in the event he was motivated in this direction, (5) respect, support, and recognition as a worker with the rights and privileges attendant thereto.

The expectations of professionals in relation to indigenous workers can be described as polarized along a continuum consisting of the "doubters" on one hand and the "idealists" on the other. The doubters were those professionals who tended to have low expectations of the aides' potential for making a significant contribution to service delivery. They tended to cast nonprofessionals in the roles of dependent clients or handymen in the service of the professionals. In this context the workers often reacted by assuming roles to fit the supervisors' expectations, thus creating a vicious circle. For example, in the teacher aide program one teacher tended to treat her aide as an overgrown student instead of a classroom assistant. Fairly early in his experience the aide perceived what was expected of him, and he played the role to the hilt. The result was that the teacher received little in the way of concrete help from him and he regarded himself as a failure as a classroom assistant.

At the opposite end of the spectrum were the idealists, who had inordinately high—in some cases unlimited—expectations of aides' capacities. Virtually all regarded the aides as practitioners. This included teachers who, in effect, believed that the aides could perform instructional tasks indiscriminately, caseworkers who voiced expectations that aides could perform intensive therapy, and so on. They seemed to view the worker as a "noble savage," who, by virtue of being poor and minimally educated, could outperform the professional, while at the same time retaining his identity as a nonprofessional person with roots in the client population. One consequence of this kind of approach was that the aide was continually expected to produce beyond his capacity. When he failed, the supervisor frequently became disenchanted. As a result, neither party got what he wanted. The aide received neither realistic nor practical skills or knowledge and the supervisor did not get the "all-American indigenous worker."

A fairly sizable subgroup of idealists were those professionals whose perceptions of their role can best be described as "warriors in the War on Poverty." They were inclined to view the nonprofessionals as potential allies in a struggle to change the human service Establishment. In many instances, the aim of these professionals was to effect change in the total agency, in which service delivery was an incidental element. Concomitant with their interest in broad-scale organizational change, these professionals also operated as advocates of the aides vis-à-vis their attempts to become integrated in the system.

An intermediate point on the spectrum was a third group consisting of professionals who might be termed "pragmatic experimentalists." These were individuals who, although committed to the acceptance of the nonprofessional's potential, took the approach that at this juncture no one could realistically "know" what that potential was, but that it should be tested out. They were inclined more consistently to orient their behavior to meeting the learning needs of the nonprofessionals as indicated in the job definitions and to try to evaluate performance on the basis of what was done on the job rather than on what ideally could have been done.

It is thus apparent that there was dissonance between the expectations of many professionals and nonprofessionals. The expectations of the latter were couched in visceral and concrete terms. They viewed themselves as consumers of the commodities or resources that professionals were supposed to supply and that they needed in order to get occupational footholds in the agency. In many cases they did not appear to share the ideological interests of the professionals or wish to enter into a compact to change systems.

On the basis of this experience, the authors would suggest that the concept of social distance as it is presumed to exist between the professional and the nonprofessional is too abstract and somewhat irrelevant in terms of the current economic and social status of most indigenous workers. The nonprofessional may not necessarily be looking for a relationship with the professional or interested in becoming *the* answer to the technical problems of service delivery. Rather, he is more likely to be concerned with getting as much concrete assistance from the professional as possible in terms of his needs for employment survival, stability, and advancement. It might be hypothesized that to the extent these needs can be responded to by the professional and to the extent that the professional can receive satisfaction from satisfying these needs, the social distance between the two parties is apt to lessen. This, then, may lead to the creation of a partnership base from which it is hoped new and more effective service can be planned and developed.

DILEMMAS AND QUESTIONS

Although the aforementioned outcomes must be recognized as tentative, they raise at least three central dilemmas relative to the professional role that will require more intensive study as future experience unfolds:

1. *Dual demand on the professional to deliver more high-quality service and simultaneously become skilled in the art of supervising the nonprofessional.* Can typically practitioner-oriented human service professionals such as social workers and teachers be expected to accommodate effectively to such demands? Can it be assumed that competence in practice is synonymous with competence in supervision? Is this perhaps an example of the "Peter Principle," wherein professionals are frequently expected to assume functions regardless of their abilities or inclinations? [3]

2. *Formulation of in-service training policy that arises from the needs of indigenous workers for intensive training and the needs of professionals for retraining.* Can agencies simultaneously respond to both pressures? If not, which combinations of "inside" (i.e., intra-agency) and "outside" (extra-agency) training and/or education for the indigenous nonprofes-

---

[3] Laurence J. Peter, "The Peter Principle," *Esquire,* Vol. 67, No. 1 (January 1967), pp. 76–77. According to the author, the promotion process in occupational life inevitably "develops, perpetuates and rewards incompetence." Each employee tends to be promoted until he reaches a level at which he is not wholly competent (but not incompetent enough to be discharged), at which point he becomes frozen. Every post tends to be occupied by an employee incompetent to some extent for the duties. The employee who is capable at one level frequently is found incompetent at a higher level. This principle was applied to social work by Robert M. Webb, "The 'Peter Principle' Applied to Social Work," *Personnel Information,* Vol. 10, No. 2 (March 1967), pp. 2, 3, 46–48.

sional are feasible in terms of costs and service production needs? A similar question might be raised in relation to the professional and his needs for retraining to meet not only the special learning and developmental requirements of nonprofessionals, but also to prepare himself for new professional tasks.

3. *Maintaining and/or enhancing quality of service and also responding to the ever increasing demand for service coverage.* What are the risks to professional standards of service in increased use of indigenous workers in practice roles? How can service units that include both professional and nonprofessional practitioners combine their talents in the interest of better service coverage? Or are there certain kinds of programs serving certain kinds of clients in which the service-rendering unit might be so designed as to place the indigenous nonprofessional in the primary practitioner role and under professional supervision? If so, what are such programs and what are the needs of the specific clientele?

Intra-agency Training of Nonprofessionals: Issues and Problems

EUNICE O. SHATZ AND SHELDON S. STEINBERG

A number of interrelated causal factors have led to current increased planning for and utilization of the nonprofessional in social service agencies. These factors include the following:

1. The increasing inability of feeder education systems to meet the demand for professional personnel.[1]

2. Increased federal legislation that has given rise to a variety of new programs demanding not only more trained workers, but also new skills.

3. The shifts in career choice of those aspiring to be social workers, not only during college years, but more important, after having worked in the field for a period of time.[2]

4. The increased expectation by and demand from the recipient population of improved service and their active participation in determining its quality and accessibility.

5. The increased recognition by social service professionals that

---

[1] Wilbur J. Cohen, "The Role of the Federal Government in Expansion of Social Work Training." Paper presented at the Annual Meeting of the Council on Social Work Education, Denver, Colo., January 1965.

[2] Galen L. Gockel, "Social Work As a Career Choice," in Edward E. Schwartz, ed., *Manpower in Social Welfare: Research Perspectives* (New York: National Association of Social Workers, 1966), pp. 89–98.

current patterns of service delivery tend to foster client dependency and fall severely short of meeting client need.

6. The militant mandate for programs that effect profound social change in environmental conditions.[3]

7. Experimental and demonstration programs that illustrate the potential for effective contributions of the nonprofessional worker in the delivery of human service.[4]

Many crucial questions related to the employment of nonprofessionals in a service delivery capacity—questions of cost and contribution to improve service—must as yet remain unanswered. While the risks involved must be recognized and studied, employment of the nonprofessional represents one realistic attempt to meet unmet and increasing client needs and demands.

The programs on which this paper is based [5] sought to do the following:

1. Select trainees, commonly referred to as "hard core," e.g., under-educated, unskilled, unemployed, or underemployed, some with histories of delinquency and/or police records.

2. Develop entry jobs with vertical and lateral career potential in a variety of human service fields.

3. Obtain a commitment from participating agencies to employ for a minimum of one year trainees who successfully complete the program.

4. Devise a training model that would in as brief a time as possible prepare the trainee for work and motivate him toward a career.

5. Devise effective means for communicating with professionals employing and supervising trainees in order to consider issues related to effective trainee supervision, work tasks, the training model, and implications for role and service change within the agency.

6. Evaluate effectiveness and modify content and job as the programs developed.

---

[3] Report of the National Advisory Commission on Civil Disorders (New York: E. P. Dutton & Co., 1968). See also Wilfred T. Ussery, "New Careers and Black Power." Paper presented to the House Committee on Education and Labor, July 17, 1967.

[4] See William H. Denham, Eunice O. Shatz, Naomi S. Felsenfeld, and Jacob R. Fishman, "Auxiliary Personnel in the Elementary School," National Elementary Principal, Vol. 46, No. 6 (May 1967), pp. 22–28; and New Careers in Human Services: A Report of a Social Experiment (Washington, D.C.: Institute for Youth Studies, Howard University, March 1969). The latter is a report of an eighteen-month demonstration project.

[5] New Careers in Human Services.

The issues covered in this paper reflect the authors' concern not only with better delivery of current service, but also with the need for different kinds of service—not only with what nonprofessionals might do, but with their relationships with the professional worker—not only with the need for further experimentation, demonstration, and research in this area, but most specifically with issues involved in training aides within the context of an agency program.

These issues specifically include the following:

1. The necessity for an agency to establish its priorities clearly when it considers the permanent employment of nonprofessional staff.

2. Administrative considerations of institutionalization of the nonprofessional worker and its ramifications for structure, table of organization, and service.

3. Program considerations that include program goals and staff functions, training control and methodology, trainee-staff relationships, and the issue of social change.

PRIORITIES

Program priority becomes a major issue in the development of any training program. For example, one problem immediately centers around budget. When federal funds are available for the training and employment of nonprofessionals, the money problems are minimal. Institutionalization of the nonprofessional employee, however, implies that sooner or later permanent budget slots must be created out of the available agency funds so that the jobs will continue after funding stops. This is quite a different order of decision-making from that undergone in initiating the experiment. While most agencies are willing to experiment with nonprofessionals, they are currently unwilling or unable to make the major budget shifts necessary to make these jobs permanent. The tendency, therefore, is to append the positions onto the regular budget in such a way that minimal problems will result if they are deleted from the table of organization.[6]

While this stance makes good sense with regard to budgetary considerations, it has a negative effect on the trainee and professional alike in that it underscores the marginality and tenuousness of the nonprofessional role. Carried to the extreme, in one school program it resulted

---

[6] Eunice O. Shatz and William L. Klein, "Training of Teacher Aides," in *ibid.*, pp. 99–138.

in the attempt to create a role for the nonprofessional as a "push-up aide."

While, theoretically, the common goal of all agency departments and programs is the provision to the client of the most adequate and comprehensive service possible, in working toward the realization of this goal each subunit in the agency tends to establish its own priorities. Especially in large agencies the nature of the bureaucratic structure paradoxically seems to encourage a narrowness of perspective around subunit priorities. Frequently the central goal of service delivery becomes clouded as each unit attempts to meet its own responsibilities. As a result, it often appears that units within an agency function at cross purposes. This anomaly underlines the necessity for agencies to have overall priorities clearly in mind so that their resources can be marshaled effectively.

ADMINISTRATIVE CONSIDERATIONS

A major administrative concern is institutionalization of the nonprofessional role and its ramifications for structure, table of organization, and service. Personnel units, for example, are faced with a major dilemma. In effect, their charge is to help create and classify positions for a new kind of employee. When the agency already has vacancies in the staffing pattern, the problem appears to be only one of reclassification and modification of qualifications in order to screen in the applicant who has traditionally been unable to qualify for a job.

However, it is often true that what may on the surface appear to be staff vacancies are, in fact, not. Often vacancies are frozen, the work absorbed into other positions and funds utilized for other purposes. The agency must unfreeze these vacancies or create new job categories. In this sense, the problems are quite similar to those faced by agencies that have no vacancies.

The job development process is made more complex when it is viewed with the intent of institutionalizing the nonprofessional role. This calls for major job re-engineering, which in many cases may imply a revolution not only for the agency, but for the profession. It may imply a change in the nature of the service offered. It may imply redefinition of agency program, task differentiation in roles, and major shifts in the practice, supervisory, and managerial functions of existing staff. When the role of the nonprofessional worker is viewed as ongoing and permanent—as an entry step into a potential career—projected budgeting must include promotion and advancement lines, which affect all employees. Simply stated, institutionalization implies that job development and change must take place on all levels parallel to that for the incoming nonprofessional worker. Given the necessary negotiations with civil service and other certifying groups, this is a highly complex and demanding task, especially when there is no assurance that the expenditure of so much time and energy will have permanent results.

Because of these complexities, the nonprofessional is generally not regarded as a permanent worker, and planning for institutionalizing his role does not take place. Just as federally funded positions are added onto regularly budgeted items, job descriptions for nonprofessional workers tend to be marginally attached to professional functions to prevent serious problems from arising if and when nonprofessional jobs must be discontinued. Thus, not only do the professional role and services continue at the status quo, but the agency need not concern itself with the major task of retraining or providing additional training for the professional to enable him to assume new responsibilities.

Administrators have used and continue to devise self-protective strategies in their resistance to institutionalizing the role of the new nonprofessional worker. One of their strategies is to fall back on the all too real and acute problem of negotiating with classifying and accrediting agencies. For example, in a program to train aides in public welfare, the agency stipulated not only that trainees had to be men, but also must have a high school diploma.[7] The rationale was civil service requirements. Aides trained to work in GS-3 and GS-4 positions entered at a GS-2 level and were then required to take an examination for the higher grades. The result was not the reassessment of what preparation was really necessary to carry out certain work tasks, but a new recruitment channel—not the creation of new roles that might lead to more effective service, but business as usual. Another example is the establishment of bogus "career ladders" designated as Aide I, II, and III, without any substantive difference among levels in role or responsibility.

Another strategy often devised in the face of real budgetary limitations is to disguise needed clerical positions within the job description of a human service aide. In one instance nonprofessionals were to be selected by virtue of their already acquired clerical skills, employed as human service aides, and given training in the theoretical concepts of human service. Essentially this is a distortion of the human service

---

[7] Naomi S. Felsenfeld and William H. Denham, "Training of Counselors in Residential Programs for Children and Youth," in *New Careers in Human Services,* pp. 159–193.

aide concept, which seeks to qualify unskilled persons. While the position may include some clerical tasks, the emphasis is on service. In fact it becomes simply a new strategy to hire skilled and qualified persons for whom no salaries previously were budgeted. In some cases this implies resistance to allowing the nonprofessional worker to participate in a direct service role. In other cases, this simply reflects an ordering of priorities in agencies committed to keeping their structure and organization intact.

The nonprofessional worker who is only marginally included in the agency organization and service frequently feels alienated—and behaves accordingly.[8] Because he is unsure that he is being actively included in agency planning and program, he tends to be less involved in his work and to learn more slowly. For example, in a program to train high school seniors for health and teacher aide positions, job commitments for health aides were made concrete more quickly than those for teacher aides. Staff observed definite differences in the attention, initiative, and behavior of the two groups.[9] The issues of institutionalization are joined when the need of the trainee for active inclusion conflicts with the need of the agency to maintain the marginality of the nonprofessional role.

PROGRAM CONSIDERATIONS

Professional staff, for the purposes of this paper, are grouped roughly into two basic categories on the basis of whether their major responsibility is training or provision of direct service to clients. Simply in the formation of these two groupings, however, the seeds for potential conflict are sown. Briefly stated, the conflict centers on the following issues: To what degree can trainers relate to service as a primary objective, and to what degree can practitioners relate to training as a primary objective? To what degree are these two objectives complementary or incompatible?

Social work has traditionally taken the responsibility for student supervision as part of the professional role. Ostensibly, then, the issue on that level should be resolved. Even in this accepted area, however, un-

---

[8] Melvin Seeman, "Antidote to Alienation—Learning to Belong," *Transaction,* Vol. 3, No. 4 (May-June 1966), pp. 35–39.

[9] William H. Denham, Eunice O. Shatz, Naomi S. Felsenfeld, and Jacob R. Fishman, "High School Training for New Careers in Human Services," *National Elementary Principal,* Vol. 46, No. 6 (May 1967).

resolved questions and disagreement exist. To what degree can supervisors of students continue to carry a case load? Are status and prestige adequate compensation for this additional and specialized responsibility? Are all professionals equipped by training and/or temperament to supervise students? What additional professional preparation may be required? Can released time to acquire it be granted?

In addition to these issues, which pertain to the training of nonprofessionals as well as graduate social work students, some major differences in training the nonprofessional as opposed to the graduate student become apparent. The student is not an employee of the agency and is, therefore, marginal to its internal life and organization, even though the student unit may be a part of the agency structure. The nonprofessional is an employee and, by implication, a part of the agency. The student's role is similar to that of the full professional worker and does not contain the strains and considerations implicit in job creation for the nonprofessional worker—the professional student "has it made"; the nonprofessional has only gained a tenuous foothold. In many agencies a pool of cases already exists that are passed from student to student, year after year. In such cases the expectation may be not so much in terms of change for the client as it is a practicum for the student. The nonprofessional, on the other hand, is expected to produce within his area of responsibility. Thus the attitudes of the professional toward the nonprofessional tend to be somewhat different.

Priorities for practitioners tend to polarize around service to the client; those of trainers, around preparation of the worker. Theoretically, as with the training of students, the primary goals seem to be compatible. Practically, however, the trainer of nonprofessionals often finds himself in the position of advocate for the trainee. This role is thrown into sharp relief when the agency regards the trainee as peripheral to its central service and the trainer is encouraging the administration and the practitioner to instititionalize the nonprofessional's function.

Issues that came to light in the training process materialized along six dimensions: (1) definition of program goals and staff functions, (2) program control, (3) training methodology, (4) trainee-staff relationships, (5) staff competition, and (6) social change. Each of these areas will be discussed in full.

Program Goals and Staff Functions

Agencies in which aides were trained tended to define their program goals somewhat broadly, in order to maintain flexibility and capacity for change. Similarly, the roles of the practitioners frequently were loosely drawn in order to maintain the possibility of flexibility as well as innovative approaches in program. A contributing factor to the resistance of professionals to specifying their own functions may have been the Topsy-like nature of their own roles as these developed to encompass unanticipated service needs or even aspects of clerical coverage. Trainers, however, sought a more precise definition of the role of the practitioner in order to (1) define a role for the trainee that was supportive of agency program and involved concrete job tasks for which he could be trained, (2) reduce the tensions and anxieties the trainee felt through having an amorphous relationship to clients and staff, (3) reduce the trainee's feelings of alienation and powerlessness by encouraging a work environment to which he felt he belonged, and (4) devise appropriate channels of supervision for the trainee in relation to those with whom he worked most consistently.

Program Control

While each staff member recognized the necessity for co-operative and overlapping activity, perceptions of responsibility for administrative control varied. Practitioners, viewing the trainees as potential employees, felt that control of the program components, curriculum content, scheduling, standard-setting, and evaluation was their responsibility. Trainers, on the other hand, viewed the training period as a special condition of employment and themselves as having the specialized skills and responsibility to structure and implement the program. An implied threat, as perceived by many practitioners, was the intent of the trainers to influence them, their professional role, and ultimately the nature of the service offered. In many cases the latter were seen as interlopers. Trainers, on the other hand, tended to be fearful that trainees would be assigned mostly clerical or marginal roles, or that service pressures would catapult the trainee into situations for which he was unprepared. Each staff group reacted strongly to what was perceived as an implied status of handmaiden to the other.

In many training programs the practitioners had responsibility for fieldwork supervision and for conducting job-skill workshops. In others, practitioners were responsible only for the former activity. Trainers maintained responsibility for conducting the rest of the program and for co-ordination and scheduling. Strains arose when the need of the practitioner for help from the trainee conflicted with planned training sessions.

Training Methodology

The training model that was developed for all of these programs consisted of the simultaneous implementation of the following five components, usually referred to as the New Careers Training Model: [10]

1. Fieldwork practice.
2. Job-skill workshop.
3. Remediation geared to job requirements and test preparation (high school equivalency, civil service, and so on).
4. Core group (discussion of issues generic to the field of human service stemming from incidents occurring on the job and in the community).
5. Seminars for professional supervisors and trainers.

This approach represents a number of assumptions based on four years of experimentation in the training of human service aides in welfare, education, health, mental health, research, recreation, and day care. These assumptions include the following:

1. The trainee, given the required information and skill, can work productively.
2. Absorption of information and skill is facilitated by the opportunity to test it out in a work situation.
3. Curriculum must be fluid to accommodate the needs of the trainee and emerging job demands.
4. The trainee is activity oriented, and teaching methods must be cognizant of and related to this learning style.
5. The role of the trainee is ambiguous and therefore he requires support and an outlet for his anxieties and frustrations.
6. Trainees will bring fresh approaches to service that might be dissonant with the traditional approaches of professionals.
7. Trainees require a forum in which they can question, criticize, and test out a variety of coping skills. The group approach will demand frankness and honesty in its capacity to provide alternatives in action and thinking from which trainees can arrive at decisions.
8. The practitioner will become involved in a personal and professional reassessment of his attitudes, methodology, flexibility, and willingness to take risks in working with the trainee.

The trainer's approach, then, was to set ground rules for the programs

---

[10] Avis Pointer and Jacob Fishman, *New Careers: Entry-Level Training for the Human Service Aide* (Washington, D.C.: New Careers Development Program, University Research Corp., March 1968).

and within those limits to confront the trainee with his activity and the limitations and possibilities of the work setting. It also encouraged trainees to discuss openly their thoughts about the system, its qualities and liabilities, interpersonal relationships, efficacy of client service, program ideas and problems and issues related to the specific job, career possibilities, the community, and talk and thought as legitimate work areas.

To this end, curricula were devised and communication channels with practitioners were developed. The programs were designed to promote constant interaction among all involved parties, encourage mutual interchange, and provide opportunities for interpretation of what was happening both to the trainee and the practitioner. Confrontation between practitioner and trainee was not only expected, but encouraged. It was hoped that through a frank and critical interchange the professional and the trainee would gain increased awareness of the problems and issues they both faced and of their individual capacities.

The practitioner, while skilled and competent in his own area, often was not familiar with or prepared for training aides. In some cases, therefore, the time allotted for job-skill workshops and supervised fieldwork was unplanned and unproductive. The trainee, unprepared for or confused about his work assignment, was frequently viewed as unmotivated or unsuited to the work. When the practitioner was faced with the task of curriculum preparation, supervision, and an implied restructuring of his own role, he frequently reacted with responses that not only maintained the intactness of his own role but tended to reinforce traditional professional responses to stress situations in worker-client relationships.

In still other cases, the practitioner felt that a kind of treatment should be intrinsic to training. It was felt that concepts of mental health and illness in particular would create a variety of anxieties and symptoms in the trainee that required psychotherapeutic intervention. At times, absence, lateness, and inappropriate or critical behavior by the trainee were viewed and diagnosed in clinical terms, as requiring treatment—frequently disguised as "self-awareness" sessions. The trainee thus was variously perceived as a person to be treated, controlled, or excluded, and the supervision and training reflected these responses.

Trainee-Staff Relationships

A great deal of ambivalence exists around the nature of the relationship between trainee and staff. The relationship with the trainer tends, for the most part, to be that of student to teacher. Here, as with the practitioner, there is a tendency to fall into a worker-client relationship, with the trainer assuming the role of problem-solver or even therapist.

One of the essential elements of successful training appears to be the commitment of trainer to trainee, that is, the degree to which the trainer acts out his faith in the trainee's potential to succeed. Ideally it is felt that commitment should lead to presenting the trainee with issues, thinking through alternatives with him, and leaving him to make decisions. Trainees tend quickly to sense the role the trainer is playing and respond by assuming the complementary role of problem child, patient, passive recipient, or worker-in-training.

The relationship between trainee and practitioner, however, is even more complex by virtue of the fact that it is ongoing, whereas that with the trainer is temporary. The practitioner must assume the role of co-worker and supervisor, whereas the role of the trainer is that of instructor and change advocate. The trainer can devote all his energies to the trainee, whereas the practitioner must be primarily concerned with service to his clients. The relationship of the trainer to the trainee is established, whereas the relationship with the practitioner is in a sense still evolving. The trainer has skills related to program and curriculum planning that in most instances the practitioner is still developing.

As a result, the practitioner is often inconsistent, shifting from an attitude that encourages the trainee to say whatever is on his mind (a freedom that few professionals enjoy) to one that is highly authoritative and directive. At times the professional is so intent on convincing the trainee that he is considered a co-worker that he inadvertently abrogates his supervisory function, only to find he must recoup it later from a resentful and confused trainee.

Staff Competition

To the degree that unresolved issues and strains relating to program control, priorities, relationships, and methodology continue, elements of competition between trainer and practitioner are heightened. Both trainer and practitioner have a vested interest in the success of the trainee, and frequently each tends to see himself as the key element in the process. At times, each finds himself vying for the loyalty of the trainee. The practitioner may become suspicious, threatened by the free-swinging and often critical nature of training group discussions. The trainer may become overly zealous in his ambitions for the trainee to take on increased practice functions.

When the channels of communication break down owing to too many differing perceptions of training approaches, work expectations, and program pc'icy, the trainees become a battleground for professional differences and finally may proclaim "a plague on both your houses!" In one program, trainees rejected a continuation of the program despite their admitted desire and need for more training, because of the hostilities that existed between the training and clinic staffs. In effect they were forced to choose sides, and appropriately they chose the practitioners with whom they had an ongoing relationship.

Social Change

There are those trainers who look to the nonprofessional worker as an agent of social change. This issue merits some serious thought. While certain organizational, structural, and even role changes do occur when nonprofessionals are employed in human service agencies, the extent of those changes depends for the most part on the agency and its perceptions of priority and use of manpower. To view the trainee as a catalyst for change is to place him in an untenable role. It may safely be stated that most institutions reflexively resist change. When change is attempted, one determining factor is the amount of influence the change agent has.

The nonprofessional coming into the agency is low man in the power structure. He has no influence. Experience has shown that when aides tried to induce practice change, professionals reacted defensively with social control measures aimed at reinforcing the marginality of the aide role rather than encouraging its flexible development. Experience has also indicated that to encourage the aide to act as a change agent is to set up an impossible dilemma for him. It means that he is told: "Fit into the Establishment, but make waves." On the one hand, he is taught how to cope with rules and regulations in the most practical sense— that is, how to adjust to the system—while simultaneously he is encouraged to alter agency practice and policy.

Finally, it forces the trainee to juggle the change-oriented trainer and the agency-aligned professional in what can only become an occupational and emotional meat grinder. It is theorized that client needs, services provided, policy, and service delivery are perceived differently by people indigenous to the client population.[11] They are inclined to be less tolerant of red tape, budget problems, and rigidity of policy than are their professional colleagues. Observation indicates, however, that many trainees quickly identify with the professional and join the Establishment.

---

[11] Arthur Pearl and Frank Riessman, *New Careers for the Poor* (New York: Free Press, 1965).

They read the system and tend, at least overtly, to fit into it. For example, while prior to employment the trainee may have deplored the long waiting lists, subsequent to employment he may rationalize the necessity for closing intake for periods of time. The extent to which the nonprofessional identifies with the system and accepts its limitations is as yet unknown. If, however, as initial observation suggests, a major concern of the trainee is to become an integral part of the agency staff and to develop the necessary protective coloration, it appears highly unrealistic to assume that he is going to view himself as changing agency policy or program. Changes that occur by virtue of his presence at present are more likely to be by chance than by design.

CONCLUSIONS AND RECOMMENDATIONS

The nonprofessional cannot be perceived of as the key to improvement of service and its delivery. Experience has indicated, rather, that he may have potential as an additional member of the service team who can enhance its capacity to provide adequate care to its clients. However, if the nonprofessional is absorbed into an agency merely as a member of one additional level of personnel, not only may service delivery remain essentially unaffected, but his unique contributions may be nullified. His contribution in terms of bettering service delivery is relevant only insofar as it may be considered part of the overall perception of how the agency perceives service delivery.

The effect of the inclusion of nonprofessionals on patterns of service delivery is predicated on several conditions:

1. The capacity of the agency objectively to define client needs both qualitatively and quantitatively and devise the kinds of service necessary to meet these needs.

2. An analysis of the specific skills, knowledge, and experience necessary to deliver and provide the service in ascending order of valence.

3. The development of a fluid continuum of task clusters, again in ascending order, with concurrent education and experience related to task proficiency, and not caste systems of staff and tasks that do not merge.

In preparing the nonprofessional worker to function within any social service system, the following areas are seen as critical:

1. *The program.* In training nonprofessionals in newly developing programs, the uncertainty of policy direction and role for all staff compounds the confusion and ambiguity that surround the nonprofessional role, even in established and well-defined programs.

2. *Agency structure.* The degree to which the nonprofessional role

is absorbed into the agency staffing pattern has immediate impact on the learning and performance of the trainee.

3. *Task definition.* Professional staff members are affected by the process of job definition for the trainee and tend to react differentially, depending on the degree to which their own roles are modified and supported by additional training or education.

4. *Practice methods.* The potential contribution of the nonprofessional depends on the degree to which agency and staff can accept the implementation of nontraditional practice methods and techniques.

5. *Training relevance.* The degree to which the training practicum is an integral part of the basic service and delivery pattern and not based on make-believe jobs has a real effect on the initiative, motivation, performance, and job longevity of the trainee.

6. *Priorities.* A viable training program is related to whether an agency views incoming nonprofessionals as dispensers of service who require training or as trainees preparing to become dispensers of service. The administrative control of the training program then evolves from this decision.

7. *Staff relationships.* Both occupational and interpersonal relationships are seriously affected by whether professional staff view nonprofessionals as trainees in a learning situation, as clients in a work-therapy situation, or as fully trained staff workers.

Nonprofessionals and the Planned Replacement Model

EARL C. BRENNEN

The growing awareness of the professional manpower shortage in the social welfare and mental health fields has given rise to a number of issues regarding the recruitment, selection, training, and deployment of nonprofessionals as helping persons. This paper will touch on several of these issues as they are reflected in programs utilizing what may be called "planned replacement." It might be best to begin with an examination of what is meant by this.

PLANNED REPLACEMENT

The New Careers model has attracted much attention as a promising strategy for service delivery, but many potential helpers—retired persons, housewives, college students, young adults "in transition," and so on—may wish to involve themselves in giving service for a period of time without making a career of it.[1] Fortunately, these sources of manpower have not gone unnoticed. Numerous programs throughout the country recruit volunteers and paid nonprofessionals with full knowledge that these workers are not going to remain for long; the Peace Corps and VISTA in particular were designed for the noncareerist.

---

[1] Arthur Pearl and Frank Riessman, New Careers for the Poor (New York: Free Press, 1965).

These programs differ from approaches that involve the employment of technicians and aides in that there is no attempt to penetrate the rather formidable professional credential system. Indeed, the planned replacement strategy has come to be an effective recruitment device for the mental health professions. Some reports indicate that college students have changed their career goals following participation in such programs.[2] These programs differ also from the traditional use of "gray lady"-type volunteers who carry out the same auxiliary tasks year after year. With planned replacement there is an attempt to capitalize on the initial zeal and freshness of helpers, and an accompanying avoidance of the "burnout" problem that has been revealed in some programs.[3] Once their initial enthusiasm is tempered by daily routine and the inevitable frustrations and disappointments, some nonprofessionals apparently lose the very qualities that once made them seem so effective.

Elusive factors such as interest, attention, spirit, and high expectations appear to account for the phenomenon that some human service endeavors, much like experimental drugs, seem to work best when first tried. Frank surmises that the various forms of psychotherapy gain their effectiveness through offering the patient a dramatically new and different interpersonal experience, and it is quite possible that such novelty has an effect on the beginning helper as well.[4] This two-way effect is merely an extension of Riessman's "helper therapy principle," with the added implication that the impact on the helper is transformed into better service for the client.[5]

In addition to the purposeful use of novelty, programs using the planned replacement approach draw heavily (but often unwittingly) on the concept of time-limited service. Shlien, a recognized therapist-researcher who has been influenced by the writings of Jessie Taft, experi-

---

[2] Milton Greenblatt and David Kantor, "Student Volunteer Movement and the Manpower Shortage," *American Journal of Psychiatry*, Vol. 118, No. 3 (March 1962), pp. 809–814. This has been the writer's experience with the Interpersonal Relations Project, which will be described later.

[3] Sherman Barr, "A Professional Takes a Second Look," *American Child*, Vol. 49, No. 1 (Winter 1967), pp. 14–16.

[4] Jerome Frank, *Persuasion and Healing* (Baltimore: Johns Hopkins Press, 1961).

[5] Frank Riessman, "The 'Helper' Therapy Principle," *Social Work*, Vol. 10, No. 2 (April 1965), pp. 27–32.

mented with Rogerian time-limited psychotherapy and found it to be more effective than unlimited therapy of the same type.[6] Presumably the shortened time encourages the client to invest more energy, courage, and wisdom in the helping process, and it seems likely that the therapist is also moved to make better use of his time. It can also be suggested that the same holds true for the nonprofessional helper who has but a year rather than a career lifetime in which to do his thing.

SELECTED ISSUES

One of the issues to be faced by administrators who use nonprofessionals in any capacity concerns the relative emphasis to be placed on selection and on training. Some believe training is in order, but that selection should be played down to prevent choosing only those who approximate the professional model. Others believe applicants should be screened carefully, but minimize training to avoid the "pitfalls of assimilation," wherein nonprofessionals devote more energy to acting professional than to being effective with clients.

There is much to be said for the training approach. In one project, a group of housewives were able to perform about as well as their professional colleagues after two intensive years of practical training in psychotherapy (although it must be granted that the housewives were superior persons to begin with).[7] However, intensive training draws heavily on scarce professional time, and the scarcity of professional time is one reason why some nonprofessionals are being used to begin with. In addition, the interpersonal skills required in many of the human services are not easily learned, and it may be more feasible to seek out natural talent than to train likely prospects. A number of programs using

---

[6] John M. Shlien, Harold H. Mosak, and Rudolph Dreikurs, "Effect of Time Limits: A Comparison of Two Psychotherapies," in Arnold P. Goldstein and Sanford J. Dean, eds., *The Investigation of Psychotherapy* (New York: John Wiley & Sons, 1966), pp. 235–238; and Madge K. Lewis, Carl R. Rogers, and John M. Shlien, "Time-Limited, Client-Centered Psychotherapy: Two Cases," in Arthur Burton, ed., *Case Studies in Counseling and Psychotherapy* (Englewood Cliffs, N.J.: Prentice-Hall, 1959).

[7] Margaret Rioch *et al.*, "National Institute of Mental Health Pilot Study in Training Mental Health Counselors," *American Journal of Orthopsychiatry*, Vol. 33, No. 4 (July 1963), pp. 678–689.

volunteers as mental health counselors do not devote much time either to training or supervision. While intensive training may be indicated for New Careerists, the planned replacement approach seems to invite the development of efficient screening devices. Later in this paper one kind of selection procedure that seems to hold promise will be discussed.

Perhaps the most sensitive issue concerns the extent of responsibility the profession is willing to delegate to nonprofessional helpers. No profession can be expected to welcome incursions into its domain, and social work has reacted predictably, evincing some fear and distrust and on occasion actually resisting the establishment of needed services when nonprofessionals were involved.[8] If giving nonprofessionals extensive responsibility is a question of trust, then we must stand in awe of the federal government, which allows free-thinking Peace Corps volunteers to serve in politically sensitive areas overseas.

One ostensibly plausible response taken by the profession has been to give consideration to the scheme developed by Willard C. Richan for the NASW Subcommittee on Utilization of Personnel, which provides for the utilization of personnel according to the dimensions of client vulnerability and worker autonomy.[9] A child requiring foster placement would be considered highly vulnerable; a normal adult seeking information about a social service would be classified as low on this variable. A service such as casework, which is given in a manner closed to observation, would be rated high on worker autonomy, while a visible service guided by set rules would rank low. The four possible combinations would serve as a way of allocating personnel with differing amounts of training and potential.

Such a system may have merit, but there are many situations to which it does not seem to be applicable. As Specht puts it: "Our professional domain is so poorly defined we could not begin to separate out levels of tasks anyway. Certainly we cannot expect nonprofessionals to do the

---

[8] David Kantor, "Volunteerism and Problems of Domain in the American Mental Health Movement," in Patricia L. Ewalt, ed., *Mental Health Volunteers* (Springfield, Ill.: Charles C Thomas, 1967), pp. 147–156. *See also* Robert B. Ellsworth, *Nonprofessionals in Psychiatric Rehabilitation* (New York: Appleton-Century-Crofts, 1968), chap. 1.

[9] "Utilization of Personnel in Social Work: Those With Full Professional Education and Those Without" (New York: National Association of Social Workers, February 1962). (Mimeographed.)

dirty work while we conceptualize." [10]   Richan's scheme also does not apply well to the tens of thousands of public assistance workers in this country. These workers are too homogeneous in level of education and amount of training to invite easy differentiation.

The writer believes that the concept of client vulnerability has had a stultifying influence on practice and ought to be discarded. It would be difficult to come to any other conclusion after an examination of the books by Ewalt and Ellsworth.[11] Their reaction to the kind of thinking associated with client vulnerability is reflected in this statement by a psychiatrist acquainted with the nonprofessonal movement:

> We used to see patients as very delicate, fragile beings in danger of a serious setback from a thoughtless word. So we had to be cautious about who was allowed to come in contact with them. Volunteers had to be screened and selected carefully. Then we trained them, with a great many hours of lectures about psychiatric illness and the behavior to be expected of patients, and the rules and regulations, and the do's and don't's and admonitions and the warnings. There were also orthodox dogmas about the kinds of jobs that must never be given to a volunteer and kinds of wards that no volunteer should be allowed on. What nonsense! The trouble is, a lot of people started programs without knowing these rules, and got away with it for years before they found out about the rules, and then it was too late; their programs had been working without the rules.[12]

The concept of worker autonomy does not fare much better. Nonprofessionals must be given sufficient responsibility if competent and committed recruits are to be attracted. They want to serve clients directly. (When one private agency decided to use indigenous workers to serve the Negro population in its area, it planned to call them social worker aides, but the nonprofessionals insisted on being called family aides instead, reasoning: "We're here to help *families,* not social workers.")

It seems, too, that nonprofessionals are more aware of the social nature of emotional problems that some professionals see as located internally, and thus the social nature of their helping efforts is viewed

---

[10] Harry Specht, address to the NASW Golden Gate Chapter, Conference on New Careers, San Francisco, May 1967.

[11] *Op. cit.*

[12] Robert C. Hunt, "The Changing State Hospital: What It Needs From Volunteers," in Ewalt, ed., *op. cit.,* p. 29.

by them as more relevant and potent than it was not very long ago. Many volunteers now share personal concerns with patients or clients and are not reluctant to venture beyond light-hearted talk. Finally, the reported use of teen-agers, institutionalized mental patients, and social deviants as nonprofessional helpers does violence to the concept of worker autonomy.

The question remains, of course: "How effective is this new breed of volunteers and nonprofessionals?" The writer is not familiar with any research reports on the performance of indigenous or other nonprofessional personnel in welfare programs, but there is some evidence from studies of mental health programs that permits cautious optimism. In the Harvard-Radcliffe program, which systematically recruits college students to work with hospitalized mental patients, a controlled study of two comparable wards revealed that in the ward served by volunteers, patients showed significantly greater advances on several criteria of improvement such as conceptual disorganization, withdrawal, and activity level.[13] A follow-up study of 120 chronic patients served by the volunteers established that 31 percent left the hospital during this period, which was ten times the expected discharge rate for chronic patients; over half of these discharged patients were considered greatly improved.[14]

A more recent investigation that has evoked considerable comment among psychologists is Poser's research comparing professional therapists with undergraduate girls who had no training in psychology and did not intend to enter a mental health profession.[15] Poser decided to test the efficacy of group therapy with 343 schizophrenic patients, and engaged the girls as group leaders merely to control for the placebo effect. The experimental sample was comprised of patients assigned to psychiatrists, social workers, and occupational therapists, all of whom had at least five years of experience. Each therapist met with his group of ten patients one hour daily, five days a week, for five months. The therapists and the untrained girls were allowed to handle their groups as they wished. Briefly, the patients of the lay therapists gained significantly

---

[13] Greenblatt and Kantor, op. cit.

[14] James C. Beck, David Kantor, and Victor A. Gelineau, "Followup Study of Chronic Psychotic Patients 'Treated' by College Case-Aid Volunteers," American Journal of Psychiatry, Vol. 120, No. 9 (September 1963), pp. 269–271.

[15] Ernest Poser, "The Effect of Therapists' Training on Group Therapeutic Outcome," Journal of Consulting Psychology, Vol. 30, No. 4 (August 1966), pp. 283–289.

more on several of the outcome measures, and a follow-up study showed that the gains were sustained. (If it is any consolation, there was no difference between patients treated by social workers and those treated by psychiatrists.) The investigator attributed the success of these girls to their "naïve enthusiasm" and "lack of professional stance," and in a commentary Rioch speculates that one factor may have been that the patients co-operated more with persons seen as closer to themselves in the social hierarchy.[16] Interestingly, Rioch also conjectures that if these girls were used much longer in the same manner, their effectiveness would taper off.

INTERPERSONAL RELATIONS PROJECT

The Interpersonal Relations Project is one example of a planned replacement program that features selection over training and the delegation of major responsibility to nonprofessionals.[17] For four years the program hired companion-counselors for emotionally troubled preadolescent boys. Each year fifty counselors and boys were paired on a one-to-one basis, meeting twice weekly for several hours over an eight-month period. Matched-pair experimental and control groups with multiple instruments and observers were used. In a number of respects the project's work parallels that described in the Cambridge-Somerville study.[18] Counselors and boys were also split into symmetrical subgroups, then matched and mismatched according to personality type in order to study the differential success of various dyadic compositions.

The planned replacement approach was to dip into an existing manpower pool—in this instance the college campus—employ these people for a year or so to profit from their enthusiasm, and then replace them with new recruits with equally high initial interest and energy. The pool is replenished by successive waves of newly admitted students, as might also be the case with newly retired persons and other suitable population groups.

To conserve professional time, the selection device for counselors consisted of a group assessment session in which the applicants them-

---

[16] Margaret Rioch, "Changing Concepts in the Training of Therapists," *Journal of Consulting Psychology,* Vol. 30, No. 4 (August 1966), pp. 290–292.

[17] This project is sponsored by the University YMCA (Stiles Hall), Berkeley, Calif., and financed by the National Institute of Mental Health.

[18] Edwin Powers and Helen Witmer, *An Experiment in the Prevention of Delinquency* (New York: Columbia University Press, 1951).

selves performed the ratings.[19]   Students formed into groups comprised
of eight applicants and rated each other after each person had performed structured tasks that called for the demonstration of certain traits
such as warmth, understanding, and openness. Applicants falling below
a set standard were rejected.

The amount of training was minimal. Counselors were paired on
programmed "teaching machines" that required them to relate to each
other in a manner designed to enhance genuineness and empathy, a procedure that did not involve staff participation. The remainder of the
training consisted of weekly discussion groups in which half of the
counselors met with a group leader (to test the effect of training, the
rest of the counselors were not assigned to groups). No regular supervision was provided, although staff members did check over visit reports
for signs of trouble and offered consultation on request.

Although the troubled boys in the program were high on client vulnerability, the untutored nonprofessional counselors were given major
responsibility for service. It might be said that they were given *sole*
responsibility, since the parents and boys were not seen by the staff
members at any time, including intake. Applications were accepted by
mail, and boys were selected on the basis of research criteria and scores
on various instruments. For example, all the fifth- and sixth-graders
in Berkeley public schools rated all the boys in their classrooms on a
behavioral inventory generating five dimensions: isolation, hostility,
likability, attention-seeking, and atypicality. Teachers did the same, and
parents described their sons on a problem checklist and a personality
inventory. These and other instruments were administered again at the
end of the program to measure change.

No counselor was given information about his boy's problems; it was
hoped that the boy could begin the companionship knowing that his
"record" would not be held against him. The purpose of the companionship was to provide a friendly, nondemanding adult who would create
an atmosphere of trust and acceptance wherein the boy could experiment
with ways of relating to another person and risk new responses without
penalty. There were few prohibitions; for the most part counselors and
boys could do what they wished. They typically went on hikes, played

---

[19] A more detailed description of Group Assessment of Interpersonal
Traits is given in Gerald M. Goodman, "Companionship as Therapy: The
Use of Nonprofessional Talent," in J. T. Hart and T. M. Tomlinson, eds.,
New Directions in Client-Centered Psychotherapy (Boston: Houghton
Mifflin Co., in press).

games, built models, had serious talks, and visited public places. Perhaps the project staff should have been more concerned about worker autonomy, but one of the major purposes of the project was to demonstrate that a mental health program such as this one could be established and operated with little professional manpower.

From an administrative standpoint the program was a success. Counselors and boys were recruited with little difficulty, about 85 percent of the companionships endured the full eight months, there were few disappointments (and *no* scandals), no boy was reported to have been emotionally damaged by the experience, and at termination parents were generous in their approval. The results are currently being analyzed, and while it does not appear at this time that boys in the program improved more than their controls as a total group, certain types of boys seem to have benefited substantially.

AVAILABILITY OF NONPROFESSIONALS

If it can be granted that the planned replacement approach deserves greater attention from social welfare organizations interested in utilizing nonprofessionals, then one can ask where suitable applicants might be found in sufficient numbers. The writer suggests the college campus.[20] Here will be found a large reservoir of potential applicants within a small geographic area. Not only are college students accessible and generally free from family responsibilities, they are also energetic and interested. Numerous mental hospitals throughout the country are engaging college students as helpers, and VISTA and the Peace Corps have come to rely heavily on recent graduates. Stiles Hall (University YMCA), which sponsors the Interpersonal Relations Project, administers an array of social welfare programs in which college students participate. One program alone, the Student West Oakland Project, currently has four hundred students offering tutorial and related services to several thousand disadvantaged children. About half of these students must be replaced each academic year, but the recruits keep the program dynamic and innovative.

It is worth noting, additionally, that many colleges are located in rural areas where human services are in short supply. Only 4 percent

---

[20] *See* Earl C. Brennen, "College Students and Mental Health Programs for Children," *American Journal of Public Health,* Vol. 57, No. 10 (October 1967), pp. 1767–1771.

of the nation's psychiatric clinics are rurally located, yet one-third of all persons under 18 years of age reside in rural areas.[21]

SUMMARY

The planned replacement approach invites the participation of non-careerists in the community and thereby contributes to service delivery. In order to maximize this contribution, it has been suggested here that more attention be given in such programs to the selection of nonprofessionals than to their training and that the concepts of client vulnerability and worker autonomy be discarded. Finally, it has been proposed that college students represent an especially valuable source of nonprofessional helpers for the human services.

---

[21] Carol L. McCarty and Beatrice M. Rosen, "Mental Health and Mental Health Services in Rural Communities," in Lee G. Burchinal, ed., *Rural Youth in Crisis* (Washington, D.C.: U.S. Department of Health, Education & Welfare, Welfare Administration, 1965), pp. 207–217.

A Sociobehavioral Approach to the Treatment of Hospitalized Alcoholics

CORDELL H. THOMAS

This paper describes a program in which a group of patients at Eagleville Hospital and Rehabilitation Center—a 100-bed facility located a few miles outside Philadelphia, Pennsylvania, and serving a heterogeneous alcoholic population—were helped to use their own strengths to improve social functioning. Through undertaking roles related to life in the external world, the patients were able to learn and practice behavior that would have relevance to their post-hospital lives.

Most of the men at Eagleville had been on Skid Row or close to it. Their ages (with a few exceptions) ranged from 30 to 50. The majority of the patients were housed in the hospital itself. The group involved in the program reported in this paper lived in a cottage, one of two on the grounds. They were assigned randomly to the study group, which ranged in number from ten to twenty-seven, but in accordance with rules established by the men in the group, were not permitted to move from the hospital to the cottage until they had met certain "membership" requirements of the cottage.

SOCIAL FUNCTIONING

For the purpose of this study, social functioning was broken down into the subparts of work, social judgment, and interpersonal relations. Most of the patients had difficulty in one or all of these areas of functioning. Even though there were signs that they had met with some success earlier in life, most of these men did not show a residual repertoire in the specified areas. Therefore, means for them to learn and practice acceptable social behavior were set up. This involved designing an operant ward. In this unit prosocial behavior is systematically reinforced and strengthened, problem behavior is extinguished, and behavioral deficits and excesses are modified. The reinforcers used were for the most part such social reinforcers as praise and approval. Primary among these was instilling a sense of self-worth. This was an intrinsic reinforcer and became highly important to those in the group. Many prosocial responses were maintained and modified because, as the residents said, "Doing that made me feel worthwhile." [1]

Work

Nearly all of the approximately two hundred men involved in the general hospital program stated that employment was their major post-hospital goal. In a group discharged in September 1966, eight months prior to the inception of the program, all thirty-two men found jobs prior to discharge. However, only three actually showed up for work. Independent studies and the staff's experience showed that this was a typical occurrence and would be repeated.[2]

The work pattern most of these men had developed had led only to frustration. Often work was endured only as a means of obtaining money, which was spent on alcohol and became a symbol of frustration because the amount earned was so small. Yet it was important to the patient to have a job because it served as a membership card to society.

---

[1] William Glasser, *Reality Therapy* (New York: Harper & Row, 1965), pp. 9–11.

[2] For example, Ken Mesic of the Diagnostic and Relocation Center, Philadelphia, Pa., accumulated data indicating that few men are able to hold a full-time job immediately after treatment for alcoholism. The center has also found the same pattern among alcoholics in a halfway house.

The author learned that membership—i.e., belonging—was important to these men, so a patient-run industrial therapy program based on a membership system was developed. Staff set out to achieve in steps a system that would allow the patient to move up, thus forming a co-operatively staffed voluntary association.[3] The line position functions were performed by the members while the caseworker took a staff position.

Each incoming patient is immediately assigned a menial job by the industrial therapy co-ordinator, a patient who has worked his way up through promotions resulting from responsible work performance. The worker is rated by the work adviser (a staff member—cook, hospital engineer, and the like) at the end of each week. When he has demonstrated that he can handle a menial task in a responsible way he receives a reward, i.e., promotion, which gives him the choice of a better job. As he progresses in his ability to handle responsibility, he will eventually become a supervisor. As a result he earns something tangible as well as receiving recognition and approval from his fellow patients.

This progression gives a man a chance to demonstrate to himself and others just how much he can do. Ultimately he is expected to take a part-time job outside the institution. He can stay at one level as long as he wants, but most choose to move upward rapidly because of the prestige and extra privileges that come with increased responsibility.

The position of industrial therapy co-ordinator is one of the top three in the organization; the person in this position is elected by the cottage members only after he has earned eligibility for it. He is one of the policy-makers, can set up committees, and has the freedom that goes with the greater responsibility of his job. Because of this, his position is an attractive one, even though he receives no pay. During the program reported here, the co-ordinator was frequently involved in working out plans with the author; other professional staff members were used as consultants.

The process of working and earning rewards appears to be a step in the proper direction. Despite the fact that few patients outside the study group were involved in industrial therapy, they all learned to take pride in the work they did. When the industrial therapy program was begun, some of the men chosen for the group wanted to know why that group was the only one. Over time, this complaining attitude shifted to a belief that they were benefiting from the program. The complaints

---

[3] Eugene Litwak, "The School-Community Manual" (Ann Arbor: University of Michigan School of Social Work, 1966), chap. 8. (Mimeographed.)

were replaced by statements such as, "You don't get anything worthwhile unless you earn it." Patients outside the group who derided them because of their work were labeled "bums." Some men took their first steps in planning a career as a result of the cottage industrial therapy program.

Social Judgment

Social judgment included the broad base of rules, duties, and problemsolving. As with work, most of the men had not exercised their own judgment in the recent past. One man said: "I'm a baby, sure, but if someone tells me what to do all the time, I'll stay one." The usual course of treatment is to tell the patient what to do. Starting with the idea that the cottage was the patients' and they could be proud of it, staff raised their level of involvement in it to the final stage of voluntary association.[4] Thus a model from the world outside the hospital—the fraternity house—emerged and with a few alterations became a therapeutic model.

Prior to this it had become clear that staff had little control over the patients' behavior. For example, drinking was viewed by them as being the staff's problem. "Ratting" on a fellow patient was taboo. It was widely believed by the staff that they could not change this situation. One can easily imagine the obstacles such an attitude represented.

This problem was attacked early in the project, because if it had not been, therapy would have remained nothing more than a charade. With establishment of the cottage "fraternity," the duty of making rules was placed in the hands of the men; they grew to share a deep sense of pride and brotherhood. The goal was for each man to report drinking incidents of which he was aware through direct contact. This goal would be considered as having been achieved when the self-imposed cottage rules made this behavior mandatory for all members. Such a rule could be achieved only through a consensus of cottage members. Modeling

---

[4] Just as specific complex responses can be achieved through sharing with an individual, the same process can be achieved with a group or collective of individuals. *See* C. H. Thomas, "Use of Real Life Models for Treatment of People with Drinking Problems." Unpublished paper presented at the Seminar on Social Pathology, Temple University, Philadelphia, Pa., May 1968.

and role restructuring were used in conjunction with the shaping process that will be described.[5]

Group behavior analysis indicated a range of possibilities of which the lowest point was refusal to become involved. The following is a condensed partial hierarchy of behavior:

1. Patient admits knowledge of drinking in the hospital.
2. He confronts a member of his group who is drinking.
3. He asks a member of his group to report himself to the group.
4. He asks a member of his group to report himself to the cottage chairman.
5. If a man refuses to report himself, he tells the cottage chairman.

Each step was discussed until there was a consensus. The consensus was reinforced by the therapist and the group members' reaffirmation of solidarity. Those who move up a step in this hierarchy are positively reinforced by the group as a result of their changed behavior.

The men eventually redefined "ratting." The man who let a fellow cottage member drink and ruin his chances for recovery was now considered the rat. The group wrote strong and effective rules and then took pride in being the first group in the hospital to face the matter squarely.

The men engaged in other prosocial behavior such as a cottage clean-up detail, an ad hoc committee that passed on readmission to the hospital and cottage as well as pass privileges, and an executive group that consulted with the therapist about plans for the growth of the cottage program. One of the most interesting innovations was a log book. Each time a man left the hospital grounds he signed out, giving his destination and expected time of return. When he returned to the cottage he was signed in by a fellow resident. This modification of the buddy system was intended to help a man see how well he could carry out his own day-by-day plans and commitments. The log book also emphasized the group's responsibility for greeting the returning member and sharing his experiences, good and bad. These techniques helped all involved measure more accurately how well they kept their commitments.

-----

[5] Modeling is what is involved when a person takes on the attributes of another—imitation is a form of modeling. It is a type of interpersonal influence. Role restructuring is the process of rearranging the structure of the expectations related to the position a person holds (e.g., teacher-pupil) along various dimensions, e.g., time, context, strength, and so on.

Interpersonal Relations

The matter of interpersonal relations posed some interesting situations. Once again many of the patients showed a deficit of skills; some may never have learned adequate skills.

All of the cottage residents were involved in committees from the time they became members. Some committees were led by elected officers, but ad hoc committees gave everyone a chance to become involved on a variety of levels. All of these committees were needed to maintain and assist the growth of the cottage. More important, however, was the increased intensity and depth of interpersonal relations. In the staffed therapy group, cottage matters came up frequently. Most of these were such everyday matters as keeping the cottage clean.

Solving the everyday cottage problems was easily transposed into solving problems of everyday life. Problems with children, sex, dating, and in many other areas started to come into therapy. The six hours of group therapy scheduled each week were not enough. Bull sessions—impromptu, small, leaderless discussions—were suggested by the residents as an answer. These were so successful that staff and patients who were not connected with the cottage program dropped in to listen and learn. Rules of therapy such as confidentiality were followed in these sessions. Such sessions would not have worked had the problem-solving committees not been so well run by the members prior to the initiation of bull-session therapy.

The area of interpersonal skills was handled largely by the social affairs co-ordinator with the help of the membership and the suggestions of the therapist. One activity was an exchange program with other institutions. These plans were made to develop social situations that involved women. The first bull session therapy was planned as part of an exchange involving female alcoholics from another institution. These exchanges awakened forgotten feelings in many men and left an indelible mark of pride on the residents.

SOCIAL ROLE

The remainder of this paper will focus on social role, although its presence has doubtless been recognized throughout.

The role of patient carries with it certain expectations, the first of which is that of dependency and compliance by the patient with hospital roles—with the daily routine and the decisions that are made for him.[6] He is not expected to fulfill his normal role responsibilities; there is also a de-emphasis of external world power and prestige—e.g., removal of valuables, driver's license, and so on and enforcement of a general or common level of status. Thomas states that to these must be added the expectation of tolerance for prognostic uncertainty.[7] Role discontinuity is built into the situation.

In the cottage this was avoided as much as possible. The basic difference was the vast contrast between the role of member and that of patient. There is or should be no counterpart outside the hospital of the patient role. As members, the men were rewarded for good work by promotion rather than by being discharged. As members they felt pride and a sense of self-worth rather than as being dependent and sick.

Each man assigned to the group made out an application for membership. He and his application were reviewed by an ad hoc committee from the cottage. These peer staffings were also used for readmission to the hospital and proved valuable from at least two points: (1) anticipatory learning is achieved as the incoming man is involved in the group and prepared for new role expectations and (2) making this choice emphasized the fact that the residents are, in the end, the ones who stand to gain or lose as a result of decisions made regarding membership. Commitments are also exchanged.

Each new member received a handbook written by the cottage members that outlined clearly the steps a man could take leading to a position of high status such as co-ordinator.[8] The handbook was as "real world" in orientation as possible.

CONCLUSIONS

This thumbnail sketch would not be complete without some comment on where the members stood a year after initiation of the program. Most are sober and functioning at a much higher level. One of the cottage chairmen is preparing to go to a school of social work.

Only three "bomb out" incidents (i.e., patients got drunk) occurred, but perhaps more important than this is that the bond of membership continued—this bond almost reached the level of a family. One group

---

[6] S. H. King, *Perceptions of Illness and Medical Practice* (New York: Russell Sage Foundation, 1962).

[7] Edwin J. Thomas, *Behavioral Science for Social Workers* (New York: Free Press, 1967), p. 62.

[8] Copies of this handbook, "An Experiment in Living," are available from the author.

of men sought follow-up treatment and together reshaped that program to resemble their cottage. Another group has moved together in an effort to set up a "cottage" or voluntary association in a series of apartments. They have persevered over a period of more than a year despite some financial and administrative setbacks.

It would certainly seem that the intended inpatient hospital services were delivered effectively through the use of external world delivery models. While the program focused on alcoholics, it seems clear that it has relevance to many groups social workers seek to serve. Some people have expressed fear that this much power in the hands of the service consumer will result in a loss of professional control or status. The writer would observe that the opposite is true and that at its best social work is a serving and enabling profession. Furthermore, the profession should strive to eliminate the traditional patient or client role and reach people on their own grounds.

PART IV

The Consumer As an Action System

The traditional principles of client participation and self-determination roll off the tongue easily. But in recent years we have become more sophisticated as to what these concepts mean in practice. Client choices are circumscribed in the typical service relationship. If there are conflicts in judgment between the professional and his client, it is the professional judgment that tends to prevail. Theoretically, the client has the option of withdrawing from the relationship. But increasingly we are dealing with clients who are required by law to continue with the agency (e.g., probationers and mental patients) or have no realistic alternative (e.g., recipients of public aid).

Self-determination has taken on a different meaning, one evolving in a political context. Consumers and potential consumers of social services are banding together to bargain with the agency or set up alternative systems. In Part IV several variations on this theme of client action are examined.

Green presents the case history of a neighborhood house that was developed with full participation of the neighborhood residents. Rosenberg and Glasgow outline more basic shifts of control to the black community. Rosenberg proposes the deliberate transfer of economic as well as political power to the ghetto residents. Subsequent events have borne out his pessimistic view about the availability of governmental and foundation resources for community action programs. Glasgow gives the example of what happened in the Watts area of Los Angeles in the wake of the 1965 disorders and how a new sense of community arose.

In view of the historic commitment of social workers and other liberals to the goal of an integrated society, these approaches that emphasize institutions of, by, and for the black community strike a jarring note. And yet we are aware that this is precisely the direction in which significant elements in the inner cities are moving. One hopes that this represents a stage along the way to eventual reintegration of society at a more satisfactory level than the traditional lopsided relationship between the races.

Specifically, what should be the stance of the professional social worker in relation to these new developments? Abels proposes a mediating role, albeit one with a bias in favor of the consumer group. Mejia and Woods, on the other hand, urge out-and-out advocacy, in a partisan sense, and activism clearly aligned with the citizen group against the social service institutions. Their paper points up the problem of obtaining the necessary resources for such operations.

Basing Community Action in a Neighborhood House

ALVIN E. GREEN

The economic, social, and psychological conditions of poverty may combine to limit severely a poor person's development of individual potential, freedom of choice, and control over normal events in his daily life. A sense of powerlessness in what may be perceived to be an arbitrary environment may influence and sustain self-doubt among the poor and afford them fewer options—including detachment and/or hostility—to meet their needs for autonomy. A legacy of hopelessness and anger may be passed from parent to child along with a rigid and inadequate set of skills with which to cope in society, and the cycle of poverty is thus perpetuated.

The neighborhoods in which the poor live often reveal their feelings of hopelessness, alienation, and isolation. Living in a neighborhood labeled a slum, ghetto, blighted area, or the like would seem to enhance one's feeling of distance from the community at large. During their lifetime, especially if they are members of an ethnic minority, the in-

---

NOTE: The content of this presentation is drawn in part from a monograph by Louis A. Zurcher and Alvin E. Green, *From Dependency to Dignity: An Exploratory Study of Some Individual and Social Consequences of a Neighborhood House,* to be published by Behavioral Publications.

habitants probably have been both overtly and covertly informed that there must be something wrong with them, a damnation "proved" by the fact that they cannot get themselves out of poverty or out of "that neighborhood." If the residents' contacts with the community's formal organizations have been only through their role as passive recipients of service, and if this enforced dependency is unacceptable, then the relationship between helpers and helped may serve further to label low-income people pejoratively and to intensify their isolation and alienation from the community at large.

One of the results of a life of poverty may be a defensive and motivated withdrawal from the community as a perceived source of psychological and physical harm. Thus it can be difficult for poor persons to allow themselves enough personal contact with formal community organizations to discover, as members of other socioeconomic groups do, that such organizations can be *used*, can be influenced and made relevant to them; that they do not necessarily have to be passive when interacting with these organizations.

How can this complex problem be dealt with? How does one stimulate changes in confidence, motivation, and skill among the poor and at the same time stimulate changes in socioeconomic structures that create and maintain conditions of poverty? In 1964 the Economic Opportunity Act proclaimed a national strategy for resolving that complex problem. A primary intent of the act was to stimulate or accelerate change in the socioeconomic structures of communities by going beyond the usual expedient of mechanically supplying material resources to the poor. The plan was to involve the poor, through "maximum feasible participation," in decisions and processes that lead to acquisition of resources. Its strategy of funds, programs, and active involvement of the poor was designed with the hope of disrupting the cycle of poverty.

On paper, maximum feasible participation was an invitation to the poor to exert power in and control over newly formed organizations that were to be concerned with their welfare. In contrast to more traditional community techniques for dealing with the poor, beneficiaries were to be among decision-makers; clients were to be colleagues. Implementation of the concept of maximum feasible participation in itself may engender significant social change. Jealously guarded professional status, safe distance from clients, coveted political and economic power, and cherished stereotypes can be challenged by meaningful entry of the previously disenfranchised poor into areas of decision-making and power within the community. Among various Community Action Programs funded by the Office of Economic Opportunity for implementing maximum feasible participation of the poor is the "neighborhood house."

OEO neighborhood-based programs exist under an assortment of names. In this paper the term "neighborhood house" will be used to refer to both (1) a specific organization studied and discussed here and (2) the general idea of a neighborhood organization that enhances opportunity for participation of the residents and encourages development in them of a sense of ownership, social roles, self-confidence, self-determination, and a feeling that they have the potential for controlling their environment and have a choice of alternatives in matters concerning their daily lives, and that provides them with an opportunity to learn new coping skills from people with different experiences and backgrounds.

The neighborhood house is not an isolated organization at war with the rest of the community or an agency-owned affiliate. Rather, it is conceptualized as a bridge, perhaps temporary in nature, between alienated poor and uninterested, misinformed, or uninvolved nonpoor. Of prime importance, the neighborhood house is seen as the property of the neighborhood people and no others. As thus idealized, it is a strategy, an agent for social change, and a medium through which community-wide services may be made relevant and delivered to a population heretofore generally excluded from or outside the reach of those services.

The Highland Park–Pierce neighborhood in Topeka, Kansas, consists of approximately four hundred acres containing some fifteen hundred residents, of whom 90 percent are Negro. The community suffers economically, 60 percent of the population having an annual income of less than $5,000 and 30 percent earning under $3,000. The unemployment rate is 10 percent, the highest in the city. The area also has the highest rates of juvenile offenses and illegitimate births. Eighty percent of the roads are unpaved. Over half the homes are more than twenty-five years old and are shacklike in appearance. This area has the highest incidence of inadequate plumbing facilities and of housing blight in the city of Topeka. The residents of Highland Park–Pierce (which is also called Pierce Addition) have felt little identification with their own neighborhood or with the community at large. One of the indigenous leaders in the area summarized the views of the residents:

> They just don't feel that they are in the mainstream of the society here. Sometimes we get the feeling that we're almost living in another country. Though it's not that we have property like they

have in the big cities where everyone is jammed all together. We
don't have that. But in some ways what we have is worse. That's
because nobody notices us. There are no big streets that come
through Highland Park–Pierce so other people can see that there
really is poverty here. This area is kind of like a whirlpool, you
know, where all kinds of cars and people go running around the
outside, but they never see the deep holes in the middle. Lots of
us have jobs in other parts of the city, but all our other activities
are right here in Highland Park–Pierce. Our kids usually play
here, too, although there are almost no organized things for them
to do. What breaks my heart is that we've got so much potential
here. Well I don't know how we're going to do it. But somehow
we've got to get attention to ourselves. Those people in Watts got
attention to themselves. I don't like that way, and I hope we never
have to do it that way. I hope we can maybe find some other way
first.

ESTABLISHING A NEIGHBORHOOD HOUSE

Through the machinery of the local OEO board, neighborhood committees were developed to serve as representative bodies of the neighborhood
on the parent body. Those initially serving on the committee were residents elected by a small community-conscious portion of the neighborhood population. The members of the Pierce Addition Committee
reviewed neighborhood and individual needs revealed by a survey they
had conducted. They discussed possible alternative programs with
Topeka OEO staff and decided that those needs could best be met by
establishing a neighborhood house in Highland Park–Pierce.

The officers and representatives of the neighborhood committee agreed
on goals stressing the facilitation of services to (1) provide a point of
contact between low-income persons and the services and (2) provide
a full range of counseling and other educational services for all age groups
in the neighborhood. For target neighborhood residents there was
another major, although unwritten, purpose for the neighborhood house
—"to give us the opportunity to run our own program."

The neighborhood committee and the Topeka OEO staff agreed that
the neighborhood house program should not be handled by a single
delegate agency. Rather, the local share of the funding was to be supplied by organizations that would not place restrictions on how the funds
were to be spent and the OEO board would be the overall sponsor,
with immediate guidance to be provided by an advisory council. The

advisory council was to consist of eight neighborhood residents and seven representatives from community agencies. The neighborhood committee members insisted that *they* choose the community agency representatives who were to serve on the advisory council. The criterion by which these individuals were chosen was demonstrated interest rather than organizational position. Furthermore, the neighborhood committee cautiously decided, with constant reference to the importance of their continuing to have a voice in the decision-making, which community organizations they would approach to help them accumulate the local financial share.

By community consensus, the three staff positions—director, neighborhood aide, and secretary—were indigenous and indigenously chosen. All were residents who were seen as committed to the people of Pierce Addition; were person oriented, empathic, and able to relate to the residents; had knowledge of the families and neighborhood conditions; and were knowledgeable about the "outside" community.

Formally, the house hours were established as 8:00 A.M.–9:30 P.M. Monday through Saturday, but informally the staff are on call twenty-four hours a day. The immediate and continuous availability of staff is felt to be essential.

Neighborhood House As a Bridge

During the initial stage, the staff viewed the neighborhood house as a bridge between community organizations and the neighborhood residents. Staff's view of the functions of the house coincided with the views held by those who came to the house for help of one kind or another. The first question asked by most of the residents was: "What can it do for me?"

Three months after the house had formally opened its doors, the staff were averaging two hundred contacts with neighborhood residents each month, including follow-up consultations. Individual problems confronted and solved were concerned with such basic matters as housing, food, clothing, mental and physical health, employment, bail bonds and legal help, loans and financing, education, family difficulties, and recreation. The staff served as a clearing house for individual, family, and community problems; provided information on individual request or by staff initiative when it was felt that a resident would be interested in some specific fact; made referrals when necessary and facilitated such referrals by introductory or clarifying letters, phone calls, or, more commonly, by accompanying the resident to the referral source. When direct services were necessary, agency representatives were invited to the neighborhood, where the service was then proffered either at the house or in the resident's home.

There is no doubt that a neighborhood house needs agency co-operation and expertise. Furthermore, many of the social problems confronted by the house have traditionally been concerns of established agencies, and the accumulation of their experiences can save the house from making costly mistakes and duplicating services. However, unless the house *invites* the co-operation of these agencies, the typical distance between the nonpoor helpers and the helped poor may be maintained, and nothing will change. If an agency exerts tight control over a neighborhood house, it may have some opportunity to improve the quality and quantity of services to low-income people, but it probably will not provide the participative process experience for the poor that can subsequently engender significant psychosocial change in them.

While making contacts, building programs, and providing services with the added purpose of enhancing the dignity of neighborhood residents, the house staff were firmly establishing themselves and the whole concept of a neighborhood house as worthy of trust. A price was expected and encouraged in order to get help from the house, that price being a commitment on the part of the resident to participate, risk himself, and engage with the staff in the helping process. Assistance was intended to conform to the individual, not vice versa. The house was on neighborhood turf and staffed indigenously. Support, in whatever form needed, was there whenever and however wanted. No restrictions, no criticism, implicit or explicit, were associated with assistance—unless the individual "tried to sell himself short."

But something more was being offered by the house than a proliferation of available services. That something more seemed to be apparent to many of the beneficiaries who lived in the neighborhood. They felt for the first time that they were initiating the contact with service organizations, and therefore felt less embarrassed about asking for help. They were able to approach relatively impersonal agencies with the personal support of the neighborhood house staff. Consequently, the agencies began to be seen as less fearsome and formidable. Successful experience in one encounter with a complex organization tended to generate self-confidence, which generalized to other encounters with such organizations.

A Sense of Community

As individuals developed greater self-confidence, along with trust in the house, they began getting together to seek to resolve concerns shared by all. At first small groups along the lines of a class or study group developed—e.g., health, homemaking, arts and crafts, adult education classes, employment counseling, and the like. Each group gained experience in organizing itself and being responsible for inviting outside resource people to "their" gatherings. With their frequently overlapping memberships, these classes increased a bond among residents and a sense of unity developed. Efforts and interests expanded from group to neighborhood concerns, and communication through regularly scheduled neighborhood town hall-type meetings was expanded by the community's development of a neighborhood weekly newsletter, hand distributed by the residents' children.

When it was learned that a proposal to rezone a section of their neighborhood was before the city council—a rezoning deemed generally unbeneficial to the neighborhood and, more particularly, a course of action being taken without their approval—the community mobilized with resources provided by the house. Using available legitimate means, they effectively blocked the action. This success encouraged greater community efforts; they initiated community rehabilitation projects such as street repair, removal of placarded housing, weed control, and so on.

The "system" seemed to them far less formidable now, far less alien. From firsthand experience of the workings of complex social structures, residents were gaining insight into how the structures affected them and, more important, how they could affect the structures. As action evolved, so also did a new set of stated goals for the neighborhood house. The first set of goals stressed facilitation of services. The second stressed more centrally purposive social change, such as (1) to develop independence, autonomy, and better overall functioning on the part of the people in the neighborhood, (2) to transform passive, uninvolved, apathetic receivers of others' beneficence into helpers and active citizens, and (3) to enhance the neighborhood by developing greater social integration and cohesion among the residents.

Initially, as the neighborhood house began to develop, residents were concerned about what the programs could do for them as individuals. As a sense of neighborhood grew, through the direct participation of about 85 percent of the residents, they began to experience the value of group efforts toward social action that would have impact on the neighborhood. Increase of self-initiated contacts with agencies and involvement in concerted social action seemed to generate among participating residents a new realization of their dignity, worth, and potency. Reinforced by their now-demonstrated competence and strengthened by awareness of membership in a cohesive community, the participants were willing to extend themselves beyond their own turf. The experience of ownership of and responsibility for self and neighborhood began to generalize to the community at large. Issues dealing with community-wide political, social, and economic conditions were now areas of interest and concern. Increasingly, statements were drafted representing the neighborhood's positions on a variety of these issues, with the result that city, governmental, and other organizational representatives increasingly began to approach the Pierce Addition community for their views and support.

"Old-timers," after a year's contact with the house, tended to view their social environment with less skepticism and more confidence than residents who were just beginning to become involved. Furthermore, the opportunity for participant democracy in house and neighborhood committee meetings invited and stimulated debate on issues important to the neighborhood. At times meetings would become heated as the participants tested their ideas and, most significantly, themselves in a climate in which discussion was free and open. In such a climate, emotional as well as intellectual restrictions were lifted, with the result that in some meetings, as one participant remembered, "it was difficult to tell what we did more, cuss or discuss."

Members differed in the degree to which they were willing to trust representatives of agencies and social organizations. They differed in the degree to which they thought the poor or the Negro could effectively become involved in the system without actually having to overthrow it. They argued not only about specific activities, but about strategies and tactics for implementing these activities.

The participants, depending on the degree and kind of experience they had had with others, varied in their future orientation, achievement motivation, activity, and willingness to gamble with something new. These differences, and the climate for unhindered expression, generated some volatile discussions, most of which were worked through to a conclusion and most of which seemed comfortable and educational for the participants.

It now seemed explicitly or implicitly understood by most participants that the purpose of the house was to stimulate social change, and that meant change in opinions, values, and attitudes about self, neighborhood, and community. Consensus and dissensus were essential to the process. The internalization of neighborhood and community identity and the evolution of a united approach toward social action did not mean that the participant had to sacrifice his individuality. On the contrary, often his individuality appeared to be enhanced by his increasing ability to operate successfully in widening social spheres.

Liaison with Other Agencies

As a result of their experience with the neighborhood house, participating residents at least appeared to be altering perceptions of themselves, the neighborhood, the system, and the community at large. Members of the system and the community at large seemed correspondingly to be altering their views of the Pierce Addition and its residents. Personnel from agencies and service organizations with whom the neighborhood house staff interacted noticeably and rather quickly shifted to a collegial relationship with the house director and staff. Increasingly, representatives from such agencies as the county department of welfare, family service and guidance center, urban renewal agency, public health department, board of education, and the small business and loan association called on the neighborhood house staff not only for reciprocal services, but for advice and consultation concerning case and neighborhood problems.

For example, some of the local schools were experiencing difficulties with a few of their students from the Pierce area and were unsuccessful in recruiting parental assistance in resolving the problems. The schools contacted the neighborhood house for suggestions about ways to engage the parents successfully. In response, the house staff reviewed in detail with the school officials the feelings that some of these parents have toward the school system, especially with regard to meeting teachers and administrative officials in the school setting itself. The director further explained that whereas school officials often imputed lack of motivation to low-income parents, some low-income parents imputed a lack of real helping motivation to the school officials. The staff suggested use of the neighborhood house as a place where parents and school officials could meet. In this way the residents could feel more comfortable, secure, and perhaps more confident. Furthermore, the school officials could openly demonstrate their desire to be helpful by having "come out of those big offices." The procedure proved to be quite successful, and subsequently other agencies availed themselves of the same opportunity for direct contact with the residents in a nonthreatening environment.

Not only were the anxieties of the residents often reduced, therefore making possible their freer use of the agencies' facilities, but simultaneously an educational process developed for the agencies' personnel themselves. Thus, statements citing lack of motivation, apathy, lack of involvement, and so on were heard less frequently. Agency personnel had successful encounters with residents who had previously been difficult to reach, which they found surprising and gratifying. Many officials verbally expressed appreciation of the house's efforts. More important, their operating policies expanded to include consultation with the neighborhood house.

Social Worker's Role

A social worker from the sponsoring agency was made available to the house on a participating consultative basis. The role model and informal training provided by the worker served to influence the director's effectiveness with agency representatives and the resident population. Briefly, this worker functioned as educator and decoder by sharing information regarding the nature, function, and language of an institution. He served as a means by which the staff and residents could share ideas and develop alternatives that previously had been perceived as being unavailable to them.

The concepts and processes of individual and group dynamics were vital in helping the staff and residents anticipate, plan, and deal with the burgeoning individual and group concepts, crises, and experiences resulting from their search for individual and community maturity. In particular, the social worker, through participating in the full range of community activities, served in an enabling role and helped facilitate communication between the neighborhood and the larger community at the behest of that neighborhood, until this was no longer necessary.

An essential task for the worker was to anticipate problems and support and help the staff and other emerging community leaders work through the conflicts they experienced in their developing marginality, from having in effect two roles—as neighborhood resident and Establishment member, of being both one of "us" and one of "them." The social worker consistently sought to enhance the staff's understanding of the residents' feelings, while the residents always served to remind them that their strength and identification came from the neighborhood.

Similarly, the role model and informal training provided by the director profoundly influenced the social worker's effectiveness with neighborhood residents. At first guardedly, but soon openly, they shared frustrations, satisfactions, and strategies associated with social innovation. The evolution of their relationship, and consequently the evolution of the relationship between the neighborhood and supporting agency, demonstrated the feasibility of indigenous leaders and organizations working closely and beneficially with professional leaders and organizations—as long as experiences can be shared by functional equals in a co-operative rather than competitive climate. It was clear that a successful relationship could only develop as each demonstrated a willingness to innovate with his own social role and tolerate resulting ambiguities, uncertainties, and conflicts. At the same time, they had to adapt to one another and to the unique task of developing a neighborhood house.

Whether the house can continue to operate with purposive autonomy remains to be seen. Will the communty resistances to and pressures on the house become more severe when and if it becomes increasingly outspoken on civil rights issues? At what point would burgeoning action orientation begin to alienate co-operating agencies and organizations? Will the neighborhood house become increasingly formalized, become more distant from the poor, and suffer the consequences of its own institutionalization?

SUMMARY

The neighborhood house appears to be demonstrating a potential for accomplishing far-reaching goals. It is serving as a training ground for the participating poor in which they develop organizational skills, new and more complex social roles, and a sense of identity with peers, neighborhood, and the broader community. The house is stimulating a sense of ownership among participants and others in the neighborhood, allowing them significant control over and immediate results from activities of which they are the beneficiaries.

The house is providing a shift in agency-client relationships—the neighborhood residents are inviting the co-operation of community agencies through *their* neighborhood house. The latter establishes neighborhood residents as the instigators of agency operations, instead of in their more typical role as passive recipients of service. At the same time, the co-operating agencies are finding new access to perhaps previously unreachable persons, and thus accomplishing their organizational purposes better. This access is being expanded even further by the provision of indigenous workers who can approach the unaffiliated poor more readily and less threateningly than agency personnel.

The neighborhood residents are becoming oriented to the neighborhood house in a fashion unlike their previous experiences with organizations. They are having a hand in determining what specific poverty programs their house will undertake, based on their perceptions of neighborhood needs, and they are beginning to understand the utility of organizations for accomplishing specific goals. The roles and attitudes developed through participation in and contact with the neighborhood house are becoming generalized to other community organizations and are encouraging the residents to interact with the latter in a less passive and dependent fashion.

The neighborhood house is demonstrating its potential for being a locus for effective and indigenously determined social action. A sense of neighborhood is emerging where little but geographic proximity existed before. The dynamics of the generative process of participation, ownership, and self-direction seem to be generalizing to residents and neighborhood associations with other components of the community at large.

From Colony to Community: Building a Financial Base in the Black Ghetto

MARVIN ROSENBERG

While social work professionals are still talking about effecting modifications in the delivery and adequacy of social services, organizations of poor people and militant blacks are talking about how to take over and control completely the entire social welfare apparatus that operates in their communities. The heretofore powerless consumers of social services have decided that the products of the various social welfare systems (and other human service systems) are so irrelevant and contrary to their self-interest that it is not enough merely to have a voice in policy-making. They believe these services must come under entirely new management. It is becoming increasingly clear to the urban poor that services managed by suburban elites and manned by trained professionals are essentially mechanisms of social control. While many social workers working with the poor would like to think they share common objectives with their clients, the ugly fact is that most of our energy is spent helping poor people adapt to intolerable circumstances.

So now we are about to be confronted by a revolt of the captives. They have found us out and know that we are the well-meaning agents of the forces of reaction and racism rather than advocates of real change. The day may soon be approaching when social workers will be barred from ghetto neighborhoods as some researchers are in Harlem. A number of citizens' organizations in Harlem have told researchers who come with questionnaires to go away unless they come back with jobs, a physician, or something they need. People are tired of being studied. They want income, housing, jobs, health care, quality education, and a voice in the running of society. This new militancy and demand for control is a direct expression of the new mood of the human rights revolution. Before getting into a discussion of issues related to funding self-help organizations, it is first necessary to trace briefly the emergence of this new militancy.

EMERGENCE OF MILITANCY

The early phases of the civil rights revolution placed a great emphasis on social status and economic reform. The massive demonstrations aimed at integrating public accommodations and housing were largely efforts on behalf of the small percentage of Negroes who could afford to travel, eat in a restaurant, or buy a house. While most Negroes identified with this phase of the civil rights movement because it attacked some forms of white oppression, it was not really their struggle. The social status phase of the movement played an important role in setting the stage for the deeper power struggles that were to come.

The next phase of the movement focused heavily on economic reform and consisted largely of a plea to extend and complete the promises of the New Deal. The leading Negro ideologists—Bayard Rustin, A. Philip Randolph, and Dr. Martin Luther King, Jr.—saw the basic problem in terms of inadequate income, unemployment, poor housing, and the lack of access to economic mobility.[1] The poverty program and other bits of New Deal or Great Society legislation were modest responses to this new emphasis. Most analysts agree that if Negroes had not been out in the streets demonstrating, there probably would have been no Economic Opportunity Act in 1964. The writer believes that such legislation succeeded primarily in raising aspirations and heightening expectations among the large masses of Negro poor. Low-income Negroes expected the programs to have some relationship to basic problems such as inadequate income, massive ghetto unemployment, and deteriorated housing. The analysis that led to the EOA focused on structural and institutional problems as the root causes of poverty. However, the programs that subsequently emerged were designed pri-

---

[1] Bayard Rustin, "A Way Out of the Exploding Ghetto," *New York Times Magazine,* October 8, 1967, p. 14.

marily to deal with individual problems and assumed family weaknesses. If the poverty program still has any meaning, it is because of its symbolic value rather than its substantive merits. It perhaps serves the function of reminding the public and policy-makers that a commitment to change has been made.

Before the summer of 1967, there was a general belief on the part of many reform-minded policy-makers that the solutions to the problems of urban unrest and disorders lie primarily in huge doses of public and private spending. Leading urbanologists such as Michael Harrington, Daniel P. Moynihan, John Kenneth Galbraith, and Leon Keyserling advocated massive spending in the public sector for projects such as housing rehabilitation, manpower training, educational innovation, and federal job creation.[2] In a number of cities such as Detroit and New Haven, large-scale reform had already been initiated by progressive mayors who reportedly understood the problems. No one was prepared for the massive, warlike character of the Newark and Detroit riots of 1967 and the lesser but significant disorders in New Haven. The ferocity and magnitude of these "rebellions" shattered the illusion among liberals concerning the simple formula for dealing with urban unrest. While to some analysts the meaning of the violence was that economic infusions were insufficient, others continued to search for deeper and more complex causative explanations.

In view of the fact that a sizable proportion of the rioters were employed men who were not living in the most deteriorated sections of the ghetto, it was clear that more than simple economic explanations had to be examined.[3] The exhortations to violence by Stokely Carmichael and H. Rap Brown went beyond the economic dimensions of the problem. They were direct appeals to manhood, dignity, and power through the use of militant social action and direct violence. They offered the ghetto resident a new route to dignity and selfhood. There was an implicit understanding on the part of Black Power leaders that power, blackness, manhood, and dignity were inextricably interwoven. It was no longer important *only* to get resources, jobs, housing, better

[2] Michael Harrington, *The Other America: Poverty in the United States* (New York: Macmillan Co., 1962); Daniel P. Moynihan, *The Negro Family: The Case for National Action* (Washington, D.C.: U.S. Department of Labor, 1965); John Kenneth Galbraith, *The Affluent Society* (Boston: Houghton Mifflin Co., 1958); Leon H. Keyserling, *Poverty or Progress* (Washington, D.C.: Conference on Economic Progress, 1964).

[3] Lee Rainwater, "Open Letter on White Justice and the Riots," *Transaction,* Vol. 4, No. 5 (September 1967), pp. 22–27.

income; it was how they were obtained and who controlled them. Control and power became the major issues—often overshadowing the quantitative nature of the resources themselves. There was a growing rejection of the paternalistic patterns of the New Deal and the Great Society, since these programs did nothing to alter power relationships and bestow dignity on those who saw dignity in terms of control of resources and institutions within the ghetto. Collective political and economic power for Negroes was seen as having a direct bearing on feelings of personal power and self-esteem for the individual Negro.[4]

Several newly emerging militant ideologists of the Black Power movement go beyond the appeal for massive resources and political control.[5] They expound the doctrine that dignity and freedom can be achieved only through direct violent confrontation with the white man and his institutions. The new ideology stems largely from the writings of Franz Fanon, a West Indian psychiatrist who interpreted the Algerian liberation struggle as a racial revolution. Fanon's *The Wretched of the Earth* is a psychological-political analysis of colonialism in which he states that self-emancipation requires participation in a struggle to bring about cultural and structural change, and that "all means were useful to this end, including, of course, violence."[6] As Don Watts, the editor of *Liberator* (a militant Black Nationalist journal) told reporters after Newark and Detroit, "You're going around thinking all the brothers in these riots are old winos; nothing could be further from the truth. These cats are ready to die for something. And they know why. They all read. Not one of them hasn't read the Bible." "The Bible?" the reporter asked. Watts replied: "Fanon . . . . you'd better get this book. Every brother on a rooftop can quote Fanon."[7]

Many liberal individuals and organizations sincerely seeking change argue that radical social reform will not be achieved through the militant pressure tactics of citizen action organizations. They argue that abrasive social action and protest, even within the boundaries of law, create

---

[4] Christopher Lasch, "The Trouble with Black Power," *New York Review of Books,* February 20, 1968, p. 5.

[5] Among the most prominently mentioned leaders are Melana Ron Karenga, the leader of a militant organization in Watts named "US," Hugh Newton, president of the Black Panther Organization in Oakland, Calif., and Max Stanford, chairman of the Revolutionary Action Movement.

[6] Franz Fanon, *The Wretched of the Earth* (New York: Grove Press, 1963).

[7] Aristide and Vera Zolberg, "The Americanization of Franz Fanon," *The Public Interest,* No. 9 (Fall 1967), p. 50.

too much resistance among influential decision-makers. Such militancy, they point out, polarizes issues and makes the opposition unwilling to compromise. While there are elements of truth in these objections, the arguments are counterbalanced by a more persuasive set of realities. For more than thirty years, liberals have been striving to achieve social reform from within a pervasively conservative political structure. Achievements such as Medicare and civil rights legislation were won only after long years of coalition-building, lobbying, and political compromise. These time-consuming, expensive approaches simply do not measure up to the climate that the new militancy has created. The pace and the method of change are now out of the hands of the liberal Establishment. The events of 1968—culminating in the assassination of Dr. King—the Poor People's Campaign, and the prospects that face the country are leaving decision-makers with an ever narrowing range of alternatives. Those in power will be compelled either to produce substantial change or resort to massive repression. The mood of the ghettos across the country is not receptive to more promises and modest compromises. The discrepancy between rhetoric and substance has reached a psychologically intolerable point. Even so-called responsible Negro leaders such as Whitney M. Young, Jr., have made it clear they cannot continue to talk about legitimate means of redressing grievances in the face of such massive intransigence in Congress. It is within this new militant context that the issue of funding must be discussed.

THE ISSUE OF FUNDING

Jesse Gray, the militant Harlem organizer, told an audience of two hundred antipoverty workers: "Take the man's crumbs but use them in your own way." [8] "The man's crumbs" referred not only to federal funds, but all the dribbles of money that church organizations, foundations, and special funding bodies dole out as their "significant contributions" to combating poverty and racism. Gray did not make the statement facetiously or in anger. He had apparently long ago accepted the fact that those seeking radical change could not expect the people and institutions needing change to supply the money to do the job.

Most of the poverty workers he was addressing were Negro and were recruited from ghetto areas. They listened attentively, but recoiled visibly at the militant call to organize and confront the Establishment.

---

[8] Speech to the Leadership Development Training Program, Case Western Reserve University, Cleveland, Ohio, March 10, 1968.

Some of these same people a few years back had been in the forefront of the battle against de facto segregation in the Cleveland public schools and had marched along with 20,000 other Clevelanders to pledge their support to an uncompromising struggle for freedom. Now these same workers—employed by the local Community Action Program agency— were too frightened even to testify anonymously before a high-level mayor's committee studying the abuses of welfare recipients by schools, hospitals, and the courts. While they still identified with the impoverishment and suffering of their neighbors, the fear of losing their jobs reduced them to settling for traditional client-by-client salvage operations.

Present Funding Picture

This example illustrates the major dilemma facing citizen action organizations that seriously want to address fundamental institutional change. The experiences of independent poverty, civil rights, and Black Power organizations with funding over the past years has been fraught with manipulation, cynicism, pettiness, and massive bureaucratic bungling. Federal agencies such as the Office of Economic Opportunity, the National Institute of Mental Health, Department of Labor, and now Model Cities have ambivalently held out the carrot of social action to militant groups. Sympathetic technicians within the various governmental agencies tried to teach grantsmanship to the applicant organizations in order to help them submit proposals that slipped social action in under such euphemisms as "leadership training," "community therapy," and "citizen participation." With a few minor exceptions, this game is over. The introduction of the Green Amendment to the Economic Opportunity Act has officially put the lid on hopes that the federal government is going to pay for fermenting social revolution. This amendment gives city officials the option of directly administering Community Action Programs. While only a handful of mayors have exercised this option, CAP directors and staff are on notice that conflict will not be tolerated.

The same general pattern applies to the mainline foundations such as Ford and Rockefeller. Every now and then these foundations dabble with a proposal that avows militant social protest activity. An example is the Congress of Racial Equality's Target City Project in Cleveland, which was funded for almost a quarter of a million dollars. Four years ago the Cleveland Chapter of CORE was the only organized militant group that had the will and stamina to confront aggressively the school system, the Public Housing Authority, and the police department. Today, CORE's well-financed Target City Project has all but abandoned mass community organization and any meaningful confrontation with abusive centers of power. Occasionally CORE issues a press release on police excesses or cosigns a statement protesting the demise of citizen participation in the poverty programs. In fairness to CORE, this disengagement from social protest is not entirely related to the fear of alienating its benefactors; it stems partly from the realization that the whole funding game must be played in a different way. They now believe the only hope for the impoverished black community lies in mass programs of independent economic development. This will be discussed in greater detail later.

From the author's limited perspective in Cleveland, the only sources of funding for aggressive social change seem to be a number of underendowed foundations and a few equally impoverished local and national church bodies. Such small foundations are bombarded with hundreds of requests. The present funding picture for independent citizens' organizations bent on aggressive social action is bleak. For more benign organizations such as block clubs and neighborhood improvement associations, the funding prospects are getting brighter. For example, in Cleveland the local federated agency, after years of virtually abandoning support of area councils, is surging with new enthusiasm about revitalizing its commitment to neighborhood organizations. While the new efforts permit the inclusion of independent action groups and also provide for a board structure composed predominantly of local neighborhood leadership, the funding is still tightly related to the suburban-dominated mother agency. The six-month accountability provision virtually ensures that no funds will be used for any activity that smacks of conflict or controversy.

There is nothing mysterious about the incapacity of chests and councils to fund social action. A recent event in Columbus, Ohio, tells the whole story. As the Poor People's Campaign was beginning its tour of Ohio cities, a rumor spread in Columbus that the local United Appeal was contributing money for buses and lodging. Within twenty-four hours a threat by labor and industrial leaders to boycott the next UA campaign was released to the local newspapers. UA officials immediately made it clear that no such use of publicly raised funds had ever been contemplated.

Prospects for the Future

Given this new mood of militancy and the pervasive unwillingness of funding sources to provide the fuel for legitimate forms of social action and protest, what are the prospects for the future? If the nation survives the next years without turning into a garrison state, several new funding patterns and new programmatic directions for self-help organizations can be foreseen. Many organizations will continue to struggle and manipulate in order to get the crumbs of money that are being doled out by federal agencies, foundations, and church organizations. Some of these organizations will become domesticated and substitute service approaches for social action in order to keep the money flowing. Others will decide that the funding game is too humiliating to continue and will find ways to become effective with more modest financial support. The main thrust, however, will come from a completely new direction —namely, community and economic development.

It is becoming increasingly apparent to the more pragmatic militant organizations that the present funding patterns are an extension of the welfare mentality or, as the militants prefer to label it, "the plantation system." In order to remain viable, organizations are compelled to keep coming back to "the man." The present expenditure of funds by self-help organizations is entirely on staff, office space, equipment, and program requirements. This precarious form of funding reinforces subordination and leaves organizations highly vulnerable to outside manipulation and influence. Those organizations that have been effective have either made the decision to use their funds without regard for the sanctions imposed by the funding body or have built up a citizen constituency that made a cutoff from the funding source difficult. This latter method is too precarious to offer as a prescription for long-range effectiveness. What is clearly needed are new models that develop independent economic bases for community organization and community development. What the writer is suggesting is that in the future seed money will be used primarily for developing independent economic bases rather than for hiring staff to engage in direct action programs. If social action organizations are to have any permanence and long-range effectiveness they must be based on sources of support over which they have control. This means that seed capital, from whatever source, should be used primarily for economic ventures that involve large numbers of participating shareholders and that will eventually net income that could be used for social and political action. This notion is entirely consistent with the new demands for control and independence. A proposal prepared by Wilfred T. Ussery, national chairman of CORE, in March 1968 spells out a massive program—the title of the proposal is "An Invitation to Cooperate in the Development of a Consortium of Black Economic Institutions Designed to Significantly Broaden the Base of Ownership by the Black Community of Productive Capital Instruments."

Strangely enough, the ideas embodied in this proposal are much more upsetting to white liberals than to white conservatives. Partly this is due to the fact that conservatives, including President Nixon, have not read the document carefully. They are interpreting the proposal as a form of black capitalism. True, it calls for the ownership of capital instruments by Negro residents of inner-city areas; however, it does not propose that this be achieved through traditional entrepreneurial means. The proposal envisions a kind of popular capitalism in which large numbers of people, including welfare recipients and other poor, are shareholders and decision-makers in various economic enterprises. The proposal envisions four types of economic activities:

1. Increased Negro ownership and employment in institutions that distribute and make automobiles, appliances, furniture, food, clothing, and building materials. Negro involvement in these areas is now exceedingly low or nonexistent.

2. Those areas of economic activity in which major funds are exchanged for various kinds of services within the black community through the purchase of goods and services that can be produced, owned, or controlled by the black community. Type 2 thus becomes the area of business enterprise in which there is potential for developing an intra-black community economic structure.

3. Those areas of economic activity that would combine the economic activity of an intra-black community economic structure with foreign, principally African, economies. This may include an African cultural center; import-export distribution firms for African clothing, art objects, and other products; a travel agency; an entertainment booking agency; and a film and communication enterprise designed to acquaint black America with black Africa.

4. Those areas of economic activity that would combine the economic potentials of the intra-black community economic structure and black Africa with the technological base of Japan or the industrial capability of other foreign countries.

These ideas are highly visionary and would, if implemented, help to reduce the growing tension between the races. It remains to be seen, however, whether government, industry, and labor are any more favorably disposed to these ideas than they are toward radical social action programs.

A NEW ROLE FOR NASW

This growing demand for independence and economic development rather than integration represents a radical departure from conventional antipoverty programs and social welfare philosophies. The new mood rejects the liberal dreams of an integrated society and says to affluent whites, "Your new role is not to lead or give paternalistic handouts. It is to support independent, autonomous black institutions." This does not mean that whites, individually and through their organizational affiliations, do not have a vital and important role to play. What is now needed to complement this newly emerging black movement is a supportive white movement.

Liberal organizations such as the National Association of Social Workers can, on both the local and national levels, become part of the vanguard for the kind of support that Negro self-help organizations need to become independent and economically self-sufficient. We can start by using our professional base to confront some obvious forms of white racism, especially those that perpetuate ghettos as colonial enclaves. We must encourage the transition of white suburban-controlled boards of agencies and institutions in the ghetto into the hands of newly emerging black leadership. This does not necessarily mean that professionals will not be employed in such agencies, only that they will become accountable to new decision-making boards of local residents. Local NASW chapters could create pools of knowledgeable and experienced professionals in different content areas who could become volunteer technical resource people to self-help organizations. They could also help in recruiting other kinds of experts that such organizations will need to launch their new programs of economic and political development.

As pointed out in a study conducted by John Turner of forty-six self-help organizations, it is at the point of negotiation and program development that most of these groups fall down.[9] They need and want technical assistance in analyzing problems and in shaping programs —provided the technicians do not try to usurp leadership.

Finally, the time has come for the professional organization to move officially into a stronger supportive position in relation to economic resources. If professional social workers are indeed as concerned as the NASW policy statements indicate, then funds should be diverted and increased for the express purpose of providing risk capital to radical

---

[9] See John B. Turner, "Epilogue," in Turner, ed., *Neighborhood Organization for Community Action* (New York: National Association of Social Workers, 1968), pp. 184–185.

reform and economic development organizations that have no other funding source to which to look.   In this connection, it is proposed that the national board of NASW increase dues substantially and divert present funds in order to create a special foundation for the purpose of matching on a dollar-for-dollar basis the contribution of any local chapter to an independent self-help organization.   Priorities should be given to those self-help organizations that seek to develop independent economic development projects that will sustain their effort after the initial grant period.   Such an action would not only have substantive importance, it would have enormous symbolic value.   It would make clear that social work's basic ethical commitments to self-determination and the dignity and worth of the individual are not empty mouthings. It would also serve the function of helping social workers as a profession to liberate ourselves from those interests that keep us captive and in opposition to the clientele we purport to serve.

The Emerging Black Community:
A Challenge to Social Work

DOUGLAS GLASGOW

This symposium was held at a most timely period, for its provides social work professionals with an opportunity to review searchingly strategies of intervention into the nation's crisis-ridden urban areas. At no time in recent history has the nation experienced so severe a cleavage as that represented by its polarization into two antagonistic camps, one black and one white. The severity of the crisis is more obvious today, in large measure owing to the black community's protest against its continued deprivation and containment in inner-city ghettos.

Various strategies have been proposed in response to the recent outbursts in the nation's ghettos. Two predominant approaches are being discussed. The first stresses containment, repressive measures, and obedience to the law; urges no capitulation to lawlessness; and places much emphasis on "humane" riot control. A second involves massive government- and private industry-sponsored programs for rehabilitation of the ghettos. An alternative view suggests a combination of both. However, in all cases control of these programs remains in the hands of the broader community.

This paper addresses itself to strategies of social intervention within the black ghetto. It reviews the structure of black ghettos, analyzes the more recent trends developing in these areas, and suggests a new orientation to underpin social work activities in the black community. The thesis of this paper is that the ghetto must undergo significant social

246

change. Transformation of its social institutions, development of indigenous organizations, and reorganization of the social patterns of
living will be meaningful only when these occur under the control of the
ghetto inhabitants. Only through self-determination will a substantial
and positive black community be developed.

This paper presents material derived from analysis of developments
in south-central Los Angeles (the riot curfew area) in the aftermath of
the Watts riots of 1965. Further, the activities of a social work agency—
Special Services for Groups, Inc.—and the emergence of the Sons of
Watts provide a prototypical model for change in a black community.[1]

THE GHETTO AS A SOCIAL INSTITUTION

Social work is unable adequately to plan intervention strategies with
people in the inner city unless there is an appropriate reassessment of the
ghetto institution. Historically, the ghetto has existed as a geographic
area in which new arrivals or immigrants initially settled. Despite their
poor facilities and low-level economies, these communities were toler-
able, since they were communities of transition. They were deemed
starting points in a socialization process—the end result was integration
into the broader society. The Horatio Alger dream of individual upward
mobility from rags to riches was operative for the vast majority of
"white" immigrants. The journey from ghetto to middle-class community living and social status was in part facilitated by the development
of institutions that assisted this acculturation process.

Social work practice has helped people achieve these mobility aspirations. One element contributing to the success of this mobility process
was the fact that in large measure it was easier for whites, regardless of
social, religious, national, or even political background, to be accultur-
ated into white American society. In contrast, the black ghetto exists
as a social structure for containment of black Americans. Clark notes:

> The dark ghettos are social, political, educational, and—above
> all—economic colonies. Their inhabitants are subject peoples,

---

[1] Special Services for Groups, Inc., is a social work agency functioning on
the periphery of the Los Angeles ghetto community with a subunit, the
Delinquency Prevention Center, within the Watts community. The developments discussed grew out of Project Escape String. The Sons of Watts
Improvement Association is an indigenous organization of young black men
who, following their participation in the Watts riots of 1965, chose to
associate in a formal organization dedicated to community betterment.

victims of the greed, cruelty, insensitivity, guilt and fear of their masters.[2]

Yet despite the innumerable actions taken by blacks protesting ghetto confinement, social scientists persist in perpetrating the myth of the ghetto as a transitory community and contend that (notwithstanding the slowness of the process) upward mobility for blacks continues and integration as a social goal is occurring. What in fact has occurred is the increased containment of blacks in inner-city ghettos.

In sharp contrast to the slum and ghetto of the 1930s, which served as communities for initial embarkation of and subsequent mobilization for whites, the black ghetto increases in size, population, and deprivation and provides only limited avenues out. As the riot commission pointed out: "Whereas in the early 1900's only 2.6 million Negroes or 27 percent lived in cities, today about 15 million or 69 percent of all Negroes are city dwellers." Further, it is estimated that "within the next 10 to 20 years, the Negro population in the central cities will increase by 72 percent, and that by 1984 over 13 major cities will have a Negro majority." [3] These facts point to an even more clearly delineated black and white society.

The inner-city ghetto is not only an area of black confinement, but also contributes to numerous social ills and to dysfunctional life-style adaptations of its inhabitants. In making survival adaptations to ghetto life, blacks have suffered cruelly as the victims of ghetto social structures. Much has been written about ghetto life as a contributing source of hard-core unemployables, school dropouts, and dysfunctional life-styles.[4]

---

[2] Kenneth B. Clark, *Dark Ghetto: Dilemmas of Social Power* (New York: Harper & Row, 1965), p. 11.

[3] *Report of the National Advisory Commission on Civil Disorders,* the U.S. Riot Commission Report (New York: Bantam Books, March 1968), pp. 236–247.

[4] *See* Lee Rainwater, "The Crucible of Identity: The Negro Lower-Class Family," *Daedalus,* Vol. 95, No. 1 (Winter 1966), pp. 172–203; Abram Kardiner and Lionel Ovesey, *The Mark of Oppression: Explorations in the Personality of the American Negro* (Cleveland: World Publishing Co., Meridian Books, 1964); Bertram P. Karon, *The Negro Personality* (New York: Springer Publishing Co., 1958); Thomas F. Pettigrew, *Profile of the American Negro* (Princeton, N.J.: D. Van Nostrand Co., 1964); Edmund W. Gordon and Doxey A. Wilkerson, *Compensatory Education for the Disadvantaged* (New York: College Entrance Examination Board, 1966).

Agencies of human concern, which cover the broad spectrum of health, education, and welfare services, have also contributed to the severity of the ghetto resident's suffering. Social agencies within the ghetto contribute to the worsening conditions; their services are often irrelevant, at sharp variance with fundamental needs, and in orientation alien to black reality. Concerning the last point, many agencies continue to view their services as being crisis oriented, as stopgap measures, and even as temporary aids in abetting individual upward mobility and assimilation of a middle-class orientation. Such programs are essentially meaningless, since social status changes and upward mobility occurs so infrequently for the inhabitant of the black ghetto. He remains part of a growing black enclave.

Examples of social services dysfunctional to ghetto communities have been documented more recently. A recent study cited the inadequacies of social services for the inhabitants of the ghetto community of south-central Los Angeles. One important factor noted is that many agencies that function in the ghetto are not community controlled, but rather are controlled by the outside community. The study noted: "Only 4 of the 42 agencies [studied] stated that their policy-making body includes representatives of the client population." [5] With respect to agencies' flexibility in responding autonomously to the special needs of ghetto residents, it was found that the two most prominently used services— "public income-maintenance and control agencies" and "sectarian organizations"—were the most limited. The study states with regard to agencies' identification with community sociopolitical currents as represented in civil rights activity:

> Only one-third (14) of the agencies reported active involvement. . . . Other than poverty program agencies, only one sectarian family agency took an official position on some aspect of the civil rights movement.[6]

Even in the allocation of professional services, it was found that "without exception the agencies not serving the 'typical' low-income Negro client were among the organizations with the highest degree of professional skills and specialized services." [7] This report further supplies

---

[5] Jerome Cohen, "A Descriptive Study of the Availability and Useability of Social Services in the South Central Area of Los Angeles," Section MR–85 of the Los Angeles Riot Study (Los Angeles: Institute of Government and Public Affairs, University of California, June 1967), p. 23.

[6] *Ibid.*, p. 24.

[7] *Ibid.*, p. 28–29.

data on the contradictions between service delivery methods and the life-style of the ghetto resident.

These findings are not exceptional, but are typical of services in ghetto communities across the nation. In speaking of one of the major institutions serving the black ghetto—the public welfare department—the New York City commissioner of welfare noted: "The welfare system is designed to save money instead of people and tragically ends up doing neither." [8] Even more indicting, the recent report of the National Advisory Commission on Civil Disorders concluded with respect to welfare:

> First, it excludes large numbers of persons who are in great need, and who, if provided a decent level of support, might be able to become more productive and self-sufficient;
> Second, for those who are included, it provides assistance well below the minimum necessary for a decent level of existence, and imposes restrictions that encourage continued dependency on welfare and undermine self-respect.[9]

Thus the patterns found to exist among social services for ghetto residents implicate agency methods, orientation, and structures as contributing to the perpetuation of ghetto life.

Even more insidious is the factor of white racism as a determinant of ghetto existence. No other factor has done more to forge the black ghetto and polarize blacks and whites. Because of race, blacks have been deprived of attainment of full citizenship, complete upward mobility in the broader community, and access to the available societal means of economic betterment. They have been forced to live in separate areas, segregated and yet encouraged to deny their blackness. Whites have perpetrated a myth of the "invisibility" of blackness, and blacks have had the task of denying this blackness as the price of marginal attainment. Complicity with this practice has served to retard black identity, integrity, and the attainment of positive ethnicity. If ever there were doubt concerning the accusation made by blacks for years that social and economic deprivation was enforced because of race, the report of the National Advisory Commission on Civil Disorders, compiled by reputable members of the Establishment, has recently confirmed that the major factor contributing to the blacks' condition is white racism. And as for ghetto confinement, they note: "White institutions created it, white institutions maintain it, and white society condones it." [10]

---

[8] *Report of the National Advisory Commission on Civil Disorders,* p. 457.
[9] *Ibid.*
[10] *Ibid.,* p. vii.

These and other factors have contributed to the isolation and confinement of blacks within the nation's ghettos. Ghetto social structure, institutions, and patterns of organization all converge to produce conditions leading to the debilitation of blacks. It is a social structure that is neither controlled by, identified with, nor owned by its residents. The governing laws and property ownership remain in the hands of extra-community forces. The interned of the ghetto do not view the institution that exploits them as theirs. They are alienated from the ghetto institution.

DYNAMICS OF CURRENT PROTESTS

Black protests against ghetto victimization traditionally remained within the accepted machinery of social protest, yet the gap between the welfare of ghetto residents and of whites continues to increase. However, a new generation of young blacks has emerged in the past two decades. Many have been raised in urban city ghettos, adjacent to affluent white communities. They have not known or experienced the intense isolation of earlier generations, who were for the better part of their youth secluded from large urban affluence. Close proximity to affluence has led large numbers of this generation to become disenchanted with a dream they see as never being fulfilled for them. Disenchantment with the American dream and alienation from ghetto life provided the condition for the riots that have erupted throughout the nation's ghettos.

The crisis of the urban community has become apparent to the whole nation. This has occurred only since the younger generation of blacks exploded in riots against the institutional practices of the ghetto. Social scientists have been reluctant to analyze riots as a phenomenon related to social change. Confusion and a broader community orientation have led many persons to view the violent confrontations of people with police, accompanied by the harsh and frightening spectacle of a burning community, as being equal to lawlessness. The reaction of open rage to enforced deprivation and humiliation is by far more functional behavior than are self-hatred and apathy. The polemic that followed the 1965 Watts explosion identified it as a riot and in some early reports as a race riot. Both characterizations tend to produce a majority response concerned with preserving broader community integrity, reestablishing traditional ghetto balances by accommodations, and ultimately contributing to the whites' fear for their personal safety. Yet deeper analysis suggests that these eruptions were different and had different consequences.

Significance of the Watts Riot

The explosion that ripped through the Los Angeles ghetto in 1965 signaled a change in relations between the black ghetto and the broader community and changes within the ghetto community itself. Four results, among others, were clear:

1. The riot served the purpose of sounding a clear alarm signal comprehensible to the broader community and the nation as a whole. It effectively gained attention and brought a halt to routine practices.

2. The riot announced the emergence of a new social force in the ghetto. This was represented by the mobilization of the hard-core unemployables, dropouts, hustlers, and young ghetto poor, many of those labeled failures, for they held none of the traditional academic documents necessary for upward mobility in society.

3. The riot forecast the emergence of new social currents from within the ghetto and also represented a new form of social protest. Differing from earlier race riots of the 1930s and '40s, the new explosions shifted from random violence against individual whites to destruction of ghetto institutions and symbols of ghetto-dwellers' exploitation.

4. The riot produced an ethnic consolidation of black people within the ghetto and focused on the whites as perpetrators of the ghetto system.[11]

The riot, although performing a warning service and providing a barometer of emergent new social forces in the ghetto, nevertheless, in and of itself produced no fundamental change in the socioeconomic structure of ghetto life. However, some of the forecast trends related to the riot have since taken on more delineated forms in the black community. The major components are a search for a positive black identity, indigenous group formation, and various coalitions composed of groups that seek to transform the ghetto into a substantial black community.

New Model of Black Mobility

The search for a positive black identity has provided Negroes with new energies. What emerged during the fires of August, expressed in terms

---

[11] Douglas Glasgow, "Effects of Riot Participation in the Life-Styles, Attitudes and Social Roles of Black Youth in the Aftermath of Watts Riot, 1965." Paper presented at the National Conference on Social Welfare, San Francisco, Calif., May 1968.

of "soul brother" (a way of signaling black identity), was expanded after the riot into a broad search for a positive identity and a positive view of blackness. This new venture has given Negroes a new purpose for existence (other than hating whites or self-hatred) and has introduced the ideal of self-fulfillment with dignity. In conjunction with identity development, socially meaningful roles have been sought through newly created social organizations.

Before Watts, blacks seeking to survive ghetto isolation operated to a large extent in an organizational void and tried to find ways of making it individually. Since 1965 the black community has seen the emergence of a diversity of organizations with goals covering a broad spectrum of social, economic, and political concerns. In the more recent period, specialized groups concerned with ghetto economics, social scientific investigation, and co-ordination of community services have been initiated. The common concern of these developments is control of black community life by its people. These new developments involve a new mobility model that sees changes in the Negro's social and economic status as being dependent on the advancement of the total black community rather than of individually exceptional persons.

IMPLICATIONS FOR SOCIAL WORK

This model of black mobility presents social work with the need to redefine its role in respect to the black community. This involves reassessing the relationship among the agency, the social work practitioner, and the client community.

The ghetto must be viewed as a social structure that has to be transformed from an area of confinement into a viable community with functional social institutions and facilities serving the inhabitants. This requires self-determined programming by the inhabitants in combination with the nation's resources. Only when the ghetto is transformed from an area of confinement into one of authentic social opportunity, operating through powerful social structures, can the broader question of positive multiracialism in society be resolved.

Agency-Community Co-operation

Some professional agencies have already undertaken programs seeking to adjust to these new currents. A model typifying this organizational pattern was recently developed between a social agency—Special Services for Groups, Inc. (SSG)—and the Watts community. This agency had its beginnings at the time of the "zoot suit riots" in 1943. Through its experiences it discovered that traditional programs had limited meaning to delinquent gangs and therefore new approaches had to be developed. After six years of effective demonstration with hard-core deviant youths, SSG was formed. It worked with predelinquent groups and delinquent gangs and supplied counseling services. More recently, developments within the black ghettos of Los Angeles have resulted in SSG's reappraisal of function. Under a special Project Escape String, a black social worker was given support to assist in developing an indigenous organization within the Watts community. This led to development of the Sons of Watts Improvement Association.

The primary function of the agency was support of the worker, providing him and the Sons of Watts with various resources. Rather than seeing its function as being a direct organizer of Negro youths or as providing the orientation for their social organization, SSG functioned as an expediting resource for materials and training skills and encouraged the development of indigenous self-directed goals. This new agency role represented a shift from early direct intervention to programs of sensitive support. It reflected SSG's recognition that social organization activities in the black community need support by broader community agencies. Further, independence in orientation and activity format of indigenous developments is essential for success.

Significance of the Sons of Watts

The emergence of the Sons of Watts as a viable force within Watts and surrounding communities in south-central Los Angeles attests to the vitality of this new approach. In a short two-year period, with the aid of a social worker and the encouragement of the community, a group of men previously characterized as unreachable, hard core, rioters, hustlers, and failures have achieved social organization and emerged as one of the community's most positive social forces working toward community betterment.

Organization of the Sons of Watts has significance in many areas. The first was social organization of the unorganized, which provided an opportunity for individuals to gain social power. Thereafter, interventions into ghetto life were not individual endeavors but carried power derived from social organization. This fact became apparent in the early formative stages of the Sons' community action development.

The program for community betterment involved many strategies of intervention:

1. Assumption of unfulfilled community roles provided the Sons with an opportunity to become community models. They undertook such activities as community cleanup and beautification, voluntarily sponsored leisure activities for teen-agers and youths, intervened in community youth conflicts, and served as guards at school crossings.

2. Another level of activity involved intervention into the social system of the community. As a social group the Sons obtained community recognition and became involved in the decision-making apparatus of the community. In this way they achieved recognition as community mobilizers, community hosts, and community change agents.[12]

3. A third strategy involved activities in which the targets for change were agencies external to the community, especially those that affect the structural patterns of the ghetto. Dialogues with police officials, private industries seeking community investments, and agencies providing community utilities such as water, gas, and electricity were directed to change, improve, and redirect these institutions' functions in the community.

Another component of the Sons' vitality was derived from a self-help orientation. Programs for job training and community business investment were initiated. The purpose was to increase attainment of salable skills by the youthful unemployed and to enrich the community by encouraging new business enterprises.

The emergence of the Sons of Watts as a potent new force for community revitalization is a unique community organization development. In a two-year period, those who were earlier vilified as rioters have emerged to become the caretakers and mobilizers of their community. In broader functional terms, they have become advocates for the larger black community. The main motivating force propelling the Sons' development has come from intimate involvement in the contemporary strivings of Negroes for selfhood and dignity. What began as a random action to destroy the ghetto has developed into a program for revitalization of the black community. The growth, social role change, and new social perspective of the Sons was derived through the search for individual dignity in the context of a black community cause.

---

[12] "Community hosts" are groups of people who welcome newcomers to a community in much the same way as would a chamber of commerce or mayor's office.

Role of the Worker

The role of the worker contributed immensely to SSG's growth and development of the Sons of Watts. Although the worker was supported by SSG, his primary association and identification were with the Sons of Watts. This was operationalized by his functions of member in and adviser to the emerging organization. Notwithstanding his role as a professional social worker, he functioned as liaison between SSG and the community. In this capacity he effected the two-way flow of communication between the agency and the black community. He interpreted the agency's function to the community and initially translated the community's orientation and needs to the agency. As the Sons gained formal organizational strength, when necessary they communicated directly with the agency and its staff. With the present disjuncture existing between the ghetto inhabitant and social welfare agencies, it is highly improbable that the role of adviser, advocate, and liaison could have been performed successfully had the worker not been black. SSG and the Sons of Watts gained invaluable knowledge of each other through the sensitive functioning of the worker.

New Orientation Is Needed

The example supplied here is presented as only one form in which a relationship can develop between a social work agency and the black community that is striving toward self-realization. The crucial components in the relationship demand that the agency encourage indigenous development, expedite attainment of community goals, and assist in the development of independently sought-after aspirations through provision of resources to enable the process to occur.

For this function to be fulfilled effectively, social work must accept that the reorganization of the black community and its people will not be accomplished by broader community agencies. This old practice is what has led in part to the profession's being identified with welfare colonialism and philanthropy. These older models are derived from an orientation that assumes paternal and caretaker roles that encourage dependency rather than independence. With the prevailing mood in the black community, such roles will be totally dysfunctional.

Aside from ideological reappraisal of agency-community relationships, social work must also review its internal recruitment policies. Heretofore social work has been viewed as a middle class-oriented profession. In many respects it has aided individuals' attainment of middle-class life-styles. In the ghetto an ethnic movement involving Negroes is

unfolding, and its ultimate goal does not appear to be attainment of white middle-class standards.

If social work is to play a part in this development, it must make substantial changes in recruitment practices, thus providing opportunity for a large and heterogeneous number of black social work aspirants to attain professional competence for leadership in their community. In the past, social work has met groups' needs during periods of severe crisis. It supported the consumer and common man against unbridled entrepreneurial exploitation during the muckraking period, it aided the poor during the Great Depression, it built and supported specialized agencies during the nation's period of greatest immigration. It is once again being called on to assist in the emergence of a most positive development, a people's search for selfhood, dignity, and freedom. It can meet this challenge with a forthright determination and further assist the nation in finding a solution to one aspect of the urban crisis.

The Social Worker As Mediator Between Tenants and Landlords

PAUL A. ABELS

There are countless organizations in the inner city, formal and informal, whose aim is to provide increased autonomy for its residents. When its goals are clear and the paths to these goals have been explicated, the group has increased its probability of success.

The idea of citizens organizing themselves for a self-help project is not new. Tenant councils, block clubs, co-ops, and numerous other action-oriented groups have been on the scene for a long time. The tenant union idea, however, *is* new. Historically, tenants have organized in order to maintain and beautify their homes or to give their local area a sense of community. The tenant union idea is to shift the basis of power and to put into the hands of the tenants a tool by which they can negotiate on a more equal footing with the landlord. Conway sees this as ". . . a new concept, a new form of institution." [1]

Buildings in inner cities are run-down and code violations are the rule rather than the exception. The lack of building inspectors, landlord-politician connections, long court dockets, and slap-on-the-wrist fines

---

[1] Jack T. Conway, "Organizing the Poor: Community Unions," *Center Diary: 18* (Santa Barbara, Calif.: Center for the Study of Democratic Institutions, May-June 1963).

258

have all but made current programs to revitalize inner-city code enforcement a farce.[2]   Under the rallying call "The tenant has no rights," tenants, indigenous workers, and professionals in Cleveland, Ohio, organized to form a new organization, the Cleveland Tenant Union.

HISTORICAL PERSPECTIVE

Plans for the Cleveland Tenant Union evolved from a program similar but not identical to that developed in Chicago in 1966 under the combined efforts of Dr. Martin Luther King, Jr., the Chicago Freedom Movement, the East Garfield Park Community Organization, and labor unions.   Criticism of and action against some of the large Chicago slumlords or their management concerns gave rise to organized meetings of tenants of slum dwellings controlled by the largest realty firm in East Garfield Park.   The number of protesters grew and a common purpose emerged.

Demands were made for immediate repairs and improved building maintenance, but the landlords refused to deal with the groups.   Because of this, picketing of the real estate office followed.   Some tenants refused to cross the picket lines to pay rents, and a rent strike developed. Managers finally agreed to meet with the tenants, who by then had united into an autonomous organization.   Collective bargaining was initiated and resulted in the first landlord-tenant contract, which stipulated rents, schedules for repairs, and recourse for grievance action. Also included was a section on tenant responsibilities.

At the same time similar action was taking place in other areas of the city, stimulated by the East Garfield Park experience.   It is estimated that by the end of 1966 approximately 10,000 tenants had been involved in or were covered by tenant union agreements.

In Cleveland the tenant union movement developed from close social worker–tenant contacts that led to a quest for some program that would permit a shift of power to the tenants.   From the start, efforts were made to involve tenants in all aspects of the program and plans for tenant take-over were built in.

In the spring of 1967 the Legal Aid Society submitted a grant to the Office of Economic Opportunity proposing a demonstration of the value of arbitration between landlord and tenant; following approval, it began to organize tenant unions in the Hough area of Cleveland, the scene of destructive disturbances in the summer of 1966.   The terms of the grant

---

[2] *See,* for example, *The PATH Report* (Cleveland: PATH Association, 1966).

permitted consultation with other tenant groups in Cleveland. Early in
June in consultation with Legal Aid and OEO, the Greater Cleveland
Neighborhood Centers Association (GCNCA) assumed responsibility
for co-ordinating the program on a city-wide basis. The primary reason
for this was the availability of its field service organizers in the major
poverty areas. Under the guidelines of its grant, Legal Aid mounted its
major efforts in Hough.

Local Involvement

Each area of the city has one or more locals of the union in order to
ensure that the needs of a specific area, block, and even apartment
building will be met. A number of landlords are being dealt with rather
than one employer (as in labor unions) and the needs of tenants in adjacent houses may differ tremendously. Each building therefore has its own
shop steward elected by the tenants. He is involved directly in any
negotiations after consultation with the tenants and the Negotiation Advisory Committee. This committee is comprised of the cochairmen of
the city-wide tenants' union, Legal Aid staff, and elected officers. It was
set up on a temporary basis to guide negotiations with the landlords and
maintain some similarity among the landlord-tenant contracts until a
unifying constitution could be formulated.

Each local selected representatives to a city-wide tenant union that
was formally established at a Tenant Union Convention in April 1968.
City-wide officers were elected and a constitution was ratified. The
city-wide structure enables the tenants to assume more control of their
own organization. Hopefully, in time the union will be completely
run by tenants, with their own structure, constitutions, and funds to
hire their own organizers. One advantage of a city-wide operation is
that it permits concerted efforts against landlords or management com-
panies with tenements in various parts of the city.

The basic program initially consisted of (1) recruiting people into
tenant unions, (2) recruiting specific tenants from houses of certain
landlords into unions, (3) a legislative program to promote legal rent
withholdings, (4) a health-in-housing program, (5) educating the community about tenant unions, (6) training recruiters, organizers, and
shop stewards, (7) being a watchdog on items related to housing that
might help tenants and tenant unions, (8) revitalizing inner-city housing,
and (9) soliciting funds and/or buildings that would allow tenants to
purchase and manage their own houses. This last point places the
unions in the real estate business; it has been implemented in Chicago.

The Social Worker and the Union

Much of the actual organizing of the tenants in the Cleveland program was handled directly by agency-trained workers hired by Legal Aid or GCNCA to organize the community. The social worker's role was administrative supervision of the program. Tenants often shifted roles and assumed the position of organizer.

In Cleveland an organizing committee comprised of lawyers, social workers, organizers, and tenants served as the strategy group that planned new steps and attempted to involve others in the initial organizing efforts. The organizing committee attempted to sell the idea of the union to local tenant groups (organizations and individuals). Teams attended various meetings to talk to any small group interested in a specific building or tenant council. Small groups were asked to gather other people together for larger meetings. During the summer of 1967, for example, as Martin Luther King, Jr., made the rounds of Cleveland housing projects, he spoke about the tenant union idea at large meetings arranged for him by the tenant union.

In service models in which the contract is primarily between consumer and social worker, tasks can be more clearly defined and assigned. Increasingly, however, the magnitude of the problems confronted by the consumer of service calls for the collaborative efforts of social work teams and a partnership with other professions. This type of assignment calls for a fairly autonomous worker who can negotiate on a number of fronts.

In the tenant union service model, the social worker is involved in direct action with (1) the tenants—the consumers of service, (2) other providers of service such as the legal profession, and (3) consumer-providers, i.e., the agency-trained tenants who become tenant agents, arbitrators, and organizers. He also provides service to another category of consumer, the landlord, helping him to learn how to be a better landlord and to find the funds and other resources necessary to bring his houses up to code requirements.

Involvement of lawyers in the union is a necessity, as the following example shows:

Recruiting Meeting—Poverty Area

The social worker spoke about the structure of the tenant union and the need for people to join together. The group was resistant to the union idea. The social worker asked the lawyer present to explain some of the rights of the tenants. The lawyer then spoke

about the legal assistance tenants might expect from Legal Aid. People relaxed and began to ask questions and relate their own personal experiences with landlords. When asked if the landlord might refuse to talk to them, the lawyer responded that often a letter or a call from a lawyer will get a meeting set quickly.

Tenants are often fearful of the possible repercussions involved if they join such a group. They need to hear about their rights from "the man," and in this case "the man" is the lawyer.

Although the organizers can become involved as quasi-legal agents in dealing with parts of the bureaucracies such as the health and sanitation departments, the landlords, and real estate groups, the entrance into the negotiations of a lawyer—even if he just stays quiet—often helps settle the matter.

THE MEDIATING ROLE

The worker is an advocate along with the lawyer in behalf of the tenant, an organizer, a trainer of other organizers and tenants to carry on the work of the tenant union, and a resource to both tenant and landlord. One model useful for carrying out this multifaceted assignment is that of social worker as mediator among the various parts of the system. This role has been proposed by a number of social workers and is most clearly defined by Schwartz. He sees the parts of the system reaching out to each other in ". . . a mutual need for self-fulfillment." The role of the worker as mediator is ". . . designed to bring together individual needs and social resources." [3] One task for the worker in this model is to help search out the common ground that will enable people to work together on their problems.

In this reciprocal relationship the landlord and the tenant need each other, and the tenant, social worker, and lawyer need each other in order to fulfill their specific functions. Not only is the worker charged with working with parts of the system, but he is affecting the entire system as well. The worker must also help the group become an autonomous organization, able to use itself as a mediator between the individual and society.[4] In order to be autonomous, the tenant must be

---

[3] William Schwartz, "The Worker with the Group," *Social Welfare Forum, 1961* (New York: Columbia University Press, 1961), p. 155.

[4] Paul Abels, "The Social Work Contract: Playing It Straight." Paper presented at a meeting of the NASW Cleveland Area Chapter, Group Work

helped to learn some basic political skills (political in the broad sense of involvement and action) such as working with others, organizing, and making himself heard. The tenants, all poor, must be helped to develop their political bargaining roles.

The mediating role is not an impartial one. All the actors know that the worker's job is to help the tenant work on his problem. The mediator acts to bring the actors together to work with each other. The social worker mediates among five major groups in the system: the tenants, the other planners, the "prime movers" (often the financers of the service), the landlords, and the field (any force being bargained with).

Mediating with Lawyers

The major objective of the tenant union is to work out a contract with the landlord, but there are some other mediating roles that must be handled between other parts of the system. One of the major tasks was to open up the lines of communication between tenants and lawyers. The following examples illustrate this:

Meeting 5

The legal representative was asked to explain the eviction procedure to the group of organizers and tenant agents so that we could better understand it and be able to give the correct information to the tenants. He replied that the tenant can be evicted without any notice and that nothing can be done about it. He then sat down. The group was extremely upset and concerned. The social worker asked him if there was any recourse at all. The lawyer

---

Section, March 1966. (Mimeographed.) The quest for autonomy is a quest for the ability to make mature decisions that affect one's life and to know that there is some possibility that these decisions may be implemented. Autonomy—the ability to make the kind of decisions that bring the rewards one seeks in life—requires that the person have a range of alternatives from which to select. Thus, for the Negro poor, race and lack of money limit the alternatives. The choices of where to work, where to live, what schools to send one's children to, what to eat, and how to live are limited. The alternatives are few, and the quest for autonomy is changed to a struggle for survival.

said no. The social worker asked if the eviction notice has to be written or if it can be handled over the telephone or tacked on the tenant's door. The lawyer then explained the various legal procedures involved, ending with the possibility of requesting a jury trial, which can often delay an eviction for three months.

Meeting 7

One item on the agenda was a suggestion to introduce legislation making it lawful for tenants to withhold rent when a building is in violation of the building code, putting the rent in escrow. The lawyer said that this has been done in a few places and he could draw up some legislation. The social worker suggested that the group think of who in the city council might introduce it. The lawyer said that this matter could not go to the city council; it had to go to the state. He was questioned about this and explained the legal complications. He maintained that it would be poor legal practice to go to the city council, that the council would only return the legislation for submission on the state level.

Following the lawyer's presentation, the tenants suggested that it would be good local strategy and publicity to present the legislation to the council: "Let them say it can't be taken up by the council." The lawyer countered this with another legal argument, but was overruled by the group. He then arranged a meeting with the appropriate council representatives, who were quite receptive to the idea. News of the meeting was leaked to the newspapers by the official public relations representative of the union, a social worker. This meeting became an important landmark in union history, forcing a number of councilmen to come out in support of the tenant unions and providing the movement with needed publicity.

Mediating with Landlords

Not all landlords who own property in the slums make a great deal of money from their houses. Some may own one or two pieces of property and live in one of them. In many cases, however, slum housing is owned by absentee landlords and often is managed for them by a realty firm.

Following the initial announcements of the formation of a tenant

union in Cleveland, the landlords formed their own version of the union. Some landlords were interested in seeing the union established because they felt it would educate tenants in proper maintenance of the buildings in which they lived.

> John Condor, a partner in the Chicago firm of Condor and Costalis, said after his firm had signed a contract covering some 2000 tenants in 25 buildings owned by the company and another 20 managed by it: "I am more or less happy about it . . . this neighborhood is in danger of rapidly deteriorating and I feel the only way to save it is through community organization." [5]

Most of the initial contacts with landlords were met with a willingness on the part of the landlords to sit down and talk over the problems. This was not always the case, and at times landlords refused to talk and coercive action was taken against tenants who were seen as troublemakers. At this point a letter or telephone call from the Legal Aid representative would remind the landlord of the tenant's right to join any group he wishes. However, although this often slows up action on the part of the landlord, with the exception of public housing he can evict a tenant without any reason whatsoever if there is no lease. (Retaliatory evictions have since been found illegal in Washington, D.C.)

The actual negotiation session usually took place between the tenant agent and the landlord, with one of the paid organizers and a lawyer also involved. Often the landlord brought his own lawyer. Initial attempts are made to present to the landlord some of the concerns tenants have about their apartments. In many of the cases, the major concern is not rent, but maintenance and code violations.

In essence the worker mediates between all the actors, although he represents the tenants. Even the landlord sees him as a mediator and looks to him for clues. Through his actions, the worker helps teach the tenant what he has to do to become a political person involved in a bargaining situation and also helps the landlord learn a new way of operating if he is going to enter into such a transaction.

Whenever possible, attempts are made to keep the negotiations out of the jurisdiction of the courts, because of the long waits and small fines given landlords for violations. Written into some of the tenant-landlord contracts are legally binding agreements to have any conflicts

---

[5] "Rent Withholding Rent Strikes, Tenant Unions, Mandatory Statewide Housing Standards," *The Journal of Housing,* Vol. 24, No. 5 (May 1967), p. 261.

over the contracts arbitrated by the American Arbitration Association (AAA). This group has also been concerned about tenant unions and has been doing research in this area to see what its role might be in relation to the tenant union.[6]

In Cleveland AAA sets up training in arbitration procedures for tenants and organizers. Hopefully, some tenants might in the future be able to assume some of the arbitrator's roles. This is in line with a new concept related to neighborhood legal services, utilizing semilegal court procedures—Legal Aid and even semi-official police forces. It is also an attempt to train the tenant in another aspect of political bargaining.

The purpose of the negotiation sessions with the landlord is to come to some agreement related to the desired change. In some cases it is actually impossible for the landlord to meet the tenants' terms and have any financial gain from the building. Part of the unions' program is to make available to the landlords information on the availability of funds with which correction of violations can be handled. In some cases the landlords have sold or turned over their buildings to the tenants because they have found them unprofitable or felt it was too much of a burden to continue to deal with an organized tenants' group.

Strategies in difficult negotiations have run from public denouncements at meetings and in the press of the kind of buildings the landlord is running, to picketing the landlords' houses, to placing rents in escrow. This last plan is legal in few areas—New York City is one of these, but elsewhere there is great risk for the tenants. The rent strike can be an effective tool, but is generally held as a last resort.[7] It has been used quite effectively in New York City, Chicago, Pittsburgh, and Cleveland. In Cleveland tenant unions have also developed strength in public housing and have worked closely with the Joint Committee on Public Housing, a coalition of groups, to bring about changes, especially with regard to maintenance and admission policies.[8]

---

[6] See, for example, "Neighborhood Housing Arbitration Rules" (Cleveland: American Arbitration Association, May 1968).

[7] For information on rent strikes see Frances Fox Piven and Richard A. Cloward, "Rent Strikes," New Republic (December 2, 1967), pp. 11–15.

[8] A complete report of the joint committee program in which the Cleveland Area Chapter of NASW was greatly involved is available in Public Housing for Cleveland Citizens (Cleveland: Joint Committee on Public Housing, undated).

In the tenant union, the actual delivery of services is part of a total service complex that encompasses the planners, financers, deliverers, and consumers of service. In essence the worker is part of a system within a system, for as he begins to operate he will find that the land-lords are also part of a system, and although the systems connect initially around the tenants, they begin to abut in other areas as well. Pressures are placed on the financers and planners of the service from the landlord system.

This type of intersystem contact not only calls for a mediating role for the social worker, but requires an extremely high degree of worker autonomy. The contract between the worker and his agency must provide for some freewheeling activity and support from powers at the central office. Even then he may have to make clear to the tenants just how far he and the agency will be able to go. Unfortunately, social welfare agencies for the most part have not been able to muster the type of support that permits many autonomous workers. Perhaps the climate is changing somewhat; as community groups in the ghetto areas start to demand and obtain funds for the programs they feel are relevant, begin to hire their own staff and do their own negotiating with the power structures, some restrictions on service may disappear. This is what has been happening in Cleveland, where the Cleveland Tenant Union has begun to search out and obtain its own funds. The social worker has a role here, too.

One model that seems to be evolving for the profession sees the professional as making the preliminary contacts in working with individuals, groups, and the like. The professional organizes the group, establishes the therapeutic contract, helps organize the agreed-upon action, and then the assignments are taken over by agency-trained workers. The lack of professionally trained social workers and the growing use of agency-trained workers suggests the possibility that trained professionals will increasingly be managers, supervisors, and teachers. The suggested model helps maintain the direct service role for the professional around the initial, formative periods of contact with people.

REQUIREMENTS OF THE SOCIAL WORKER

The role of the social worker as mediator in this type of system calls for a worker who can act in the following capacities:

1. Enabler in the area of communications, helping the various sub-systems deal with each other. In a community action program such as

the tenant union, communication is seen primarily as the process of transmitting and receiving information, the purpose of which is to get some type of action. The first ingredient necessary for successful communication between people is trust.

> The pathetic notion that you can improve communications by giving more and better information should surely be allowed to die a natural death; you will not get any reception if you are not trusted.[9]

Nothing of significance will happen between people if a feeling of trust does not exist. Unfortunately, the feeling of trust between those who want to help and those who need help is at a low state. But this trust can be developed and maintained if the worker maintains his service contract with the people with whom he is working, both consumers and other providers of service.

2. Provider or searcher of resources related to housing that can be made available when needed. These resources may be for tenants, landlords, and at times lawyers who need help in the area of organization and communication skills.

3. One who helps the tenant focus on the job to be done, negotiating for better housing. The tenants have many problems, but the focus must be on building the tenant union so it can negotiate and achieve its goals and helping the tenant learn the skills necessary to participate in the union and bargain actively. This becomes his area of expertise and the area in which both he and the tenants have agreed to function.

4. Teacher and trainer, helping both organizers and tenants to improve their bargaining skills.

5. One who helps the group in its efforts to work and demands work from all parts of the service system.

6. Specialist in behavioral science; the member of the team most prepared to help the members work together. Bion points out that the fundamental nature of the group is that it has two simultaneous kinds of impulses: work and emotionality (nonwork).[10] Each group always

---

[9] T. M. Higham, "Basic Psychological Factors in Communication," in S. G. Hamergager and J. L. Heckman, eds., *Human Relations in Management* (Cincinnati: South Western Publishing Company, 1967), p. 533.

[10] Wilfried Ruprecht Bion, *Experiences in Groups* (New York: Basic Books, 1961).

has both impulses, but at times one seems obviously more in command than the others. Bion refers to these impulses as the culture of the group. Emotionality is nonwork and it includes three ways of avoiding dealing with the task: fight-flight, pairing, and dependency. The role of the worker is to help the group maintain its work culture.

7. The agent who maintains a therapeutic stance on behalf of his client with all parts of the system. The worker carries with him the value system of the social work profession. He also maintains the meaning of various experiences, positive and negative, for people, and he can help the team tune in on this aspect of their work. His major concern must be what will best help the tenant and the system to use each other. The goal is to help the tenant become more autonomous, able to make mature decisions and see that these decisions are implemented. The tenant cannot be pushed into the decisions. He must work at his own pace. The tenant union is the tenant's tool.

Relating Community Organization Practice to Social Change

ROBERT P. MEJIA AND LYN WOODS

For the past several decades the entire social service system in the United States has been based on false assumptions. It clearly has not served the needs of the urban Negro poor. Any community organization effort that serves their needs must be geared to helping them to engage in the decision-making processes that affect their lives and their community, to overcoming their powerlessness (i.e., estrangement and exclusion), to realigning the community's power resources so that they, the consumers of social welfare services, can define their needs and negotiate on their own behalf.

If the social work profession has any professional commitment to this goal, we must develop a social action–social change practice model and become actively involved in the struggle for Black Power. This paper will deal with the critical reasons why community organization services must be changed and will present a practical application of the advocacy and activist roles inherent in a social action model.

THE NEEDS ARE DIFFERENT

The assumption has been that the needs of the urban Negro poor are the same needs other poor ethnic minorities felt in the past; in fact they are entirely different. The poor immigrants arrived in this country

270

with a group solidarity derived from strong religio-ethnic communal forms. Their autonomous (i.e., separatist) institutions were transformed into vehicles for political and economic power. Political support was bartered for the advancement of group needs and interests, ethnic solidarity was used to achieve control of local governments, or ethnic groups actually set up their own separate service structures or their own governments.[1]

During the process by which ethnic solidarity was being transformed into power for social mobility, social welfare structures were needed for protection of economic gain. One such structure was organized labor, which was as Marxist as any movement to date and should have proved the necessity of collective action and conflict strategies to achieve social reform. Furthermore, labor's organizational efforts were met with violence, similar to the violent response to collective actions that the Negro's efforts have evoked.

These ethnic coalitions also forced passage of federal social welfare programs designed to protect them, such as the 1935 social security program, 1937 public housing acts, 1946 full employment legislation, and the 1949 housing act. All that was left for the social work profession was to offer services that would socialize the ethnic minorities for assimilation into the American melting pot, services that taught how to speak English inconspicuously and how to make oneself "acceptable." Being white, of course, made the assimilation possible. The unorganized Negro poor, who do not have the political muscle to effect changes in these institutions, continue to be left out.

The Negro poor have been subjected to welfare programs not of their own choosing, and the grim reality is that they spend the major portion of their lives in a continuous battle to achieve a decent existence. How can they believe they have a say in what happens to them, their children, their homes, and their futures in the face of a racist and brutal police force, unjust and repressive welfare structures that deny as many as they purport to serve, a paternalistic school system with prejudiced, frightened, and inferior teachers? Grosser maintains:

---

[1] There are at least two examples of this in Detroit alone. When the Detroit city government excluded and disenfranchised them, the Polish set up what became in effect their own separate city within a city, Hamtramck, and the Armenians did the same in Highland Park. Similarly, religious groups have established their own social service systems. But any effort on the part of Negroes to develop separate institutions is considered "reverse racism."

> . . . the institutions with which local residents must deal are not
> even neutral, much less positively motivated, toward handling the
> issues brought to them by community groups. In fact, they are
> frequently overtly negative and hostile, often concealing or dis-
> torting information about rules, procedures, and office hours. By
> their own partisanship on behalf of instrumental organizational
> goals, they create an atmosphere that demands advocacy on behalf
> of the poor man.[2]

The perception that these repressive structures are maintained and perpetuated by service professions because of institutionalized racism is
inescapable.

To offer meaningful services would mean to help poor Negroes acquire group power, and that would mean the white structures would
lose control over black communities or client groups. And control,
not money, is the issue. Why else is this country the only industrial
nation that does not have a family or children's allowance, although the
administrative costs would be far less than for the present system of
Aid to Families with Dependent Children? Why do we not have a
negative income tax, which top economists such as Leon Keyserling
and Walter Heller say would be much cheaper to administer than present
income maintenance programs and less demeaning?

In practice, community organization services have consisted of planning and co-ordination and a little community development. The basic
assumptions of traditional services and inherent "professional roles"
are that needed resources are available and all that is required is "expert
allocation," better use of resources, or making the needs known to the
proper agency. The accepted roles (enabler and broker) demand complete professional neutrality and have been geared to process rather
than goals. These self-imposed limitations are really a way of evading
the responsibility to commit fully social work knowledge and skills to
help black communities build power for self-determination.

The reluctance, couched in ethical terms like "professional neutrality,"
"objectivity," "loyalty to an agency," and "serving the interests of the
total community," is in reality due to the fact that to provide relevant
services would mean direct involvement in political organization, advocacy, and activism—involvement that must surely result in the necessity for assuming controversial positions. The irony of the situation is
that to offer these needed services, i.e., to help the Negro poor to

---

[2] Charles F. Grosser, "Community Development Programs Serving the
Urban Poor," *Social Work*, Vol. 10, No. 3 (July 1965), p. 18.

achieve economic and political power, would mean helping them to achieve true self-determination (as other ethnic groups have been allowed to do), and true self-determination is supposed to be the basis of social work's ethical structure.

NEW SOCIAL FORCES DEMAND NEW SERVICES

It has also been assumed that the civil rights movement, through a nonviolent appeal to moral conscience, has been effecting the necessary basic structural changes in society. But these changes have been only symbols or tokens as another look at the statistical picture of the Negro poor will demonstrate. They did not effect basic changes in social and economic structure, and Martin Luther King was fully aware of this.[3] The movement has failed because no attempt was made to form a viable infra-structure for political organization, so the gains did not include what is most needed—the giving up of control by white society and redistribution of national wealth. What the civil rights struggle did achieve was to make it possible for "acceptable" Negroes to be co-opted into the white structure, robbing the black community of potential leaders for possible organization of politically viable groups.

What we fail to realize is that riots (the preferred term is "insurrections") and violence are the natural reaction of powerless and unorganized people to oppression. This has been proved in the course of world history. When people feel oppressed and government does not respond to their needs, they have only a certain number of ways to react. The Negro poor have tried an appeal to moral conscience, and it has failed. They are now beginning to attempt to organize the separatist institutions that were avenues of power for other groups, but this is being thwarted as funding or support of such efforts is discontinued.

We have begun to experience the third alternative. Reverend Albert

---

[3] In planning the Poor People's Campaign, Dr. King said: "The American black man, after centuries of suppression, achieved finally his basic social and political rights. . . . We can now see ourselves as the powerless poor trapped within an economic oriented power structure. We are those men and women with certain inalienable rights, but without the means to express them. . . . Our insight into the structure of American society teaches us that the right to vote or to eat in any restaurant, while important, does not penetrate the 'power plant' and therefore does not actually affect conditions of living." "Statement of Purpose: Poor People's March," Washington, D.C., April 1968.

Cleage, Jr., a militant leader in Detroit, has spelled out the choices clearly: Whites can either begin now to turn over control of black communities to black people or prepare for guerilla warfare in the cities.

The significance of all this for social workers is that client groups will no longer allow us to provide services that they now realize are irrelevant. To understand this one must be aware of the extent of the cry for self-determination or Black Power—this cry is being expressed by nonmilitant groups as well as by militants in specific terms.

NEW PROFESSIONAL ROLES

It must be recognized that effective community organization efforts will have to be directed at helping community residents to coerce branches of local government and other social agencies to redress social injustices. As a matter of necessity, the worker's stance, both to the community residents and to the service bureaucracy with which he negotiates, must be that of advocate for the client group's position. Grosser makes the point dramatically:

> Striving toward the equitable distribution of these resources is the programmatic strategy that must accompany any bona fide effort to encourage the residents of the inner-city slum to help themselves.[4]

He goes on to define the advocacy role:

> . . . to provide leadership and resources directed toward eliciting information, arguing the correctness of a position, and challenging the stance of the institution.
>
> . . . [The worker] is, in fact, a partisan in a social conflict, and his expertise is available exclusively to serve client interests. The impartiality of the enabler and the functionalism of the broker are absent here.[5]

Often the advocacy role is not enough, especially when the organization, through inexperience, is choosing ineffective strategies. It is then the responsibility of the worker to assume an activist role, urging the group toward a specific strategy or goal. To paraphrase social scientists such as Grosser, Cloward, and Morris and Stein, the community must be taught that city agencies control the distribution of the re-

---

[4] *Op. cit.,* p. 16.
[5] *Ibid.,* p. 18.

sources they desperately need, and that these agencies must be forced to respond to their demands. This kind of partisanship cannot be avoided, for to do so is to sanction the criminal state of neglect that exists.

Example of the Advocacy Role

The Positive Neighborhood Action Committee (PNAC), a Detroit, Michigan, community group, had spent six futile months trying to engage the city Department of Parks and Recreation in negotiations that they hoped would lead to the inclusion in the department budget of some desperately needed facilities and services for their community. Finally, the department's general superintendent was forced to meet with PNAC.

A fact sheet was prepared for the community residents, listing possible arguments and excuses to be expected from administrators and possible rebuttals. This sheet also included a statistical and graphic analysis of parks and recreation resource distribution clearly showing that virtually all present resources and proposed federal programs were deployed in outer-city white areas.

Unfortunately, because of the lack of negotiating experience and uncertainty of their position on the part of community residents, coupled with the ability of the agency representatives to filibuster, conceal facts, dodge questions, and intimidate the community people, the fundamental injustices were not pressed by the residents. The bureaucrats were skillful in sidetracking the discussion with excuses like "Legislation is too complex for you to understand," or "There is not enough money to go around." Their attitude was one of indignation at having to be present at the meeting, and the effect of this was intimidating.

The worker entered the discussion by strongly pointing out that all of the responses from the parks and recreation staff were excuses, and these excuses were irrelevant to the purpose of the meeting, which was to decide how the documented recreational needs of the community were to be reflected in the budget appropriations for the present year and the years to come.

During the ensuing heated exchange (by this time two residents had gain enough confidence to join in the fray), it was pointed out that the community was not asking for more money. The worker repeatedly cited the discriminatory pattern of the allocation of resources, staff, and money. The department was accused of insulting the intelligence of the community residents by stating that they could not understand a piece of legislation. The community group was urged to demand reasons

why the department's resources were being distributed in such an unjust pattern, showing prejudice against Negroes.

What were the objectives achieved by this advocacy role? First, attention was dramatically focused on the department's unjust (if not racist) resource allocation policy and on the fact that control over resources was solely in the hands of the department. Second, irrational, angry responses on the part of the department's administrators resulted in their loss of the illusion of authority and thus broke down their "professional" intimidation of the residents. Third, the worker's strong advocacy position made it possible for the community group to accept conflict as a legitimate tactic for use in confronting institutions. Finally, the revelations brought out in the worker's exchange with the staff and their hostile responses served to infuriate community residents, and they made a more united and determined effort that persists to the present.

The morning following the meeting, the general superintendent called a United Community Services administrator to complain about the "unprofessional" behavior of the worker. He said: "After all, we are all professionals and one should not attack the other in front of community residents."

Example of the Activist Role

A local junior high school parents' group had for two years attempted to convince the principal and the Board of Education of the systematic breakdown of student behavior and the lack of a just and effective disciplinary policy. Student and teacher morale was nonexistent. Over half the teachers by their own admission feared for their safety and could not control their classes, let alone teach anything. Parents feared for their children's safety. Thus, a small handful of problem students were keeping the school in complete chaos. Efforts to meet with the principal on this problem were delayed and several attempts to outline the problems to the Board of Education were ignored.

Finally, one morning the school exploded—students roamed the halls and classrooms breaking windows, desks, and other equipment until they got tired and walked out. That evening the parents' group invited the principal to a meeting to be held at the school. (The principal did not attend since it was his naval reserves night.) The parents' demands of the administration (the assistant principal was in attendance) were (1) joint efforts at restoring order so they could feel safe in sending their children to school the next day and (2) assurance that the school administration would involve the parents in long-range solutions to the problems and that these solutions would be acted upon. Since the assis-

tant principal and board representatives could guarantee neither demand, the worker strongly urged the parents to keep their children out of school until they had the necessary commitments from the school administrators and the Board of Education.

A state representative in attendance that evening later charged the worker with "inciting people to riot, in effect excluding the democratic process." His position was that "our children need all the schooling they can get!" What child can learn or teacher teach when both are in constant fear of physical harm?

HOW CAN AN AGENCY ACT?

In the cases reported here, the worker was assigned to specific community groups on a formal contract basis, his professional behavior controlled by the sanction of either the community groups or the agency. The agency did this to protect itself from actions of the community group that might become threatening to the agency and from anticipated reactions from its board or other institutions to controversy arising from the performance of the advocacy-activist roles. Inherent in this social action practice model is the fact that the community is an employer and thus has the power to decide type, frequency, and standards of practice. This model is similar to the detached gang worker model of group work and also approximates the client-lawyer relationship.

If the social action practitioner has been successful, an organization will emerge that will begin to confront and threaten service institutions. When this happens, the logical tactic for the embarrassed or harassed institutions is to "get the agitator" through charges of unprofessional conduct or an attack on his personal life. This is a familiar tactic that has also been used against citizens who perform their roles too well in this country's "participatory democracy."

Thus the agency must formally accept its responsibility to protect its commitment to social action by educating its own board of directors and legitimating the practice model with other relevant publics such as the funding source.

Other problems that have not been fully dealt with in this paper include these:

1. The fact that the agency can withdraw services or break the contract with the community group. One solution to this would be a legally binding contract.

2. The most significant problem is that the repercussions of successful practice have interfered with other agency business. For example, one community group has for the past two years been exerting consider-

able pressure on local schools, resulting in a number of policy changes from the school board, including removal of three principals. These actions have been threatening to local school administrators and, as a result, most local principals are reluctant to allow the settlement's unit to operate in their schools.

The only solution to this problem seems to be for the agency to achieve legitimation as being exclusively a social action agency. This would not require that its entire staff be community organization practitioners, but the advocacy role could be used in the agency's other areas of practice as well.

The reality is that controversial social action services are cut short to protect the service delivery structure, although reasons are couched in ethical terms. But the real ethical issue is that deliberate withholding of needed services for the sake of vested interests perpetuates racism and poverty in society. Morris and Rein point this out: "The question for us is whether our commitment to professional neutrality and noninvolvement is to continue to sustain our professional practice." [6]

---

[6] Robert Morris and Martin Rein, "Emerging Patterns in Community Planning," *Social Work Practice, 1963* (New York: Columbia University Press, 1963), p. 174.

PART V

Breaking the Grip of Agency Inertia

If social workers are to change social services, they must change the agencies that provide the services. Having said that, we might, like the old church mouse, leave to others the best means for belling the cat. In point of fact, this is essentially what the profession has told its members for years. "Go out and change the agency—but you figure out the means and provide your own means of survival while you are doing it." We should not be surprised, then, that social workers have had little success in changing their agencies from within.

Originally, social agencies were looked on as benign allies in the job of helping people. They were our source of support and our link with society. One was expected to identify with the agency. In reaction, we have sometimes gone over to the other side and seen the agency as the villain of the piece. That has had its own escape function, for how could one expect unalloyed evil to become good?

But we eventually have to come back to face reality. Most social workers are employed in agencies, and there is every indication that they will continue to be. Agencies respond to interests, some of which are irrelevant or even hostile to social work professional values. And they are hard to move. The papers in Part V consider a range of strategies for coping with these hard realities.

Morris's overview of the problem of changing social service institutions provides a number of clues as to how to go about the process. His paper is an especially concise presentation of major considerations in change strategy.

Weinberger examines the role of the executive in institutional sta-

bility and change. He provides a useful reminder that, despite some views of bureaucracies as being inaccessible to human control, the individual administrator has significant opportunities for bringing about change and should not abdicate his responsibility on the assumption that he can do nothing.

The next two papers deal with attempts to overcome organizational problems in Mount Sinai Hospital in New York City. Rehr and Goodrich describe a wide range of planned innovations and the factors that impeded their implementation. Ravich and her two colleagues offer the hospital Ombudsman as one means of coping with organizational inertia. Being a creature of the bureaucracy, however, the patient service representative can only partially fulfill the Ombudsman function.

Levin suggests that problems of financing are a major factor in failure of social agencies to be more responsive to changing needs. Tax-supported agencies maintain monopolies in designated sectors of the social services, while voluntary agencies' preoccupation with budgetary problems diverts their attention from problems of service effectiveness. He proposes the use of social insurance coverage for social work services as a means of lessening these tendencies, while at the same time protecting against unanticipated risks under conditions of dignity.

Agency inertia is usually thought of as emanating primarily from the upper and middle ranks of an organization. But it is frequently the line worker who sabotages the best-laid plans for agency change. Blickstein and Leyendecker describe an attempt to prepare the casework staff of a large welfare department for liberalized eligibility requirements.

Strategies for Innovation in
Service Delivery

ROBERT MORRIS

This paper is intended to consider strategies for innovation—ways of implementing better service delivery through changing the institutions that provide services. This implies knowledge of what constitutes a better system or set of goals and also of ways of changing the social work profession and social welfare institutions—implications that may be misleading and frustrating. Whatever we know about change, the process is complex and calls for a sophisticated technology. Unfortunately, social work's approach to change has been idealistic (which is necessary), and it has also been simplistic, which forecasts failure in a complex world. Social work has relied overmuch on the rightness of its views, on a generally humanistic value stance, on intermittent educational efforts, and on sporadic outthrusts of activity.

Many new ideas have been introduced recently, but they have been in the nature of a laundry list of possible actions. They have not yet been unified or informed by a sense of strategy. Some of the more promising of these ideas will be considered here, to see if they can be put together in such a way as to constitute a strategy for innovation. *This will not be a prescription for any specific project. It may be a framework by which a useful strategy can be shaped.* But first it is necessary to agree on the term strategy itself.

281

A SENSE OF STRATEGY

A sense of strategy requires an honest acceptance of the complexity of man's organizational life. When we speak of "challenging social institutions" or, for that matter, "changing social work institutions," we are not speaking simplistically of wiping out everything that exists and replacing it by something ideal. We are speaking about making changes yet to be specified, by persons yet to be defined, using steps not yet ordered, and directed against targets or objects not yet named.

A sense of strategy is acquired most easily by asking ourselves the answers to a few simple questions each time we want to start a campaign—who? what? where? how?—and probing deeply for answers.

Clarity About Goals

Clarity about goals is a central element. Does one goal contradict another? What is being sought? Most social work goals are expressed in cloudy generalities to cover their contradictions. Consider the recent statement by the National Association of Social Workers on income maintenance. Its preamble is an excellent rallying cry about which people can easily agree. When one gets to details, however, the internal contradictions weaken the strategic sense.

The association is interested in expanding the general economy, improving the social insurances, reforming the public assistance program, and also administering either a universal benefits system (negative income tax) or a demogrant—a children's or family allowance. These are not goals for a strategy. Instead, they represent a compromise among the differing forces within the profession, each of which has been satisfied by a statement of what *it* considers to be of primary importance. But a goal for strategic purposes is not arrived at by adding together the contradictory ends of many parties in order to achieve what must be a spurious consensus. Any major strategy to reorganize public assistance, for example, is bound to deflect and divide the energies of those who are interested in a negative income tax or a family allowance system.

Another example of contradiction is seen in federal policy itself. The U.S. Department of Health, Education, and Welfare has recently enacted a major reorganization in which income provision and service delivery have been divided administratively. Almost immediately the Congress introduced a policy of work incentives which virtually requires that services and public assistance be closely attached to the payment of income. Both policies presumably are binding on the delivery system and each contradicts the other.

Such examples are introduced to suggest that rationality is needed as much as passion to produce a reasonably clear statement of purpose for innovation, and that goals must be consistent with each other, not contradictory.

Where and How of Strategy

When we ask the question: Where is our action or strategy directed? we are talking about the targets of change, which means changing our own institutions—the social agencies that employ us. And if innovation is to mean anything, we are talking about changing them even when they do not want to be changed.

Such action involves attacking not a single target, but a succession of targets. Decision-making in American society is, by and large, dispersed among a number of interlocking centers. Great enthusiasm for a single battle is patently insufficient.

The *how* of strategy is determined by one fact—that nearly all social organizations resist change and do so for various reasons, not necessarily solely because of ignorance. It may be due to vested interest, philosophy, ideology, a commitment to alternate ends, and prejudice. If the resistance to change is universal and has various explanations, then the strategies to overcome this resistance must be more than educational, since education is best directed primarily at ignorance.

A sense of strategy has two other characteristics: willing flexibility with regard to the means to be used coupled with a patient persistence about the ends to be achieved. Strategy is worked over time; it is not an instant problem-solver.

Limiting Social Work Commitments

When we try to act out this sense of strategy we confront more sharply than we like the fact that we ourselves have limited our performance. Many of the limitations in the range of tools and methods that might be used to enhance our effectiveness as change agents are self-imposed by three social work commitments:

1. *The commitment, inculcated by professional social work training, to education and the creation of a consensus to a controversy as the major acceptable strategy for professional behavior.* Consensus and education cannot be objected to per se, but they can be questioned when they become the exclusively acceptable pattern for social work behavior. They are necessary, but are not sufficient for innovative change. Social work as a profession has seldom considered seriously the boundary

beyond which consensus is counterproductive to the changes the profession seeks. However, lacking attention to this boundary, social work education has done little—if anything—to prepare the profession for additional kinds of steps that will be outlined presently.

2. *The preoccupation with professional integrity.* Social workers have reached out to collaborate with other professionals and with social work's clientele tentatively and only comfortably when that collaboration is on our own terms. However, effective collaboration with others can become effective only if we match our concern with our own professional values with open-minded readiness to consider the values and views of others in achieving commonly desired goals. To seek to impose on others our specific value stance, without being ready to give serious consideration to theirs, ends up in our being narrowly sectarian or presumptuously dictatorial. Beneath our general aims there lurks a defense of our professional status. The more social work attacks broad problems that trouble many people, the more effective it can be.

Examples can be seen in many social workers' suspicion of our easiest allies, economists and social scientists. We reject the economists' use of money as a measure and resist administrative efforts to use such tools as costs-benefits analyses. And when social science researchers introduce other objective measures of behavior, we are equally suspicious. Skepticism is useful, but so is open-mindedness when we seek colleagues in an action enterprise.

3. *A latent, if not manifest, commitment on the part of social work toward protecting the employing agencies.* This latent and often hidden protectiveness obviously makes it difficult for social workers to act freely to change those institutions. A close reading of NASW's Code of Ethics, for example, uses such statements as these: "I use in a responsible manner information gained from professional relationships," "I . . . use appropriate channels to express judgment . . . ," "I distinguish . . . between my statements and actions as an individual and as a representative of an organization." None of these statements taken by itself need be questioned. However, a review of cases appealed for violation of the Code of Ethics will uncover few instances in which the profession has defended individuals who have openly and vigorously attacked the policies or practices of an established employing agency. The interpretation of "appropriate behavior" is subjective and often made by defenders of the status quo.

There are honorable individual exceptions, but as a profession, social work has taken little initiative in redirecting efforts of its own agencies to deal with two of the most pressing problems of the times, racial discrimination and poverty. There are few instances in which employees

of the major counseling or helping agencies have fought vigorously to reverse the scale of priorities of their own employers in order to introduce neighborhood health centers or counseling services for the most poor. Similarly, there are few cases in which social workers have vigorously and persistently attacked the unwitting, if not conscious, tendency of their own public and voluntary agencies to avoid employing Negroes in sensitive and critical policy positions.

These are not mentioned to malign the intentions of colleagues. The point being made is that the redirection of social agencies' efforts requires that the present work of these agencies be challenged as a prelude to change. And in this task we are too likely to challenge someone else's agency rather than our own.

ADDITIONAL STRATEGIES

To strengthen social work's capability, seven additions to the present approach to innovation are suggested that it is hoped combine the best of our heritage with a disposition to experiment.

Diversify Strategies

The first approach is to diversify and make more exact a wide range of strategies, effective in specified cases and useless in others. Hokenstad has developed a useful model for sharpening a sense of strategy.[1] Instead of relying on general slogans and one-track means, he suggests five explicit types of service problems: services that are inadequate, inaccessible, underused, fragmented, or discontinuous. Each problem has an appropriate high-priority goal that differs from the rest. And fifteen specific strategies are outlined, assigned to the goals for which each is considered most effective. Social work's armamentarium can indeed be enriched and diversified.

Update Conventional Approaches

The social work tradition of consensus-building and education can be strengthened by a major investment in the updating of conventional approaches. This can occur mainly through allocating a larger share

---

[1] Merl C. Hokenstad, Jr., "Planning for Improved Service Delivery in Urban Neighborhoods." Paper presented at the Second NASW Professional Symposium, San Francisco, Calif., May 1968.

of monetary and manpower resources, however limited they may be, to active research and development.

If social workers are to continue to persuade others, our powers of persuasion must be greatly improved. It is no longer sufficient to argue that our cases reveal the need or that Judeo-Christian ethos requires this action. Our audience has become too sophisticated. It knows that our ethical inheritance sanctions several roads to salvation, not just our interpretation of the proper road. It also knows that professional and agency experience is subjective, and that it is subject to self-serving biases. An audience now asks for more-objective data to support professional experiences and biases.

A combination of applied and rigorous social research may give the objectivity needed for greater persuasive power. Although lip service has long been given to this ideal, few if any social agencies have invested any significant part of their income in such research. It has been customary to complain that there is not enough money for service and therefore research cannot be afforded—we have been on a downward spiral of persuasive effectiveness.

In the voluntary field about 2 percent of expenditures are made for all of central planning and administration, which leaves precious little for research, and service accounting, which is included in this total, is not developmental research. Local public agencies have virtually no research funds.

The federal agencies do a little better in some of the newer emergency programs, but when it comes to that bedrock of public social welfare— the public assistance program—a fraction of 1 percent of expenditures is earmarked for research and little of that is obtained by social work, in a university or in an agency. The National Institutes of Health and specifically the National Institute of Mental Health have more funds, but only a tiny fraction ends up in a study of social welfare issues and institutions.

It is clear that ways must be found of using service and administrative funds for research if that service is ever to be improved by our own persuasiveness. A goal might be the earmarking of from 1 to 5 percent of all welfare funds for research, depending on the size of the program concerned. Since individual agency budgets are often too small to make this meaningful, pooling these amounts can be tried. Such pooled funds can be allocated to a social research institute acting under instructions of the donors, or they can be used as a pool on which research can draw for social work projects. Control will be a problem, but not an insurmountable one.

Stance Against Agencies

An adversary stance must be taken against, as well as for, social agencies. Social workers can broaden their ethical practices vis-à-vis the responsibility each worker has to his employer. The tendency is to protect and defend agencies on the grounds that they have more than enough enemies as it is. Limits of money and public understanding are serious at all times. Still, our own agencies are an integral part of any innovation we seek. This calls for full professional acceptance of employee action taken against their agencies to alter certain policies. What we could benefit from is a certain amount of freedom to widen the range of interference in order to achieve ends that may turn out to be socially useful. It is not possible to prejudge what will or will not be useful in advance of the test. One need consider only the extent to which the profession today, through its heavy reliance on supervisory and administrative superstructure, provides sanctions against and deterrents to employees who seek to challenge agency-determined policies.

One need only consider the twin trouble spots of the times: civil rights and poverty. Are agency structures to be considered so fragile that social workers as employees are to be prevented from pressing their own agencies to make an aggressive and active search for minority group members for employment in key professional positions?

A classic example is public assistance, with the private family agency not far behind. Social work should either abandon all responsibility for public assistance or get serious about it. If we are to be serious, then social work, within and outside public assistance, can launch a campaign to expose the central flaws in this program, as Comanor has.[2] These are flaws in our own and in society's way of viewing the poor. Action is required in each city and state, as well as in Washington. Until we substitute a radically better program, our hopes for a better society remain vacuous. To substitute a better program means completely discarding kid-glove treatment.

Similarly, it speaks not too well for the profession if some agencies and most social workers concentrate their services on the nonpoor and counseling on the grounds that these are the population and the method for which the profession is best equipped. Such a stance only increases social work's inflexibility.

It is not satisfactory for the profession to ask others to change with-

---

[2] Albert Comanor, "Social Service Delivery in the United States," this volume, pp. 27–49.

out changing itself. Social workers should make it uncomfortable for their own agencies to maintain traditional policies; they must expose agencies to the pressure for change that the profession can bring to bear on its own employers.

Use the Courts and the Law

The social work armamentarium should be enlarged to include the use of the courts and the law as an instrument for altering or changing policy. Historically, social work efforts have been devoted to the legislative process to enact new laws. The fact that perhaps 90 percent of the service function is carried out through administrative processes that are presumed to execute the legislative intent has been ignored. But the present-day scene is cluttered with illustrations of well-intentioned laws that have been undermined and destroyed, not only by unsatisfactory funding, but by unsatisfactory administrative policies and practices.

The profession is grateful to attorneys and others who use the courts to reverse harsh administrative regulations that result in forced labor for welfare clients, arbitrarily restrict freedom of movement across state lines, or arbitrarily support unjust denials of assistance. It is only regrettable that it has not been social workers who have initiated most such action.

The civil rights movement in this country is a classic example of how the courts can be used to set policy and to put in motion a vast process of social change. It is quite possible that the courts, in carefully selected situations, can also be used by social workers to alter the forced labor practices and the arbitrary restrictions on privacy and movement that are now embedded in administrative regulations and legislative authorization. It would be beneficial if the new work incentive program enacted by Congress could be bird-dogged by some persons in the profession, so that socially indefensible forced labor by AFDC mothers might be challenged in the courts. It is even possible that the movement toward simpler administration of eligibility and the granting of relief itself might, here and there, be challenged by taxpayers in the courts. It is grand that a social work administrator in New York City advocates determination of eligibility for assistance by affidavit, but it is possible that in more recalcitrant parts of the country legal process might serve the same end.

The use of legal means by social work could be made real in several ways. Planning councils and large voluntary agencies could agree to finance a legal office to act as a voluntary Ombudsman or as a social

welfare liberties union. Alternatively, local professional groups could organize such services financed by local dues or local foundations and mounted in co-operation with university professional schools. Or the creation of an official Ombudsman office could be pressed for each locality, but this would require some means to ensure that the Ombudsman is free from constraint to act on behalf of welfare clients.

Publicly Visible Accounting of Programs

It is necessary to face quite frankly the fact that accountability for social welfare is of two orders. First, it consists of Madison Avenue-type promotion of the wonders of social work programs. Second, real accountability as to results is buried under a layer of obscuring reports and service statistics that do more to hide than reveal what programs accomplish. The writer is not talking about social indicators, which are primarily a baseline against which to measure change. Rather, what is meant is the development of some means by which the achievements of agencies in relation to their professed program goals can be brought into high public visibility. Much professional attention in recent years has been devoted to the protection of professional practice. What is much more urgently needed today is a program of accountability for agency results. If social work skills accomplish the results they claim, the profession need have little to fear from this kind of visibility.

Lest this be considered an easy tool, it is worth noting that several efforts to develop regional data banks for the centralization of agency information have run into the most vigorous and violent opposition from all kinds of health and welfare agencies, which object to the sharing of any information that might conceivably, and in any circumstances, be used to cast any kind of doubt on their operations. In many places data have not been shared simply because agencies do not retain the right to censor whatever is reported about their program.

Social workers share this reluctance. We are happy to report how many persons we have helped. We are reluctant to look at social problems such as delinquency, poverty, and divorce to see whether our work has had any impact on the incidence of such problems. And we resist public testing to ascertain whether our methods help individuals and families more or less than other approaches. For example, are disengaged youths helped more by counseling, group activity, employing them as youth leaders in settlements, getting them industrial jobs, getting them into the army, using untrained indigenous counselors, or leaving them alone?

Studies of public welfare have, by and large, been directed to better

ways of using unavailable professional workers and of relieving the
manpower shortage by use of bachelor's degree holders. Little has been
done to make visible the likely link between inadequate income and exclusion of 75 percent of the needy from relief by investigations on the
one hand and infant mortality, deviant behavior, and disability on the
other.

It is doubtful whether this kind of subtle censorship by omission should
be tolerated any longer. What it does, of course, call for is the courage
to talk about social work's failures as well as its successes, and this can
become an incentive to alter programs. Perhaps in each city there can
be an independent social audit corporation—a kind of better welfare
bureau acting like a Better Business Bureau.

Abandon Preoccupation with Service Duplication

The preoccupation with duplication of services and co-ordination is
based on the mistaken assumption that somehow social work's scarce
resources may be dissipated by duplication. A wide accumulation of
evidence now reveals that social work is plagued by a shortage of
resources rather than a misuse of them. Co-ordination in its essence
involves agency monopoly. It involves carving out territories, refining
them, and allocating them to single agencies in the mistaken belief that
in this way efficiency is maintained. In a number of places competition
among agencies might be much more salutary if innovation and change
are really desired.

Hamish Gray of the Institute of Economic Affairs, London, England,
proposed recently that an income maintenance system based on the
negative income tax be accompanied by a certificate system for social
service to ensure competition or to reduce tendencies to monopoly.
Certificates might be given to or sold to anyone who has the need for
service, for example, if day care, nursery, or health services were to be
considered a public utility, certificates would be made available to all
in the population with children. These certificates could be redeemed
whenever the recipient wished to use them. Instead of clients being
forced to go to an assigned agency to make an application to be accepted
for service, providers of services are free to organize themselves and to
compete for clients against the city-wide or regional market of consumers who would go where the best product is available.

Neat agency boundaries are already breaking down in a sense. Out-
reaching neighborhood service centers in urban ghettos usually duplicate
services offered by city-wide agencies, despite the fact that each claims to
use the other. Self-help efforts often replace service efforts by formal
agencies.

The certificate idea presents a great many difficulties, but it is valuable mainly as a stimulus to real innovation as compared with merely reworking the old service system without any substantive change. Experimentation at least is called for. Will the profession try it or something better? Or will initiative be left to others?

It would be equally interesting if some voluntary agencies would abandon their latent, if not open, interagency agreements requiring that applicants must of necessity be referred to a sectarian agency of their religious persuasion. The same might be said about settlement houses and the network of medical, character-building, youth, and adult leisure programs that often impose territorial boundaries on eligibility for use or membership. There is no reason why such agencies—including the Boy and Girl Scouts—could not have pioneered more than they have in a sort of busing program, breaking down racial barriers so that Negro youths who are interested in a program might be encouraged and even helped to go some distance away to a white "Y" or scout troop in order to break down the segregation that is inherent in the present residential pattern of eligibility and service allocation.

It is hoped that the time will come when such measures that destroy neighborhood integrity will not be necessary. But it *is* necessary to consider the contemporary situation when strategies are discussed. The particular situation requires a particular strategy appropriate to a specific end.

Forging New Coalitions and Alliances

Forming new coalitions and alliances constitutes a final strategy. If social workers are not powerful themselves, perhaps a coalition will strengthen the profession. There is some slight basis for this in Washington among various organizations and representatives. But throughout the country the relationships between social workers and other groups is tenuous and intermittent at best.

There are a few essential guides to forming such alliances, since the idea is an old one, but it has seldom been acted on with vigor.

1. Building coalitions will require long and persistent effort.

2. Alliances can be ad hoc, formed around specific aims; they need not be uniform for all plans and all times.

3. Allies will have to come from outside the customary boundaries of social welfare. It is necessary to reach out, case by case, city by city, to whomever the profession can connect with.

4. Reaching-out will work only if the profession is open-minded about approaches and solutions that potential allies can contribute. We will not be successful if we insist that allies adopt our solutions and

methods in every case.   We can be clear about our aims but open-minded
about means.

5. It is necessary to resist illusions about the value of any potential
ally.   The current investment in alliance with organizations of the poor
and of minorities needs to be weighed with the time scale for our
strategy: Do we want results now or in a future generation?   If action
now is the aim, some allies will be valuable in helping to fix goals, but
will they be equally powerful in reaching those goals?   Few poor people
and few minority organizations can enhance action potentials *now*; only
a few are organized or can be organized quickly for exerting influence.

Many campaigns have been lost because of a naïve belief that the
poor or deprived have a mystical power and share social work values.
Sometimes they have only apathy, and more often they want quite different things from what the profession hopes to achieve, often wanting
too little.   Social workers have sometimes sought elaborate plans for
urban development, housing, progressive schools, or many public welfare
services, while the residents of an area may only want the garbage
collected, a more disciplinary school system, a small neighborhood park,
or intervention by the social worker as the price for a straight relief
check.

What is necessary is to keep separate our identification with some
allies because of shared values, identification with others because they
have power for limited purposes even if their values are different, and
identification with still others that simply represents an empathy with
their suffering rather than a useful alliance to relieve that pain.   In these
times of outreach to clients, they are first of all vital in helping us select
goals.   Whether they are also capable of implementation needs to be
checked in each case.

The work of alliance-building has consistently been led by a minority
of social workers.   This minority was often suspected of instability and
unprofessional conduct by employers and colleagues.   More effective
coalition-building requires abandonment of this labeling approach to
those whose actions are unconventional.   Instead, behavior can be
evaluated against the ends articulated by the profession.

CONCLUSIONS

The discussion of possible innovative strategies has continued far enough
to suggest some possible directions.   It is evident that few of these ideas
are new, and even fewer of them promise easy or quick solutions.

The very definition of "strategies for innovation" requires the development of a professional stance that is both logical and clear as well

as impassioned. It demands that social workers become fully aware of the intricate complexity by which social institutions are bound together. This complexity argues against any closed system for social work strategy that is to be judged solely by an appeal to social work values that may be inadequate. Social work's values and standards are broad and estimable, and they are shared, in fact, by a large segment of the educated population of the country. It is necessary to avoid the self-defeating and self-limiting tendency to interpret these standards narrowly and in such a fashion as to prevent us from developing strategies appropriate for achieving the desired goals. Building blocks for a strategy for innovation include the following:

1. Developing a sense of strategy.

2. Freeing social workers from self-imposed and arbitrary limitations on inventiveness.

3. Updating social work's persuasive powers by an allocation of service and administrative funds to independent community and national pools for research development.

4. Interpreting the social work Code of Ethics to protect maverick individuals who challenge the policy priorities of their own agencies.

5. Creating local centers for social-legal action to promote policy ends through the courts—a local social welfare liberties unit or an Ombudsman.

6. Establishing independent local and national social audit centers to give high visibility to professional agency deficiencies as well as achievements.

7. Replacing agency monopoly with some modest competition, thus releasing the straitjacket of agency boundaries and residential eligibility procedures.

8. Actively pursuing coalitions on an ad hoc basis, with allies appropriate for the action planned, being skeptical about the value of each alliance, but also open-minded about the contributions from each ally.

This list is neither perfect nor complete. It is offered to stimulate an active search for a viable strategy good enough for the general and humanistic aspirations social workers share with so many others in the world.

Executive Inertia and the
Absence of Program Modification

PAUL E. WEINBERGER

There has been a dearth of empirical research in social work about the relationship between needed new social service programs and the readiness of organized social welfare to meet emergent needs. Many impressionistic explanations have been offered for the slowness that characterizes program innovation. In this paper the focus of analysis is on one source of resistance to program modification: the social agency executive.

Based on a review of the social work literature, research findings, and selected interviews, it is the thesis of this presentation that it is the social agency executive, generally an individual with professional social work education, who shares major responsibility with the agency's board of directors in allowing "the dead hand of the past" to circumvent the implementation of needed new programs. The rationale for his conduct and suggestions for change will be discussed.

An analysis of selected voluntary welfare federation allocations shows a rather remarkable absence of change in funding patterns despite important innovations in federal and state legislation and in community social service needs.[1] Dinerman conducted research on the budgeting

---

[1] The passage of federal legislation providing medical care for the aged and for the medically indigent did not result in substantial voluntary welfare fund allocation changes to nonprofit hospitals. *See Annual Reports,* 1963–68 (San Francisco: United Bay Area Crusade, 1963–68).

294

process of public and voluntary social welfare agencies in Los Angeles County and found a heavy reliance on past experience together with an unquestioned acceptance of the status quo.[2] This obviated the possibility of any radical shifts in allocations in response to changing community needs.

A recent empirical study found a slight *negative* correlation between the allocation decisions of two Jewish welfare federations and the allocation choices made by two samples of Jewish religious leaders in the same geographic area.[3] Such indications of a disturbing lack of consensus between fund allocations and perceived service needs do not appear to be isolated examples. Rather, it would seem that the problem has not been sufficiently studied in the past.

EXECUTIVE'S DECISION-MAKING POWER

Conceptions of the decision-making power of the executive in the social agency have shifted over time. Before the massive infusion of organizational concepts and theories into social work, the agency executive, although technically subordinate to his board, was generally viewed as the partner of the board in a mutually harmonious undertaking.[4] The partnership concept was in harmony with the democratic value system of the social work profession and was based on the assumption that there is a community of interest and purpose among board, executive, and staff.[5]

More recently, using the framework of organizational theory, Senor advanced the view that in many work situations the executive is superordinate to the board.[6] He described several structural variables that

[2] Beatrice Dinerman, *The Dynamics of Priority Planning* (Los Angeles: Welfare Planning Council, 1965), p. 219.

[3] Paul Weinberger and Eugene Brussell, "Religious Leaders' Assessment of Jewish Social Service Priorities," *Journal of Jewish Communal Service,* Vol. 44, No. 2 (Winter 1967), pp. 184–191.

[4] *See* Harleigh B. Trecker, *Group Process in Administration* (New York: Woman's Press, 1950); Ray Johns, *Executive Responsibility* (New York: Association Press, 1954).

[5] Trecker, *op. cit.,* p. 5; *see also* Frank J. Hertel, "Administration Defined," in Florence Hollis, ed., *Some Dynamics of Social Agency Administration* (New York: Family Service Association of America, 1945).

[6] James M. Senor, "Another Look at the Executive-Board Relationship," *Social Work,* Vol. 8, No. 2 (April 1963), pp. 19–25.

enhanced the decision-making power of the administrator vis-à-vis his board. Empirical research findings document this point of view. In a recent study, administrators expressed a high degree of satisfaction with their ability to implement program changes regardless of whether their board initially concurred with new plans. Selected comments indicated board acceptance of program changes and innovations in those situations in which the executive informed and explained to the board the rationale for policy change.[7]

In the public welfare field, it has been shown that in a number of states welfare administrators have developed innovations in determining eligibility for public assistance that not only simplify procedures but also respect the client's dignity.[8] These changes were inaugurated without specific legislative mandate. They provide support for the thesis that the administrator has considerable autonomy to implement program changes if he is committed to the necessity for such a course of action.

ROLE OF THE EXECUTIVE

The definition of the executive role in the social welfare agency is that of the person who is responsible for and carries out implementation of the agency's goals and programs within the general policies established by the board. He also provides professional expertise to guide the board in relation to decisions that influence program planning. The professional training of the administrator and the usual requirement of practice and administrative experience prior to assuming an executive position are designed to provide the executive with professional know-how to help the board arrive at decisions.

Difficulties in clearly defining goals for social welfare agencies may prompt many administrators to favor the role of mediator rather than that of planner in dealings with their boards.[9] This tendency is pronounced among fund and federation executives, but it appears to characterize the executive-board relationship in voluntary social welfare

---

[7] Paul Weinberger, "The Job Satisfaction of Social Welfare Administrators." Unpublished doctoral dissertation, School of Social Work, University of Southern California, 1966.

[8] George Hoshino, "Simplifications of the Means Test and Its Consequences," *Social Service Review,* Vol. 41, No. 3 (September 1967), pp. 237–249.

[9] Roland L. Warren, "Types of Purposive Social Change at the Community Level," *Brandeis University Papers in Social Welfare,* No. 11 (1965).

generally. The executive de-emphasizes his role as professional expert and focuses on minimizing discord among board members. One technique used by the executive toward this end is to screen out items from board consideration that might be controversial. This process has been described as "non-decision-making," in that conflict is repressed through the executive's habit of introducing only "safe" issues for board consideration.[10]

EXECUTIVE'S JOB PERFORMANCE

The rationale of the social agency executive in minimizing conflict through an adherence to the status quo is a straightforward one. Administrators concerned with maintenance of their agencies seek to promote board loyalty, which in turn is seen as maximizing contributions from board members both financially and in terms of goodwill from other persons and organizations with which they have contact. In line with the consensus orientation of executives, past allocation decisions are the logical point of departure for future decisions because they have been validated by boards and have been found to be politically feasible. This strategy ignores the variable of changing community needs. It is based on the untested assumptions that board members and donors concur with past allocation and program decisions and might reduce contributions if funding patterns were changed.

In the service agency, the same rationale can be used to defer practice modifications because board members may be unaccustomed to changes in professional practice. The situation is frequently one that may be characterized as presumed cultural lag—the stress that occurs when related patterns change at different rates of speed.[11] The executive assumes that it may be unwise to present ideas about program modification in order to avoid disturbing the existing balance. It may be that the executive has an unduly negative perception of the ability of board members to take new developments in stride. Since many executives were influenced by the Marxist class struggle concepts prevalent in the post-Depression era, they may be unconsciously, and perhaps incorrectly, stereotyping board members as stand-pat conservatives. Also, the executive may be caught up in his role of enabler or facilitator instead of professional expert and guide toward needed program changes.

---

[10] Ralph M. Kramer, "Ideology, Status, and Power in Board-Executive Relationships," *Social Work*, Vol. 10, No. 4 (October 1965), p. 111.

[11] George A. Lundberg, Clarence C. Schrag, and Otto N. Larsen, *Sociology* (3d ed.; New York: Harper & Row, 1963), p. 697.

The absence of change in allocations to voluntary hospitals provides a case history in how welfare budgeting ignores social reality. Medical care for the aged and indigent was provided in 1965 under Titles XVIII and XIX of the Social Security Act. While the federal government assumed financial obligation for the care of the medically indigent, this has not resulted in any substantial reduction of welfare fund allocations to voluntary hospitals for clinic patients. In the case of one hospital studied by the writer from 1965 to 1968, the welfare fund allocation dropped from $206,000 to $190,000, while the fund executive responsible for allocations freely admitted that the number of clinic patients not covered by governmental funds was negligible. The allocation was explained off the record as a gesture to keep major fund donors who were also hospital board members happy.

The same point was underlined in a discussion of substantial allocations to Jewish-sponsored hospitals. It was noted that "hospital boards as groups represent the largest contributors to the [Jewish] Welfare Fund campaign, ranging as high as 30 per cent of the annual amount raised." [12] The inference apparently drawn by welfare fund executives is that donors who are also hospital board members might reduce or eliminate their contributions unless the hospital remained a major beneficiary of the welfare fund campaign. There are, of course, no empirical data to support this supposition.

VARIABLES INHIBITING POLICY-MAKING

It has been shown that the executive has ample decision-making power, as well as professional expertise, to utilize in promoting program change, but his characteristic stance tends to be that of a mediator. In view of the definition of his role, the executive has a professional responsibility to advise board members and other decision-makers about changes in communal service needs and to suggest remedial approaches.

This obligation to render a professional planning and consultative service to the board is frequently not met by the administrator. Since the social work profession is currently engaged in a major effort to remove obstacles to client service, all hurdles in the way of service delivery need to be identified, including the role performance of social work executives.

Among factors that might inhibit the executive from functioning as planner and advocate of change are the following:

1. Because of the vagueness surrounding goals in social work organi-

---

[12] Ben Rosenberg, as quoted by Samuel Spiegler in "Fact and Opinion," *Journal of Jewish Communal Service*, Vol. 42, No. 3 (Spring 1966), p. 289.

zations, the executive may rationalize the desirability of the status quo on the grounds that the advantage of change in funding or program often cannot be documented.

2. The values of social work have long been in the direction of trying to achieve consensus. This value applies to the executive-board relationship as well. However, research data show that conflict may be functional for the operation of an agency.[13]

3. Radical program innovations might produce board antagonists for the executive who could cost him his job. This possibility exists, as it does in line social work positions in which workers are sometimes penalized for championing unpopular positions.[14] A balance is provided by the fact that both line and executive positions are plentiful in social work and that people who lose out in the wake of a controversy can relocate in another position.

4. The male social work executive has been shown to choose board members as role models instead of other members of the social work profession.[15] This may inhibit executive initiative vis-à-vis the board since the executive may strive for harmony and acceptance by the group he emulates.

5. Fear of the unknown may be a factor in that the executive knows the boundaries of his present work situation, but may be anxious about modifications that could change the dimensions of his job.

It has been indicated that social work executives have frequently failed to include consideration of new community needs in their dealings with their boards. A number of assumptions and variables have been discussed that explain but do not justify the status quo orientation of many social agency executives. Since the dictates of professional conduct—to give primary consideration to client need—are honored in

---

[13] For example, nurses and physicians who had opposing philosophies and attitudes toward patients worked better together than those whose attitudes were homogeneous. See Herman Turk, "Social Cohesion Through Variant Values," *American Sociological Review*, Vol. 28, No. 1 (February 1963), pp. 28–36.

[14] Refusal to carry out so-called night raids led to suspension of a social worker in Alameda County (California). On appeal to the California Supreme Court, the decision was reversed and such unscheduled searches were declared unconstitutional. See *Parrish* vs. *Alameda Civil Service Commission*, Cal. Sup. Ct. 35 Law Week 2583 (1967).

[15] See Louis Goldstein, "The Social Agency Executive—A Study of Organizational Isolation." Unpublished doctoral dissertation, Department of Sociology, University of Minnesota, 1960.

the breach, new organizational arrangements are required to produce a better balance between communal social service needs and welfare funding.

TOWARD RESOLVING THE PROBLEM

In the voluntary welfare field, a persistent problem has been how to reconcile rational planning for social service needs with the reality that allocation of funds is based on past precedent and political considerations. One working assumption underlying social agency structure has been that agency administrators would provide information and professional expertise to enable lay boards to make planning and budgeting decisions. The writer's analysis of the job performance of the social welfare executive indicates that this assumption is incorrect and that lay board members do not possess sufficient expertise to make complicated allocation decisions on their own.

Another assumption has been that welfare planning councils would supply recommendations that could serve as the basis for decisions about social service priorities. In the past, operating either as independent agencies or as divisions within United Funds, such planning bodies have been impotent to effect implementation of new programs, agency mergers, dismantling of unnecessary services, and the like. The planners lack enforcement powers and are funded by the same source that allocates money to agencies for which they are to make recommendations for change. Since the very existence of planning councils is bound up with the fund-raising machinery that provides their income, the possibility of far-reaching, change-oriented activity by such planning groups is limited.

In an effort to come to grips with the problem, it is suggested that panels of objective, detached professional experts be selected by local chapters of the National Association of Social Workers. These panels would assess the need for existing and projected service programs and compare their findings with the recommendations of the agencies concerned. When discrepancies exist, the panel could make its recommendations public and would be authorized by the profession to exert veto power over the flow of funds until a mutually satisfactory reconciliation is arrived at. Since adverse publicity is harmful to voluntary fund drives, it is in the interest of the agency system to avoid public controversy. Panel members could be drawn from universities, nonprofit research institutes, and the professional social work community; would have no ties with the affected agencies; and would be rotated periodically to prevent formation of personal alliances. They could be paid by NASW through a system of dues collected from professional agencies.

The function of such a professional review board has points of congruence with that of a tumor review board in a hospital and with the provision for mandatory assessment of project effectiveness in War on Poverty programs. It locates control over social service priorities within the social work profession through use of qualified specialists not connected with the agency system and not dependent on it for their major source of income. The proposal is similar to the evaluation and accreditation process for professional schools in colleges and universities.

The panel would be able to rectify imbalances in allocations, suggest the inception of new programs if such recommendations do not emanate from existing agencies, and recommend the removal of programs or agencies that no longer meet a community need. Essentially, the panel would serve as an objective warrant for social work and the general public that there is a reasonable balance between service needs and allocations.

This proposal combines the variables of professional expertise and legal sanction to promote optimum delivery of social services.[16] Since conflicting requests for new and existing programs have strained available financing, the choice among program alternatives has become more complex and increasingly requires professional judgment. This development, together with the growing emphasis on empirical data as the basis for planning decisions, enhances the influence of the professional expert.

It is suggested that the variable of professional expertise be tied to a system of legal sanction. The scope and status of the review panel have to be defined and supported by the National Association of Social Workers and adhered to by social work agencies. Implicit in this proposal is the use of sanctions against noncomplying agencies. Such a plan for objective outside evaluation of the social services would constitute a clear indication of the profession's intent to put client service ahead of other considerations. Further, it would lodge with the profession full responsibility for its acts and omissions.

CONCLUSION

The social welfare scene has been characterized by a process of "muddling through": decision-making based on small incremental changes

---

[16] For a discussion of these variables, see Edmund M. Burke, "The Search for Authority in Planning," Social Service Review, Vol. 41, No. 3 (September 1967), esp. pp. 255–258.

that are closely related to past experience. Its essential ingredient centers around a preoccupation with maximizing security at the expense of incurring those risks that inevitably accompany radical change. This acceptance of the past as an unfailing guide to the future constitutes a serious barrier to improved policy-making in welfare and substantially weakens the administrator's role as a catalyst for innovation in response to changing social conditions.[17]

This paper has described reasons that explain, but do not justify, executive inertia. To improve the static situation in welfare budgeting, the injection of an objective review panel with veto power over funding decisions has been suggested. Such a panel can provide not only expertise and detachment, but can also serve as a spur to remind the executive of his professional commitment to client service. Thus, this new arrangement provides the possibility of nudging the social service system to arrive at decisions that provide greater harmony between community welfare needs and the financing necessary to implement needed services.

The inertia of the social welfare administrator has a great deal to do with the lack of program innovation and change in social welfare. An alternative has been suggested that addresses itself to this urgent problem of improvement in service delivery.

----

[17] Dinerman, *op. cit.*, pp. 221–222.

Problems of Innovation in a
Hospital Setting

HELEN REHR AND CHARLES H. GOODRICH

An article in a recent issue of the Sunday *New York Tim s* dealt with "laws" that have entered into common language. Two of those mentioned seem especially pertinent to the planning and implementation of multidisciplinary multiservice programs: (1) Fitz-Gibbon's Law, "Creativity varies inversely with the number of cooks involved with the broth," and (2) Weiler's Law, "Nothing is impossible for the man who doesn't have to do it himself." [1]

This is a tale of a "social health" program and its planning and implementation as a new ambulatory care system in a large general hospital located in an urban area in which there are both great economic deprivation and small pockets of extreme wealth. While the emphasis will be on the hospital social service department's approach to planning and its contribution to a social health program, the paper will describe the extent to which overall goals for ambulatory care have been accomplished, how they compare with the original goals, and what can be learned from the experience.

Under the impetus of Medicare, a new ambulatory care program was introduced in Mount Sinai Hospital, New York City, a large medical teaching center. The new Division of Ambulatory Care was committed

---

[1] "Faber's Law," *New York Times Magazine,* March 17, 1968, p. 117.

to the development of a program comprehensive in scope, including preventive and rehabilitative services, serving families in one unit of care, personalized in approach, and with continuity and co-ordination assured. This was to replace an antiquated, fragmented outpatient care system that was typical of many large medical institutions. The basic clinic system of hospitals in the United States has been described in the literature in the following terms: depersonalized, fragmented, with long waits, providing generally poor care or only sporadically good care, disinterested and frustrated staff, and hostility and lack of effective communication between patients and hospital staff members.

When social service has followed the medical model, it has encountered problems similar to those medicine is now facing. Fragmentation of care not only characterizes the delivery of medical services, it also characterizes the delivery of social services.

REORGANIZING THE DEPARTMENT

The plan for reorganization of the outpatient department was intended to overcome this ad hoc, fragmented, and splintered care by establishing a multispecialty group practice with comprehensive services co-ordinated and available twenty-four hours a day. Each Health Care Unit, as they were later called, was designed to serve about 1,000 families, or an estimated 2,500–3,500 persons. The adults' and children's sections were to be housed side by side, ensuring the proximity of the internist and pediatrician. The unit was to share key personnel such as a psychiatrist, nurses, social workers, social health advocates, and administrative staff, who were available to serve families in the same physical location. Frequently called-upon medical subspecialties such as gynecology, neurology, and orthopedics were to be located nearby so that patients referred to them would not have to leave the floor or make new appointments. Specialist opinion would thereby be immediately available to the patient and his doctor.

To assure continuity of social health care from out- to inpatient status, one social worker was to follow a family wherever members were to be treated. In addition, the unit nurse was expected to notify inpatient area nurses of her patient's admission. An appointment system, drop-in hours, and a telephone answering service similar to that used by doctors in private practice were features of the plan. The emergency room staff was to be on special alert for unit patients. Other projections for the overall ambulatory care program called for home care, day care for those in need of rehabilitation, and home support aides to assist patients with special needs at home. In addition, the program would provide transportation service either to the hospital for patients or to patients' homes for staff. Satellite storefront walk-in programs and special liaison with the local health department services were planned. A community worker was to develop better liaison between the hospital and its neighborhood.

Existing general medical clinics were to become Health Care Units. When specialty clinics existed, they would be available for consultation to the parent Health Care Unit and for continuing care to patients with special needs, such as hemophiliacs. These clinics could conduct approved research in relation to the Health Care Units, which served as the patient's "parent clinic." Guidelines and standards of care would be developed with the clinic chiefs.

The social services to be integrated into the ambulatory care program were evolved by the senior staff members of the department, who also projected the staff development needs. In anticipation of implementation of the general plan, social service in-service training began almost immediately. The training involved lay and professional leaders in programs serving low-income groups, professional and lay leaders from the local community, public health planners, and a number of lay persons who lived in the area. The staff learned about the local community, the different people who lived in it, and the nature of services available within the institution and in the local community, and heard new ideas about working with low-income groups. Staff also learned to what extent the neighborhood residents were unknown to them and that the social service department served comparatively few families from nearby areas. Later in the program, the Division of Ambulatory Care introduced a weekly series of informative talks along similar lines. It also undertook to learn in detail who was using the hospital's outpatient services.

SELECTED SOCIAL SERVICE PROGRAMS

The social service projections introduced the concept of social health to the program planners. This was perceived as incorporating those known somatic and multisocial, environmental, and emotional factors that comprise the social health of an individual in his family constellation. The Health Care Unit's concern was with illness, disease, or disability; the patient's physical and social functioning levels; and those other factors that affect his health. The social health concept was promulgated in the belief that sound medical care cannot be administered separately from an awareness of the social-emotional environment in which the individual lives. Data about this can contribute to medical diagnosis, while to be effective, treatment and rehabilitation goals require knowledge of the patient's social health. James noted, in testifying before the House Subcommittee on Health Services for the Elderly, that people are prone to support or modify health habits to the extent that their environment is well adjusted, self-sufficiency is maximally maintained, and decent family life and human dignity are achieved.[2] It was in the social health context that social services for general ambulatory care were conceived. Space permits only a brief description of selected programs.

Screening Mechanisms

Screening mechanisms for determining social need were seen as essential no matter what the point of entry into the medical care system. The existing case-finding methods, dependent on referrals by others, are inadequate, since the perception of need depends on those least equipped to make such a determination.

At the present time the Social Service Department is testing two case-finding screening mechanisms. One is based on an interview schedule conducted by nonprofessionals with parents of children receiving ongoing treatment for illness or disability. If the device is successful, it will permit some assessment of social problems directly or indirectly related to the child's medical condition.[3] A second screening method is utilized through a program the department offers new patients to facilitate their orientation to institutional services. For example, it is used with mothers of new pediatric patients and unmarried multiparas registering for obstetrical care. Each group session of eight to ten new persons results in two or three clients for social service.

---

[2] Dr. George James, dean, Mount Sinai School of Medicine, in his testimony before the Subcommittee on Health of the Elderly, U.S. Senate Special Committee on Aging, June 23, 1967, Part 1 (Washington, D.C.: U.S. Government Printing Office, 1967), pp. 71–76.

[3] Alma Young is responsible for the design and testing of the instrument. She first projected it in a final report to the Health Research Council of the City of New York, "A Co-ordinated Program for Out-Patient Care of Handicapped Children," December 31, 1966.

Other Program Aspects

The Patient Service Representative Program, a sort of Ombudsman for the sick, was created to meet the needs of persons encountering obstacles in obtaining medical care.[4]

A program of social health advocacy, originally proposed to serve ambulatory care patients and now serving out- or inpatients in all parts of the hospital, including the psychiatric division, has become a fully accepted program of social services, with at present five advocates (several bilingual), drawn from the local community with the assistance of community action groups and other social agencies. To orient them to the resources of the institution and the community, the advocates are specially trained in a prepared curriculum involving not only hospital social workers, but also doctors, nurses, administrators, and personnel from different community agencies.

Advocates help designated families residing in the local area to deal with needs that affect their social health status, such as shopping, diet, food preparation, household budgeting and management, school and welfare department relationships, baby-sitting, and escort services, if needed. They offer orientation to medical services available to new patients and families, assist the hospital's community worker in programs designed to help people to use health care services soundly, and aid in attempting to bring in patients and their relatives requiring medical or psychiatric care who fail to keep or have difficulty in keeping appointments. They also work alongside other hospital personnel, taking responsibility for information-giving, "steering," and advocacy services on behalf of patients and families in relation to agencies outside the institution, while the patient service representative program carries a similar function within the institution.[5]

In addition to some of the social service programs that have become

---

[4] See Ruth W. Ravich, Helen Rehr, and Charles H. Goodrich, "Ombudsman: A New Concept in Voluntary Hospital Services," this volume, pp. 311–320.

[5] For the concepts of patient service representative and social health advocacy programs, the authors are indebted to Alfred J. Kahn. We have borrowed freely from his Neighborhood Information Service proposals, adapting them to a medical institutional setting. See Alfred J. Kahn et al., Neighborhood Information Centers: A Study and Some Proposals (New York: Columbia University School of Social Work, 1966).

operational, a community relations co-ordinator now represents the hospital in the community, a well-run pediatric acute care (emergency) unit has been opened, administrative processing of clinic patients is smoother, and one Health Care Unit has been housed in the outpatient area, providing service to approximately 500 patients—about 20 percent of whom are known to the social workers in the unit.

On the other hand, only limited pediatric services are available within the unit. A family-oriented approach to patients is in operation for cases known to social service, but total inclusion of families under medical treatment in the unit remains to be achieved. Continuity of medical services on an outpatient basis is accomplished by each patient having his own doctor. A family-type record or card file system is under discussion. Selected patients are discussed in multidisciplinary clinical conferences. A weekly administrative conference serves to iron out old procedures and to introduce new ones. Some services for patients in the Health Care Unit, such as drop-in hours, emergency care, the inpatient co-ordinator, and the proximity of specialist consultation remain to be developed.

PRELIMINARY SPECULATIONS

Almost three years from the day planning began, it is realized that only part of the goal has been achieved. What has stood in the way of greater changes in the outpatient department? What follows are preliminary speculations; it must be kept in mind that the institution is undergoing major change.

1. Belief in a program of better services to people is not enough, nor is money to set up new programs sufficient in itself. General plans have to be translated to fit the specific environment. It is necessary to know that environment thoroughly and time the change process appropriately. The community medicine staff brought with them a model for ambulatory care designed for another institution. The pressure for making changes as quickly'as possible prevented the staff from learning enough about the hospital organization, its personnel, and the stake they had in the system as it existed. The existing staff had well-established lines of relationship and communication within the medical and administrative systems that had to be learned and related to.

In addition, information regarding the users of the hospital was not available, and systems for collecting data had to be created at no extra cost to the hospital. "Make-do" data-collection methods were initiated while proposals were designed and entered into the slow machinery of granting agencies to reach final approval a year and a half later.

2. Any change requires an investment in the change process on the part of those who will be involved in it. Such investment can be through either direct participation in the planning or indirect participation by endorsement of the plan and commitment to hold one's staff accountable for its actions. The writers have suggested that many cooks stirring the pot make for no easy planning operation. However, if future participants are not represented early enough and one profession attempts to speak for another, resistance can be anticipated. A plan for a multiservice program, co-ordinated and comprehensive, manned by different medical specialists and other professional staff, requires changes in clinical practices.

3. The question is raised as to how explicit power and control have to be made in any change situation. The position of the Department of Community Medicine, the newest of the twenty-four hospital medical departments and the one under which the Division of Ambulatory Care operated, was not made clear. The medical field has already defined the functions of its traditional subdivisions but has not yet clarified the role and function of community, preventive, environmental, or social medicine, as these departments are also called. Is the sphere of interest of community medicine the administration of sound medical care? If so, how does that differ from the concerns of administrative medicine, hospital administration, and medicine itself?

4. To implement its new ambulatory care program, community medicine was dependent on all other medical specialties, as well as on other departments. A change process of the proportions required takes a long time and invariably means conflict and confrontation. The mandate for change was so broad that alliances and alignments requiring full knowledge of the environment had to be created and solidified before the specific changes could be tackled. The power to achieve the mandate had not been invested in the director of ambulatory care. Under the existing system, such power could not be decreed, but would require an evolutionary change.

5. The authors have suggested that social work needs to look at its own system of service delivery and ask whether it mirrors the splintering practices of the medical model. Our unwitting support of fragmentation by our own practices has been noted. We credit ourselves with knowledge about dealing with crisis situations, but does it not become episodic care as we open, transfer, or close cases in rapid, successive steps? What about those families who face chronic ongoing problems with no continuing supportive assistance to offset anticipated crises? Do we not need to rebuild open-ended programmed services that have been co-

ordinated to invite people to use them before marked deterioration has become irreversible?

In the early stages of development of the ambulatory care program, staff spent a great deal of time in the community, meeting with the neighborhood residents. We agreed with people when they said they received poor care, and we tried to learn something about them and what they wanted from the hospital. We spoke of ideas for better services for the distant future and tried to tell the truth. Then we returned to the institution to work for change and left the people outside. We are no longer certain that the primary task of change is within the institution. We have begun to ask if one can successfully use inside instruments to change the inside or if one should look to outside instruments. Have we paid enough attention to the consumer and the role he can play? In returning to work on the inside, have we overlooked our engagement with the consumer to help him understand his rights to good medical care, to encourage him to be articulate, to acknowledge with him that he is receiving poor care? If we encourage the consumer's expression of his feelings, it means living with open and expressed conflict, which is not in keeping with either the conventional view of the social work profession or with established departments of institutions.

Ombudsman: A New
Concept in Voluntary Hospital Services

RUTH W. RAVICH, HELEN REHR, AND
CHARLES H. GOODRICH

Mount Sinai Hospital is located in one of the most heavily populated ghetto areas of New York City—East Harlem, which has an estimated population of 183,000, constituting over 10 percent of the people of Manhattan.[1] The hospital provides care for 34,000 inpatients and 60,000 outpatients annually and employs almost fifty different occupational groups ranging from professionals to unskilled workers. Over the past few years the institution has grown rapidly in both size and complexity. A concomitant of this rapid growth has been increasing difficulty in providing individualized services to patients. In addition, the hospital, which had previously been isolated within the developing ghetto, committed its resources to serving the health requirements of the community. While the Ambulatory Care Division serves patients from any section of the city, almost 50 percent of the outpatients live in the immediate vicinity of the hospital. Many of these people are underemployed and suffer from poor housing, overcrowded conditions, and inadequate educational opportunities. A large percentage are Spanish-

---

[1] These figures were provided by the Bureau of Records and Statistics, New York City Department of Health, July 1967.

speaking, which is an additional barrier to communication with hospital staff.

Recognizing the problems associated with expansion of service and seeking to be more responsive to specific difficulties encountered by patients in obtaining medical care, the hospital's social service department proposed creation of the position of Ombudsman, or patient service representative, to provide a means by which the many special requests, issues, and complaints regarding Mount Sinai's services could be registered and processed. The idea for instituting this service at the hospital was received enthusiastically by the Division of Ambulatory Care and by hospital administration, and the patient service representative program was put into effect in January 1967.

MODEL FOR THE PROGRAM

A model for such a program was the Citizens' Advice Bureaus, organized in London during World War II to aid the disrupted urban dweller. Kahn and his associates state the purpose of these centers:

> To make available to the individual accurate information and skilled advice on the many problems that arise . . . to explain legislation; to help the citizen to benefit from and use wisely the services provided to him. . . .[2]

Reuss and Anderson have described the Scandinavian concept of Ombudsman as

> . . . an agent of Parliament who receives and may investigate citizens' grievances versus bureaucracy. His powers are to recommend, to publicize and to report. . . . The Ombudsman meets the general need . . . for a means of resolving citizens' unique, individual problems with a depersonalized administration.[3]

The patient service representative program attempts to combine these two concepts—the Citizens' Advice Bureau and the Ombudsman. Its

---

[2] Alfred J. Kahn et al., *Neighborhood Information Centers: A Study and Some Proposals* (New York: Columbia University School of Social Work, 1966), pp. 33–35.

[3] H. S. Reuss and S. V. Anderson, "The Ombudsman: Tribune of the People," *Annals of the American Academy of Political and Social Science,* Vol. 363, No. 1 (January 1966), pp. 44–51.

two major purposes are to facilitate delivery of services to individuals encountering obstacles and to develop a system of appropriate feedback concerning impediments within the institution that tend to delay or prevent the delivery of comprehensive medical and social services. By providing a centralized office for registration of complaints and problems, staff can identify those obstacles to services, investigate their source, and contribute to the initiation of changes to eliminate them.

The program makes available to patients, staff, and community organizations a centralized source of information about the hospital and its services and offers direct consultation, referral, and advocacy. It keeps informed about community resources that can be used by Mount Sinai patients and staff. It also acts as liaison between the hospital and community agencies on behalf of their clients, facilitating use of the hospital by people living in the area.

The program was organized under the joint auspices of the departments of community medicine and social service. Its administration is under social service, but it is separated from all other programs of that department. The co-ordinator has free access to all levels of staff throughout the hospital and is able to provide feedback to the medical, paramedical, and administrative services so that procedural changes can be initiated.

The place of the program co-ordinator in the hospital hierarchy has been the subject of considerable discussion. Some administrators expressed the view that the position should be under the aegis of hospital administration. Others realized that if the patient service representative were to deal successfully with problems affecting more than one department, negotiation across departmental lines must be permitted. Establishing the position in two departments, social service and community medicine, both of which work in concert on the program, allows great freedom for the representative to contact hospital staff at all levels.

However, the program has no authority to effect change when such change is resisted. If it is to affect the Establishment at all, it must be through voluntary means involving persuasion and the documentation of problems to serve as a repeated reminder of the system's deficiencies. It must be kept in mind that when feedback is operating, other administrative and medical departments may view social service and community medicine as initiating complaints around their operations, procedures, and staff. Whether this critical role should be assumed is one that must be given careful consideration.

SERVICE USE BY STAFF

The first step in organizing the program was to talk with department chiefs and other key personnel in all areas of the institution in order to acquaint them with the program's objectives and to learn about services and procedures of the various divisions. An information file was compiled and is kept up to date as new information becomes available. Through group meetings, individual discussion, a personnel bulletin, and an announcement in the hospital newspaper, hospital staff—including nurses, administrative personnel, social workers, and physicians—were invited to use the services. Meetings were held with settlement house personnel and community action groups in the local area to alert the community to this new service and to invite them to use it.

The orientation of nursing and clerical staff in the clinic to the program took place at a time when many changes were occurring in the outpatient department. The Medicaid legislation was just being implemented and the department was undergoing reorganization, which required the department staff, both nursing and clerical, to be subjected to many questionnaires, surveys, and examinations of their procedures. At first the patient service representative seemed to be just one more annoyance. With time and patience, the staff were made aware that the program centered on the patient and on facilitating his use of the hospital and that its purpose was to pinpoint hospital procedural problems, not problem personnel.

Group meetings with the nurses and clinic staff yielded few referrals to the program. However, when the representative was present in the clinic, patients would approach and ask for help. On-the-spot talks with staff members about ways in which specific patients were helped to negotiate the system brought the program to the staff's attention and they began to make use of it, both when the representative was in attendance and later when he was not present.

Communication with the social service department was much easier. Small unit meetings were set up early in the program and staff began to use the services immediately. Social workers have found that the program provides a centralized resource for information about the hospital and community, can arrange special clinic appointments, and can solve problems about hospital fees.

Different methods of orientation to the program seem more effective for different groups of personnel, but in all departments experience has shown that frequent reorientation is essential to remind permanent staff and to inform new personnel about the purposes of the program.

TYPES OF PROBLEMS

Data were compiled after the program had been in operation nine months and again after fourteen months of operation. The number of referrals increased from an average of thirty-three a month during the first period to seventy a month. (For the first six months of 1969, new cases averaged over one hundred a month.) The largest source of referral—about one-third of the cases—was the social service department. During this period, referrals by hospital administrative staff dropped from 25 to 13 percent, a decrease that may be due to more direct referrals to the patient service representative by other sources such as nurses, community agencies, and physicians, and to an increase in self-referrals. The percentage of referrals from each of these latter groups increased slightly during the second period.[4]

In order to describe the situations most frequently coming to the attention of the program, the referrals have been divided into three categories according to type of presenting problem: services to individuals, problems regarding hospital policies and procedures, and requests from educational and social welfare agencies in the community regarding health concerns. Overlapping of categories exists, since individual requests frequently led to the uncovering of a problem in hospital procedure or to a community need.

Services to Individuals

Of the 650 cases reviewed, the majority—557—dealt with services to individuals. When these were further divided into patient care and non-medical problems, 84 percent were found to involve patient care. Of these, 27 percent had to do with the unavailability of medical records, which impeded sound medical care or prevented the delivery of medical information to requesting agencies; 26 percent involved problems with medical services such as dissatisfaction with staff attitudes, failure to provide sufficient medication to last until the next scheduled clinic visit, poor clinic co-ordination for patients requiring the care of different specialists, and delays owing to unavailability of clinic appointments; and 17 percent were requests for information and assistance in registering for

---

[4] Data for the first nine months of the program appear in Ruth W. Ravich, Helen Rehr, and Charles H. Goodrich, "Hospital Ombudsman Smooths Flow of Services and Communication," *Hospitals,* Vol. 43, No. 5 (March 1, 1969), pp. 56–59.

clinics and in making clinic appointments (the largest proportion of cases referred by community agencies fell into this category). Other requests reflected a need for interpreters to assist staff in communicating with patients, financial problems, including Medicaid information, requests for referrals to private physicians, and other needs.

The most frequent requests made by nurses were for help in locating interpreters, finding missing records and reports, handling difficult patients, and finding baby-sitters and escorts. Nonmedical requests were most often for help with housing relocation, finding homemakers, locating special services in the hospital, and providing information about employment opportunities.

Procedural Problems

The second group of cases dealt with hospital procedures and policies that were seen as blocks to patient care. Many requests were received for interpreters to help staff communicate with patients. While it was not possible to determine the exact extent of this need, the frustration of staff, especially nurses, was evident. In many instances communication took place through young children and at other times strangers sitting in the clinic area were asked to translate information of a highly personal nature. A notice in the hospital newspaper elicited a response from thirty-seven volunteers speaking fifteen different languages who were available to help occasionally by telephone or in person by appointment. This service is now in the process of being expanded. All employees who speak a second language will be registered with the telephone operators. Working hours, locations, and telephone extensions will be listed so that requests can be handled quickly and efficiently. The Personnel Department will initiate the "interpreteam" register and will keep it updated.

Another problem was the unavailability of medical records and laboratory or X-ray reports for patient care. When the medical record was not in the clinic, the physicians were often unable to continue treatment. Patients' records were sometimes unavailable for a period of several clinic visits because of incorrect filing in the Medical Record Department, delay by doctors in dictating inpatient hospitalization summaries, charts requisitioned for research that were kept for many months, and records that had been subpoenaed by the courts. This problem was discussed with the director of medical records. It was agreed that at the request of the patient service representative, laboratory and X-ray reports, when available, would be duplicated to start a new record for patients whose records were missing. A note in the new chart would explain the situation and direct the physician to take a new history of the patient. The unavailability of medical records was also a problem in the pediatric allergy clinic, where many children had to be retested before injections, which were discontinued when their charts became missing, could be resumed. This problem was resolved when arrangements were made for tests to be recorded in duplicate and one copy kept in the clinic.

The lack of communication between two medical services having joint responsibility for patient care often created difficulties. Occasionally patients were discharged by one service, which failed to notify the other of its actions. When the same social worker was assigned to both these services, better co-ordination of discharge-planning was achieved.

Community Concerns

The third category of cases led to the provision of various community services. A request for information about hospital facilities resulted in tours of the institution being arranged for community groups. Talks on birth control were given to neighborhood groups. Preschool, precamp, and pre-employment physicals were performed at the hospital or in the community. The response of community agencies to the program has been positive. Agency staff members have indicated the value they find in having a central resource—one person to whom they can go with all questions involving the use of the institution, and who can also be consulted about other health problems.

A Typical Case

Various aspects of the Patient Service Representative Program can be seen in the following case example:

> Mrs. B was almost blind, and although she could manage by herself in her own home, she could not get to the hospital without an escort. She had been brought to the emergency room by a neighbor, and emergency oral surgery had been performed. Mrs. B stated that she would have to see the oral surgeon at least four more times. She asked if someone could escort her to the hospital so that she could get this needed care. Arrangements were made with a local community action group, Massive Economic Neighborhood Development (MEND), to have one of its workers bring Mrs. B to the hospital.

A review of Mrs. B's medical chart showed that she had diabetes and glaucoma. Although she had been followed at monthly intervals for years, at the time of this contact she had not been seen by a doctor in over four months. Arrangements were made for her to be seen in the diabetes clinic for specialist evaluation in regard to the oral surgery that had been performed. By co-ordination of appointments, Mrs. B was seen in the diabetes clinic, the eye clinic, and by the oral surgeon in a single hospital visit. Clinic appointments for her were made at the convenience of the MEND worker.

During the course of these contacts it was found that Mrs. B was living at a minimal financial level, using limited resources to pay a neighbor to do her shopping. She was referred to the hospital's social worker for help in working out financial aid and better living arrangements.

Because the clinic staff have no way of flagging the chart of a patient such as Mrs. B who is well known to the hospital but has not returned for some time, the case was discussed with the assistant directors of ambulatory care and of nursing in the outpatient department. They agreed that follow-up of patients who missed appointments should be instituted in certain clinics. [Implementation of this suggestion is still to be worked out.]

Thus, for Mrs. B the program facilitated needed medical and dental care, while for the hospital it served a case-finding purpose for the social service department and alerted clinic staff to the need of finding ways to assure continuity of patient care. This case also illustrates the value to patients of close community agency–hospital relations.

REVIEW OF THE PROGRAM

In a review of the Ombudsman program it has been pointed out that the system is generally willing to effect change for individuals when problems are clarified.[5] Experience confirms this impression. The program's major impact has been on behalf of the individual patient. The co-operation of the hospital staff in response to requests has been gratifying. The patient service representative's position has been scaled at a level at which he can be in contact with the person in each depart-

---

[5] Reuss and Anderson, *op. cit.*

ment with the authority to solve whatever patient problem is presented. Almost every suggestion for facilitating care for individuals has been responded to affirmatively. (It is possible that this co-operation exists not only because staff members are interested in solving patient problems, but because they are also eager to smooth over individual incidents and thereby avoid a demand for major changes that might "rock the boat.")

When impediments to patient care are identified, discussion is opened with the appropriate person around procedures that need analysis and possible revision. This process has been accepted readily by some department chiefs who see the program as an aid in evaluating their departmental training and procedures. In other cases, however, the implications of the problem have been resisted. Some department heads have responded by fending off discussion and have expressed concern about being confronted with documentation of problems in their department. In other cases the need for change is acknowledged, but change is resisted on the basis that "the timing is not right" or "personnel are not of the caliber that could be expected to handle these problems efficiently." The patient service representative must be aware of and resist the temptation to bypass the complicated channels to successful feedback and instead deal with the problems of individuals.

While it is known that some changes have been achieved by feedback, overall evaluation is difficult. In some cases discussion or additional dialogue on revision of procedures and policies has resulted, and although movement on many of these issues is slow, it is under way. Hospital staff may view the Patient Service Representative Program as "taking the heat off the system" by solving individual problems and it may therefore prolong the change process. The question is whether it is necessary to permit situations to reach the point of conflict or confrontation between the system and the consumer before change becomes inevitable. This promulgates the idea, suggested by some, that it may be necessary to allow the situation to deteriorate rather than to continue to temporize with ameliorative methods. There is no question that the sick must be served in a personalized way and with every courtesy, not only by paramedical staff but also by medical professionals, who, because of increasing specialization, are guilty of becoming more and more removed from the care of the whole person.

The patient service representative's concern must be to continue to improve services for the individual patient and at the same time allow the problems enough visibility to result in change. It is anticipated that patients will find ways to band together to deal with their common problems and assure themselves of their entitlements as welfare recipients in some communities have already done. So far, when a community voice exits among medical care users, it has been primarily in relation to Medicaid cutbacks; interestingly enough, the community and the hospital have joined together in their efforts to sway the legislators. It is possible that if patient advisory groups come into existence, some of the problems the patient service representative confronts will no longer be in evidence. However, even without this pressure, as more comprehensive health care services become available in the institution, the obstacles to good patient care should diminish. Even when changes in delivery of health care are accomplished, an Ombudsman who is empowered to move freely within the hospital to hear a patient in need or a community request, to uncover a procedure that impedes service, and to highlight obstacles to care, is an invaluable asset in any institution.

Financing Social Work Services Through Prepaid Social Insurance

ARNOLD M. LEVIN

Life is tough and full of risks. Similar risks are faced in varying degrees by the privileged rich, the modestly comfortable, and the deprived, with the risks generally inversely proportional to income and privilege. Increasingly, especially in the United States, protection against individually unpredictable risks is sought through private and public insurance.

The varieties of insurance Americans may buy for protection against the financial costs of certain risks are too extensive to list here, but among others are included protection against the costs of illness, fire, tornadoes, crop damage, auto collision, professional malpractice, loss of income owing to illness, unemployment, old age, and so on. Even lawyer's fees may soon be covered; according to the *New York Times:* "Thousands of people who now get low-cost medical care through their company or union doctors or group insurance policies, may soon obtain legal aid in much the same way." The article went on to discuss the possibilities of prepayment plans for legal services. In April 1968 Dr. Robert E. Cooke outlined a proposed insurance plan to help families meet bills for mentally retarded children and adults

> to meet the catastrophe of a seriously handicapped child. . . . it
> would be a compulsory public plan, and it might end up part of

321

the social security program for those who become disabled anytime from birth to age 65.[1]

The need for most, if not all, social work services is a risk to which all families and individuals are exposed in the course of a lifetime. (The operant words here are "need for." Hopefully, receiving social work services is not of itself risky.) Some of the more obvious individually unpredictable circumstances requiring family, individual, or group social work services are marital conflict, disorganization, or divorce; disabling or crippling illness; overwhelming reactions to death, loss, accident, or rape; serious childhood crises such as loss of parents through death, desertion, or neglect; mental retardation; overwhelming reactions to aging; inability to cope with geographic or social mobility; unmarried motherhood; and the like. So long a listing may seem labored, yet it reminds us that social workers do in fact work with people whose need for service springs from an unpredictable circumstance, a problem to which anyone may be exposed, a situation in which all are at risk.

Although it may be impossible to insure against the problems necessitating social work intervention, it is possible to devise insurance to pay for the services required to cope with them. Before proceeding to examine the possibilities of an insurance method for financing social work services, it may be wise to take a brief historical excursion in order to achieve a perspective.

HISTORICAL BACKGROUND

Social work services have, of course, traditionally been offered through community-sponsored private agencies and paid for by philanthropic contributions or tax moneys. (Some economists would probably say that all payments are essentially out of tax moneys because of income tax deductions for donations.) Most of these institutions originated as instruments for the distribution of charity to the needy. Gradually, as social work became professionalized, the poor were joined or sometimes, unfortunately, even displaced by the middle and upper classes as recipients of the "benevolence" of nonconcrete services.

Fee-charging by social agencies, private and public, especially by the "counseling" social agencies such as family service, adoption, child guidance and others, which began in the late 1940s and early 1950s, introduced a new dimension to the financing of social work services.

---

[1] *Chicago Sun-Times,* April 29, 1968, p. 11.

By the mid-1960s even the private practice of social work had been professionally legitimated and became "respectable." [2] The concept of consumer purchasing of social work services rather than of clients receiving "benevolence" was gaining credence.

During the 1960s poverty in America was "rediscovered" and the attention of professional social workers was riveted on the poor, especially on those caught in the welfare net. By November 1967, the National Association of Social Workers adopted as official policy support of ". . . proposals which involve a separation of income security measures from social service functions . . . whether within or outside the present public welfare structure. . . ." [3] In a sense, policy changes regarding social work services for poor people were being recommended to catch up with what had already in fact taken place for those financially better-off persons who were seeking social work services from non-public welfare agencies.

WAYS OF FINANCING SERVICES

The present is always a crossroads in tomorrow's history. What roads may be taken in financing social work services while separating income maintenance from social services for the poor and what are the possible ramifications of each choice? The traditional combination of public and private agencies is certainly one way of doing this. Another direction, following the "social utility" model, might be to support all social work services with taxes and offer them free to all through government agencies in the same way as public schools, libraries, and the like are provided. A third way is to devise a system of insurance to cover a large share of the cost of social work services.

Public-Private Agency Combination

The first method is well known and has existed for a long time. It has, however, many drawbacks:

1. Perhaps its greatest drawback is that it tends to perpetuate separate but unequal treatment for the haves and the have-nots. American ex-

---

[2] "Handbook on the Private Practice of Social Work" (New York: National Association of Social Workers, 1967). (Mimeographed.)

[3] Policy Statement on Separation of Social Services and Income Security Programs, National Association of Social Workers, Document 9854/2/S, November 22, 1967.

perience with private versus public hospitals is paralleled in social work services. Even if the separation of income maintenance from social service is achieved but the service function continues to be part of the welfare agency, the basic drawback remains.

2. The private sector has tended to shrink as the demand has increased and philanthropic contributions have become harder to obtain.

3. This method has resulted in a crazy-quilt pattern of service delivery that is hopelessly irrational. Geographic eligibility boundaries drawn arbitrarily or related to funding leave a painfully huge uncovered population. Incalculable professional time is squandered in establishing eligibility or finding makeshift alternatives.

4. Scarce professional time is wasted in fund-raising activities. Private agency executives sometimes come to feel their major function is to help their board members fill their time in at least a semblance of creative activity. Public agency administrators also invest heavily in dealing with (seducing, cajoling, begging) their funding bodies.

5. Finally, such a system is inconsistent with the generally accepted philosophy in relation to poor relief whereby money is given directly to the poor to purchase goods and services because of the degrading aspect of giving them goods and services in place of money.

Tax-Supported Services

The social utility method is somewhat new for social work, with the exception of group work services and social work in schools. It seems, however, fundamentally unfitted for the delivery of services needed to meet unpredictable individual risks. It is perhaps a better concept for the delivery of community services such as day care, which resembles the public school model, or for informational services, neighborhood centers, and so on.[4]

It is conceivable that community centers placed strategically throughout the nation and encompassing a complex of functions ranging from day care to mental health, rehabilitation, and employment might be desirable and even usable by a significant portion of the population. But such a plan would require a gigantic investment, redesigning of the total social agency structure, and incredibly skillful individual managers.

---

[4] Alfred J. Kahn, "Social Services in Relation to Income Security: Introductory Notes," *Social Service Review,* Vol. 39, No. 4 (December 1965), pp. 381–389.

Insurance

The insurance plan is consistent with the main thrust of means to protect against risks. It is fundamentally better suited to financing services for a population in need that represents a relatively small fraction of the total population at risk at any one time. Further, it enhances human dignity by promoting the consumer-purchaser point of view as opposed to that of the recipient of a benevolence.

It can also be designed, in conjunction with various supporting steps, to place greater control over the delivery of services into the consumer's hands. In most communities, for example, when social work services are delivered at all, they are provided by an agency that holds a monopoly on that specific service. In a system in which the consumer has control of the money required to pay for the service, agencies or individuals offering it are likely to be more responsive to his needs. If they are not, he may have more flexibility in turning elsewhere and even in promoting the development of alternative service organizations.

The insurance method essentially provides an opportunity for using the same funds that are currently expended for social work services in a more dynamic, flexible way. To illustrate, suppose that a certain sum is appropriated by federal and state governments to provide services for welfare recipients other than income maintenance. Suppose further that this money is used either to purchase private insurance coverage for all individuals in that group or is contributed to the Social Security Administration's insurance pool to be used to pay for services as individually sought (within certain reasonable limits). The service user would be free to decide whether he wanted a service, and he could seek it from private or public agencies or private individuals as he chose. The same money contributed directly to agencies on a straight agency budgetary basis would perpetuate agency control and inhibit the consumer's choice. Impetus for use of service would continue to come from the agency rather than from the consumer.

Thus far, payment for services to the poor has been stressed, perhaps because the principle of insurance payment for social work services to the nonpoor is already well on the road to acceptance. For example, the government-wide service benefit plan covering all federal employees provides payment for members of a "Mental Health Team (i.e., physician, psychologist, psychiatric nurse, psychiatric social worker)" for in- and outpatient care. Similar coverage exists for members of some unions, employees of certain large corporations, and executives of many industries protected by major medical policies. Medicare, which has the most potential for mass coverage, does provide for social work services, but under certain conditions only. A plan called CHAMPUS, which covers servicemen and their families, already pays for social work services.

Unfortunately, all of the private insurance plans have been developed with little or no planned participation by social workers or by NASW. Generally they have been shaped by physicians, and the social worker is treated as ancillary to the physician. Almost all require medical supervision or referral. Social work service is perceived as part of a medical model and its practice content is fitted to that model. Since large sectors of the U.S. population are affected by such plans, the implications for the social work profession are, in truth, staggering.

BASIC ASSUMPTIONS

It might be well to make explicit certain assumptions on which this paper is based.

1. There is a profession of social work; there is a body of knowledge, skill, and technique identifiable as social work practice and communicable through an educational process; and there are individuals who can be identified as professional social workers by virtue of their training, experience, adherence to ethical standards of behavior, and personal attributes.

2. A professional person takes responsibility for his practice.

3. There are people who need social work services and, therefore, if there were no social work profession extant, something like it would have to be invented (no matter what it might be called).

4. The existing system for distributing this professional service influences heavily the content of that service and, in turn, is heavily influenced by the method of its financing.

5. Private practice is only one of several distributive mechanisms, not necessarily the most or least desirable.

6. The insurance method of financing social work services is not an insidious design to promote private practice, but is a proposal aimed at making more rational, reliable, and modern the basic means of financing all social work services.

The validity of any one or all of these assumptions may be debated. However, this paper attempts to build from them rather than to defend them.

IMPLICATIONS OF AN INSURANCE PLAN

An insurance base holds broad implications for the entire delivery system of social work services. To focus delivery patterns in relation to population priorities instead of in relation to availability of financing sources would be a delightfully novel opportunity for all. Bright, energetic executives, board members, and consumers could devote more of their time to consideration of service policy issues and much less to concern with raising money. The role of state and federal governmental granting agencies could more clearly and realistically become one of stimulating and encouraging experimentation, co-ordination, and geographically and demographically comprehensive planning.

The feasibility of such a plan is, of course, immediately open to question. Objections similar to those raised by groups like the American Medical Association to Medicare or by insurance carriers to coverage for mental illness are likely to be voiced to this plan. A few of these might be abuses of usage; disappointment of potential clients owing to the professional manpower shortage; total costs beyond the economy's limits or beyond individuals', industries', unions', or governments' willingness to pay; impossibility of computing a sound actuarial base; and so on. The actual experience with Medicare, however, belies the predictions of its critics, inasmuch as abuses have been minimal and systems for policing have been undergoing refinement. There is no reason to think it would be different with social work. The issue of the manpower shortage is difficult to assess. However, to quote Glasser:

> Supply rises to meet demand. We have found that in many of the communities where we had an abysmal lack of resources, the introduction of the program [insurance coverage of mental illness for union members] . . . caused an increase in the availability of services, a reorganization of the use of the time of professional people and has encouraged professional people to associate with each other to maximize such time.[5]

Glasser went on to cite the need to develop and institute quality controls in insurance programs in co-operation with the professional associations.

---

[5] Melvin A. Glasser, "The Psychologist and Voluntary Health Insurance," p. 17. Paper presented at the meeting of the American Psychological Association, May 1966.

As to the issue of the country's ability to support such a plan, the economists will have to provide answers. Certainly it would have a considerable number of advantages. For one, a federal plan would reduce the burden on individual states and localities already paying for services and would shift the burden more equitably to federal tax funds and payroll taxes. Administration of such a plan would be vastly simpler than the present morass of funding systems; considerable money and time savings could be expected.

While it is unlikely that providing social work services has as high a priority as such grave national problems as income maintenance, racism, basic health care, public education, and unemployment, it is nonetheless not among the lowest in priority. If a basic change from the present public assistance system is effected with services separated from income payments, the proposed insurance plan seems most compatible and deserving of high-priority assignment.

An important issue that is much too broad to be dealt with here extensively is what to do with existing private community-sponsored fundraising apparatus. By cutting income tax deductions for charitable donations, the apparatus could be encouraged to contract. The tax money so realized could be used partially to fund the insurance plan. Or the apparatus could be retained with the money used in different ways than at present. One possible use might be to pay for organizing new delivery structures, with ongoing operating expenses paid for by the insurance method. The entire question of the fund-raising apparatus deserves broader treatment elsewhere. Meanwhile, how can an insurance plan for financing social work services be investigated?

1. NASW should take leadership in promoting it. A basic requirement of the profession would be to articulate clearcut, understandable, legally definable definitions and standards of social work practice backed by state licensing laws.

2. Study of several general approaches would have to be undertaken to determine which would be most desirable. Coverage under existing medical insurance packages, extended and modified, might be one approach. Statutory regulation of insurance carriers might be sought to insist on inclusion of social work services in certain types of major medical policies (an approach being considered by psychologists). At the present time, this type of insurance applies only to the working, middle-class, and managerial segments of the population. Conceivably, such a package could be purchased for other less-fortunate population segments with tax moneys. However, since it is medical insurance, there might be more difficulty in shaping social work services, were they to be included, in other than the medical model.

Another possible approach might be a general insurance plan specifically covering social work services, made part of the social security system. Perhaps a strategy could be formulated initially for its adoption to cover limited population segments such as welfare recipients.

3. Having decided on an approach, a strategy for its implementation would need to be outlined. Close collaboration with other professions, labor unions, management associations, and the like would be essential.

A beginning organizational step for NASW would be the appointment by the national board of a high-level committee to study insurance payments for social work services. Such a committee would be charged with developing proposals applicable to the separation of income maintenance from services. The board could instruct the committee to establish contact with the Family Service Association of America, the Child Welfare League of America, and other major professional groups and organizations, possibly pooling funds to employ staff to make a feasibility study and suggest specific detailed proposals. Early consultation with the President's Committee To Study Income Maintenance could be sought.

Failure to act in relation to insurance payments for social work services will have serious, damaging impact on the future of social work practice and of social work agencies. For the working and middle-class populations, availability of insurance coverage for services of psychiatrists, psychologists, and other mental health professionals (although payments for social workers are not covered) will inevitably encourage use of the other specialties even at the cost of unrealistic definitions of illness and treatment. If social work is to be covered, the profession must have a voice in establishing the conditions of such coverage. Failure to act may well be an unrecognized, unacknowledged decision to let much of social work practice, especially casework and group work, fall by the wayside to be picked up by other professional groups. At a time when there is almost universal accord about the desirability of increased participation of consumers in the organization of services, the insurance mode seems especially consistent and appropriate as a system for realizing this desire.

SUMMARY

Insurance is a basic and culturally acceptable method Americans use to protect themselves against the costs of unpredictable risks.[6] The

---

[6] Evelyn S. Myers, "Insurance Conference Woos Steelworkers," *Psychiatric News*, Vol. 3, No. 3 (March 1968), p. 1.

need for social work services to deal with a wide array of social and emotional problems is a risk for which insurance payment plans can and should be devised. It provides a mechanism by which the consumer has greater, more direct control over the financing of services and, therefore, greater potential control over how they are organized and offered. The consumer gains in dignity, while funding becomes more efficient, reliable, and flexible.

A public social insurance scheme offers a means of implementing the principle of separation of income maintenance programs from service functions for people who are financially deprived, without perpetuating separate but unequal institutional patterns. The mushrooming of medical insurance plans for the working and middle classes, which sometimes cover social work services, demands the profession's participation to help shape them. NASW is called upon to exercise leadership in influencing such plans and to initiate proposals for public social insurance coverage of social work services for people not otherwise covered.

Participation of a Voluntary Agency in a Public Agency Program

IRENE BLICKSTEIN AND GERTRUDE LEYENDECKER

The public welfare field today reflects some of the profound contradictions that exist within society. In response to multiplying crises, governmental institutions pull in opposing directions. In public welfare a regressive pull is expressed in the senseless and arbitrary exclusion of some families from financial assistance and service, increasing the gap between the government's promise to fulfill some basic needs of its citizens and the realization of this promise. A contrary thrust also exists —if only at this time as a blueprint of social planners—toward provision of guarantees of income and service for all families as a right. A small but important initial step toward development of these guarantees is the elimination of archaic and dehumanizing means tests. Under such circumstances the client is transformed from helpless recipient to claimant.

This paper will describe the introduction by the New York City Department of Social Services—on an experimental basis—of significant changes in eligibility procedures and the staff training program that accompanied this experiment. Community Service Society of New York (CSS), a nonsectarian family agency serving a wide range of families, participated in the development and implementation of this training program at the request of Mitchell I. Ginsberg, then commissioner of the New York City Department of Social Services.

331

ELIGIBILITY BY DECLARATION

As an alternative to the humiliating means test, the client's signed statement or "declaration" of his needs was to be the main basis for granting assistance, in contrast to the traditional system in which the burden of proof is placed on the client to establish his eligibility. Some objectives of this new method were to enhance the dignity of the client, to reduce enormously wasteful procedures, and in turn to free staff time for other urgently needed services to families. The New York declaration experiment was the first of its kind in the United States. While a similar approach to eligibility was used in three other states—California, Colorado, and West Virginia—it was used only with Old Age Assistance applicants. In developing this experiment, the department's assumption that applicants could be trusted to give accurate and complete accounts of their financial situation was bolstered by studies showing that only 2 percent of the 7.5 million people receiving public assistance do so as the result of deliberate dishonesty.[1]

The declaration system was introduced in April 1967 on an experimental basis in two welfare centers, to be tried for a period of one year, with the hope that if successful this could then be extended to all twenty-six New York City welfare centers. Research was to be conducted by a group independent of the Department of Social Services, with the major objectives of research to include evaluation of the effectiveness of the declaration procedure in determining eligibility, assessment of its efficiency in relation to costs and service objectives, and examination of its impact on the nature and extent of services given to clients.

The essential difference between the traditional form of eligibility determination and the proposed declaration program lay in the acceptance of the applicant's statements regarding his financial situation and family composition without verification or documentation. A decision to grant assistance, with a few exceptions, would be made at intake without a field investigation. In the traditional method the applicant is asked to document or present verification of every statement concerning his past and current financial status. The same information is then reviewed during a subsequent home visit. This duplicative and time-consuming practice frequently created long delays between application for assistance and its receipt, even though there may have been no basis for questioning the applicant's veracity.

---

[1] Jonathan Spivak, "Treating the Poor," *Wall Street Journal,* November 17, 1966, p. 1.

STAFF TRAINING PROGRAM

CSS was chosen for participation in this tradition-breaking program because of its long and varied experience in work with families of all income levels and the understanding of family diagnosis and treatment developed and tested in the course of these experiences. One of the deciding factors in the agency's decision to participate was its conviction that the declaration program was an important step in the direction of sound social policy and planning. CSS agreed to provide highly skilled staff members who, together with Department of Social Services training staff, would teach basic understanding of family life to the staff of the two welfare centers. This would be a beginning way of preparing them for the shift from eligibility-checking to provision of some basic services to families. In describing the training program the emphasis will be on the trainers' experiences, reactions, and conclusions as seen from CSS's vantage point as an "outside agency."

CSS training staff met regularly with trainers from the Department of Social Services prior to the inception of the training program to discuss and develop the content of the training course. As part of CSS's orientation to the full gamut of the department's policies and procedures and to the learning needs of staff, CSS trainers read selected case records. A vivid awareness was thereby gained of the magnitude of each worker's task, of the mountains of forms to be completed and procedures to be followed, and of the vast and frequent turnover of staff.

While the records of many workers reflected their concern for people, there was often little understanding of family life in its most elementary and basic terms. Health needs of the majority of families stood out starkly and were often overlooked or met in piecemeal fashion. Here, too, forms and procedures tended to obscure, delay, and confuse the giving of meaningful and timely help to families. Reading these records further confirmed the difficulty of the task of developing an approach to training that would take into account the great variation in understanding and experience of the workers. Trainers were most appreciative of the task facing the department's staff at all levels, in trying to move an antiquated system and develop one more responsive to the needs of families, coupled with the anxiety involved in the acceptance and incorporation of a fundamentally different approach to eligibility and provision of service.

The teaching staff, totaling twelve persons, was drawn equally from the Department of Social Services training division and from selected CSS staff. The training course was to consist of fourteen sessions for each group. The staffs of the two welfare centers, approximately 450 persons, the majority of them without professional training, were divided into groups of approximately 25 persons each for ongoing training. Staff members were grouped according to their job responsibilities, with separate classes for intake workers, service workers, and supervisors. Among the major training goals were understanding of objectives of the new program and development of attitudes and skills necessary for its implementation. The department staff's initial reaction to the experimental proposal was one of grave doubt regarding the possibility of fundamental change within the department. This was expressed in their union newspaper in an article headed "Declaration Training Clouded by Skepticism."

Problems with Workers

CSS trainers quickly became aware of the intense degree of anxiety that pervaded the trainee groups. Despite trainees' recognition that eligibility checking was a sterile and frustrating way of dealing with family needs, the giving up of these checks was nonetheless not easy for them. Forms and eligibility checks had become a way of life for many workers, and at times a protection against the tremendous demands of the job. Anxiety was expressed directly regarding the administration's expectations in the new program. Did the administration think that in fourteen sessions they could really be prepared to give service? If clients were not honest under this new system, would the workers be held accountable? Would supervisors really approve the service workers' recommendations regarding their clients' budgetary needs or would it be "the mixture as before"?

Intake workers had great concern because the full initial brunt of the declaration procedure would be borne by their group. They now had to accept clients' statements without the usual documentation, make a full determination of the client's need, compute the budget, and grant assistance—all on the same day. This placed a greatly increased responsibility on this group, requiring a quicker shifting of gears for them in relation to basic procedures and attitudes.

An additional serious complication during training was the fact that the program had not been made operational prior to the beginning of the training period. Procedural changes and unresolved procedural problems became intermixed with and at times inseparable from the basic learning task. In fact, policy and procedural questions were still being resolved long after training was completed. Staff, used to detailed directives, fell into a veritable sea of confusion as they grappled with a changing program and shifting directives.

In beginning as trainers, the CSS staff were mindful of their role as outsiders and as a voluntary agency that they lacked intimate knowledge of policies, pressures, and the climate of a public agency. In addition, CSS was incorrectly viewed by many of the trainees as accepting for treatment only highly motivated and articulate middle-class families. A heavy aura of suspicion hung over the training sessions. Face value was not sufficient. The trainers had to demonstrate that they had knowledge of and know-how in work with low-income families. One of the greatest challenges was how to impart highly complex, technical knowledge in a way that would be useful and practical for the public welfare worker without professional training. The other challenge was to navigate between their need for specific knowledge and their need to talk about and handle the daily frustrations of their difficult jobs. The trainers needed to make clear that they had no special magic that could eliminate these frustrations, and that they could not reduce the confusion and chaos attendant on introduction of a new program.

Developing Teaching Content

Because of the tremendous diversity in age, experience with the department, and degree of interest and ability of the trainees, the first task was to get a sense of the group's knowledge and understanding, and then to aim the teaching at this diversity. Instead of a didactic approach, trainers actively elicited and promoted group discussions and an interchange of experiences. This served as a basis for offering specific teaching content that took into account their knowledge and learning needs. Trainers utilized their own experiences with families and their questions regarding clients' behavior and its meaning to provide content transferable to families in general.

In developing basic content that would increase their understanding of families, CSS trainers felt that it was first essential to tackle entrenched attitudes regarding clients. Even sensitive workers had many subjective and stereotyped ideas about welfare recipients. The thinking of large segments of the community, which holds, for instance, that Negro and Puerto Rican women are promiscuous or have babies in order to obtain relief, that fathers are disinterested in their wives and children and callously desert them, that such people do not want to earn their own living, was all expressed blatantly and directly in many instances, described as "cultural values" of clients. Workers frequently perceived minority group children and their parents as having different aspirations from theirs, as lacking ambition and the desire to achieve. As stereotyped and judgmental thinking surfaced again and again in discussions of individual families, the trainers engaged the groups in lively discussions of families under stress and of the purposes served by various kinds of behavior, offering new ways of looking at behavior.

In addition to stimulating workers to examine their views of clients, trainers also offered specific help in relation to basic interviewing techniques for exploration of family problems. Workers were well accustomed to ask questions freely about finances, but did not know how to explore other problems or understand the purpose of such exploration. Trainers therefore concentrated on the ways in which exploration and discussion help the client to sort out problems and consider different solutions.

Workers found it difficult to understand why people did not always behave logically. In discussing employment and employability, an important recurring group theme, a question that arose time and again, expressed directly and indirectly, was: "Why don't people follow through on our suggestions regarding employment when they say they want to work?" A client was often referred to the department's own employment counselors or to other community resources with little or no advance preparation and before he had defined for himself even minimally what kind of help he wished. When clients did not keep their appointments, this reinforced the workers' view that they were apathetic and ambitionless. Discussion of individual clients helped to illuminate the conflicting forces working on clients, the low self-esteem many of them felt, the fear of failure that retarded their action. Without expecting that the workers would necessarily understand all of the forces affecting behavior, trainers tried to help them, through discussion of individual situations, to observe and listen more sensitively, to help the client voice his own reactions rather than make advance judgments regarding clients' needs.

One of the emphases of training was on how to achieve a view of the whole family. While workers had been accustomed to doing what was called a "study" prior to the declaration program, this frequently failed to highlight the most urgent and pressing needs of the family. In their case records situations were found that dramatically illustrated the great resilience of both individuals and families despite tremendous stress. Focus was placed on families' strengths as well as stresses and on ways of promoting these strengths.

While the major thrust of teaching with intake and service workers was to offer basic practical knowledge that would sensitize them to the needs of families and help them to determine priorities of need, the emphasis with supervisory staff was on how to offer more orderly and systematic teaching. Some were providing sound but piecemeal teaching or were unduly hung up on technicalities, which in turn created delay in service to families. Many supervisors, while wanting to adapt to a new and more viable approach, clung to old and more familiar ways, operating essentially as before, with stress primarily on eligibility. Others were able to view the new system more creatively and flexibly, and used what they learned in training sessions to offer real leadership to their workers in the provision of increased services to families.

Workers' Reactions to Program

As might be expected in a program involving people with such diverse backgrounds and abilities, reactions of many intake and service workers to the declaration system remained mixed until the end, with some continuing to be essentially contemptuous of the new approach. The entrenched and judgmental points of view about people and behavior continued to characterize the thinking of some trainees, who participated little in the discussions or, if they did so, gave examples from their case loads to support their stereotyped thinking.

It was gratifying, however, to see the ability of many workers to try out new approaches and to utilize new insights. Many had expressed great trepidation at the beginning of training regarding the nature of clients' responses to their offers of service. Under the declaration plan, the first home visit was no longer for the purpose of checking but to offer service. Would clients view the workers as anything other than eligibility investigators? If clients had the option of accepting or refusing their offers of service, would their choice be to refuse? Some expressed this fear quite directly, asking: "What do you say if the family says, 'I don't need any help'?" "How do you change the image they have of caseworkers as people who are there only to check up on them?" As the workers began to get a sense of how to listen, elicit information, and observe the overt signs of distress within a family, clients in turn began to experience the helpfulness of the more sensitive workers and to open their doors actually as well as symbolically.

At the final class session trainees were asked to evaluate the training program. The response was mixed, with some viewing the program as helpful, others seeing it as of little value. Among the latter, what stood out was the fact that continuing daily problems within the centers made them skeptical that the declaration system would or could really work. It was hard for them to separate training from their on-the-job experience and the frustrations that had not abated. Others, while equally conscious of these frustrations, pointed to a beginning change in the climate of the Department of Social Services, to a new sense of dignity on the part of workers as well as clients. They were ready to opt for the declaration program even though they knew that many operational changes still needed to be made before the program could really work. In describing areas of training that were especially helpful, some workers identified the following: the changed attitudes of some workers toward welfare recipients, discussion of how to listen to the client, open discussion and exchange of opinions and experiences, a basic approach to people under stress.

AGENCY RECOMMENDATIONS

Following the completion of the training program, CSS trainers shared some of their observations and conclusions with the Department of Social Services. A major recommendation concerned the staffing and training of the department. As public welfare moves toward establishment of guarantees of income and service, it is expected that this will lead to eventual separation of income payments from service. Under these circumstances, responsibility for an even wider range of community programs and services will then come under the public welfare umbrella. These programs may die aborning unless public welfare staff can meet these vastly increased responsibilities. One overriding issue, then, is how to select and train the personnel who will be the major providers of service, recognizing that in the foreseeable future it is unrealistic to expect to have a fully professional staff.

In the New York City Department of Social Services, as is true with so many public agencies today, one of the major drawbacks to any training program is the enormous staff turnover. Unless turnover can be ended, training is an almost hopeless task, since the efforts devoted to it are lost with the departing staff member. In view of this constant exodus of workers, it was recommended that the department make every effort to retain those persons with greater ability and an interest in a career in public social services and concentrate on their development. While the adoption of programs such as the declaration system will help to attract a higher level of staff, unless sound in-service training is provided workers will continue to leave because of the frustrations created by the disparity between the promise and the reality.

It was also clear from work with the supervisory staff that a much greater investment was needed in the selection and development of supervisors, since they hold key positions in the department. Many of these supervisors had little preparation for their job; the greater degree of preparation and training of others was far from sufficient for the task at hand. Supervisors needed help with the whole range of supervisory functions, including learning to select priorities in teaching, how to plan time for regular conferences, how to offer greater support and stimulation to workers in their emotionally demanding assignments. Some first-rate teaching was seen, but it was fragmented and not properly related to what caseworkers knew and needed to know. Adequate supervision was a far greater need than formal training of casework staff. A better quality of supervision would contribute significantly to improved staff morale and would make it possible to develop good staff potential currently being wasted.

A significant problem in relation to staff development in the declaration program was the fact that key administrative personnel were not involved during the planning phases of the program. It was recommended that such personnel be brought into planning as early as possible. It is also of vital importance that training efforts have the full backing of all administrative personnel. When such backing is lacking or insufficient, training efforts are subverted or negated. This may be expressed through insufficient provision of time for training or in viewing the content of training as an unnecessary frill.

While as trainers CSS staff felt that they had made a contribution, it was not felt productive for an outside agency to be involved in training of a public agency's staff at a time when many procedures and practices were undergoing change. The contribution of a voluntary agency to in-service training in a public welfare department could be both more effective and less costly if more generic in scope and less specifically related to major program changes. In the latter case, outside training staff are inevitably caught up with policy and procedural issues that they lack the authority to resolve.

A final but vital conclusion comes from the knowledge of families on public assistance developed by CSS, not only in the training program but in its own long history of service to families receiving assistance. Training of staff at any level within an experimental program or a traditional one will be of little value in providing significant service to families as long as assistance grants remain at their present low level. This is not only the conviction of CSS but one that is shared by the Department of Social Services' trainers and administrative staff.

PART VI

Is Social Work Equal to the Challenge?

If the vitality with which social workers have been arguing the above question is any indication, we are indeed a vital profession. And yet we know that much of the self-criticism for which social workers have so long been famous is reserved for national meetings, with about as much carryover to our daily lives as the proverbial Sunday morning sermon. Characteristically, we lay ourselves out in lavender at such affairs, then, as if concerned that we have stripped the profession of its defenses, we wind up reassuring ourselves that all is still well.

It was the determination of the people who planned the 1968 NASW symposium that there should be no false note of hope struck at the end of the program, that the participants should go home a little unhappy with the present state of affairs. Here, then, is the most disturbing question, for we risk a negative answer and with it a negation of an institution to which social workers are devoting their lives. So be it; we serve ourselves poorly if we avoid the question and its deeper implications.

Kraft's eloquent and biting critique of the profession poses the question in its baldest terms. It is a relatively long article, but the reader is assured that it will not be boring.

Any consideration of the social work profession's role in the delivery of services must include NASW. Wade assesses where NASW is now, suggests where it has to go, and offers some guidelines for getting there. It is fitting that the book closes with this paper, for in sponsoring the 1968 symposium and this volume of papers, NASW has demonstrated its readiness to examine its own relevance.

The State of the Social Work Profession

IVOR KRAFT

Although harsh things will be said in the course of this paper about the established leadership of the social work profession, it must be acknowledged at the outset that, in the context of contemporary American society, it is an essentially healthy profession. There is much wrong with social work today, but it must be pointed out that in its long pre-history, reaching back to the days of seventeenth-century New England puritanism and the severities of a Judeo-Christian ethic operating in an often strange and threatening new world, and in the time of its much shorter history proper, which begins in post-Civil War nineteenth-century America when the nation was making giant, often swashbuckling, strides toward an industrialized civilization, the social work profession has been almost consistently on the side of the angels—lacking in militancy perhaps, overtimorous perhaps—but almost invariably on the side of the constructive forces in history and almost invariably abjuring the destructive forces. Social work is a profession with integrity. Its past is worthy, its present is free of major corruptions, its future can be promising. That is an accolade that not every American profession can accord itself.

WHERE ARE THE FRONTIERS?

Having said as much, we must turn to less self-congratulatory reflections. When historical matters or comparisons with other professions are put to one side and we consider the kind of direction this country needs as we approach the eighth decade of this century, social work assumes a distinctly less heroic aspect. Indeed, it gives the appearance of being weak and devitalized, a rather dessicated and ineffective calling under a leadership without talent or deep conviction. Sad to say, these days no one seems to expect much from social work, including social workers themselves.

There are certainly frontiers of social planning, environmental reform, and system change in American society, but it is hard to find frontiers in social work. They have been appropriated by others. There is a tedium in social work that is reminiscent of the tedium in mid-twentieth-century religion, which has been gradually boring the intelligent public to death since the days when enlightened and crusading clerics dropped by the wayside, abandoning the religion of the social gospel from the time of Walter Rauschenbusch and Washington Gladden (the latter of whom once attained notoriety by urging the Congregational Missionary Society to return a large sum of money to John D. Rockefeller on the now quaint grounds that it was "tainted"). There has been a slight revival in our day, and some among the clergy are bestirring themselves. Similarly, social work has its handful of outstanding personalities and its cadres of quiet, dedicated practitioners, but as a profession it appears derivative, imitative, weakly adaptive, utterly nonthreatening, and well padded in layer upon layer of dull rhetoric having to do with dull abstractions ("method," "knowledge base," "the helping process," "community organization," "research").

But let this rhetoric be applied to a major problem, and the irrelevence of much of social work's contribution becomes evident. The population question, for example, is among the great social issues of the epoch, and it has direct impact on social work concerns. But who turns to social work's knowledge base, helping process, or research for enlightenment on this question? Almost no one. Family planning is one aspect of the population crisis, but in it social workers play a minor role.[1] Even more important is a crucial debate now shaping up on the limitations of family planning and the need to consider more vigorous and far-reaching

---

[1] Dr. Mary Calderone, executive director of the Sex Information and Education Council of the United States (SIECUS), in reviewing the role of the professional in programs of sex education and family planning, pointed out that "in schools of nursing and social work—a lot of them— they aren't even learning about planned parenthood." The *Plain Dealer* (Cleveland), April 10, 1968.

program interventions.[2]   The preoccupation with family planning to the exclusion of other strategies may itself be a negative influence in developing suitable action programs to limit population growth.   But there are probably not more than two or three specialists among the fifty thousand academically trained social workers who are competent to take part knowledgeably in this portentous debate on population policy; the curricula of graduate schools of social work hardly touch on these matters.   There is a frontier in planning for human welfare through population studies, but it is not a frontier for social work.

Consider also the matters of income maintenance and the reconstruction of the welfare apparatus, now seriously out of date and out of whack. Here the situation is slightly more encouraging.   There are perhaps ten American social workers who have made themselves competent to do authoritative analysis, research, and planning concerning alternative schemes of income maintenance.   But at least fifty times that number could be used, probing the issues far more deeply than has been done to date.   The reason why we lack these specialist cadres is that for the past thirty years the Establishment within American social work has been tightly locked in with the 1935 revision of the American poor law system—the Social Security Act—a revision that was intended not to abolish poverty, but to save the economic system from the potential onslaught of the poor.

Obstinately (and perhaps necessarily) committed to defending this system against reactionary detractors, and at the same time continually

---

[2] Kingsley Davis, director of International Population and Urban Research at the University of California, Berkeley, offers the following provocative judgment: "The things that make family planning acceptable are the very things that make it ineffective for population control.   By stressing the right of parents to have the number of children they want, it evades the basic question of population policy, which is how to give societies the number of children they need.   By offering only the means for couples to control fertility, it neglects the means for societies to do so."   "Population Policy: Will Current Programs Succeed?"   *Science,* Vol. 158 (November 10, 1967), p. 738.   For a contrary view, *see* a letter from William D. Mc-Elroy *et al., Science,* Vol. 159 (February 23, 1968), p. 827.   For a position statement giving the views of the Committee on Science and Public Policy of the National Academy of Sciences, *see The Growth of World Population* (Washington, D.C.:   National Academy of Sciences, National Research Council, 1963).   Suggestive as a historical treatment is David M. Heer, "Economic Development and the Fertility Transition," *Daedalus,* Vol. 97, No. 2 (Spring 1968), pp. 447–462.

exaggerating the nature of its achievements as a rehabilitator of the impotent poor and a pecuniary fortress providing proud comforts for the worthy and able-bodied poor (which it never did), the established social work technicians of the act never got beyond the Great Depression mood of 1935. They rested on their laurels, dug in their heels, settled comfortably into their niches in the federal-state welfare structure, and simply assumed that as the years rolled by and the federal welfare amendments rolled out, all would go well with the world, progress would be made, and the poor would be contained. This welfare Establishment notion may be called the myth of "assured progress through Social Security Act amendmentism."

Because social work has failed to meet the ideological challenge in the schools where recruits to the field are trained, and because this challenge has largely been neglected in the social action wing of social work over the past thirty years, there are today not five hundred social workers expert in planning beyond the welfare state, and not twenty-five graduate centers of social work where teams of social planners are being trained to reconstruct social welfare theory and practice in America; instead there is a potpourri of professional aggregates where social planners are isolated and where they must shout to be heard over the babble of derivative Freudian theory and tired clichés about "community organization." This is not to denigrate the counseling-psychotherapy stream in modern social work. It is an important stream, even though it can never fulfill a genuinely preventive and re-creative social function, but it needs to flow in a separate channel from social planning and community development. It also needs to be enriched and joined to the mainstream of counseling and psychotherapy.

THE PATH OF THE PROFESSION

This point was not arrived at by choice. Social work blundered into the quagmire; it did not leap into it. Let us sketch briefly and quickly the path the profession has followed over the past few decades.

Since a tightening and consolidating hegemony of the social-political-moral dimensions of daily life, heretofore looser and less constrained, was becoming a predominant reality in this period, no general review of programmatic and ideological commitments of the profession in post-World War II America would be complete without reference to the major political and economic trends in society, as well as the major events in the areas of finance and international relations. It is an overwhelming order, and not within the competence of the writer. Still, a few comments must be offered.

In an ideological sense, the essentially nonintegrated subfields of social work, while insignificant within the larger domains of professionalism and education, were being effectively drawn into this hegemony, and the prevailing conservative, bloodless, official ideology cast its dead shadow over the entire field, where thrusts of social reform and psychological meliorism could hardly be allowed free play. Somewhat resembling the atmosphere of the 1920s, it was unfashionable even to speak of these matters in social work circles. One is reminded of Jane Addams's comment:

> Throughout the decade this fear of change, this tendency to play safe, was registered most conspicuously in the field of politics, but it spread over into other fields as well. There is little doubt that social workers exhibited many symptoms of this panic and with a kind of protective instinct carefully avoided any identification with the phraseology of social reform. . . .[3]

To this day, it is not stylish to mention this view.

It would be far beyond the scope of this paper to analyze those ideological commitments, but a few brief comments will be offered. By far the predominant ideological-political factor in this era (roughly 1945 to the present) has been the rise and continuation of the cold war, which dates to the Truman Administration. America became a global imperium, a bastion of fierce anticommunism. In the heyday of McCarthyism, even the mildest of reformist impulses could be challenged as an insidious component of the communist conspiracy. All social work-type undertakings—legislative action, local health and welfare campaigns, personnel practices, the contents of journals, the curricula of schools of social work, even the justification for the Peace Corps—were contaminated by the mood of the times. Innocuous demands for system change could be interpreted as invitations to disaster, as threats to any hope for pragmatic achievements. The times were (and still remain) gravid with self-censorship. Thus, genuine probings of ideology were perfunctorily avoided; harmlessness became the preferred image of the social work Establishment. In an antirevolutionary environment it would have been the kiss of death for social work to assume even the flimsiest mantle of revolution. As Toynbee put it:

> America is today the leader of a world-wide anti-revolutionary movement in defence of vested interests. She now stands for what

---

[3] *The Second Twenty Years at Hull House* (New York: Macmillan Co., 1930).

Rome stood for. Rome consistently supported the rich against the poor in all foreign communities that fell under her sway; and, since the poor, so far, have always and everywhere been far more numerous than the rich, Rome's policy made for inequality, for injustice, and for the least happiness of the greatest number. America's decision to adopt Rome's role has been deliberate, if I have gauged it right.[4]

No doubt it is difficult for the younger generation of social workers, now emerging from the universities, to grasp the somber, noxious, and sometimes ludicrous ideological aura of the twenty years following World War II. But while the mood is now beginning to dissipate, the fruits of a generation put to suck on the pacifier of anticommunism are all around us: a highly conservative Congress, an entrenched and primitive rightism in lower middle-class America, consolidated white racism, a moribund public sector, laggard social services, rebellious black ghettos, and an unpopular war being lost in Vietnam at an annual expenditure of $30 billion.

The evolution of social workers during this century is the evolution of a professionalizing class of "fixers." When social processes break down, they need to be fixed. The chief fixes that needed to be applied to the culture were those that had to do with handling and containing the poor.

But there are social services that are not intended exclusively for the poor: services for the aged, handicapped, mentally retarded, troubled youths, children in need of placement, and the like. The wealthiest prefer to buy these services from private sources. For the less wealthy, public services have been provided. Social workers took a hand in delivering many of these services—which is another way of saying that those who took on these services came under the heading of "social work," actually a catch-all category that could accommodate any worker who thought of himself as "helping people in need."

Then professionalism set in. The more differentiated the tasks became, the more professionally conscious and elitist the academically trained social workers became. Instead of acknowledging that in a society that has attained a state of affluence, while at the same time remaining beset with deep social problems, there are and have to be pro-

---

[4] Arnold J. Toynbee, *America and the World Revolution and Other Lectures* (New York: Oxford University Press, 1962), pp. 92–93. *See also* Walter La Feber, *America, Russia and the Cold War, 1945–1966* (New York: John Wiley & Sons, 1967); and D. F. Fleming, "Who Won the Cold War?" *The Nation*, April 15, 1968, pp. 508–510.

found differences among social reformers, providers of social services, and counselors of the psychologically troubled, the established leadership of the field—for largely careerist purposes—saw advantages in a generic image of the social worker. Like the one god within the trinity, social work became a grand unit within a triplet—or, for that matter, a quadruplet or even quintuplet, depending on how many "methods" could be identified. But even then the distinction was not according to whether one was helping individuals to adjust or seeking ways to alter social systems. The distinction was by number and degree. If you worked with one person, you were a caseworker. If you worked with two people, this was enough to make you by definition a group worker. But if you worked with committees, for the most part fulfilling policies set by boards made up of people who were not social workers, then this made you a community organizer. And if you had a master of social work degree, you were a trained and fully professional person.

Just as the community organization component of social work largely missed the boat after the recent raising of banners for the War on Poverty (actually a series of petty skirmishes) so the counseling-psychotherapy component largely missed the boat after World Wars I and II, when significant numbers of veterans requiring neuropsychiatric and psychotherapeutic treatment returned, making it impossible for the psychiatric profession alone to cope with the tide. Social workers lost out, but psychology filled the breach. The upshot was that psychology, formerly a chiefly academic-laboratory enterprise confined to a narrow field of expertise, was able to claim for itself a major and emancipatory piece of clinical territory. For years psychological counseling has been gaining popularity in the United States. This same territory could have been shared effectively, constructively, and overtly with psychiatric and counseling social workers had the latter been able to overcome their irrelevant agonizing over the differences between casework and therapy, clients and patients, deep and not-so-deep probings of the psyche. Social workers became so boxed in by their preoccupations with a careerist struggle to maintain a professional image and status separate from the established clinical fields—as well as the illusion that they were creating a generic and self-contained helping profession—that they failed to accept obvious challenges from the clinical field on the one side and the social action field on the other.

One other point may be added. Impelled by honorable motives, many social caseworkers were misled into thinking that the highly refined and specialized techniques of dynamic (Freudian) psychology could serve as the cornerstone of a special treatment approach to victims of poverty. This misconception, which became institutionalized in the 1930s, has remained as the peculiar albatross of contemporary social work. An ironic corollary to this state of affairs is that social casework is the only profession that trains its would-be practitioners in one misnamed "method" (dynamic counseling and psychotherapy) and then sends many, if not most, of them off to practice something quite different (low- or middle-level supervision and administration of individuals who have not themselves been schooled in social casework).

In short, most social workers straddled; they played it safe. They refused to become full-blooded counselors and psychotherapists. They refused to become full-blooded social activists. The humbler direct service tasks were left to the so-called untrained workers. The clinical field was all but abandoned to the psychologists. The immensely difficult social action tasks were left to those who had the courage and audacity to undertake them. (And few did.) Some social workers became caseworkers to the lower middle class. The majority settled comfortably into slots as low- and middle-level supervisors, administrators, and managers presiding over the provision of generally ineffective services to the poor—a slightly updated version of charity organizers and caretakers of the troubled and distressed. Thus, if we dig beneath the surface, if we scrape away the fashionable patinas of cant and rhetoric that are now churned out wholesale by phalanxes of writers, consultants, academicians, researchers, workshop organizers, and public relations specialists—all of whom are fed and watered expressly for this purpose under the rationale of "extending the knowledge base of the profession"—we find that the work of the social worker has changed little over the past thirty or forty years, although it has increased greatly.

THREE WORLDS OF SOCIAL WORK

Today there are three worlds of social work. The first and largest is a world of poverty, squalor, inadequacy, and frustration; a world of massive state institutions poorly staffed and poorly budgeted; of welfare departments sweeping back the sea of poverty with a broom; of festering slums on the verge of exploding; of welfare case loads of 50, 100, and even 150, no matter what the federal guidelines may stipulate; of probation officers, truant officers, and child welfare workers barely managing to keep their heads above water; of somewhat shabby, somewhat dilapidated, somewhat genteel neighborhood centers and settlement houses where part-time workers play ball with the children, chat with the elderly, provide custodial care for the children of working mothers, and where used clothing may still be distributed on the last Thursday of the month, known as "opportunity day."

This is a world of deteriorating and depressing conditions, a world where still prevail the familiar principles of "less eligibility," of public assistance according to a means test, of relatives' responsibility, of the dole-plus-moral-uplift—a cluster of principles that first emerged in the sixteenth and seventeenth centuries, when England was making its transition from feudalism to capitalism. But within this first world of social work there serve, often with great skill and great patience, large numbers of dedicated and effective human beings, who nevertheless up to now have not been eligible for membership in the National Association of Social Workers and are not dignified with the title "professional social worker." They are social work's own "unworthy poor," the undeserving victims of our own elitist version of "less eligibility."

The second world of social work consists chiefly of private agencies and the more specialized and prestigious public agencies. The major specialties of these agencies (often funded in whole or part by the United Funds or Community Chests) include counseling, psychotherapy, recreation, and selected kinds of intermediary or advocacy functions (quality adoption agencies, work with middle-class delinquents). By and large the clientele of these agencies are working- and lower middle-class families and individuals. Social caseworkers predominate in these services.

Some evidence of the relative importance of these two worlds of social work can be found in the differential amounts of money available to them. It must be kept in mind to begin with that most welfare expenditures in America are not administered by social workers. In 1965 over $28 billion was expended by the government for social insurance, and almost $6.5 billion for veterans' programs. More clearly in the area of social work as commonly apprehended were expenditures having to do with public assistance, child welfare, certain health and medical services, and miscellaneous welfare programs. In 1965 these totaled about $6.5 billion. In contrast with these figures, the total amount raised by United Fund campaigns in 1965 was $585 million. This is 9 percent of what are here being designated as social work-type expenditures.[5]

Tiny in dimension is the third world of social work. It is a small but relatively influential realm of higher administration, federal-state bureaucratic leadership slots, prominent deanships and professorships in schools of social work, and the like. People who occupy this realm are typically

---

[5] These figures are based on U.S. Bureau of the Census, *Pocket Data Book, USA 1967* (Washington, D.C.: U.S. Government Printing Office, 1968).

many years removed from baseline practitioner concerns and function chiefly as intermediaries between the profession and the lesser power centers of American society. While this third world of social work is essentially congruent with the recruitment pool of what can be termed the leadership or the Establishment of the profession, and while it is a constantly shifting assortment of individuals who are upwardly mobile and status conscious, it does not thereby command great amounts of power or prestige, and it is considerably less influential than other professional Establishments in America (medicine, law, education).

The medical profession commands power and prestige because it is a high-salaried and supremely high-status entrepreneurial calling— the average medical practitioner earns about five or six times the income of the average social worker—and thus has access to sources of governmental and business power. The educational Establishment wields power not because teachers are well paid (they are poorly paid) but because education involves the expenditure of $50 billion annually and is now the biggest "growth industry" in America. Social workers are not well paid entrepreneurs, they treat a generally undistinguished clientele, and they are not part of a mainstream growth industry expending $50 billion a year. Thus, the social work Establishment commands only fragile power, is less hagridden with hatchet men and ambitious infighters, and is somewhat more responsive to the rank-and-file members of the profession.

These three worlds are intertwined, but they still have little in common. Professional social workers are concerned with the first world chiefly as administrators and consultants; in effect, they have abandoned it to the nonprofessional workers. The most skillful practitioners in the second world are not really social workers; they are counselors and psychotherapists who happen to have received their training as caseworkers in schools of social work. Their concern about the first and third worlds of social work is largely peripheral and their actual knowledge about these worlds is frequently skimpy and unreliable. As for the establishmentarian realm of the field, now being sniped at from all sides, it is a polite but nervous coalition of conflicting interests, made up as it is of bureaucrats, social planners, educators, and a handful of social critics.

It is in the nature of Establishments to make a virtue out of necessity, to pretend that what is expedient is a desirable goal, and to celebrate every petty gain as if it were a triumphant victory. It is no different when the Establishment happens to be a social work Establishment.

In the last century, for example, the charity organization societies made an ideological virtue out of the need to police the poor, preach self-restraint, and attach cost accounting to moral uplift; in part they called it "friendly visiting." And when somewhat belatedly they learned to handle charity dispensation more efficiently, making use of some of the new principles of orderly management and sound retailing being introduced by the large department stores and supply houses at the turn of the century (for at this time the itinerant peddler and nomad merchant were being replaced by modern-style tradesmen), the charity organizers glorified these minor achievements by fabricating pompous theories about "scientific charity."

The Establishment's policies must be defended at all costs, even if this means a retreat to nineteenth-century bootstrap philosophy and an apologetic stance in the face of what is now by far the most destructive and poisonous force in American domestic life, white racism. The truth must be suppressed, not confronted. In this regard we are naïve if we imagine that a social work Establishment, tied into a vast network of local-federal prestige, power, and status, with deliberately manipulated apparatuses of punishment and reward, is different from any other Establishment. It is probably no worse, but is certainly no better.

WOES OF THE LEADERS

We must not be too harsh on the social work Establishment, because it means well. But meaning well and effectively doing good are separate matters. The criticism that must be leveled against the social work Establishment and NASW as well is that it does not do enough good.

The most important thing to say about a leader of social work is that he is not. He cannot be a social work leader, because there is no longer a unitary profession of social work. To be sure, there are welfare department administrators, marriage counselors, psychiatric social workers in mental hospitals, social planners who work for the federal government, organizers of community action projects in inner cities, statisticians and researchers who work for health and welfare councils, Peace Corps and VISTA volunteers, Black Power advocates who organize the ghettos, and college students and housewives who work in Head Start centers and tutorial projects. Theoretically they can all claim to be social workers. But they require entirely different kinds of leadership and different kinds of spokesmen. And they are getting them.

Another characteristic of the established leaders is their lack of deep concern about the effective and democratic provision of social services. Until quite recently their major preoccupation was with career advancement, professional prerogatives, and image-building, none of which would have been promoted by attacks against the status quo. But an overhauling and upgrading of America's social services cannot be achieved without forthright assaults against the status quo. We cannot make an impact with cozy words of comfort, platitudes about helping people to help themselves, and Community Chest-style rhetoric.

Today the old platitudes can be attacked more openly and the failures of the past generation can be more openly confronted. This is healthy, but we should not forget how easy it is to retreat to quiescence.

For years the profession was tranquilized with a false faith in gradualism. The professional literature of the 1950s rarely mentioned such things as festering inner-city ghettos, proliferating AFDC case loads, and sodden welfarism as a way of life for second- and third-generation paupers, the vast internal migration, rural areas reduced to derelict status, the miseries of Appalachia, scandalous care in state institutions for the retarded. In those years everyone knew that social work had passed from cause to function, that it was the proper mission of schools of social work to train 80 or 90 percent of their students in the "science" of social casework, that the profession was destined to become more and more "generic"—whatever that might have meant. The preferred style was cool professionalism, the approved image one of polite and constructive comment on the need to broaden the profession's knowledge base and deepen competence. The *Social Work Year Book* for 1960 is as optimistic, buoyant, and sprightly a catalog of achievements of American society and the social work profession as anyone could hope to encounter.[6]

In this edition sweetness and light are the ambience in which most topics are discussed. The word poverty does not even occur in the index. The article on "Public Assistance" never bluntly informs the reader that payments are niggardly and most programs wretchedly administered and hopelessly understaffed, so that public assistance as a "social service" was approaching a shambles, which was certainly the case in the 1950s.[7] (At that time more than half of the states had *official* case loads in excess of two hundred, and in a good third of the states the average was closer to five hundred.) But the author blandly informs us that "emphasis on the broad rehabilitation potentials of the public assistance programs is beginning to show results" in many of the states, although he is concerned about the "lack of professional training."[8] The

---

[6] Russell H. Kurtz, ed., *Social Work Year Book 1960* (New York: National Association of Social Workers, 1960).

[7] Jay L. Roney, in *ibid.*, pp. 460–470.

[8] *Ibid.*, p. 468.

timorously composed article on "Community Organization for Social Welfare" informs us that "in recent years the impact of dynamic psychiatry has been permeating the thinking" of community organization practitioners and that the task of the social worker is to provide not direct or forthright but "indirect leadership." [9]   The reader is warned against certain undesirable types who may intrude themselves into the community organization field:

> The "promoter," the "cause reformer," and the "authoritarian personality" have no more place in professional community organization practice than in other areas of social work, yet because of the planning and promotional features of community organization work they may naturally gravitate to this field despite professional advice to the contrary.[10]

Thus, the reader is not warned against bigotry, apathy, conservatism, and entrenched vested interests—the classic obstacles to community development—but against social workers who may be overly devoted to social reform.

THE NEWER CRITICISM

Today the bottom has dropped out.   The profession is angry and aroused.   A New York City welfare commissioner publicly declared the system he administered to be "bankrupt" and nobody batted an eyelash; it was obvious, why bother to deny it?   The letters to the editor columns and book review sections of social work publications bristle with rapier thrusts, polemical outcries, and on occasion downright insults, and there is no sign of a letup in the near future.

An adroit lunge was taken recently by Scott Briar.[11]   He deplores caseworkers' preoccupation with therapy, their failure to do today the sort of things that were done by their antecedents in pre-World War I America (brokerage, advocacy, social reform).   Briar is wrong.   If the truth were told, it hardly worked with yesterday's poor, and it certainly will not work with today's.   Caseworkers cannot return to an America in which only 4 percent of the population graduated from high school, 70 or 80 percent grew up in rural environments, millions were

---

[9] Campbell G. Murphy, in *ibid.*, p. 186.

[10] *Ibid.*, pp. 190–191.

[11] "The Casework Predicament," *Social Work,* Vol. 13, No. 1 (January 1968), pp. 5–11.

immigrants not literate in English, and two-thirds qualified as lower class. The kind of casework supposedly fitted for that world is truly dead.

The sophisticated casework of today does not merely resemble counseling and psychotherapy; it *is* counseling and psychotherapy. It should be honored for what it is, no matter what took place or failed to take place with the girls at Vocational High.[12] As for the kind of work performed by those who deliver social and human services without engaging in individualized psychosocial meliorism, that is still another kettle of fish. Not purely education or counseling or group work or old-time casework, it is a peculiar blend of all of these, a blend that has not as yet been suitably defined. Of two things, however, we can be certain: it is far more an art than a science and it can be performed with complete adequacy by practitioners with four or even two years of college preparation.

It is time for us all to face up to the fact that social casework of the old school, or the new-old school, has played out its role on the stage of American social history. It should be allowed to depart painlessly. But at the same time we do need to return to a style of direct and vigorous dispensation of human services, which entails more than therapeutic listening from behind the desk. If this, in the final analysis, is what Briar means to say, he is quite correct.

Students in schools of social work pass resolutions condemning NASW for its failure to provide effective leadership, and no one is vexed (or pays much attention, for that matter).[13] An organization called the Association of Black Social Workers recently came into existence.[14] Any American who has tried all of his adult life to adhere to a strict ideal

---

[12] Henry J. Meyer, Edgar F. Borgatta, and Wyatt C. Jones, *Girls at Vocational High* (New York: Russell Sage Foundation, 1965).

[13] *See*, for example, "Minutes of Policy Meeting, October 28, 1967," East Central Regional Organization, Graduate School of Social Work, University of Pittsburgh. (Mimeographed.)

[14] *See* "A Segregated Professional Association?" *Social Service Review*, Vol. 41, No. 4 (December 1967), p. 435. Social workers are not the only ones to be afflicted by such developments. Recently a group of Negro Catholic priests assembled in Detroit to form the Black Catholic Clergy Caucus, at the same time declaring that the Catholic Church in the United States is "primarily a white, racist institution." (Among America's nearly 60,000 Catholic priests there are said to be not more than 150 Negroes.) *See* the *Plain Dealer* (Cleveland), April 19, 1968, p. 7.

of racial integration can hardly welcome the implications—but how can we in all fairness criticize such a development when we know that for generations white social workers have managed to live quite untroubled in a racist society and a racist system of social services? Given the mood of the times, this development might have been predicted.

Indeed, the bottom has fallen out, the lid has blown off, and there is much jostling and pushing among us. Gone are the days when social workers were bright-eyed bearers of glad tidings, wrapped in the enabler's bag and tied with a generic bow. And so, having glanced at the scenario, and having confronted a bit of the worst in our past, let us cast a jaundiced eye at social work's very own: the National Association of Social Workers.

NASW: SOCIAL WORK'S OWN

Three good things can be said about NASW:

1. Compared with most other professional associations, NASW is a paragon, both with respect to vocational virtue and political liberalism. For example, the National Education Association until quite recently was a haven for old-fogeyism, and the American Medical Association has always been a headquarters of stuffy conservatism. As for the American Bar Association, until just a few years ago it was both a haven and a headquarters for the aforementioned specialties.

2. NASW is honestly administered and has an able staff.

3. Unlike many professional associations, NASW is fairly responsive to the expressed viewpoints and felt needs of its rank-and-file members.

Main Purposes

A professional association has two main purposes: to enhance professional functions and services across the board for the eventual betterment of the entire community and to protect and advance the legitimate interests of the professionals who make up the association. It was presumably for these reasons that NASW came into existence.

The merger of the seven constituent bodies (American Association of Social Workers, American Association of Psychiatric Social Workers, and so on) into NASW in 1955 and the de facto emergence of weak but nevertheless consolidated social work Establishments in loose confederation was from the vantage point of today a regressive episode in the history of American social work. Coming during one of the most stagnant and conservative periods in twentieth-century American history, and meaning as it did the co-optation and muzzling of a debilitated and beleaguered social reform impulse in the profession so that the safely strident official voice of American social work became the voice of psychosocial meliorism (in the guise of social casework), the creation of NASW signified a preoccupation with the format and packaging of professionalism rather than the programmatic content of the laggard social services in America.

But it is difficult to see how it could have been otherwise. Any profound analysis of social service delivery in America implies not only a liberal and liberating humanism, but a radical political-economic critique of American society. This would hardly have been tolerated in America in the early 1950s, when the government welfare structures and the private agencies were irrefragably glued to the status quo. The cracks that are now beginning to appear were not then present. Today it is at least viable, but hardly popular, to recommend that we might be served better by separate professional organizations—one carrying the commitment to reconstructed human and social services and uniting all those practitioners who in fact deliver such services, and the other carrying the commitment to militant social reform and the reconstruction of community life. (Certain individuals might choose to join both.) The two professional organizations would of course require leadership and official spokesmen, but today there is at least the prospect of their being free of government agency domination and unburdened by accommodationist and status quo Establishments.

There is not space here to explore in detail aspects of the second purpose of the professional association, that of advancing the legitimate interests of its members. No doubt certain gains have been made. NASW sponsors insurance schemes for its members, issues regularly a publication listing available jobs, and publishes another containing many names and pictures of members and mentioning various honors, awards, tributes, laminated plaques, gatherings, and the like; it must be assumed that this is a source of satisfaction to those individuals who provide source material for the publication.

As for the all-important matter of the salaries of social workers—completely overlooking the matter of those social workers without the MSW degree—this is more difficult to assess. The median income of graduate social workers is not impressive and does not compare favorably with that of many vocations requiring less academic preparation and presumably less professional skill. It is not possible to judge whether the economic status of social workers today would be higher or lower given the nonexistence of NASW.

When it comes to the other purpose of a professional association—that of community service and social advancement—NASW's record leaves a great deal wanting. The association does not seem to have its priorities straight. *Goals of Public Social Policy* is not a bad statement, as such documents go, but it is not clear how the activities of NASW, as expressed in its budget of nearly $1.5 million, relate to these goals.[15]

According to NASW's statements on housing, civil rights, income maintenance, and the like, one might expect the national office to rise to the occasion when a prominent body affirms viewpoints that support and even go beyond its own. But weeks passed after the appearance of the report of the National Advisory Commission on Civil Disorders, strongly affirming the need for multi-billion-dollar investments to arrest deterioration in central city ghettos and to forestall urban apartheid—and nothing of significance was heard from NASW. Surely an immediate and enthusiastic endorsement was called for, and that endorsement should have been promoted to a major campaign, taking precedence over many lesser projects of the association.

There is a fairly good statement on peace, and NASW is certainly not happy about the war in Vietnam. Still, a recognized social work figure went to Vietnam and then issued an embarrassing statement that, while it was probably not meant to do so, in effect whitewashed the American presence there and for all practical purposes gave the impression of passively committing American social workers to an endorsement of America's abhorrent and tragic involvement in the Vietnam conflict. When this superficial and misleading report was challenged by other social workers, rather than repudiating this statement with dignity, Establishment spokesmen saw fit to make excuses for it.[16]

The April 1967 Delegate Assembly adopted a position statement on income maintenance and there is now a modest association pamphlet devoted to this matter.[17] The guaranteed income may be a tactically necessary demand at this time, but is hardly a cure for poverty, and it needs to be presented in a proper way. It would probably be more fitting for social workers, in making appeals or ceremonial statements to the public, to probe the meaning of poverty on the deepest levels.

The body of this pamphlet opens with this question: "What would it

---

[15] Rev. ed.; New York: National Association of Social Workers, 1968.

[16] *See* editions of *NASW News* for May 1967, November 1967, and February 1968.

[17] "So All May Live in Decency and Dignity" (New York: National Association of Social Workers, 1968).

mean if no family in the United States had to live on less than a minimum standard for a decent existence, for example, $3,200 a year for a family of four?" It is only the first sentence, but already we are off on the wrong foot. Is there a single social worker in the United States who thinks that he personally can provide "decently" in 1968 for a family of four with $61.54 a week (before deductions)?

The idea of a guaranteed income has been admitted to the routine conference-and-report circuit wisdom of blue-chip financiers and corporation giants. In a recent report to New York's Governor Rockefeller, twelve leading and conservative industrialists formally endorsed the negative income tax. They said of the present welfare system that it is "demeaning, inefficient, inadequate, and . . . encourages continued dependency."[18] Conservative Republicans may be found in favor of the guaranteed income. Six years ago an economist who served as adviser to Barry Goldwater came out in favor of the negative income tax,[19] and the idea of a general floor on income has for years been considered old hat among European social planners. In America poverty is preeminently a *relative* matter, and it can never be ended with the device of an income floor alone.

This is the message about poverty that social workers should have been bringing to students and fellow citizens all these years. We should have been revealing, analyzing, and exposing the inner workings of the system that keeps almost 20 percent of the wealth in the hands of 5 percent of the population and that compels 20 percent of the population to make do with less than 5 percent of the wealth.[20] We should have been informing the American public in and out of season that only basic income redistribution and a fundamental commitment to economic justice and egalitarianism will ever salvage the poor and reclaim society. We should have been challenging all the Establishments and demolishing all the conventional wisdoms that failed to come out vigorously on the side of economic egalitarianism.

There is a view to the effect that NASW is weak on "social action," that it must budget more in this area, that it needs to affirm more robust

---

[18] A. H. Raskin, "Negative Income Tax: Support for a Plan To Replace Welfare," *New York Times,* May 5, 1968, p. 4E.

[19] Milton Friedman, *Capitalism and Freedom* (Chicago: University of Chicago Press, 1962).

[20] Herman P. Miller, *Income Distribution in the United States,* a 1960 Census Monograph (Washington, D.C.: U.S. Bureau of the Census, 1966), p. 21.

stands with respect to the urban crisis, and so on. There is much to be said for these criticisms. Still, it is not clear that they lead of necessity to any major implications concerning the present role of NASW. The upshot might be an added mite to what is essentially a minimal program of system change.

It would be an entirely different matter if an expanded and strengthened NASW were to adopt, publicize, and strenuously advocate a really ambitious program of social reform. Such a program might include planks like the following: an income floor of $5,000 a year for a family of four; an absolute income ceiling (whether earned or unearned) of $75,000 a year; guaranteed jobs to all, with minimum wage rates pegged to cost of living and rise in Gross National Product indexes; the nationalization of all military production in order to put it on a genuinely nonprofit basis and to eliminate profiteering in military procurement; total overhaul of the income tax system to eliminate loopholes now routinely exploited by the rich; complete redoing of the social security system; a federal law making racial discrimination a crime; an end to de facto segregation and a radical upgrading of educational services to minority groups; massive rehabilitation of black ghettos; rapid de-escalation of the arms race; new and massive investments in the social services. Also, a price tag would have to be attached to this bill of particulars. The rock-bottom floor on any tactical antipoverty program for the nation at this time would probably be in the neighborhood of $40 billion annually. Short of this we are in the realm of tokenism. Even the Full Opportunity Act (HR 14492) now pending before the House Education and Labor Committee does not meet the minimum needs with its total annual cost of about $30 billion.

Some such program as this would be worthy of social workers, if by social workers is meant men and women militantly committed to a policy of social reconstruction and system change. But it is extremely doubtful that the leaders or members of NASW possess the ideological maturity and political daring to adopt such a set of goals of social policy. And if all that can be expected in the sector of social action or advocacy is the espousal of a set of goals that might soon be acceptable to the liberal wing of the Republican party, it hardly seems worthwhile to labor so mightily. After all, it can be predicted that this country will in the near future get a new system of income maintenance based on some version of the guaranteed income even if every social worker *opposes* the move.

Perhaps we do not want to become the bearers of this message; perhaps we do not have the skill to convey it with the sophistication and élan needed to gain the ear of the people. If so, we can confine our efforts to a more restricted but equally important mission: that of becoming bold advocates of high-quality social services for America. This is chiefly an educational task, a fierce, often competitive struggle for the attention and support of the public. There can be no quarrel with the need for effective public relations in this sector. A chief goal in this enterprise is to capture the attention of the public, to explain patiently, to educate ceaselessly, to plan creatively concerning understaffed and underbudgeted social services.

But neither of these two major roles seems to define what NASW is about. Rather, an analysis of the activities, budget, and structure of the association shows that its primary efforts are directed toward polishing professional competence and probing the knowledge base.[21] Is it not time to call a halt to this sacerdotal outpouring of talk about social workers' competence, the need to promote deeper communication, social work's unique values (in what way unique?), our role as supervisors and consultants, intervention strategies, and all the rest? Who is listening? Who cares? There must be more useful ways of spending a budget of $1.5 million a year.

NASW As Spokesman for the Social Services

The profession's job is service—it provides social and human services. Very well, then: let NASW speak to the needs of these services in America. Let us bring the message of the social and human services to the American people, let us tell the truth about the still wretched state of these services, and let us fight to make them better. We all know that it will not be an easy fight, and that we will have many defeats. But far, far better that we should fight these battles and endure these failures than that we should say publicly only what the Establishment deems politic.

This is a good point to dispose of another myth that relates to competence, the myth of the indispensability of the MSW degree. The issues have been debated too often to require an airing here. Suffice it to point out two facts: (1) There is a great need for tens of thousands of new

---

[21] Lack of space prevents a full discussion of organizational and structural aspects of NASW. For interesting comments on these aspects, *see* Chauncey A. Alexander, "NASW National-State-Local Relationships." Paper presented at the Washington State Council of NASW Chapters conference, Seattle, Wash., March 17, 1967. (Mimeographed.)

people to provide services in the areas of child welfare, community health, corrections, mental retardation, old age, youth work, and day care. (2) There is ample evidence that this work can be performed routinely with satisfactory competence by practitioners with under-graduate education and suitable on-the-job training. Why, then, do we insist so illogically on making the MSW degree the hallmark of profes-sionalism? Surely the answer has something to do with self-seeking careerism, a distrust of the wisdom of practice, and plain academic clubiness, if not snobbery. It is difficult to see how any of this can benefit clients, the vast majority of whom now receive direct, face-to-face services from non-MSW social workers and will continue to do so for the foreseeable future.

NASW should become the major professional voice speaking for all of the social services in society. That is to say, there is a need to represent the interests of all those services that have historically been assigned to the profession and in which social workers work, but which are now represented in various scattered and fairly weak organizations and special interest groups. It would certainly be useful to have an association made up, say, of 200,000 members who would speak with one strong voice to advance and uphold the interests of the social services.

The social services are starved, abysmally underfunded. This is not the fault of social workers. The nation is so implicated in other pursuits, so involved in military spending, and so committed to a life-style that involves the use and waste of goods in often harmful pursuits that it must be called forcefully to account on this score. The potential chief sources of support for research and development in the sector of social planning are the government, foundations, and industry. The actual support given has been miniscule. Thus, major blame for this state of affairs can hardly be assigned to social workers themselves. They have been meagerly supported in their efforts to develop expertise as social planners. The vast discrepancies here must be pointed out again and again.

There is now a ratio of about one social worker to one thousand people in the population. This is totally inadequate, but no one knows what a more equitable ratio might be. If we were to assume that the country needs one social service worker for every two hundred people, this would mean that we require five times the present number of social workers (of whom only one in four is academically trained). This is the kind of message that NASW should bring to the public.

The public must also be informed that its expenditures are prejudiced against its own interests and must be remedied. About $16 billion a year is spent in military, space, and allied research. (All told the staggering sum of nearly $90 billion is spent for current military activities.) In comparison with this, the nation spends about $1.5 billion a year for biomedical education and research. But probably not one-fifth of this amount is spent for research and education in the social services. This information must be brought to the American public—loudly, clearly, in unmistakable terms.

ACSW: A Regrettable Case

Many of the points made are reflected in the sad case history of the Academy of Certified Social Workers, and it will pay to conclude this discussion of NASW with a glance at some of this evidence. ACSW was brought into being in 1961 for the purpose of strengthening, extending, and improving the "quantity and quality of social work services" by way of "setting standards and establishing criteria for sound social work practice." [22]

There is ample evidence of the spurious or "paper" nature of ACSW. It does not command genuine and specific policy-making authorities. It does not function under its own board of directors or trustees (the NASW board fulfills this function in implicit violation of the bylaws of ACSW itself). It does not possess an adequate staff. There is no self-policing process to protect against improper use of the ACSW designation. There is no consistent definition of the supervisory requirement. There is no official definition of any sort with respect to the matter of practitioner competence, although an enormous amount of importance seems to be attributed to this matter. Finally, any member can retain his ACSW status indefinitely by the mere device of retaining membership in NASW and paying an annual renewal fee of $1.00.

There are relatively few cases of individuals being censured or excluded by NASW (and hence ACSW) as a result of ethical or other violations. In contrast with this pristine record it may be pointed out that American physicians, by no means excessively stern in their self-governance procedures, in the course of one year alone (1966) brought no less than 579 disciplinary actions before state examining boards. (No doubt there was a much larger number of internal reprimands and informal actions that never reached the state bodies.) This resulted in 197 official reprimands, 45 active suspensions, and 69 revocations of

---

[22] "Bylaws of the Academy of Certified Social Workers" (New York: National Association of Social Workers, 1964). (Mimeographed.)

license to practice.[23] Can it seriously be claimed that ACSW was brought into being to "protect the public against abuses and incompetence" when there is not a single case on record of the Academy's actually doing this? Can we seriously believe that ACSW ever carried promise of facilitating and encouraging the "highest possible standards of professional performance" when to this day there is not even so much as a blueprint for a mechanism to define, establish, and monitor the aforementioned "standards"?

ACSW cannot be credited with a single significant achievement. Even the designation "ACSW" is used by only a handful of social workers, conveys nothing to the public at large, and amounts to nothing more than a pretentious and largely spurious badge of professionalism. The Academy in its present form is incapable of being salvaged and should be forthrightly dissolved. The "academification" of the profession of social work at this stage of its development ought to be the least of our worries and the lowest of our priorities.

To be sure, ACSW is not a conspiracy: it is merely a farce. It would hardly be worth the attention here being devoted to it, were it not for the fact that ACSW provides a revealing case study of the self-deception and collective vanity that have made regrettable headway in the profession since World War II. The preoccupation with building an image, with accumulating merit badges and official testimonials of high social sanction, whether in the form of laminated plaques or gold seals or legal prerogatives, has been so eagerly pursued among establishmentarian sectors of the profession that it has led us into the preposterous stance of first creating an "academy" and then seeking a justification for its existence—a justification that has not as yet been found.

Need for Review

In the absence of evidence to the contrary, it must be assumed that the chief mission of NASW seems to be the perpetuation of NASW in the style to which it has grown accustomed. And that style seems principally to be a species of conspicuous if plodding consumption: busywork and self-exposure. It is not the first or the last example of organizations falling into the trap of existence for the mere sake of existence. One can imagine NASW trudging along for another ten years without so much as causing a ripple, without registering the slightest effect on the actual quality or content of social services in American society.

---

[23] *The House Physician Reporter*, Vol. 8, No. 1 (January 1968), p. 12.

In short, the social work profession has in NASW an honest but thoroughly ineffective organization. Social workers are deserving of a far bolder leadership, a far more enterprising program of professional advocacy than NASW has over the past decade shown itself capable of providing. The implication is clear: NASW must be submitted to a full-dress review and critical study. A special study commission should be appointed at the earliest possible date—a commission not dominated by Establishment voices—and entrusted with the task of redefining membership rules, structure, publication policy, principles of budgeting, and program priorities. NASW needs to be remodeled from top to bottom.

As the writer affirmed at the outset, the profession is at root a healthy one. Since we are committed to the ideal of growth and change in the lives of others, we ought to be capable of such growth and change in our own professional evolution.

In Pursuit of Community:
A Platform for NASW

ALAN D. WADE

For the second time in less than five years, a major public figure has been assassinated.[1] Violence in one form or another will long continue to be a part of our way of life in this surely the most savage of modern nations. The violence and destruction that erupt in city ghettos will attract morbid attention and interest and, with the help of the news media, will be mistaken by many for revolution. But these are only symptoms of radical social change. The true dynamism of revolution lies not in the burning of a few blocks or even a few square miles of decaying inner-city slums, but in our ethics, our technology, and our social institutions. It is here that the revolution is taking place, and social workers are a part of it, whether we know it or not and whether we want to be or not.

The aim of this paper is to speculate on the emerging nature of the world, which will be calling for social work services in a shape radically different from what has been known in the past, and to suggest some of the ways in which the profession, and particularly the professional association, may take the initiative in preparing to become relevant to the needs of this society in radical transformation.

---

[1] ED. NOTE: The NASW symposium was held following the assassination of Dr. Martin Luther King, Jr., and prior to that of Senator Robert F. Kennedy.

SOCIAL WORK IN THE YEAR 2000

The preceding papers have made clear what has long troubled us—that the social work profession has not made much real difference in the public life of America. We have dutifully played our role as agent-technicians, working residually to patch up human ills here and there in support of economic progress and urban and industrial growth. This symposium may well represent an important turning point for us, because we have come here goaded by terrible discomfort. That discomfort is based on the dawning awareness that the services we have given as agents of the old economic order have had little impact on the fabric of society in the past and must suffer the fate of becoming irrelevant or worse in a world undergoing dramatic change.

Charles Dickens's *Tale of Two Cities* begins with the observation: "It was the best of times; it was the worst of times." Wheeler cogently perceives the nature of our current revolution within the "two cities" framework:

> They [revolutions] take place when societies have divided in two. During revolutionary times the established social system persists a long while before it finally disappears. It continues to go about its business very much as it always has. It maintains a certain integrity, in the sense of holding itself together and of remaining devoted to its traditional ways and beliefs. At the same time it is host to a second city that lives and flourishes inside it. This is the society of the future. Together these two cities comprise the revolution.[2]

The social work profession must of necessity have one foot in the old city and one in the new. But it has a special responsibility to understand the conditions of the new and to play a part in hastening its coming and shaping its capacity to provide for human well-being in ways thus far only occasionally visualized and hardly ever realized.

Planning for the future of the profession can only take place in the context of thought about the shape of society to come. Recently, efforts to predict the future have moved from fiction and fantasy to the status of serious academic enterprise. Currently in progress is the work of the American Academy of Arts and Sciences' Commission on the Year 2000. In a progress report, its chairman, Daniel Bell, reminds us:

---

[2] Harvey Wheeler, "The Politics of Revolution," *The Center Magazine,* Vol. 1, No. 3 (March 1968), p. 49.

. . . the world of the year 2000 has already arrived, for in the decisions we make now, in the way we design our environment and thus sketch the lines of constraints, the future is committed. Just as the gridiron pattern of city streets in the nineteenth century shaped the linear growth of cities in the twentieth, so the new networks of radial highways, the location of new towns, the reordering of graduate school curricula, the decision to create or not to create a computer utility as a single system, and the like will frame the tectonics of the twenty-first century.[3]

The commission's work rests on recognition of four basic sources of social change, none of which is especially difficult to chart. These are the following:

1. The expansion of technology, including such diverse but related phenomena as biomedical engineering, investigations into the source of life itself, organ transplants, control of the weather, the impact of the artificial intelligence of the computer and the diffusion of data systems, and the growth of intellectual rather than purely machine technology, e.g., simulation, model construction, linear programming, operations research, and so on.

2. The diffusion of existing goods and privileges in society, including both tangible goods and more abstract claims on the community, such as the spread throughout society of the heretofore largely middle-class urge to participate in decision-making.

3. Structural developments in society, including centralization or decentralization of authority, a shift from production of things to production of services, the shift of sources of innovation from the old industrial complexes to universities and research organizations, and the concentration of power as well as new forms of human misery in the cities.

4. The relationship of the United States to the rest of the world, marked by the tension caused by the gap between rich and poor nations, the problem of color, and the changing balance of world political forces.

These four sources of change bear important implications for social work. Before these can be understood, however, another ingredient, less tangible and far more difficult to chart, must be dealt with. That is the ethical context in which these forces operate. Within one such con-

---

[3] Daniel Bell, "Toward the Year 2000: Work in Progress," "The Year 2000—The Trajectory of an Idea," *Daedalus*, Vol. 96, No. 3 (Summer 1967), p. 639.

text, society by the year 2000 could become an efficient, sanitized, and monstrous engine for the control and ultimately the destruction of human beings—an advanced technocracy the outlines of which may have been recognized but dimly by Huxley and Orwell. We must face the fact that social work could play a key role in such a state, utilizing the new technology of human engineering to manipulate people in the interests of the monolith.

But there is another possibility, given substance by the new generation of students and young people (including our own social work students), who, being the first in human history to grow up in an immediate environment free of material want, have a vision of the world that frequently transcends ours. This vision has been cogently expressed by Green:

> The moral vision that is emerging insists upon human well-being as the central moral category and requires that each law or authority justify itself through the contribution it makes to this end. It rejects the subordination of emotional, aesthetic, and sensory experience to the rational faculties, and holds that human well-being requires the cultivation of intelligence and the sensibilities, a greater capacity for rich erotic experience, heightened sensory awareness, and a cultivated aesthetic sensibility. It denies that non-affective modes of human intercourse, mediated by decency of manners, constitute an acceptable pattern of human relations. Such modes of association, it holds, explain our tolerance of suffering and the exercise of power for merely selfish ends. Men must learn, we are being told, to develop a network of affective relationships that go beyond decency to genuine involvement in the well-being of others.[4]

Let the social work profession, then, join with the nation's students in the choice of a society in which all planning for change is measured against a standard of what it does to and for people in the pursuit of community.

The second city flourishes and lives within the old. The general outlines of the twenty-first century are already in sight. Social work as we now know it, the creature of an expansive nineteenth-century individualism that called for meliorative services for casualties of the system, will continue to exist for some time. Direct services to small groups and

---

[4] James L. Green, "The New Student Morality," *Antioch Notes,* Vol. 45, No. 6 (March 1968), pp. 4–5.

individuals will be required, but at a diminishing rate, for perhaps the next thirty years. The rate of need for the services that most present-day social workers have been taught to provide will decrease, however, as new social institutions are developed for the purpose of anticipating and providing for the variety of quite predictable human needs that arise in the course of both ordinary and unusual life crises.

We have been willing to provide services without careful attention to their consequences, their relationship to total community need, or their potential for instructing us in the alteration of social institutions for the nurture of life. Content to place children in foster homes, we have neglected to pursue basic questions concerning the relationship between family breakdown and its social context. Intent upon the provision of counseling and psychotherapy for the few, we have not addressed ourselves systematically to the conditions that cause multitudes to require it. Blinded by an uncritical faith in individualism, we have banked on the offering of services in a gigantic public welfare system that compounds social illness among those we intend to serve. Above all, we have failed to use the full potential of our knowledge to clarify for the larger community the intimate relationship between individual stress and the environmental and to collect the data required and initiate the action needed to develop social institutions that can effectively mediate between human want and the community's capacity to respond to it.

It is necessary to make clear that recognition of serious limitations in current modes of service delivery is in no way to be construed as meaning that casework and group work are out of date, irrelevant, and ready for the scrap heap of rusting social institutions. None but the most fatuous optimist could suggest with conviction that people will not have serious individual problems that need therapy or other forms of help by the year 2000. It is in fact likely that, by that time, psychotherapy for treatment of serious disturbance in some as well as for "preventive maintenance" for all may be regarded as a part of the birthright of all Americans. A sharpening of the knowledge and skills relevant to establishing such services as rights for all must take place, along with the recognition that the bulk of such services must be offered in the future by those to whom we now refer as nonprofessionals.

GOALS FOR THE PROFESSION

The real issue today, and for the next thirty years, is not whether casework is dead, but whether we can find ways of stopping this mad gallop toward the destruction of human beings by our archaic social institutions. The demand is not that we stop bandaging the wounded or reducing the fevers attributable to the swamps of society. These activities will always be required. But we must immediately set about the task of spraying those swamps and ultimately draining them of the noxious fluids that give rise to the disease-bearing agents. We must talk not about eliminating what we are doing now, but about establishing priorities for the most effective expenditure of efforts based on old and new knowledge.

We need to take seriously the action of the 1964 Delegate Assembly calling for an end to the means test and setting the goal of an income guarantee for all Americans as a first step in eliminating absolute poverty. Once this is done, we can proceed to initiate a range of social services planned and organized around the life-cycle needs of human beings. In a sense, we must return to the wisdom of the primitive society that, through rites of passage and a variety of institutionalized social supports, recognized the interaction of biological needs and social requirements. Having passed through the period of rapid industrialism when individualism was a prerequisite for growth, we are now theoretically, technically, and economically free to establish on a large scale a range of social services that will anticipate the periods of high vulnerability to pathology that occur among most people during the life cycle.

We already know what is needed: adequate nutrition and medical care for all; multiservice centers; neighborhood self-help programs; citizens' advice bureaus; prenatal maternal counseling and infant welfare services; effective mental health services in major social institutions such as factories, offices, and schools; pre- and postmarital counseling for young adults; day care and sound programs of preschool education for all young children; home help and recreational services for the aged; completely reorganized and humanized correctional and mental institutions; and many others.

If we are to make a difference in the current revolution, we must decide now what we ought to be doing by the year 2000, then proceed systematically toward that goal. We cannot wait for others to tell us what to do.

We must commit ourselves during the next thirty years to a gradual phasing out of those professional services with their roots in nineteenth-century individualism, beginning with a continued, planned decrease in the emphasis placed on services to individuals and small groups and in the numbers of professionally educated social workers committed to such service modes. If 80 percent of students currently enrolled in graduate schools of social work plan to be providers of direct service, with only 20 percent committed to the organizational, administrative, research, and policy activities of the profession, then by the year 2000 we should plan for a direct reversal of these proportions. As institutional and social provisions for human life-cycle needs increase, and as we along with many others work toward the development of a society whose reason for existence is the support of human well-being, more and more of those who are now called social workers must become strategists, tacticians, and technicians devoted to bringing about these ends.

This is a large, if not a staggering, order, one that, expressed in these terms, seems too grandiose even for comprehension, let alone for achievement. In fact, the assumption by the profession of a leadership role in the pursuit of a goal as vague as "human well-being" could become a horror. A possible assignment for the profession is the development of increasingly efficient techniques for modifying human behavior in the interests of manipulation of people and subordination of their search for community to the requirements of a new fascist state. It must be faced squarely that social work, or whatever its twenty-first century successor may be called, could be enlisted in the business of repression of movement toward the true human community. Social work could become a major supplier of the manpower and the know-how to "adjust" people to an increasingly dehumanized social environment or, to put it more bluntly, to narcotize and socialize people on their way to the next century's equivalents of this century's gas chambers and concentration camps. Strategists, tacticians, and technicians—indeed, but for what? It is an old dilemma for the profession, one that has commanded the attention of its greatest leaders. It haunts us in new and more urgent form today.

An Old Dilemma

In a series of papers written in 1902, Jane Addams stressed the sanctity of human life and the necessity for social conscience, at a time when social work was all too often employed in a mission of rescue rather than restoration of the capacity for self-determining behavior.[5] Porter R. Lee wrote in 1929 of the dangers inherent in confusing cause and

---

[5] Anne Firos Scott, ed., *Democracy and Social Ethics* (Cambridge, Mass.: Belknap Press of Harvard University Press, 1964).

function—the process of making ends out of means that leads to professionalism or technicianship.[6]

Speaking of the "enlightened participation of the commonwealth" in the pursuit of the intertwined goals of political democracy and human welfare, the late Gordon Hamilton wrote in 1940:

> Social work is still engaged . . . in furnishing the "commodities" of welfare: assistance, board of children, institutional care, recreational and neighborhood activities, and the like, but this is not its sole purpose. It is deeply concerned with programs, social planning, and social change which will make for a better social order, but this is not its entire contribution. The participation of labor in industry, of staffs in their own administration, of groups in their own education, of communities in social planning, of informed and responsible forces in social action, are constructive only as they involve self-determined, cooperative and altruistic behavior. All these movements are interdependent and all rest ultimately on the possibility of socializing the individual personality within the family and the group, for the development of a truly good society.[7]

In one of her last papers, Charlotte Towle wrote of the importance of "knowing ourselves in terms of ethics and values for use in the adaptations we make as social work increasingly becomes world cause." [8] She observed:

> It is held that social work is based on humanitarian democratic ideals. They are the foundation and framework of our value system. Concern and efforts to make our society one in which democracy as a way of life would be realized has been a long struggle and it will be a continuous one. Its partial realization only will be kept alive and grow through conscious safeguarding and cultivation of the conditions of life which nurture man as a social being. Social work

---

[6] "Social Work: Cause and Function," *Proceedings of the National Conference on Social Work, 1929* (Chicago: University of Chicago Press, 1930), pp. 3–20.

[7] *Theory and Practice of Social Case Work* (New York: Columbia University Press, 1940), p. 371.

[8] "Ethics and Values in Social Work," Fiftieth Anniversary Symposium on *Ethics and Values in Social Work* (Chicago: Loyola University, School of Social Work, April 3, 1965), p. 24.

early was absorbed in assuring man's bare survival, but the writings of our pioneers show concern beyond this and awareness of the part played by social conditions in implementing democracy as a way of life, as well as of the significance of such a life as preparation for citizenship in a democracy.[9]

No matter how expressed, the problem has remained the same throughout the history of the social work profession: the urge to rescue rather than to restore, the confusion of means with ends, the failure to bridge the gap between the commodities of welfare and social programs, and a sort of hovering on the brink of a breakthrough in perceiving and acting on the relationship among social conditions, the nurture of man as a social being, and the full flowering of the good society. While the problem is by no means new, social revolution forces it to the surface with more insistence than we have known in the past, and helps account for the present state of affairs within the profession, which seems to be marked at the same time by profound cleavages and by a deadening anomie.

As we attempt to spell out goals for the profession for the year 2000, only three things seem quite clear: (1) the technician without an ideology rooted in democratic values is the most dangerous man alive, especially when his techniques are directed toward changing people, (2) the ideologist without method or technique is fatuous, and (3) those who would retreat to the rescue of individuals are as fundamentally valueless in the creation of the good society as are the "power boys" in community organization who omit human life-cycle needs from their lexicon.

A New Conception

What is needed is a new ecological conception of human needs and how they may be gratified—in effect, an entirely new world view that constitutes "the most arresting of the many faces put forward by the revolution of our time." [10] We continue to fight old battles with old conceptual tools. The terms we use show that we have not yet developed the new social ecology, that we have not emerged from the thought systems of classical physics, materialism, and the logic of Descartes and Bacon: band-aids versus social revolution, social treatment versus social action,

---

[9] *Ibid.*, p. 17.
[10] Wheeler, *op. cit.*, p. 59.

income maintenance versus social services, and so on. Our very thought systems act to draw a seemingly impenetrable curtain between what we have learned through many years of work with individuals and small groups about what people need and what helps them change, and what needs to be done to incorporate these things into the social system.

Ecology is the branch of biology that deals with the relation of living things to their environment. It is increasingly coming to be understood also as the patterns of culture whereby people adjust to their environment and through which they initiate new political systems and social institutions. The new ecology is emerging in the thought of the new breed of city planners who are concerned with the construction of buildings, transportation and communication networks, and the creative use of open spaces in support of human needs. Small but encouraging signs are emerging within the social work profession that we are beginning to develop a conception of human life that is more organic than mechanistic and to operationalize it in our social structures. The many fine papers presented by the membership of the National Association of Social Workers at this symposium indicate serious and increasingly effective efforts to translate the ethical insights derived from services for our social casualties into structural changes in agencies and neighborhoods designed to provide opportunities for freedom, creativity, and citizenship in its most complete sense for large numbers.

REJUVENATING NASW

This analysis suggests that there is much in the profession that is good and strong, but that strength and virtue are not effective without goals. We must, in effect, decide what we want to do and how we want to do it. While the social work profession and NASW are not one and the same, the professional association does represent the major voice of the organized profession. While there are many avenues, both organizational and individual, through which members of the profession may work in moving us toward the new ecology, toward working ourselves out of the job assigned to us in the last century, and toward more effective means for translating our insights into social provision in the development of the new city, NASW can become the most important among them.

But at present NASW is hamstrung. It suffers from a basic malaise that is, in its broadest sense, political. There are no means by which goals can be established that are consonant with community need and membership commitment and by which effective planning can be initiated to achieve them. The chapters are anomalous appendages and, with few exceptions, largely defunct. The Delegate Assembly is a debating society that, although preserving some of the more tedious outer symbols of democracy, bears little relationship to membership opinion and that sees its occasional statesmanship in the setting of social policy goals frustrated by board and staff inaction and general confusion. The Board of Directors is never certain what or whom it represents and to what larger social purposes. Staff, isolated from the membership, receive only conflicted and confusing messages. Commissions and committees spend large sums of money moving people about the country in a search for professional truth in a vacuous process that seldom seems to get tied to the aspirations and needs of the majority of the membership. The elective process, both locally and nationally, is a travesty of democracy, which, to be effective, insists upon the selection of leadership on the basis of clearly differentiated positions regarding issues of great importance to the citizenry.

Organizational renewal of the association is required if the profession itself is not merely to survive (although that too is an issue), but to become significant. The following steps are suggested for consideration:

1. Move the national office from New York to Washington, D.C. There is no excuse whatsoever for maintaining national headquarters in the country's financial and cultural center, when the major decisions affecting the nation and the profession will continue to be made in its political center.

2. Politicize the association. Widespread democratic participation, both in the nation and in its myriad of voluntary organizations, is the only answer to the making of wise decisions in a complex society. It is only through the articulation and presentation of varying points of view that the organization can become viable. The only alternative, one that has already gained support from some quarters, is the balkanizing of the association through the formation of competing groups that do not hesitate to advance their viewpoints on social issues.

3. Reorganize and expand the staff, retaining either on a permanent basis or for ad hoc assignments the top specialists in or related to the profession's various concerns. Make these specialists, either as teams or as individuals, available to "high-cost high-gain" areas of the nation as problems arise that need expert consultation and mobilization for action.

4. Decentralize the staff. A series of regional offices with the best paid staff available should be established in areas of the nation that are determined not primarily by geography, but by their character of political and economic interdependence. These regional offices should provide

membership services to all members in their area through the most effective automated devices available, and should offer intensive consultation
and services designed to mobilize the potential power of maximum
numbers of social workers in a region when a specific problem needs
attention.

5. As long as the future of the nation depends on what happens in
the cities, the major efforts of regional staff must be focused on urban
areas. Everything cannot be done at once, but high-priority areas can
be selected in accordance with the planning process suggested. The
heaviest possible concentration of staff and membership power must be
focused on bringing about change in high-payoff areas.

6. Develop information retrieval systems at the national level that will
enable the association literally to have at its fingertips means for identifying those members who have the knowledge or skill to address themselves to selected issues at the moment when action is required.

Because so many things need to be done, it is hard to know where to
start. But the organization is in crisis, and a little leverage can go a long
way in moving an organization in such a state. It is suggested that 50
percent of the current operating budget of the association be devoted
immediately to (1) moving the national office to Washington, D.C., and
(2) initiating the planning process referred to.

The complaint will be heard that such a step would cripple the
association's ability to do what needs to be done now. The fact is that
we are not doing anything so important or so relevant now that it cannot
wait for a few years. The next four or five years of our national life will
be miserable. They cannot be otherwise. We have lost our chance really
to make a difference in the short run through our procrastination in the
past. What we must do now is to bend the bulk of our resources toward
rejuvenating NASW, politicizing it in the development of an effective
process of planning that grows out of the real concerns and best thinking
of the membership, and focusing our energies on what we wish to become and how we wish to have influenced national life by the end of the
next thirty years.

Along with the nation, whose hopes, dreams, and hatreds they share,
social work and NASW are in serious trouble. For too many decades
social work has been a passive profession, waiting for its assignment
from others, occasionally protesting, too little and too late, the social
forces that we know to be damaging to people, but seldom initiating
action. Social work must begin to lead the way in advocating radical
means for rebuilding society. We must use the full potential of the
profession toward the courageous and creative wedding of individual
need and social requirement.

An important place to begin is with the reorganization and renewal of NASW. Bell underlines the importance of the voluntary association in the modern world as follows:

> In the modern world, politics is inescapable as one of the arbiters of life. But an open society—one which necessarily lives by the give and take of bargaining—can only survive by maintaining the distinction, so firm in Roman Law and Western tradition, between the public and the private, and sharply defining the scope of each. The political world can only be sustained by voluntary associations which freely provide the underpinnings of a common order; the private sphere is the precious one in which the individual works out his own will and his own destiny.[11]

[11] Daniel Bell, "Toward a Communal Society," *Life,* Vol. 62, No. 19 (May 12, 1967), p. 124.

NASW Task Force on Service Delivery

Second NASW Professional Symposium on
Human Services and Professional Responsibility

Division of Practice and Knowledge

Titles of the task force members are those at the time of the symposium
(May 1968)

Chauncey A. Alexander (Chairman), Associate Director, Program
Development, UCLA Regional Medical Programs, Los Angeles,
California

Bertram M. Beck, Executive Director, Mobilization For Youth, and
Executive Director, Henry Street Settlement, New York, New York

Arthur Blum, Professor of Social Work, School of Applied Social Sciences, Case Western Reserve University, Cleveland, Ohio

Richard A. Cloward, Professor, Columbia University School of Social
Work, New York, New York

Wilma I. Gurney, Chief Clinical Social Worker, Center for Health
Sciences, University of California, Los Angeles, California

George W. Magner, Associate Professor, The Jane Addams Graduate
School of Social Work, University of Illinois, Chicago, Illinois

Rex Ragan, Director, Foster Home Services, Family and Children's
Services, Los Angeles County Department of Public Social Services,
Los Angeles, California

Willard C. Richan, Associate Professor of Social Work, School of Applied Social Sciences, Case Western Reserve University, Cleveland,
Ohio; Consultant, NASW Service Delivery Project

Edward E. Schwartz, George Herbert Jones Professor, School of Social

Service Administration, University of Chicago, Chicago, Illinois; Chairman, Council on Social Work Research, NASW

Elliot Studt, Research Social Worker, Law and Society Center, University of California, Berkeley, California

Fernando G. Torgerson, Dean, School of Social Work, University of Texas, Arlington, Texas

---

Bernard Russell, Assistant Director, Model Cities Administration, Department of Housing and Urban Development, Washington, D.C.; Chairman, Division of Practice and Knowledge, NASW

Mrs. Mildred Kilinski, Director, Department of Social Work Practice, National Association of Social Workers, New York, New York

4M 11/69–10/71—P&K
1M 6/74—P&K